PRACTICAL WOODWORKER

Practical
WOODWORKER
CARPENTRY
AND HOME MAINTENANCE

BLACK CAT

First published in Great Britain in two volumes, *Practical Carpentry*
and *Practical Home Maintenance,* in 1984
by Macdonald & Co (Publishers) Ltd.

Reprinted as a single volume in 1989,
under the Black Cat imprint
Reprinted 1991, 1994

Little, Brown and Company
Brettenham House
Lancaster Place
London WC2E 7EN

ISBN 0 7481 0240 X

Printed in the Slovak Republic
50816/2

Contents

Part 1:
CARPENTRY
Percy Blandford

Chapter 1
WOOD

Wood is one of the most widely-used and versatile constructional materials. Fortunately for us, it regenerates and what
we use is replaced by new growth. Today trees do not
replace themselves as quickly as wood is used, but supplies
are plentiful still, even if some of the particular species we
would like are not always available when we want them.
Sometimes wood has been taken in excessive quantities, as
when English forests were denuded of oak trees in the days
of the building of wooden warships. The slow-growing oaks
have not yet recovered. Sometimes nature takes a hand: in
many countries the terrible plague of Dutch elm disease, for
example, has removed that wood from common use.

With modern methods of transport timber may be brought
to almost any port from almost any part of the world. This
means that we can now use woods that were unknown to
carpenters even only a few years ago. Many of the traditional and well-known woods are still available, but others have
been added to them and it is sometimes difficult to know the
characteristics and suitability of the woods we are being
offered. It was sometimes difficult to identify even the comparatively few woods in general use up to a few years ago.
Now it is increasingly difficult, particularly if you want to use
a common name. For instance, there are some widely-
different species that are all called 'mahogany'. Even a
prefix in front of it may not be sufficiently specific. A name
like 'Brazilian mahogany' can be used to embrace a group
rather than refer to one type. There are scientific names,
which are essential if you need to state exactly which wood
you mean. But, if you use them when buying wood, it is
unlikely that the average timberyard man will know what
you are talking about. Fortunately, the woods on offer are
usually sufficiently limited in range for each type to be iden-
tified by a common name, and the seller will probably know
enough about the characteristics to tell you how a new wood
compares with another you know already. There are many
thousands of different species of tree yielding timber suitable for various branches of woodworking, but those avail-

able at any particular time or place will be comparatively few.

Anyone with a little experience can identify some woods by their appearance, if only in very general terms. But even amongst the common woods there are varieties that show subtle differences when you work them. The only true way to identify wood is by microscopic examination, and as most of us do not have facility to do this, we have to take the word of the suppliers.

Trees can be broadly divided into hardwoods and softwoods. In most cases that is a fair description of relative hardness, but there are a few softwoods harder than some hardwoods. Most softwoods come from coniferous, needle-leaved trees that keep their leaves during the winter. Hardwoods have broad leaves, and in more severe climates these tend to be shed during the winter. Softwood trees are commonest in the colder parts of the world, while many hardwoods grow in the tropics, but there is a considerable range of both varieties in all sorts of climate.

Softwoods grow quickly, maturing in 20 to 50 years. Some of them are grown to be pulped and made into newsprint. Hardwood may take hundreds of years to grow large enough for conversion to timber. The relative density of hardwoods is much greater than that of softwoods; some hardwoods are so dense that they will not float in water, which obviously makes them unsuitable for use in boat-building or similar work.

CONVERSION

When a tree grows it develops from the centre outwards, producing a ring of grain each year. The earlier rings become compressed and hardened as they form the strong heartwood around an almost invisible pith. The newer sapwood outside is not as strong or as durable as the heartwood. In some woods there is a very obvious division between heartwood and sapwood, but in others it is more gradual and therefore less obvious. As far as possible, sapwood should be avoided, but in some woods the difference in quality is slight. Wider boards will usually be cut across the heartwood, although there may be some sapwood at the edges. Narrow battens and strips may come from offcuts near the outside of the log and be entirely sapwood. If you want to ensure having heartwood, it may be better to cut down your own narrow pieces from wider boards.

The outside of a log is no use for general woodwork. Usually, the bark and the cambium layer under it should

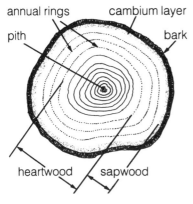

annual rings   cambium layer
pith   bark
heartwood   sapwood

1.1 *As a tree grows it forms annual rings outwards and these are the visible grain markings in cut wood. Bark is usually removed from the outside.*

have been removed (fig. 1.1), but for decorative outside woodwork these outer layers may be retained, giving a board with a waney edge.

The part of the log from which a board comes can be found by examining its end grain. This is better grasped if the methods of cutting are understood. The simplest way to convert a log to planks is to make a series of cuts straight across (fig. 1.2a). Another way is to turn the log through 90° between cuts, so that its section as it is reduced is square (fig. 1.2b). With both of these methods you can examine the end grain and see, to fairly close limits, where the board came from and how far it was from the centre of the tree. This could be important in relation to warping possibilities.

Another method of cutting is radial or quarter-sawing (fig. 1.2c). Making every cut truly radial is wasteful and cutting is usually done in steps with a quarter section (fig 1.2d). With this method only a few pieces are near radial. In addition to the annual rings around a section of log there are medullary rays, which radiate from the centre. They occur in all woods, but in most they are too fine to be seen with the naked eye. Oak is the best-known exception. The medullary rays can be seen at the end grain and when cut radially they produce a pattern known as *figuring*. Wainscot, or figured, oak is cut in this way.

SEASONING

The lifeblood of a tree is sap, which becomes excess moisture in the wood when the tree is felled and converted to boards. Most of this moisture must be removed before you use the wood, and this process is called seasoning. The traditional way is called 'air' or 'natural' seasoning, when the boards are stacked with spacers between them (fig. 1.3) and left to dry out to an acceptable level of sap content. The rule of thumb is one year of drying for every 2-3 cm (1 in) of thickness, so natural seasoning is a slow process. There are several ways of speeding the drying, usually with some form of kiln, which can reduce the period to weeks. Too hasty drying, however, causes warping, cracking and some other problems.

A small amount of moisture is normal and acceptable in wood, and, as wood is a natural material, it will always absorb and lose moisture, according to the temperature and relative humidity of the atmosphere. As wood dries, it shrinks, so if wood is stored in a workshop that is normally unheated, and then an object made from it is kept in a well

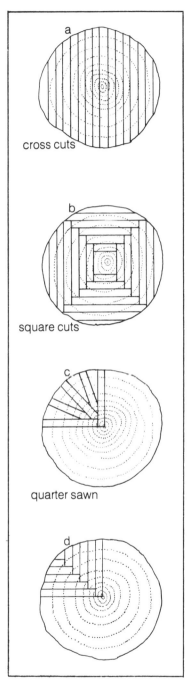

cross cuts

square cuts

quarter sawn

1.2 A log may be cut 'through and through' (a), it may be cut in alternate directions for different grain markings (b), it could be cut radially (c) or near radially (d) for the sake of figuring, particularly in oak.

1.3 *For natural seasoning boards are stacked so air can circulate.*

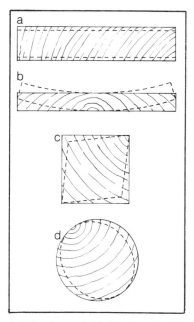

1.4 *Wood may shrink the direction of the grain lines as seen at the end, so a board with lines across gets thinner (a), one cut away from the centre of the tree will warp (b), a square will become a diamond section (c) and a round will become elliptical (d).*

heated room, parts may shrink or warp enough to spoil appearance or construction. Before making an object, it is advisable to store the wood for some time in the same sort of atmosphere, and temperature, as that in which the finished object is likely to be kept. In any case, it is always good practice to buy a stock of wood well before you need it, and to keep it for further natural seasoning before making something from it.

Shrinkage tends to reduce the length of the annual rings. If the board has been cut radially, with the annual rings appearing across the end from top to bottom, it will get thinner as it dries (fig. 1.4a); but any cross-wise shrinkage will be negligible. If the grain lines on the end show that the board was cut across the trunk of the tree further out from the centre, it will cast or warp as it dries. You can anticipate what may happen by imagining the grain lines trying to straighten out (fig. 1.4b). If you start with a square section, shrinking in the direction of the annual rings will pull the shape towards a diamond section (fig. 1.4c). Similarly, a circular cross-section will reduce to an elliptical section (fig. 1.4d).

Those examples suggest what may happen. If the wood has been properly seasoned, it may never shrink or warp enough to be noticeable. If you are aware of what might happen, you can allow for it during construction. For instance, a wide solid wood top can be held to rails with wood buttons engaging in slots, so that the top may get slightly wider or narrower without causing splits or joint failures.

SIZES

The maximum width and thickness of boards that can be cut from a tree must depend on the size of the tree. When allowance has been made for cutting off the bark and the outer sapwood, the available width may not be as great as expected, and further allowance must be made for the taper of the trunk and for cutting out any flaws. An extra charge is often made for particularly wide boards, so do not order wood wider than you need. In fact, you may get a better result by gluing together two narrower boards to make up a required width, as you can arrange the end grains so that any tendency to warp in one is reversed in the other.

Some wood is available in very long pieces, but for convenience in transport and storage it is usually supplied in lengths of about 6 m (20 ft) or less. If you need a single piece longer than the maximum normally available, you will probably have to place a special order. Do not order timber that is longer than you need. For example, if you want four pieces 4 m (13 ft) long, do not order one piece four times that length. A piece that long might not be in stock, while the yard man could probably find wood to cut the four pieces and you might gain some extra ends that he did not think worth cutting off.

If you buy your wood already planed (PAR), the sizes quoted will refer to dimensions as measured before planing. With power planers of the sizes used, your wood will probably be about 3 mm (⅛ in) undersize in each direction.

Knots in a board come where there was a branch leading off the trunk. A tree grown in a forest will have few knots because there were no branches in the lower part of the trunk. A tree grown in isolation may have many knots due to· branches in its lower part. Knots must be accepted and may even be regarded as decorative in the grain pattern of polished work. However, knots weaken the wood. If the part is load-carrying, a knot that is large in relation to the wood section should not be accepted. In softwoods, in particular, a black ring round a knot indicates a 'dead knot', one that is no longer bonded to the surrounding wood. A dead knot may fall out, and whether it does or not it contributes nothing to strength, so discard the wood or use it where this weakness does not matter.

Trees develop shakes, which are cracks due to the tree swinging and twisting in the wind. They may radiate from the centre or follow the lines of the annual rings. They are not apparent until the tree is felled and cut into boards. Usually wood can be cut to size around them. End cracks may occur during seasoning, but these should be cut off before the wood is sold.

Before ordering wood, prepare a cutting list showing all the pieces you need, correct to section, but allowing a little extra on the lengths. If you show this to your supplier, it will save him time and trouble in finding suitable pieces from his stock – and the saving should be reflected in the price. If you expect to be making considerable use of your workshop and have a good idea of the types of project you will undertake, it is worth buying more wood than you need for the immediate job, so that some can go into stock. This gives you something to draw from, and stops you having to go out again for just a small amount. Storing the wood in your workshop will also stabilize it by further seasoning. Aim to reach a stage where you have enough wood on your racks to tackle some projects without having to buy wood specially.

SOFTWOODS

Besides being soft, most softwoods are light, both in weight and in colour. Because they come from tall straight trees, boards tend to be available in good lengths, but the sections are not very wide. Some softwoods have many knots, which are acceptable if they are small – although knotty pine panelling, in which large knots are a feature, has enjoyed a vogue. In many softwoods the grain lines on the surface are not very obvious. In some woods there is a considerable amount of resin, which imparts durability and causes dark and light grain lines. Resin may not show up much in the paler softwoods except where it comes to the surface at knots. The knot can be sealed, usually with shellac (see p.185), then painted or varnished over so that the resin does not spoil the finish.

Softwoods are confusingly named and the common names are not always the same in every place. Spruce, fir and pine may be found applied to the same woods. These are the names of trees as well as the cut wood. Sitka spruce is the lightest and straightest-grained wood with the minimum of knots. Because of this it has been used in aircraft construction and in making wooden yacht masts, although its durability in wet conditions is poor. Firs are mostly natural poles, stripped of bark and used for rustic and other outdoor purposes. The word pine is not always correctly used, but it has found a place in furniture as 'stripped pine'. Yellow pine is a stable, easily-worked softwood that has been popular in patternmaking for metal casting.

At one time the common softwoods in Britain were red deal and white deal, with the red version being the better quality. The names have changed, and they are now known as Baltic redwoods. In America there are giant redwoods, which are not to be confused with the Baltic woods.

Most softwoods are not durable in damp conditions, although the modern method of impregnation with preservative makes them suitable for outdoor use. Larch is a softwood that is more durable outdoors than many others, and it can be used for boat planking. Several varieties of cypress have similar properties and are used instead of larch, particularly in America.

The wood with the most resin is pitch pine, which is obtainable in large sizes. It is strong and heavy, but the amount of resin makes it unsuitable for painting. Columbian and Oregon pines are straight-grained and have less resin, and can be used for spars and other parts requiring strength in the length with small cross-sections.

Cedar is a name given to both hard and soft woods, most of which are soft and light with a fragrance that makes them attractive for lining linen chests. Parana pine is variegated, with brown and occasional red streaks, and may be used as a general-purpose softwood.

In general, softwoods are not furniture woods, although they can be used internally and for parts that do not show. They are the woods for general carpentry and tend to be much cheaper than hardwoods. Such things as floors and roof trusses in ordinary buildings are made from softwoods, as is much domestic woodwork – usually painted, rather than given a clear finish. However, although softwoods suffer more from wear and tear than hardwoods do, it is possible to protect them with tough modern clear finishes. If the object being made has to be as light as possible, softwood should be used. Softwoods are more amenable to nailing, and can be used in situations where hardwoods would need joints cut or the parts screwed together.

HARDWOODS

Hardwoods of furniture quality mostly come from specialist suppliers, who are often knowledgeable on their stock and its properties for cabinetwork. This is important because there are many woods on the market, sometimes for short periods only, that are welcome alternatives to some of the more established furniture woods, and we need to know their characteristics before using them. With the enormous numbers of different hardwood trees growing in the world, and the different names applied to some of them, it is not always easy to find details in reference books, so accurate information from the man on the spot is invaluable.

The seasoning of hardwood is important, but it is a comparatively slow process. It is advisable to buy hardwoods well ahead of your needs, if possible, so that the wood can dry or stabilize in your store for a few months. The yard expert may be able to give you an idea of how the wood was seasoned, how long it has been in stock and what its present state should be.

Such things as shakes and knots will show, whether the wood is bought planed or unplaned, but it is not always easy to visualize the final appearance of the woodgrain if it is bought 'from the saw'. If you are unfamiliar with the type of wood, it is advisable to buy it planed or have one surface planed so that you can see the grain pattern. You are not necessarily looking for straightness of grain or freedom from knots and other flaws. If the purpose of the wood is structural, straight grain may be important, but in furniture much of the beauty of the wood is in wavy grain and other markings, provided that you are able to plane and work them smooth.

There is a great variety of hardwoods available. The ones listed below may be regarded as the standards for comparison if you are offered woods with which you are unfamiliar. You need to know the qualities of a new wood before you use it, and, if you are planning to make several matching pieces, whether supplies of it will be maintained.

English oak is a darkish brown, fairly hard and with many pockets in the grain. It is rather coarse and tended to be used for fairly massive furniture, although it can be carved in quite fine detail. The medullary rays are quite prominent and quarter-sawn boards show them cut through to make the well-known figuring. English oak is a strong structural timber and very durable, and there are examples of its use in architecture and furniture surviving after many centuries. Japanese oak has a very similar appearance, with prominent medullary rays, but it is softer and much easier to work. Chestnut is a wood sometimes used with or in place of oak. It comes from the sweet chestnut tree, not the horse chestnut. Its appearance can be matched closely to oak, but as its medullary rays are invisible it cannot be used where figuring is required. It is less durable, but for indoor furniture it will last as long as required.

Elm has almost disappeared from the market because of Dutch elm disease. In fact, the disease only affected the outside of the tree, so a good deal of useful wood could still be cut from the logs of a diseased tree. Elm has a similar brown colour to oak and has similar hardness. Much of its grain is very twisted, and finishing a surface can be difficult. It is a good wood for outdoor furniture, particularly as it is available in very wide boards, and with a waney edge, if required.

Because of its complicated grain an elm board has fairly equal strength in all directions; other woods, with straighter grain, are weaker across it. This makes elm suitable for seats and other broad expanses that may have to take loads in all directions. It is used for seats of Windsor chairs as well as milking stools.

Beech, another widely-used timber, is reddish-brown, and the reddish tinge may be intensified during seasoning. Once seasoned, it is very stable, which has made it the choice for wooden planes, mallet heads and many other tools. Beech does not have the sort of grain that makes it a feature on the surface of furniture. It is close and not prominently marked, and although medullary rays may be seen on the end grain, they are only visible as small flecks on a surface. However, it is good structurally and as a backing for veneer. It is one of the most easily turned woods, cutting fine detail with little risk of the grain breaking out. It is not very durable, so is unsuitable for outdoor use, unless treated.

Ash is a greyer brown than oak, but with a similar open grain. It is not durable, but in the past its flexibility and springiness, made it the best wood for shafts of a cart, hammer hafts, and similar applications where the springiness was needed to cushion the load. It is still used for furniture – although usually very wide boards cannot be obtained – and tools and farm implements. Ash can be steamed and bent to tighter curves and in thicker sections than most other woods. Hickory, smoother than ash, but with similar springy properties, is often used for hammer and axe handles instead of ash.

Mahogany is a name that covers a large range of woods, some of which are not truly of the mahogany family. This is the wood of the great cabinetmakers. All mahoganies come from the hotter countries, and species are usually known by their country of origin. Honduras mahogany is sometimes considered *the* high-class furniture wood, but very similar types come from other Central American countries. All have a reddish tinge that tends to intensify with exposure to light, but it is common in furniture-making to stain mahogany redder before finishing. These mahoganies come from large trees, so wide boards are often available. The woods are mostly used in the rather short lengths needed for furniture. Some furniture is made with choice mahogany veneers on a plainer and cheaper wood backing.

African mahogany is a browner red and straighter-grained lighter wood than these. Some of it, such as Gaboon, does not belong to the same family as the mahoganies from the other side of the Atlantic. With longer straighter lengths available, it is used in boat building.

Walnut has been used extensively in furniture and there are plenty of antique walnut pieces around, but its use now is not as common as it once was. It is brown or brownish-red with a close, fairly hard-textured grain and little prominent marking. The darker variety may be called 'black walnut'. Both varieties are strong and fairly easy to work, so surfaces can be brought to a good finish.

Teak is fairly costly as a solid wood, but it has become better known as a veneer on commercially-produced chipboard panels. It is a light brown wood with fairly straight grain. Its characteristic is an oiliness, which has a good preservative quality and makes teak one of the best woods for use in boat building. Because of the oiliness teak is better not treated with any of the usual furniture finishes. Sometimes it is left untreated, or given an oiled finish.

Afromosia comes from Africa. It looks similar and is very similar in character to teak, and can be used in place of it, usually at a lower cost.

Maple is a light-coloured furniture hardwood, chiefly seen only as veneer. It can be cut to show an attractive 'birds-eye' figuring, and such boards may be sold as 'birds-eye maple'.

Sycamore and plane are names for similar trees, although the wood from either may be called sycamore, or buttonwood. This near-white close-grained hardwood has a clear, smooth appearance. It stains easily and is sometimes matched to other woods. It is stable, but not very durable. It can be turned easily and is used in making some musical instruments. Large sizes are available and a board makes a good bench-top.

Lime is not used much today, although it is one of the easiest woods to work and was used to create some of the famous carvings of the past. It is lightweight and near white, without any strong markings.

Obeche is one of the woods that are technically hardwoods, although it is actually lighter and softer than some softwoods. It has a uniform cream colour with little prominence to the grain, which may interlock and be difficult to chisel across. It can be stained to match other hardwoods, and can be used for shelving and similar purposes instead of softwoods.

PLYWOOD

While solid wood has its attractions, it also has some limitations, particularly when wide, thin pieces are required, as can be seen in some of the cracked distorted panels and backs in old furniture. Plywood gives wide stable panels of wood in sizes bigger than most woodworkers will require. For door panels, cabinet backs and similar purposes, plywood is the material to use. Much early plywood was made of three plies held with glue that was unreliable, and that gave plywood a bad name, but modern plywood is nearly all bonded with a synthetic resin glue that holds well and is either water-resistant or fully waterproof.

Plywood is made with at least three veneers glued together with grains crossing (fig. 1.5a). There may be any number of veneers and they can be of different thicknesses within one overall thickness. A larger number of thin veneers is stronger than a smaller number of thick ones in the same total thickness. For example, five thicknesses (fig. 1.5b) within an overall depth of 9 mm (⅜ in) is stiffer than three thicknesses in the same total depth (fig. 1.5c). The total is always an odd number, so the grain of the outside veneers goes the same way – normally along the length of a sheet.

Many woods are made into plywood, provided that they can be cut from a rotating log with a knife to make veneers. A softwood used in large quantities is Douglas fir which has a coarse open surface, but most other plywoods are fairly smooth. Plywood can be given an extra face of choice veneer, either by the craftsmen or during manufacture, and in this way a plywood panel can be made to match a surrounding frame of solid wood.

Building-quality plywood may be bought with knots and other defects in one or both surfaces. In better plywood knots have been cut out and patched, or the veneers are of a type that is free of knots. Exterior-grade plywood is used for outdoor work. It should be a durable wood bonded with fully-waterproof glue. In some inferior plywood, joints in inner plies show gaps, which are weak spots. Of better quality than exterior-grade is marine-grade plywood, in which the core plies as well as the outside ones are of good quality and close-fitting. Marine-grade and much exterior-grade plywood are made of mahogany-like woods.

Metric measurements are usually used to specify the thickness of plywood, but imperial measurements are often used for standard surface sizes. Common thicknesses are from 6 mm (¼ in) to 25 mm (1 in) or more, but other boards now are usually used in place of the thicker grades. Although 3 mm (⅛ in) is usually the thinnest plywood available, some aircraft plywood goes down to three plies within an overall thickness of 1 mm (1/24 in). Sheets can be made up to suit needs, but the usual maximum size is 2400 × 1200 mm (96 × 48 in), that being the largest that one man can reach across and carry (a woodworker's reach was considered standard before metric measurements were introduced). Plywood is good stock and it is much cheaper to buy standard size sheets to cut yourself than to ask the supplier to cut pieces to suit your immediate needs.

1.5 *Plywood is made with veneers having their grains crossing (a) – either a large number of thin veneers (b) or a greater number of thick ones (c).*

HARDBOARD

Hardboard must not be confused with hardwood. Hardboard is made from wood that is pulped and compressed to make sheets usually 3 mm (⅛ in) thick. The face surface is smooth and hard, and the other side is rougher, with a pattern of crossed lines. Some hardboard is little better than cardboard, but other boards are compressed to a very hard state. The toughest hardboard is treated with oil and described as oil-tempered. This kind has a resistance to damp, but the other grades soften and deteriorate if they get wet.

The chief advantage of hardboard is that it is cheaper than plywood or any other form of board. It takes strain and can be used with solid wood, but it cannot be disguised because of its lack of grain. It can be used for such things as the backs of cupboards and the bottoms of drawers, and for side or door panels in less-important painted assemblies. Sizes are similar to those of plywood.

Hardboard can be bought with a regular pattern of holes, either for a ventilating panel or for use with hooks on which to hang tools. It may also be found in a form that has a pattern on the surface, such as a series of ridges, which can be cut across and used as moulding. This may suit something like a bar front, but is not a traditional furniture treatment.

Softboard is similar to hardboard, but deliberately made softer. It is sometimes used for insulation. Pins can be stuck into one grade, and this may be framed for use as a noticeboard.

BLOCKBOARD

1.6 Blockboard is thicker than most plywood and has a core of solid wood strips.

Instead of plywood being made up to a great thickness, the inside may be made of solid wood strips – giving blockboard, battenboard or solid-core plywood. Usually blockboard has two veneers on each side, their grain going the same way, with strips of a solid wood laid together on the inside (fig. 1.6). Thicknesses are from about 19 mm (¾ in) upwards. Thinner boards are more likely to be like normal plywood – all veneers. Blockboard provides a stiff panel suitable for table-tops and similar large areas. Compared with solid wood, blockwood and plywood are stable, so there is no fear of a broad top expanding and contracting in relation to the supports below. This means that, although in solid wood the joints used have to take account of this factor, a plywood or blockboard top can be fixed down rigidly.

CHIPBOARD

Boards made with particles of wood embedded in synthetic resin are sold as chipboard or particleboard. Usually the proportion of wood to resin is enough for edges to be sawn and planed in a similar way to wood. The untreated surfaces are smooth and level, but an unattractive drab grey in colour. In that form the material is used in place of floor boards and in other situations where appearance is unimportant. For household and furniture use chipboard is sold already surfaced in many ways. A common finish is a white plastic veneer on surfaces and edges, so a board may be bought already suitable for use as, say, a shelf. There are plastic surfaces that have simulated wood grain effects, which are often seen in mass-produced furniture. While that treatment may be acceptable for some purposes, wood-grain plastic cannot be used alongside. real wood. For use in furniture making, there are chipboard panels available already veneered with wood, but the range of veneers is limited, so it may be necessary to start by selecting other woods to match what can be obtained on chipboard.

For furniture making veneered panels are available – usually veneered on the surfaces and edges, but not the ends. There is not much choice of thickness. That most commonly available is about 18 mm (¾ in). Many stock widths and lengths can be had, and it is best to design the other parts around these.

For covering cut edges, strips of self-adhesive veneer can be bought. These are made slightly too wide, to allow for trimming after fitting (fig. 1.7), and can be pressed on with a hot domestic iron.

Chipboard is heavier than comparable solid wood or plywood, but it provides broad stable panels of reasonable strength. Any furniture shop shows how the material has revolutionized the mass-production furniture industry. The individual craftsman may not want to make one-off copies of the product of a factory, but within the limits of good design veneered chipboard has a place in furniture construction.

1.7 Chipboard made from wood particles and resin may have veneer on the surfaces and edges.

LAMINATED PLASTIC

What was originally designed as an insulating material made of paper embedded in resin has been developed into an attractive hard-surface material, a well-known trade name being *Formica*. This gives a hard kitchen top or similar working surface. It needs a stable base, such as plywood or blockboard, to which it is attached with a special contact adhesive. The regular plastic surface supplied on chipboard is not hard enough to stand up to kitchen and similar work, but laminated plastic is the treatment to use in making anything of that sort.

Laminated plastic is no more than 2 mm (just over 1/16 in) thick. Until it is fixed down the material is brittle and can be cracked, so careful handling is necessary.

Chapter 2
HAND TOOLS

Not very long ago all woodworking had to be done by hand methods. Some of it was very laborious and time-consuming and was mostly concerned with the preparation of wood for the skilled processes involved in finally fitting together and applying a finish to a piece of work. Fortunately, we now have power tools that can not only take out much of the hard work in the preparation of wood but also do certain later processes – often with greater precision than might be achieved by hand methods.

However, there is still an important place for hand tools. It may be possible to make some furniture and other wooden assemblies almost entirely by machine, but those designs are planned to suit the method, and lack the features that indicate craftsmanship. The pieces will be identical mass-production products, which have a place in modern life, but they cannot compare with the one-off products of a skilled craftsman. Even if similar pieces are made to the same plan, there will be slight subtle differences.

Anyone who wants to call himself a craftsman in wood needs hand tools. They are more important to him than power tools, as it is possible to buy wood already machined, so that a project can be completed by hand work. But it is advisable to have *some* power tools, if much work is to be tackled without outside help. Mostly, hand tools are accumulated and we discover from the work being tackled what we need. But a bewildering array can be had, so it is possible to be attracted by a tool and buy it – to discover later that, although it might be appropriate for more limited uses, it is not the best for the general run of work being tackled. Of course, no good quality tool is valueless, but in some cases another might have been a better buy.

Hand tools are only good investments if they are good quality. Tool catalogues show what is available. British woodworking tools have a reputation for quality, and they are often used in preference to locally-made tools in many countries of the world. If a few catalogues are examined, some manufacturers' names (not always of the large firms) will be found to occur often in connection with certain types of tools: some specialists, for example, make only carving tools. This shows they are the recognized makers of those tools for craftsmen. Their tools are not usually cheapest, but in general price is a good guide to quality.

Many woodworking tools have to cut. It is the quality of the steel in them that controls their ability to take and keep a sharp edge. A good tool by a recognized maker can be given a sharper edge and it will hold it longer than a cheap tool from an unknown source. So if it is necessary to be economical when buying tools, it is advisable to spend what you must to get good cutting tools, while settling for something cheaper when buying tools for other purposes. It may even be better to spread the purchase of tools, getting good ones at intervals as funds allow. Most tools will give a lifetime of service, so get the best you can and make sure they are appropriate to your needs.

SAWS

Heavier cutting of wood to size may be done with power tools, either before you buy the wood or with your own workshop equipment, so some of the larger traditional handsaws are no longer essential. For cutting along the grain a rip saw – with large teeth sharpened for such cutting – used to be used. If one is available it is worth keeping in your kit, but lengthwise cuts are now normally made with a circular saw. For cutting across the grain you will still need to use a hand or panel saw, 500 mm (20 in) to 650 mm (26 in) long and with teeth about 8 per 25 mm (1 in) (fig. 2.1). If most of your work is in hardwoods, it is better to use saws that have slightly finer teeth than the ones used on softwoods. You may still use a circular saw for many cuts across the grain, but there are times, if – for instance – you are away from a workshop, when the handsaw is essential. It is interesting to note that although most Western craftsmen use saws that cut on the push stroke, in the Far East it is more usual for saws to be sharpened so that their teeth cut on the pull stroke. With normal saw handles you get the best control if you hold with your forefinger pointing along the blade, and allow the teeth to cut without putting excessive hand pressure on the saw.

Your most important handsaw is a backsaw, for precision cuts when working at the bench (fig. 2.2). The larger version may be called a tenon saw and a smaller one is a dovetail saw, but both saws are used for many things besides cutting those joints. The most expensive saws have brass backs,

2.1 A hand saw is the general-purpose tool for cutting to size.

2.2 A backsaw is the benchwork tool for precision cuts.

2.3 A coping saw is for cutting curves in thinner wood.

2.4 A compass saw may have several blades to fit the handle for cutting curves.

2.5 A keyhole saw is used for fine internal cuts.

2.6 A marking knife is used instead of a pencil for greater accuracy in marking out.

which are heavier than the cheaper steel backs. Apart from the attractive appearance, the extra weight is an advantage. The teeth are sharpened for cutting across the grain and should be fairly fine. About 15 teeth per 25 mm (1 in) will suit a tenon saw, and a dovetail saw should have slightly finer teeth. There is no need to buy both saws in the first instance. A 300 mm (12 in) tenon saw will do its own and a dovetail saw's work, although the latter has advantages for small and delicate cuts.

Curves are most accurately and conveniently cut on a bandsaw, but if at first they have to be cut by hand the most suitable hand tool is a coping saw with some spare blades (fig. 2.3). These tools are all the same size, and the normal blades have rather coarse teeth. There are limitations, particularly in the distance a cut can be from the edge, but the blade can be turned in relation to the frame and with a little ingenuity it is possible to use the tool in many applications.

If you have a power bandsaw or a jigsaw, the coping saw need be the only handsaw for curves in your kit. But, if you want to cut curves far from an edge or in thicker wood than a coping saw will manage, there are narrow-bladed hand-saws, often sold with three blades of different widths to fit into one handle, which may be described as compass saws (fig. 2.4). If of good quality steel, they are worth having, but more than the usual proportion of inferior standard goods may be on offer when you are looking for this tool.

A useful narrow one-ended saw is a keyhole saw (fig. 2.5). Its name describes its purpose. It is possible to get a pad handle with a slot through it that will hold a keyhole saw or a metal-cutting hacksaw blade. Saws very similar to keyhole saws are obtainable to fit into some holders for disposable knife blades. Any of these are cheap and give you the means of tackling awkward internal cuts. All are soft, bending instead of breaking if the cut does not go as you wish, so do not expect the same stiffness as in other saws.

EDGE TOOLS

Much hand woodwork is done with chisels and other tools with sharp edges. It is in this sphere that the most bewildering variety of tools is offered. When getting a tool kit together, it is best to start with a few basic cutting tools and add to them as the work shows a need. As with other tools, it is unwise to accept any collection sold as a kit – you may be buying tools you never use.

All woodworkers have uses for knives. The cutting edge at the point is most important in a knife used for marking out across the grain: the rest of the knife can be almost any shape. There are special marking knives (fig. 2.6), but many craftsmen use ordinary pocket knives or one of the types sold with replaceable blades (fig. 2.7). A broken-off table knife can be sharpened to have a sloping cutting end for use as a marking knife. Some marking knives are sold with pointed awls at the other end. That can be dangerous, unless it has a cover. A marking awl has some uses, particularly for getting into places where a marking knife cannot go, such as around dovetail pins, but any pointed steel rod can be used for this (fig. 2.8). A sharpened steel knitting needle in a handle is suitable.

2.7 An alternative to the marking knife has replaceable blades.

Chisels and gouges

The general-purpose chisels are usually described as firmer chisels. They can have square or bevel edges (fig. 2.9). The bevel edges allow the chisel to get closer into corners. They may be slightly less stiff, but in modern woodworking they do not get such tough treatment. New chisels bought should have bevel edges. For a first purchase, four chisels should be enough: 25 mm (1 in), 19 mm (¾ in), 12 mm (½ in), 6 mm (¼ in).

2.8 A fine awl has uses in marking out.

Longer and thinner chisels are called paring chisels (fig. 2.10). Thicker chisels are called mortise chisels (fig. 2.11), from their original use in chopping out mortises. Both types still have uses, but purchase should be left until the work justifies it.

2.9 Firmer chisels are for general use and may have square or bevel edges.

Many chisels are offered with plastic handles moulded on. These are tough and strong enough to stand up to hammering, but most craftsmen prefer wooden handles with brass ferrules. Traditional woods for chisel handles are beech and box, but others are used. If you have a lathe, you can buy chisels without handles and make your own – individual and cheaper. With individually-turned handles you soon get to recognize them easier among shavings on the bench. The tapered tang goes into a hole tapered in steps, so that it drives in tightly without splitting the wood. There may be a leather washer between the chisel shoulder or bolster and the handle if it is likely to have its end hit.

2.10 A paring chisel is longer and thinner than a firmer chisel.

Further chisels bought will be of intermediate sizes, with some larger ones. A broad long paring chisel is often useful, but you have to remember that it is not stiff enough to be hit. If you cut many mortise and tenon joints, it is worth getting chisels the same width as the mortises most commonly cut – 9 mm (⅜ in) is a popular width. Here you may prefer a square-edged chisel to a bevel-edged one.

2.11 A mortise chisel is thickened to withstand levering.

2.12 A paring gouge is sharpened inside.

2.13 A gouge sharpened outside is used for hollowing.

2.14 A turning gouge is long and mainly used for roughing work to shape in a lathe.

2.15 A turning chisel is long and is mainly used for finishing turned surfaces.

2.16 A parting tool separates turned parts.

Gouges are chisels with curved cross-sections. You can do a considerable amount of woodwork without owning a gouge or finding a need for one, so purchase might be left until you feel the need. If a gouge is described as in-cannelled its sharpening bevel is on the inside of the curve (fig. 2.12). If it is out-cannelled the bevel is on the outside (fig. 2.13). The first type is used for paring to curved outlines, while the other is needed for scooping out hollows. If you decide to start with one in your kit, you are likely to find most use for a 12 mm (½ in) in-cannelled gouge.

Carving tools are specialized and of no use for general woodworking, so do not buy them unless your work will include carving. Carving tools include gouges in many widths, with different curves in each width, and with many shapes in each length. The variety of carving gouges alone may total more than one hundred, and this does not include chisels, 'V'-tools and others. A carver certainly need not start with them all, but he needs quite a large assortment.

Tools for use in lathe work

Wood turning may come within the general woodworker's scope and it can add considerably to what he can make. The basic tools for turning are few. There are now many special tools offered, but they should be avoided, at least until you have mastered the basic tools, which will do almost all the turning you require.

The general-purpose roughing tool is a gouge that is sharpened on the outside with a curved finger-nail end (fig. 2.14), although some turners favour a square-ended one for some work. For most turning of furniture parts a gouge 20 mm (13/16 in) or 12 mm (½ in) will do almost everything, but another 6 mm (¼ in) wide is also needed. Finishing work is done with a chisel, using slicing cuts. Its edge is angled and sharpened from both sides (fig. 2.15). Only a small part of its edge is cutting at any time, so width is not important – one 12 mm (½ in) would be a good first buy. A parting tool is like a narrow thick chisel (fig. 2.16). It cuts straight into the wood being turned, to cut off or mark a depth.

Turning tools do not have to withstand having their ends hit, so they are not given a shoulder where the tang enters the handle. However, leverage is important and the blades of turning chisels and gouges are much longer than the ordinary bench types; these are then fitted to long handles for even more leverage. Although handles may be bought with the tools, most turners buy them unhandled and make their own. Differing forms or woods make identification of tools easier among the chips of wood on the lathe bed.

The standard tools are made either in ordinary strength or 'long and strong'. The latter are for heavy work as the size and stiffness damp down vibration, which causes 'chatter marks' on the work. Most furniture turning can be done with the ordinary strength tools.

It is necessary to measure and compare diameters when turning. You cannot put a rule across the work, and the tool to use for this is a pair of callipers. They may have a screw adjustment, as used in engineering, but a cheaper simple pair with a friction joint – if you can get it – will serve just as well (fig. 2.17). There are also inside callipers, with their points turned outwards, but these are rarely needed and should not be included among first purchases.

For bowls and similar items, the turning tools cut with a scraping action and are given obtuse angles. Ends may be square across for outside curves (fig. 2.18), or curved for use inside the object being turned (fig. 2.19). they may be bought, but can be adapted from chisels or straight pieces of tool steel, by grinding the ends. Some are made by grinding worn-out files. One straight and one curved scraping tool of somewhere near 25 mm (1 in) may make the start of a bowl turner's kit.

2.17 *A simple form of calipers for checking diameters has a friction joint.*

2.18 *For bowl turning a straight-ended obtuse-angled tool is used for scraping.*

2.19 *A scraping tool is given a curved end for work inside a bowl.*

PLANES

Traditional British planes have nearly always been made of beech. There are many still about and secondhand ones may be worth having, but any new planes bought should be metal. There is something to be said for the feel of a wooden plane and the way it slides over the wood being worked, but modern metal planes remain flat and have adjustments lacking in the wooden planes, which needed an acquired skill to deal with their crude means of setting.

Much wood is now machine-planed, so the heavy work of hand planing to prepare wood has gone. But the machine surface has to be followed by hand work to get the best results, and there are parts that cannot be machine-planed, so a craftsman still needs all the general-purpose bench planes.

The planes made by leading manufacturers are often similar, and vital parts suit various makes within a range of sizes. A minimum bench set consists of smoothing plane (fig. 2.20), a jack plane (fig. 2.21) and a trying plane or jointer (fig. 2.22). These planes differ only in the lengths of their soles, and if at first only one plane is bought, it should be a jack plane. The name comes from 'jack-of-all-trades': it is the

2.20 *A smoothing plane is a finishing tool for bench use.*

2.21 *A jack plane is the general-purpose bench plane.*

2.22 A trying plane is longer and is particularly used for making straight edges.

general-purpose plane. It can be used for removing machine plane marks from surfaces, and straightening edges or cuts across end grain. But the smoothing plane would be better for removing machine plane marks, and the long sole of a jointer is more suitable for bridging hollows and getting an uneven edge level.

In all these planes cutting is done by a blade, often called a plane iron. Although this is now made of steel, old wooden planes had blades of iron, with steel welded on to make the cutting edge. Over the blade goes a cap iron or chip breaker. This latter name, used in North America, is more appropriate, as the chip breaker breaks up the shavings as they come off the wood and prevents the surface tearing. For finishing work it is set quite close to the edge (fig. 2.23), but for coarse cuts it is brought back a little (not more than 1-2 mm ($\frac{1}{16}$ in)).

2.23 The cap iron in a plane breaks off chips and is set close to the cutting edge.

The planes also have adjustable mouths, and this is a control often ignored by users. A screw inside the sole behind the blade allows it to move the support of the cutting edge backwards and forwards a small amount, and so alter the width of the space ahead of the cutting edge. For fine finishing of hardwoods the mouth should be narrow, while for coarse cuts on soft woods, besides moving the cap iron back, it would be better to widen the mouth. If only one plane is available, these adjustments will have to be made to suit uses. But, if three planes are available, the jack can be kept set for coarser work, while the jointer has its cap iron closer to the edge and the mouth narrower, with the smoothing plane normally set finer than that.

The planes have a screw adjustment for depth of cut and a lever to regulate the tilt of the blade crosswise, so once the blade has been put in and the cap iron secured, adjustments may be made with the hand holding the tote or handle.

2.24 A block plane is held in one hand for fine trimming and cuts across the grain.

One other plane worth having is generally described as a block plane (fig. 2.24). This has a single iron, with its bevel upwards, fitted at a lower angle than in the other planes. This is a one-hand plane, particularly intended for use across the grain, but it can often be used to take off a sharp edge or make some other small cut. In the simplest block plane you have to adjust the cutter by moving it about by hand before locking it, but the better block planes have screw and lever adjustment as well as a means of altering the width of the mouth. They are worth the extra cost.

There are two operations that you may be able to do with power tools instead of using hand planes. These are cutting rabbets and making grooves. If you have suitable power facilities, purchase of the hand planes can be delayed; but in some woodwork you may reach a stage where you would be glad of the hand tools to follow, or take the place of, machine rabbeting (rebating) or grooving.

To cut a rabbet, the plane needs to cut the full width of the sole. There are planes made like the bench planes just described, but with the ends of the plane irons brought out through notches in the side of the sole, to give this effect (fig. 2.25). There are also narrower rebate planes to give the same effect, but in neither case is there any control of the depth or width of the cut. For this the plane is called a fillister (fig. 2.26). It is a rebate plane with a depth stop at one side and a fence on an extension at the other. The stop fence can be removed to make it a simple rebate plane. The type commonly available has a second position for the cutter close to the front of the plane, so that it can become a bull-nosed plane to get close into the end of a stopped rabbet, leaving only a small amount of wood to be removed with a chisel. The fillister may have a little side cutter ahead of the main edge, to sever the grain fibres and prevent the surface tearing up and leaving a ragged edge when a rabbet is being cut across the end of a board.

This desirable facility is not shared by the plough plane, the tool used for cutting grooves (fig. 2.27). It has a sole as narrow as the smallest of its cutters, but cutters from about 3mm (⅛in) to 12mm (½in) can be fitted. Like the fillister it has a depth stop, and a fence to regulate the distance of the groove from the edge.

There are combination planes that will make rabbets, plough, cut mouldings and form other sections. One is called a '55', since that is the number of planing functions it has. Although this obviously has some attractions, most craftsmen prefer a plane specifically suited to each job, and a combination plane should certainly not be an early purchase.

2.25 A rebate plane has its cutting edge the full width.

2.26 A fillister is a rebate plane with depth and width guides.

2.27 A plough cutter has several cutters for making grooves of many widths.

2.28 *A hand router will level the bottom of a groove.*

2.29 *A spokeshave is a form of two-handled plane for use on curves.*

2.30 *An older spokeshave is made of wood with a cutter that slices.*

2.31 *A brace holds bits for drilling and may have a ratchet for use when the swing is restricted.*

The word 'router' is now accepted as referring to a power tool, but originally it was a type of plane with a projecting blade for levelling the bottom of a groove, such as a housing joint. Because of its appearance it was also known as an 'old woman's tooth'. The modern metal version (fig. 2.28) does not look so much like that, but it is a cheap and useful tool for this particular purpose.

Spokeshaves are like planes with handles at the sides. The modern metal version (fig. 2.29) has a wedged iron like a plane, but the older wooden type (fig. 2.30) has its cutter at a much flatter angle so that it makes more of a slice, and this may be found preferable when the tool is used to follow a curve. A spokeshave with a small flat sole is used on outside curves. One with a sole curved front to back is used on inside curves.

Much of the work of spokeshaves can be done with *Surform* tools. Spokeshaves belong to traditional craftsmanship, but *Surform* tools are quite effective, so the individual woodworker will have to decide which to buy and use.

DRILLING TOOLS

Old-time craftsmen talked of boring rather than drilling, but the latter term is more widely used. Almost up to the beginning of this century, when better drill bits for hand work began to appear, making holes was one of the less efficient processes in hand woodworking. By then, in any case, power drilling was becoming more common. Today it is probable that a craftsman who may have no other power equipment will have an electric drill. A hand-held electric drill or one of its more advanced variations takes much of the labour out of drilling and should produce cleaner and more accurate holes than boring with a brace and bit. However, there are steps in woodwork construction where a brace is necessary and a craftsman should include one in his tool kit.

It is worth getting a ratchet brace (fig. 2.31), as this allows you to turn the bit even when there is insufficient space for the handle to make a full circle. It also allows maximum leverage in a stubborn situation, as you can apply more turning power at some parts of the sweep than at others. Braces can be obtained with different lengths of sweep. A long sweep gives you more power, but you need more room to turn a full circle. The brace chuck is intended to take a standard square tapered end of a bit, but there are chucks to hold other shaped ends.

If an electric drill is available, most bits will be bought to fit that. These cannot be used in a brace. If bits are bought for the brace, they should be of the twist type, such as the *Jennings* type (fig. 2.32). These will drill shallow holes. An expansive bit to adjust to any large diameter hole is valuable, but not necessary as an early purchase. The usual bits have a central point that goes deeper than the main hole and may penetrate right through when the main hole is intended to be blind. The point is necessary to guide the drill as it penetrates. *Forstner* bits (fig. 2.33) are different, as they are guided by their circumference and have no extending central point. Besides making full holes, they can be used at an edge, where the circle breaks through the side. They are expensive, but should be remembered if the need arises.

Countersinking – hollowing for a screw head – is better done at the slow speed of a hand-turned brace than the high speed of an electric drill, so a suitable countersink bit for screws is worth having (fig. 2.34). A screwdriver bit should also be bought (fig. 2.35). More leverage can be applied to a stubborn screw with a bit and brace than by any other means.

Small holes for screws or other purposes, under about 6 mm (¼ in) diameter, are usually made with metalworking bits driven by the electric drill, but for the smallest sizes, under about 3 mm (⅛ in), this is rather clumsy and it is too easy to go too far. A simple wheel brace (fig. 2.36) gives better control and you are less likely to break the bits. The smallest wheel brace, with a chuck capacity of up to 6 mm (¼ in), is better than a breast drill or other large tool.

Gimlets are sold, but they should be avoided as they pull into the wood with a splitting action. An alternative to a small drill, for screws up to about 4 gauge, is a bradawl (fig. 2.37). Its chisel-shaped end is pushed in across the grain and quarter turns are given each way as it is pressed in. This severs the wood fibres and clears the way for the screw, but leaves the fibres ready to spring back and grip the screw threads, giving a stronger grip than in a hole where a drill has removed some of the wood as dust.

TOOLS USED FOR MEASURING AND TESTING

Apart, of course, from metrication in some countries there have been other changes in the way wood is measured and tested. The many versions of the folding carpenter's rule are almost obsolete. They have some uses, but should not be bought new. Most measuring is best done with an expanding tape or rule (fig. 2.38). Incidentally no craftsman talks

2.32 A twist bit draws itself into the wood and keeps straight in a deep hole.

2.33 A Forstner bit is guided by its circumference and can make part holes.

2.34 A countersink bit prepares holes to take screw heads.

2.35 A screwdriver bit gives increased leverage on stubborn screws.

2.36 A wheel brace can be used instead of an electric drill for small bits.

2.37 A bradawl will make holes for small screws.

2.38 *An expanding tape/rule serves for most measuring.*

2.39 *Try squares are for marking and testing squareness.*

2.40 *A combination square measures and tests mitres and levels as well as squareness.*

2.41 *For special angles an adjustable bevel can be set and locked.*

about a ruler – there is no final *r*. The rule's length depends on your requirements, but for bench use 2 m or 6 ft should be sufficient, with another longer one for use elsewhere on large projects. Even with metrication some measurements will be required in Imperial measure, so both scales should be included.

Straight steel rules have two uses. They will measure, but they are also good straight-edges. A 300 mm (12 in) size is convenient to handle, but one twice that length is worth having. It can be sprung to draw curves as well as being a straight-edge. Markings on it should not be too fine – not less than 1 mm or $\frac{1}{16}$ in for most of the length (although there could be finer markings for a short distance from one end) – and deep enough to be easily visible. Marks close together have to be shallower, which is one reason for close markings not extending too far along a rule. Stainless steel has attractions, but some stainless steel rules have very shallow markings.

Carpenters' pencils have rectangular section leads, so that they can be sharpened with a chisel end. Used on edge, it lasts longer between sharpenings than a round point. For accurate marking, where the cut line will not spoil a finished surface, it is better to cut distances across the grain with a knife, but pencils are frequently needed. Get them brightly coloured so as to be easily seen among shavings on the bench.

Angles and curves

Next to rules come try-squares, for marking and checking right-angles. This is another sphere where it is better to go for an all-metal square (fig. 2.39) than a wooden one with a metal blade. The all-metal square comes true and stays true. The truth of a square can be checked, even in the shop, by putting its stock against a straight edge and marking along its blade. Then turn it over and see if the mark matches.

A square with a 300 mm (12 in) blade will cope with most needs at the bench, but for marking out strips of wood of smaller section a smaller combination square (fig. 2.40) is more suitable. This is basically a rule with a sliding head on it that can be locked at any position. One side of the head is at 90° and the other is at 45° to the rule. Usually there is a spirit level in the head, so that it can be used to check whether something is vertical or horizontal. It may also have a small awl or scriber pushed into a hole in the head. Additional heads are available, less important for most woodworking. One is V-shaped, to allow the tool to be used to find the centre of a circle or draw a line square to a curve. The other is a head that can be adjusted to any angle to the rule with a built-in protractor. The basic combination square is more use than a small try-square; the other heads may be regarded as desirable, though not essential in a first tool kit.

The usual tool for marking angles other than square is an adjustable bevel (fig. 2.41). Some are made of wood, with a metal blade, but an all-metal one will stay accurate longer. There are various ways of locking the blade in position once it has been set. Some involve projections, such as levers or wing nuts. A flush screw that needs a screwdriver is better, as any fixture sticking out will stop it lying flat. Most angles to be marked or tested are fairly small, so a small adjustable bevel will do. If there is a need for a large one, it can be made from wood. Very large adjustable bevels are not usually available.

2.42 *Dividers must be stiff and lockable for marking wood.*

Large dividers are useful, not only for scratching circles, but for stepping off divisions along a line or around the circumference of a circle: a pair with 300 mm (12 in) arms will do (fig. 12.42). They should have stiff legs and a firm pivot, with a quadrant that locks firmly. Shaky dividers are no use. They are often called compasses, but a pair of compasses has one pencil point. For similar use, but a greater reach, trammel heads can be mounted on a strip of wood (fig. 2.43), but a strip of wood with two nails knocked through it serves the same purpose.

2.43 *Trammel heads will mount on a strip of wood for use as large compasses.*

Distances from an edge

2.44 *Notched wood and a pencil will make a line parallel to an edge.*

2.45 *A combination square can be used in a similar way.*

2.46 *A marking gauge is the general-purpose tool for scratching a line parallel with an edge.*

2.47 *A mortise gauge scratches two lines parallel with an edge, particularly for marking out mortise and tenon joints.*

2.48 *A cutting gauge cuts instead of scratches and is used for slicing veneers or marking cleanly across the grain.*

When lines have to be marked parallel to edges, gauges can be used to ensure accuracy and speed. It is possible to use a notched piece of wood with a pencil against it as it is drawn along (fig. 2.44). The end of a combination square can be similarly used with a pencil (fig. 2.45), but a marking gauge is more commonly used. Marking gauges are usually of wood with brass reinforcing on the face to take wear (fig. 2.46), but there are all-metal gauges. The thumbscrew in the wooden head is usually plastic, although older gauges have wood screws. The steel point is round, to scratch the wood.

A mortise gauge has two points (fig. 2.47), so that it can mark both sides of a tenon or mortise at the same time. Usually, one point is fixed to the stem, but the other is on a slide let into the stem, with a hand or screw adjustment to alter the distance between the points. Some of these gauges have a single point on the opposite side of the stem to the pair for mortises, so that they can be used as an ordinary marking gauge. It is not difficult to put a point in a mortise gauge bought without one, so avoiding the need to buy two gauges at first, although eventually you will probably be glad of more than one marking gauge.

A similar gauge, which may be needed as your work gets more ambitious, is a cutting gauge (fig. 2.48). Instead of the scratching point there is a blade sharpened on its end like a knife and held in place with a wedge. It will slice strips of veneer to width, cutting thicker strips by repeated passes from opposite sides. It can also be used as a marking gauge across the grain, making a cut instead of tearing the fibres as a round point does. A less-common marking or cutting gauge has a rotating wheel with a knife edge on the end of the stem. Besides its value for marking across the grain, it can be used close inside a rabbet or other obstruction – where the projecting end of the usual marking gauge could not reach.

CRAMPS

There are frequent occasions when you have to hold, pull or squeeze things together. Some improvisations are described later, and some devices are part of the bench or other fixed equipment, but there are a number of holding and gripping devices that are separate hand tools. Most prominent in your needs are 'G' cramps (fig. 2.49). They can be had in many sizes, described in terms of their capacity. Large ones are clumsy for holding small things, and some large cramps do not close fully, so a range of sizes is desirable. It helps to have two of each size, as cramping is often done in pairs. Much depends on the type of work being undertaken, but two at 75 mm (3 in) and two at 150 mm (6 in) could be your first purchases.

2.49 G cramps, in many sizes, are general-purpose tools for squeezing parts together.

There are several makes of adjustable cramp, and these allow one head to be slid to a convenient position (fig. 2.50). These can take the place of some fixed 'G' cramps. The cramps must hold their shape and the better ones are cast steel, but for light holding of small items bent strip metal cramps – sometimes described as fretwork cramps – can be used. A use in the workshop can be found for discarded domestic equipment with cramp action.

2.50 An adjustable cramp, with one head movable, can take the place of several G cramps.

For a greater reach than is possible with a 'G' cramp there are several versions of bar or sash cramps. Usually there is a sliding head on a bar, with a means of stopping it at many places, and a fixed head on the end of the bar to squeeze parts held between the heads (fig. 2.51). Much furniture is framed, and bar cramps are the best tools for pulling the joints together. Two with 900 mm (36 in) bars are needed for most work on furniture. Improvisations are possible (see Chapter 4), but if much furniture or other framed woodwork is to be made, bar cramps are quicker and more reliable. Extension bars are obtainable, but unless you need these it is better to start with plain bar cramps. A few bar cramps can have their heads turned round to provide an outward thrust if necessary.

2.51 A bar or sash cramp is used where a greater reach is needed than is possible with a G cramp.

As a cheaper alternative to bar cramps, or a means of supplementing them with this extra facility, there are loose cramp heads for mounting on the edge of a board (fig. 2.52). They are effective, and allow a cramp to be made up to any length.

2.52 Sliding cramp heads can be fixed on the edge of a board for setting to any distance.

2.53 A dog cramps when driven into the end grain of two boards.

2.54 Circular spring clips are for cramping picture frame mitres.

2.55 A corner cramp holds a mitre while it is being joined.

2.56 A general-purpose woodworking hammer has a Warrington-pattern head.

2.57 A claw hammer can withdraw nails.

Not all cramping needs are massive. Boards can be pulled together with joiners' dogs (fig. 2.53). These are made with wedge-shaped legs, parallel outside and tapered inside. When driven into the end grain of two boards that have to be pulled together they apply considerable compression on the joint. For a picture frame corner, or other light mitre, there are sprung circular clips (fig. 2.54), that have to be opened and positioned with a special tool with a pliers action. There are corner cramps (fig. 2.55) that hold mitres together, using screws in the same way as 'G' cramps do. 'G' cramps can be bought with a screw working through the body at right-angles to the main thrust, to put on a three-way pressure. These and other special cramps may be considered when your pattern of work has been settled, but plenty of 'G' cramps and at least two bar cramps should be given priority.

For smaller cramping needs there are tools with a pliers-like action. Simple pliers have limited uses, but the type that can be locked into position with a screw and lever action serve as small cramps to hold parts being worked on or while glue sets.

DRIVERS

At least one hammer is needed. Many modern hammers have the head and handle in one piece, with – in most cases – a rubber grip. These have no resilience, and shocks are transferred to your hand with every blow. That may not matter for occasional hammering, but a woodworking craftsman prefers a steel head on an ash shaft, where the wood cushions any shock. If the head is properly wedged and sealed, there should be little risk of the joint loosening or parting. For most woodwork on a bench a cross-pein hammer is usual, with a Warrington pattern head (fig. 2.56). There is a satisfactory balance, and the thin pein will get into restricted places. It is advisable to test the weight and balance of a new hammer, to suit yourself.

A claw hammer (fig. 2.57) is more the tool of a general outdoor carpenter, who assembles parts with nails and sometimes has to pull one out. If that is what you plan to do, get a claw hammer, but otherwise the Warrington pattern is more likely to suit you. As well as a hammer for general use, a very light similar one is useful for driving pins and tiny nails, if that is the sort of work you will be doing.

Pincers often have to be used with hammers. Some are made with narrow heads. Probably that was the easy shape for a blacksmith to make, but you get more leverage from a wide head (fig. 2.58). See that the ends meet and are bev-elled inside only, so as to get close to the wood, but not so sharp that they cut off the nail-head.

Also used with hammers are nail punches or setts (fig. 2.59). They may be round and knurled for a grip, or of ta-pered rectangular section. The end should be slightly small-er than the nail head it is to drive, and some ends are hollow to prevent slipping. A few nail setts might be bought, but they can be filed from steel rod or even thick nails. It is worth getting a centre punch (fig. 2.60), which is really a metalworking tool but can be used on wood to locate with a positive dent the point where a drill bit should enter.

A tool with a steel head is a hammer, but if the head is of wood or any soft material it is called a mallet. The traditional English mallet has a squared beech head, with the handle as a taper through it. Centrifugal force then keeps the head tight on the handle (fig. 2.61). This is a fine tool to buy or make. It can be used on chisels or on wooden parts being assembled. The alternative is a cylindrical head on a wedged handle (fig. 2.62). The boxwood head on an ash shaft can swing a considerable weight in comparatively small bulk. Other mallets now have plastic heads, some with removable faces and others with lead shot inside. A carver uses a mallet with a round head in line with the handle (fig. 2.63) and this can be used with ordinary chisels if you wish. If you have a lathe, you could make such a mallet as a turning project.

Screwdrivers

Screwdrivers play a large part in some branches of wood-work. Ideally, you have a screwdriver that is an exact match for each size of screw being used, but in practice it is poss-ible to make each blade work with a few sizes. Even then you need several screwdrivers. There are combination tools, in which you change the ends, but if many screws have to be driven it is more convenient to have a screwdriv-er that does not have loose parts, so in general it is best to start with plain screwdrivers. There are ratchet screwdriv-ers and some very good pump-action drivers. Both are use-ful if you have to drive hundreds of screws quickly, as may happen when building a boat, but – for occasional screws in normal assembly work – simple screwdrivers are cheaper and more effective.

Most screws for general use have slotted heads. There are screws for mass-production work that have star-shaped sockets and other patterns in the heads. Some of these may

2.58 *Pincers grip and pull nails.*

2.59 *A nail punch has a small flat or hollow end for driving nail heads below the surface.*

2.60 *A centre punch will make a dent in wood or metal for starting a drill.*

2.61 *The traditional woodworking mallet has a squared head on a tapered handle.*

2.62 *A mallet with a cylindrical wooden head can also be used for general woodworking.*

2.63 *A woodcarver favours a mallet with a round head.*

2.64 *A screwdriver with an oval handle is best for driving woodscrews.*

be used by hand driving, and drivers with matching ends are needed. For the screw sizes likely to be used there are three sizes of sockets to be matched. Other screws have square sockets. For these special screws, which may be used only occasionally, you could use a driver with interchangeable ends, but it is better to avoid these screws and use only slotted ones.

To drive a screw you need leverage. Not much may be needed to drive a small screw, but a long driver exerts more leverage than a short one – because of the slight movement out of line as you turn – so get long screwdrivers. Choose oval heads for the same reason (fig. 2.64) (wood gives a better grip than plastic, but you may have to accept plastic). Another way of applying extra leverage is with pliers at the flat section at the top of the shaft just below the handle on some screwdrivers. There will be places where you cannot use the increased leverage of a long screwdriver, so have a few short ones. One should be broad in the handle and the end, for turning large-headed screws like the one in a plane cap iron. There are offset screwdrivers for awkard places, but they are rarely needed.

FILES AND SCRAPERS

2.65 *Surform tools in many forms have disposable perforated blades.*

At one time a carpenter used files very similar to those used on metal and rasps for coarser work. A file has teeth cut with lines across. A rasp has teeth individually cut. These tools are still of use, but their place has mostly been taken by *Surform* tools (fig. 2.65). The cutting parts have holes making teeth through sheet steel, and the strip blade is replaced when blunted. The common tools take flat or curved blades, but there are others. Their effect is very similar to that of planing, and the tools are particularly useful on shaped parts, such as rounded ends or hollowed edges for gripping.

2.66 *A cabinet scraper is a flat steel plate sharpened with burred edges.*

When grain is wild and tends to tear up whatever way it is planed, the tool for smoothing it is a scraper. The traditional tool is a flat rectangular piece of tool steel (fig. 2.66) of a size to hold in both hands. Its edge is sharpened, so that a slight burr is turned over (see Chapter 8). If the scraper is held so that it is slightly bowed and tilted to get the burr cutting, a very thin shaving is removed. Scraping in this way may follow planing when the finest surface is required on hardwood. The scraper edge is maintained by rubbing with a hard steel burnisher, which is a piece of round, flat or elliptical section steel in a handle (fig. 2.67). It may be possible to use the back of a chisel or gouge, but a proper burnisher should be made or bought.

There are tools with bodies like planes and spokeshaves that will hold a cabinet scraper correctly, but hand holding is usual. Other scrapers are made in a hook form to mount in a handle, for pulling. The best-known make is *Skarsten.* The handles take several forms, but the actual cutter hooks into a holder and can be driven out and replaced when blunt (fig. 2.68). Some blades are intended for paint removal and other purposes, but with the appropriate blade the effect on wood is similar to using a cabinet scraper.

2.67 *A hard steel burnisher is used to turn over the burred edge of a scraper.*

Sanding follows scraping, or may follow on directly after planing. There are ways of power sanding, but for hand sanding a flat surface the paper is wrapped around a block, usually of a size to take one quarter of a standard sheet, which is coated with glass or garnet – not sand. The block needs some resilience and cork has been found to be very suitable. These blocks may be bought, but one could be made by facing a wood block with hard rubber or something similar.

SHARPENING EQUIPMENT

Methods of sharpening are described in Chapter 8. Tool catalogues show a large range of sharpening devices, some of them very expensive, but sharpening any tool consists of rubbing the cutting edge thin with successively finer grits. That is all – the back-up equipment is not important.

2.68 *Skarsten scrapers have disposable hooked blades.*

If much metal has to be removed, some sort of rotating abrasive stone is useful (see Chapter 3), but a coarse flat stone will do the same thing almost as quickly. Abrasive stones may be lubricated with water or oil, and as oil and water will not mix, you must settle for one or the other. In most countries oil is preferred – this must be very thin lubricating oil or even paraffin. Old-time craftsmen had their own special mixtures of oil, but any oil that does not clog the pores of the stone or keep the tool edge away from it is suitable.

For general sharpening, a stone should be about 200 mm (8 in) by 50 mm (2 in) in surface area – and preferably mounted in a box or a hollowed block, which you can make yourself (fig. 2.69). In this case the tool is rubbed on the stone, but other smaller stones, called slips, are rubbed on the tool – inside a gouge for example (fig. 2.70).

2.69 *An oilstone for sharpening tools is best mounted in a case.*

Sharpening stones may be natural or manufactured. The manufactured stones give a control of grit size. Several grades are available and it is possible to get a combination stone, fine on one side and coarse on the other. This may be a good buy for a first stone. Manufactured stones produce an

2.70 *A slip is an oilstone shaped for sharpening inside curved edges.*

edge good enough for most purposes, but for the finest edges they should be followed by a natural stone.

For the very finest edge the tool may be drawn along a strop, which is just a piece of leather on a wood backing, dressed with a special honing paste. For most woodworking there is no need to strop a tool, but you may need to use one when carving.

Chapter 3
POWER TOOLS

These are tools in which some power is provided to supplement the user's skill: they do not do all the work. It is wrong to think of them as production machines, though something of the sort may be used in industry for quantity-production. When used by a craftsman a power tool simply speeds his work, as well as lessening the labour and increasing accuracy in some processes. As with hand tools, there is a bewildering variety of power tools on the market and you should take care to select tools that suit your needs. It is no use paying extra for a particular facility, only to find that you rarely use it or that it does not do exactly what you want, so that you have to follow with hand work that could have accomplished the whole task with little more effort.

At one time power tools were not individually motorized and had to be driven by belts from shafting powered by one motor or engine. Those days have gone and it would be unwise to acquire a secondhand machine that needed outside power, unless that could be arranged compactly near it. Modern power tools have individual electric motors, built-in or closely connected by a belt or other drive mechanism. The power needed for many woodworking machines can be taken from a domestic supply via a simple plug, although it is better to have some machines wired in permanently.

Electric motors are graded in terms of their horsepower. For most machines this is expressed in fractions – ¼, ⅓, ½ etc. If a machine is offered with a choice of motor, it is usually better to choose the higher power. The initial cost may be more, but running costs are little different. The lower power may be sufficient for occasional and light use, but the more powerful motor is best for long and heavier use.

Many machines have a switch built in, and that will have been matched to the motor by the makers. If a switch has to be provided, do not choose a simple on-off one, but go for a push-button type with a cut-out that protects you and the motor in emergency. These have a prominent red button that you can feel, as well as see, to switch off quickly. If wiring has to be installed and connected, it should be done by an expert.

Power tools are broadly divided into portable and fixed ones. In general, besides being light enough to be lifted and moved about, a portable tool is taken to and moved over the work, while a fixed power tool has the work brought to and moved over it. Both types have their place, and the fixed ones can usually deal with heavier and larger work more successfully. For some work both types are suitable and a particular craftsman has to decide which will suit his purpose. There are a few machines adaptable to both functions. Much depends on the work being tackled. If what is being made is all done in the workshop, more fixed machines may be used than if outdoor carpentry or built-in furniture are the main products.

DRILLS

3.1 *A portable electric drill is the most-used power tool.*

Portable electric drills are the most commonly-used power tools (fig. 3.1) and purchase is justified for most woodworking activities. Many that are offered are aimed at the amateur do-it-yourself market and have quite low prices. These have their uses, but if the drill is intended to be a craft investment, it is better to buy one intended for professional use: the motor will be better able to stand up to prolonged and heavy use.

An electric motor only develops maximum power if it can revolve at high speed. That means it must be geared down, and in many drills there is a selector at the chuck that gives a choice of two or more speeds. This is desirable, as if you want to drill large diameter holes in wood you need a lower speed than is suitable for drilling small holes in metal.

3.2 *An electric drill takes metalworking twist drills for use in wood and other materials.*

The chuck on an electric drill is self-centring, to take drills with round parallel shafts. The smallest usual capacity is 6 mm (¼), but many chucks open to take 9 mm (⅜) or more. The larger chucks go with increased power in the tool. If the main use for your drill will be in making holes for screws, the lighter small-capacity drill is more convenient to use, but for large holes, particularly in hardwood, the better reserve of power of a bigger drill is worth having. It can also be used for screw and similar small holes.

3.3 *For larger holes an electric drill is used with a spade bit.*

As the three jaws in the chuck have to grip a round shaft that will slip if not firmly held, their grip must be tight. Usually a key is provided, and it is important that it works in a way that puts adequate pressure on the chuck jaws. If a drill slips, it and the chuck jaws can be damaged. The key should be attached to the drill with a cord or in some other way, as the drill is no use without it and searching for a loose key is a waste of time.

For ordinary drilling of small holes, where smoothness of the hole is unimportant, metalworking twist drills (fig. 3.2) are suitable. These can be obtained in sizes differing from screw sizes by much less than will matter in woodwork. There is no need for the more costly high-speed steel drills, but the cheap short 'jobber's' drills should be avoided. Carbon steel drills in standard lengths are suitable.

Drill bits for use in wood at the higher speed of an electric drill have a different form from those used in a hand brace. For fairly shallow holes there are spade bits (fig. 3.3) in diameters from 6mm (¼in) to upwards of 25mm (1in). Three flats on the shaft end reduce the risk of the chuck jaws slipping when subjected to the considerable torque of drilling with the larger diameters. For deeper holes there are drills with twists along their length and shafts whose diameter is usually 6mm (¼in) (fig. 3.4). They can be used to drill shallow holes too. Countersink bits are available for power drills, but this work is better done at the slow speed of a hand brace.

3.4 *For deeper holes there are special twist drills for power driving.*

DRILL STANDS

For accurate control of a drill bit, it should be mounted and driven in a stand. Ideally a separate drill press should be used, but the expense of this would be justified only in a large comprehensively-equipped workshop. For most purposes, satisfactory results can be achieved with a portable electric drill mounted in a stand (fig. 3.5). This can easily be removed for use freehand, although the state of work may justify keeping a second electric drill in the stand most of the time.

The main advantage of using a stand is that holes drilled with one are known to be square to the base in all directions, as is necessary in, for example, holes for dowels. The stand is usually equipped with a depth stop, so holes can be made to uniform depth. For freehand drilling there are depth stops to put on the bit. They work, but are inclined to rub the surface of the work, which the stop on the pillar of a stand does not.

Some bits are unsuitable for use freehand. A forstner bit is more easily controlled if a stand is used. The rather similar saw tooth centre bit is also designed for use with a pillar stand (fig. 3.6), although both bits can be used with suitable equipment in a lathe. They make clean holes from 9mm (⅜in) to 50mm (2in) in diameter. Another bit that can be used only with a drill in a stand or a drill press is a plug cutter – which is a sort of hollow drill (fig. 3.7) that cuts a ring

3.5 *A bench stand for an electric drill allows drilling with precision and permits other functions besides drilling.*

3.6 *A saw tooth bit can only be used with a drill in a stand.*

3.7 *A plug cutter, used with an electric drill in a stand, cuts small cylinders of wood.*

3.8 *The plugs cut by a plug cutter can be made to match surrounding wood when used to fill counterbored holes.*

3.9 *A hollow mortise tool, driven by an adapted electric drill, cuts square holes, so several adjoining holes can form a mortise.*

3.10 *A mortise miller bit cuts on its side and may be moved along to make a mortise.*

in the wood, so that the plug at the centre can be broken out and used with its cross grain matching surrounding wood, over the head of a counterbored screw (fig. 3.8).

A drill press or an electric drill in a stand can be used for making mortises. The tool used is a sort of hollow square chisel, down which a twist drill can work (fig. 3.9). With a suitable attachment the outer part is forced downwards to cut a square hole, while the twist drill removes the waste. The mortise is made with a series of adjoining square holes. Sizes available are from 6 mm (¼ in) to 18 mm (¾ in) across. You also need a sharpening tool, like a large countersink, to sharpen the square chisel.

There are alternatives to that mortise tool. If you are cutting only a few mortises, you may first drill and then use a hand-held chisel: your budget for new tools may not allow you to buy specialist tools at first. It is possible to use a router cutter to make a mortise with a rounded end, which can be squared off with a hand-held chisel. There are mortise miller bits (fig. 3.10), which quickly cut mortises when used with suitable equipment in a lathe or other machine. The method and equipment chosen will depend on your needs.

DRILL ACCESSORIES

A large number of accessories is offered for use with electric drills. Mostly they are aimed at the amateur, and most of them are unsuitable for the serious woodworker. Apart from the fact that many accessories are not sturdy enough for anything but light work, which may often be more easily done by hand, changing uses of power tool can be time consuming and it is better to aim at having one tool for each sort of job as soon as possible.

There are some attachments that allow you to groove and shape with an effect similar to that of a router, while the electric drill is still on its stand, but the router and its cutters are preferable. Pairs of cutters are available for making tongue and groove joints, but router or spindle cutters are better, as would be cutting by hand with fillister and plough planes.

If you expect to drive large numbers of screws, there is a screwdriver attachment that freewheels after the screw has been driven tight, but a hand-held pump action screwdriver may be preferred, as less likely to slip and mark the surrounding wood.

A rubber backing disc for a sanding disc is worth while (see the sanding section, pp.52-3). A circular wire brush mounted on an arbor to fit in the drill chuck is also useful for removing rust and for other cleaning jobs. A bench stand to hold the drill so that it is horizontal can be useful, with the above attachments and others. A stand that extends to form a lathe is of doubtful value, although if you do not have a lathe as well it allows you to turn small parts, up to the size of tool handles. Adaptors to make the drill into a portable circular saw, a jigsaw or even a planer, tend to be cumbersome and lacking in power.

One useful accessory is a dowelling jig. There are several types, of varying degrees of complexity, but their purpose is to guide the drill squarely, and at regular pre-set intervals, into both pieces to be joined (fig. 3.11). You can get the same results by careful marking out and drilling, but the jig ensures accuracy and is particularly useful when making dowelled joints in chipboard. Simple alternatives are a set of little pointed plugs (fig. 3.12). To use these you drill the holes in one part, put the plugs in the holes, and press the drilled part against the other to mark the centres to drill there. For many assemblies they are as effective as a jig.

A dovetail jig (fig. 3.13) allows you to use the electric drill to cut accurate dovetails, similar in appearance to those seen in mass-produced furniture, with the pins and tails the same width. If that is what you want, this is fine, but the mark of hand-cut dovetails is wider tails than the pins between them. If you want your drawers and similar parts to show the marks of hand craftsmanship, this jig is not for you.

POWER SAWS

Next to an electric drill, among the power tools needed in most woodworking shops, is one or more power saws. Which to choose from the variety available depends on the work done. Of the hand-held power saws there are circular saws, which do much of the work of handsaws with little effort, cutting with the grain or across it, and jigsaws – which cut curves and will do a certain amount of straight cutting.

The best known fixed saw is a circular saw, available in capacities up to more than will be needed in most individual workshops. A bandsaw cuts curves in much thicker wood than a jigsaw can and it is also capable of straight cuts. It may be more use than a small fixed circular saw as the first power saw to be fitted in a workshop. A radial arm saw is a circular saw that can be moved across the wood on an arm. It may have a greater number of possible joint-cutting and similar functions, but the fixed saw – which may be called a table saw – is probably more use for cutting wood to size, and radial arm saws are not universally popular.

3.11 *A dowelling jig can be set to ensure holes matching in meeting parts.*

3.12 *Dowel points can be used in one set of holes to mark matching holes in another part.*

3.13 *A dovetail jig and its cutter driven by an electric drill will cut the parts of a dovetail joint.*

3.14 *A hand-held circular saw does general sawing that would otherwise be done with hand saws.*

Portable Circular Saw

A hand-held circular saw has the saw blade in a protective case, with below it a sprung guard that pushes out of the way against the wood being cut. There is a handle above the case and the motor projects to one side (fig. 3.14). A small one might be used in one hand, but most need two hands. The saw blade has much larger teeth than on a handsaw and they are usually of a form that is a compromise between cross-cutting and ripping along the grain. The sole through which the blade projects can be adjusted so that it is possible to limit the amount of blade projecting, for cutting grooves or rabbets or for tilting. There is an adjustable fence to guide its cut parallel to an edge, and a mark on the front of the sole serves as a guide for freehand cutting.

The power for some small circular saws is based on an adapted drill motor and this is unlikely to stand up to prolonged heavy use. Larger portable circular saws have more powerful motors, but are heavier; for some jobs you may find it simpler to use a handsaw or take the wood to a fixed circular saw.

A portable circular saw blade revolving rapidly can be dangerous: beware of the teeth below the wood as it cuts across. Its guard keeps it covered except when cutting, but care is needed to prevent the wood worked on from moving.

Jigsaw

The basic jigsaw has the motor horizontal and a handle above it, while a saw blade projects below a sole at one end, operating with a reciprocating motion (fig. 3.15). the cut is normally square to the sole, but in some jigsaws this can be tilted either way for angled cuts. A fence may be fitted to make cuts parallel to an edge, or the whole tool may pivot on a centre for cutting circles.

The blade cuts on the up stroke, so any roughness left is on the top surface of the wood. Some jigsaws have a blower to clear dust. The blade is held at the top by a clamping device, which is not the same in all makes. Blades are made with different teeth spacing, and in types suitable for plastics and metals as well as wood. There are wide blades for easier cutting of straight lines. The actual reciprocating motion is small, so on thinner woods only a few teeth get worn. In some saws it is possible to break off a blade and grind its top again to fit the clamping arrangements and give further use to the blade with other teeth.

A jigsaw is mainly a freehand tool and you can cut intri-

3.15 *A powered jigsaw is a hand-held tool for cutting curves.*

cate shapes down to about 12mm (½in) radius anywhere on a sheet, or follow a straight line reasonably well. The cut may wander from perpendicular to the surface, so some trimming of edges may be needed. The jigsaw lacks the precision of a bandsaw in this way, but gains by being able to be used at any distance from an edge.

Circular Saw

A fixed circular saw is often the first static power tool to be installed in a workshop. For one to be of maximum use there should be plenty of clear space all round, as at the start of a cut boards being ripped have to extend their full length at one end, and at the finish they must extend the same amount at the other end. There is a similar problem with cross cutting. Ideally, it should be possible to move a full standard 8ft × 4ft plywood sheet into position for a cut to be made anywhere on it. It may be impossible to achieve this, but this is the working area to be aimed at. If the table of the saw is higher than the things around it, it will be more versatile.

A circular saw is mounted on a spindle driven by a motor usually via a belt. It projects through a slot in a table and wood is pushed against it for cutting. The cut breaks through downwards, so any raggedness is on the underside. There is a fence alongside the saw to guide wood for parallel cuts. There is often a groove parallel with the blade, and an adjustable guide slides in this to hold wood being pushed through at an angle.

The table may be adjusted in height or the saw assembly may move up and down. The former is usual and preferable. This allows any amount of saw blade to project. The table may also tilt for making angled cuts.

The whole tool can be mounted on a bench (fig. 3.16) or be given legs or a stand to the floor. A considerable amount of sawdust is produced, and this must be led away via a chute or other means. There may be sealed bearings, or you may have to lubricate frequently.

Over the saw there is a guard that can be lifted and tilted, but it should be kept in position during cutting. At the far side of the saw is a riving knife, which is a steel plate that keeps the cut open as the wood passes across the blade. If you want to cut a groove, or otherwise use the saw only partly through the wood, the guard and riving knife must be removed. In some machines they swing out of the way, but in others nuts must be slackened.

A large table is an advantage, as it steadies large pieces of wood, but space available will limit this. Some machines

3.16 *Circular saw benches are made in many sizes and can be adjusted for cuts additional to straight cutting to length or width.*

have extending arms. With others you can make or buy stands with rollers at the same level as the table. These are particularly valuable when you are working single-handed.

Circular saw blades have central holes and are clamped between washers in these and portable power tools. They are made with many tooth spacings and shapes. A saw with a combination blade will do most general cutting of solid wood, but you may need a finer one for a cleaner cut in plywood, laminated plastic or chipboard. Blades are made in tool steel, but more costly ones have carbide or other tips, which keep their edge much longer. A tool steel blade can be sharpened by the user, but tipped blades have to be dealt with by an expert with special equipment.

The capacity of a circular saw depends on the projection of the blade through the table. With a 200 mm (8 in) blade you can expect about 50 mm (2 in) cut, but much depends on the wood and on the sharpness of the blade. Considerably more power is needed to push a blunt blade through hard wood, and overloading could cause the motor to stall even though it might have functioned easily with a sharp blade.

Bandsaw

A bandsaw has a continuous narrow blade passing over two or more wheels, with most of it enclosed, but the cutting part exposed through a table (fig. 3.17). The capacity in width depends on the throat between the blade and the solid support. Having three wheels allows this to be wider in a small machine. But, with two large wheels, less strain is put on the blade – so that it is less likely to break. For general woodworking the throat depth should not be less than 300 mm (12 in). The capacity in depth depends on an adjustable guide above the table, but in a small machine could be up to 75 mm (3 in) depending on the size of saw blade used.

The body of the tool opens to allow blades to be changed. They run on rubber rims on the wheels and the tension of the blade can be adjusted. Several widths of blade can be used on a machine: wide blades are stronger and suitable for straight cuts as well as moderate curves; narrow blades – 6 mm (¼ in) – will cut tighter curves. Several tooth sizes are available, but a useful type is 'gap tooth', in which there is a straight recess between teeth, which therefore make cleaner and freer cuts.

Cuts are clean and perpendicular, with any raggedness underneath. The table may have a tilting adjustment and it may be grooved to take a guide or fence for controlling the wood as it is cut. Besides its obvious use in cutting curves,

3.17 *A bandsaw has a continuous flexible blade and is used for cutting external curves.*

the bandsaw is convenient for simple cutting off from strips, or for many other cuts that might otherwise be done with a tenon saw on the bench, provided that the edge of the board to be cut does not project more than the depth of throat of the machine.

Fretsaw

Intricate dust-catching patterns used to be cut from thin wood, often by hand with a fine blade in a long frame like a coping saw (see p.24), or with a treadle machine. There are power fretsaws that can be used with blades from hair-like thickness up to those like coping saws. If you are concerned with fine shaping this would be a useful tool, but otherwise a jigsaw or a bandsaw is more useful.

Radial Arm Saw

A radial arm saw may be likened to a portable circular saw mounted on an arm above the bench that supports the work being cut (fig. 3.18). In use the saw is moved along the arm. It has guards that open against the wood, and it can cut through partially into the surface of the work.

Adjustments give a precise control of depth, angle and direction of cut. It can crosscut or rip, squarely and at angles. With other attachments, the tool will cut grooves, mouldings and some joints.

It is necessary to weigh up the value of this against that of a table circular saw as a first buy: for straightforward cutting the table saw should be preferred. The radial arm saw has other features, but making use of some of its other capabilities involves changing equipment, so in the workshop it may be more convenient to use a router or some other tool.

3.18 *In a radial arm saw a circular saw cuts when it is moved along a controlling arm.*

PLANER

A power planer is the obvious complement to a circular saw. Once you have sawn wood to the width you want, it is convenient to move to the planer and put a smooth surface on the edges and faces you have just sawn. The planer may be a separate machine, but it could be combined with a circular saw, to use the same motor and conserve space. It can be housed below the level of the saw table so that it does not interfere with overhanging boards.

A planer, sometimes called a jointer, uses blades mounted on a cylinder that rotates at high speed between two tables that can be adjusted in height to regulate the

3.19 *In a planer the wood is moved over two tables each side of rotating cutters.*

thickness of cut (fig. 3.19). With a fixed planer, wood is fed over the tables and the cutters remove tiny pieces – leaving a series of ridges across the grain. In careful fine cuts these are not very obvious, but in quick coarse work they are very apparent. Such a surface is acceptable for some purposes, as it is basically flat and true, but in other cases some hand planing or sanding is necessary to produce a furniture-quality finish.

A planer is described in terms of the width of the cut it can make. The weight and size of castings, as well as the power needed (and therefore the price) increases considerably with cutting capacities, so a machine capable of dealing with wide boards may be desirable, but not justified within a given budget. A 125 mm (4 in) cut is useful, and the smallest planer worth buying has a capacity of at least 150 mm (6 in).

A planer has a fence to hold boards against when planing their edges. It is normally set square to the table, but can be adjusted for planing bevels. Guards go over the cutters and should be used. With this and the circular saws, push sticks of various sorts should be used, instead of bringing fingers near cutting edges.

One table can be dropped in relation to the other so that rabbets can be planed with the edge of the cutters. The machine may be equipped for 'thicknessing' – planing one surface, then putting the wood through to plane the other surface and bringing the wood to a set thickness – which is convenient if you want to prepare a large number of pieces of wood of identical section. some simpler machines do this with guides above the cutters. In others the wood can be fed back underneath.

There are portable planers with soles and handles something like normal hand planes, but blades on a cylinder similar to those of a fixed planer do the cutting. Portable planers are comparatively narrow, and their scope is little different from that of a hand plane, so they are not worthwhile alternatives to a fixed planer. They make similar small ridges, so for a quality finish they have to be followed by hand treatment.

Vibration can spoil the work of a fixed planer. It is important that castings should be robust in relation to their size, to ensure rigidity. Table length helps in maintaining the truth of a surface being planed. Practical considerations affect both requirements.

ROUTER

Modern powered routers are comparatively recent tools. They have a vertically-mounted electric motor, with a cutter bit gripped at the end of its shaft and a base through which the bit projects (fig. 3.20). The cutting edges, on its sides and sometimes on its end as well, must be sharp and must rotate at high speed. The name comes from the similarity to a hand router, and it is used chiefly for cutting housing or dado grooves across boards. But there are a large variety of cutters now available for doing other things.

In a standard router the base is adjustable for depth of cut and it can be used with its own fence or against guide pieces to get cuts in the right places. A plunge router is similar, but the cutter can be held above the surface and lowered or raised through it before and after cuts.

3.20 *A router has a vertical motor that takes cutters for grooving and shaping.*

Bits have standard shafts to be gripped by a special chuck. The simplest makes grooves in any direction of grain. Others will make round or 'V' grooves and decorative moulded patterns. For edge decoration, from simple chamfers to various mouldings, the cutter has a projecting pilot to run along the plain part of the edge (fig. 3.21).

There are several pieces of equipment for use with a router and special cutters. A dovetail fixture allows for the cutting of dovetails similar to those possible with an electric drill (see p.45). A pantograph arrangement allows the router cutter to repeat a pattern from a guide: this can be used for cutting letters in signs and house name boards. A device something like a lathe uses the router to make round things and to cut patterns like spiral flutes on them. It will copy another piece, to make such things as identically turned legs.

Whether the variety of cutters and special equipment is justified or not depends on needs and the availability of other tools for doing the same work. A router is a versatile tool and much of its supplementary equipment may be justified if full use is to be made of it, but it cannot take the place of other power tools in all their applications.

A spindle moulder is a tool like a router, but with the cutter projecting upwards through a table and with an adjustable fence. A piece of wood pushed along the fence can have moulding or other pattern cut on its edge. This is a similar action to that of the router, with the wood being moved instead of the tool. A spindle moulder may have uses in a large production workshop, but a router is certainly the more generally useful and versatile power tool for the small domestic workshop.

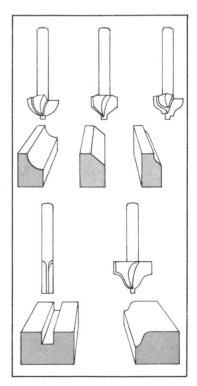

3.21 *Router bits will make mouldings as well as cut grooves.*

3.22 A flexible sanding disc can be driven by an electric drill.

3.23 A flat sanding disc can be used for smoothing and shaping.

3.24 An orbital sander is a finishing tool.

SANDING

Sanding is primarily a finishing process, but there are some situations where abrasive can be used for stock removal on the surface or for shaping edges. However, for good craftsmanship coarse abrasive should not be used as a substitute for planing and other cutting processes.

Simplest is a sanding disc that is held with a central screw and washer to a flexible backing on a short arbor to fit into a drill chuck (fig. 3.22). The disc may tear away at the centre, so might not last long. It makes curved scratches on the wood, so is unsuitable for many applications. However, it is cheap and worth having, provided that you do not expect too much from it. Another disc is rigid or has a flat, padded surface. With a table in front of it to support the work, small pieces can be manipulated against it for sanding shaped edges (fig. 3.23). There are abrasive metal discs as alternatives to paper or cloth sanding discs.

For finishing sanding there are orbital sanders (fig. 3.24). The base takes a flat piece of abrasive paper and the motor and handle are set above it. The paper is moved rapidly with a small oscillating action and the effect on the wood is very similar to hand sanding. A dust-collection bag and an extractor for dust is attached in some cases.

A flap sander is a wheel with a large number of abrasive pieces that project radially as loose flaps (fig. 3.25). It may have its own portable motor, be used with an electric drill or be bench mounted – with wood being moved over it. This will sand into intricate shapes. It will also remove paint and do other coarse work, when fitted with flaps of suitable grit.

A belt sander may be portable or fixed. The portable type is handled something like a plane and the belt runs over a pair of rollers and a pressure plate between them in the opposite direction to which the tool is pushed (fig. 3.26). Depending on the grit used, this will level off rough surfaces or provide a finishing cut. With the lengthwise action the effect is more like hand sanding along the grain. However, on wide surfaces care is needed to keep the edge of the belt from cutting into the wood. The belt sander is particularly effective where end grain adjoins side grain.

Fixed belt sanders are more specialized. A rather longer endless abrasive belt works in a similar way to that of a portable sander, but its working surface is upwards or sometimes at an angle nearer vertical. It may have a flat pressure plate, so that wood held against the belt is sanded flat, or the whole or part of the exposed belt may be unsupported. With that sort of belt it is possible to hold wood against it to shape it. For instance a knife handle could be shaped completely from a square block by manipulating it on the belt. Much depends on what sort of work you intend to do. For most woodworking, the expense of acquiring and fixing a belt sander is not justified, but a portable belt sander may be useful.

3.25 A flap sander uses a large number of abrasive pieces.

LATHE

Whether you have a lathe or not also depends on what sort of work you intend doing. Some round things, such as bowls and lamp standards, can be made entirely on a lathe, but you can also make tool handles and such spindle work as table and stool legs. A lathe makes possible the production of parts of furniture or other assemblies that might have had to be bought, or for which a square part would have had to be substituted. The principle on which a lathe works is that the wood is mounted between centres and rotated, while tools are used on a rest to shape it by making circular cuts. For a bowl or similar shallow thing of large diameter the wood is mounted with a faceplate or chuck, without the aid of a second centre.

3.26 A belt sander has the advantage of sanding in a straight line.

A lathe has a headstock, which takes the power from a motor. This is mounted on a long bed, on which slides the tailstock, carrying the other centre, and the adjustable tool-rest (fig. 3.27). There are differences in construction between makes, but the principles are the same. For spindle turning, the capacity between centres should be 760 mm (30 in) or more, so that table legs can be turned. The height of the centres above the tool-rest attachment to the bed determines the largest radius that can be swung. This is usually more than enough for most spindle work, but if bowls have to be turned over the bed, the diameter is limited by the clearance. The specification of a lathe may give the

3.27 A lathe is used to rotate wood, against which a tool is used for shaping. For discs and bowls too large to fit over the bed there may be a faceplate at the outer end of the spindle.

centre height above the bed (radius), or the diameter that can be swung.

In many lathes there is provision at the outboard end of the headstock for a faceplate to be mounted there, so that a bowl or wheel of considerable diameter can be turned. There may be a mounting on the lathe end for the toolrest, and that will set the maximum size that can be swung. But in some cases the toolrest has a stand on the floor, so it should be possible to turn such a thing as a large round table top (which depends also on the power and speed adjustment available). A much slower speed is needed on a large diameter than on a small spindle. The load on a tool cutting at the edge of a large diameter is much more than it is with a smaller diameter. Lathe speed is usually controlled in the less ambitious machines by cone pulleys on motor and headstock spindle: moving the belt gives a choice of speeds – probably four. For very large diameters there may have to be some other arrangement for stepping down the spindle speed.

Turning is more a hand process than some other machine work, and the tools needed have been described in Chapter 2, but there are several pieces of equipment that go with the lathe. Drive for work between centres is provided by prongs pressed into the ends of the wood to be turned. At the tailstock the centre tapers to form an axle as it goes into a hollow in the wood. A plain centre there causes wear in the wood and has to be adjusted occasionally. It is better to have a revolving centre, with a bearing that lets the point rotate with the wood.

A screw centre at the driving end will hold small things, like egg-cups. For some lathes there are special small chucks for the same purpose. For larger diameters there are faceplates, to which the back of a disc of wood may be screwed while its face and edge are turned. If there is provision for turning discs on the outboard end of the headstock spindle, the thread there has to be left-handed to prevent the faceplate unscrewing in use; so faceplates cannot be changed round.

A drill chuck to mount at either end in place of a centre is almost essential. With a drill bit fixed at the tailstock end, wood can be drilled while it revolves, either to take a dowel or full length for the wire of a lamp standard. Having the drill chuck at the driving end, the lathe becomes very similar to a drill press for accurately making holes for dowels or other purposes, with the wood mounted on a pad at the tailstock or on a special table on the lathe bed.

Several lathe makers provide additional equipment to

mount on the lathe for other functions. As with other multiple tools, it is necessary to consider the time it takes to change from one purpose to another and the effectiveness of the machine when set up – in comparison with that of an independent power tool. Anyone concerned in the long run with doing serious woodwork should normally aim – as with other power tools – at separate machines for different jobs. But adaptations to a lathe have the advantage of compactness, so – if space saving is very important – they may be worth having.

GRINDER

Tool sharpening is dealt with in Chapter 8. Most of it can be dealt with by hand and with suitable coarse-grit stones you may do all of it. If grinding is needed, you may take tools occasionally to a specialist. However, it is helpful to have some means of grinding in your workshop.

The traditional means of grinding woodworking cutting tools was by use of a large sandstone. No modern way is better, but you are unlikely to find such a stone.

There are smaller sandstone grinders driven at a suitable speed with a motor (fig. 3.38). There are other grinders with the wheel on a vertical spindle, so that grinding is done on the side of this cylinder. Both are good for woodworking tools.

3.28 *Tools are best ground on a slow-turning sandstone wheel.*

The alternative is a smaller grinding wheel, used dry and protected with a casing, that revolves at high speed on a spindle projecting from a bench-mounted motor (fig. 3.29). Usually a second wheel or a polishing mop is mounted at the other end. This is really an engineering grinder, but many woodworkers use one. Care is needed to keep the bevel uniform and to prevent overheating. A container of water alongside can be used for cooling. Some grinders have a trough included, but that is for dipping tools, not for wetting the wheel, as is done with sandstone. The wheel should have a diameter of at least 150 mm (6 in).

3.29 *A high-speed grinder requires care to avoid overheating and softening a tool being ground.*

There are geared hand- and foot-driven engineering wheels, but it is almost impossible to drive them fast enough to sharpen properly and avoid rapid wear of the stone, so they should be avoided.

A possible alternative for occasionally grinding tools is a disc sander, using a suitable grit on a rigid backing. This makes a true flat bevel easier to obtain than on the edge of a small grinding wheel, but the tool must still be dipped in water frequently to prevent overheating.

Chapter 4
EQUIPMENT

Tools are not much use without somewhere to use them. Some work may have to be done in position on site, but most woodworking processes are better performed in a workshop or, at least, on a properly-equipped bench. The surroundings and equipment can make a considerable difference to the quality of work, and to the ease and speed with which it can be done. If work has to be done in a room that is also used on other occasions for other purposes, that should be regarded as a temporary expedient if you mean to produce good work. But, even then, something better than a shaky table is required for working on.

4.1 *The Workmate is an alternative to a bench and vice for some purposes.*

There has to be a good flat solid surface that will withstand hammering and not bend or move under planing and other processes. In temporary accommodation you might use a stout plank on trestles. Besides the flat surface there is a frequent need for something to hold wood on edge, and the best thing for doing this is a vice. There are vices that cramp onto a plank, and they are suitable for light work, but a more substantial permanently-mounted vice is preferable. It could be fixed to the plank, to be put away with it when the area has to be cleared.

Ideally, work is done at about table level. But some things can be done at a lower level, so it is possible to manage with a board placed across stout trestles. An ingenious form of folding trestle, obtainable in several forms, is the *Workmate*. Its main attraction for anyone wanting a compact woodworking support is in the top, which opens like a long vice and can be used for holding and clamping wood (fig. 4.1). Other stops and attachments permit the gripping of wood in various ways, and there is provision for using your own weight to steady the trestle. For anyone who has to make do with temporary quarters for woodworking, or – even when your base workshop is well equipped – if you have to go out to do work on site, the *Workmate* is worth having.

BENCHES

A strong rigid bench is the most important piece of a woodworker's equipment. No matter how elaborate the assortment of power tools and the range of hand tools available, much work has to be done on a firm flat support. There has to be a surface known to be level, larger than the things that have to be assembled, and there must be provision for tackling the many hand operations that are involved.

Much of the work is done on the front part of a bench, so that is where the thickest and strongest part has to be. Even if other parts are of lighter section or less dense wood, the front should be very strong. Beech is most popular for bench-tops. It is dense and even-grained, with little tendency to warp or split. Ideally, the bench front board should be 75 mm (3 in) thick – certainly not less than 50 mm (2 in) – and about 300 mm (12 in) wide, with its top level and without twist, and its front edge square and straight.

For the average worker a height of 800 mm (32 in) is about right. You are unlikely to need it higher, so – if you make or buy a bench of that height, and then find it would be better shorter – you can cut off the bottoms of the legs. From back to front may be 600 mm (24 in) or more, if the bench is to go

4.2 *A bench should be heavy and rigid, with at least one vice.*

against a wall. For some work there is an advantage in being able to work all round the bench, for dealing with large assemblies, sheets of plywood and similar big things. In that case it helps to have a wider one.

There are many benches for sale in many sizes and with various arrangements of stops and vices. They are attractive and obviously worth having, if you find one to fit your space and needs. But prices are considerably more than the cost of material to make your own, and that would have the advantage of being tailored more exactly to your needs. A

4.3 *An end vice is useful for an additional grip on some work.*

bought bench may have one vice, a drawer and tool rack (fig. 4.2). Sometimes there is a second vice at the end (fig. 4.3). The substantial legs are framed for stiffness, and the framing could be made into a tray. For some work it is convenient to have a bench that is level for its full width, but it is more usual to include a thinner plank to form the base of a tool well (fig. 4.2a), with the rear edge level with the front for supporting wide things. If the bench is to be used at both sides, the well is in the middle (fig. 4.2b). Sometimes the board forming the tool well can be lifted out. That allows cramps to be put through, to hold wood being worked on or to pull joints together.

4.4 A tool well goes at the back of a single bench (a) or between the sides of a double one (b).

Making your own bench

If you make your own bench, plan sizes in relation to where it is to be used. If you are able to attach it to a wall, that will help in maintaining rigidity – assuming that the wall is strong enough. But it may be advisable not to rely on the walls of – say – a wood-framed shed to take the place of legs or other framework, which must take the strain of working loads. Besides, you may want to re-organize your workshop one day, or take the bench with you when you move. Bear this sort of thing in mind.

Ideally, all of the bench (fig. 4.5) is made of beech or other hardwood, but it is possible to have a satisfactory bench with legs and underframing of softwood – provided that they are of large enough section, and that the vital working surfaces are hardwood.

It is better if you start with the front working surface and design other parts around it. It is also worth providing an apron, which is a vertical hardwood piece below its front (fig. 4.6a). Dowels may join these pieces squarely together. Besides providing a true surface for boards on edge to bear against, this gives rigidity to the bench, particularly under

4.5 *A bench can be made in your own workshop.*

Note: Measurements in millimetres are given in **bold type**; measurements in inches are given in normal type.

the frequent lengthwise loads that are applied in planing and other processes. Many benches without aprons flex in the length after much use.

For a bench up to about 2 m (6 ft) long, two pairs of legs will be enough. For a longer bench there should be an intermediate pair. Legs may be 75 mm (3 in) square for a small bench, but 100 mm (4 in) would be better. Rails can be the same section or 100 × 75 mm (4 × 3 in). Deep rails provide stiffness from back to front.

The rails are best tenoned to the legs (fig. 4.6b). At the front, the leg is partially cut back to take the apron piece (fig. 4.6c). Treat the leg at the back similarly for the piece behind the tool well (fig. 4.6d). For a simpler construction, the parts may be halved and bolted (fig. 4.6e). In any case, be sure to get both leg and rail assemblies square and matching each other.

The top parts provide all the links that are needed between the leg assemblies, but lower down arrange lengthwise rails at a different level from those set across (fig. 4.7a), so that their tenons clear the others. If the lengthwise rails are notched instead of tenoned, do not halve them fully (fig. 4.7b), so as not to weaken the legs by cutting out too much. Allow for a small overhang each end, but not more than 150 mm (6 in) if the bench is free-standing.

The apron can be fixed with counterbored and plugged screws into the legs, and the back piece may screw into the legs. To hold the working top down screws may be driven upwards in deeply counterbored holes in the rails (fig. 4.7c). The holes should not be plugged, so that you can tighten the screws if ever necessary. It is best to avoid driving screws or other fasteners down through the top. But if you have to, counterbore and plug them, to make sure that there is no metal anywhere near the surface.

The tool well can be made with a thinner board, either fixed permanently or arranged to lift out. Supports on the front and back pieces are needed for such a board (fig. 4.7d). If it is to be lifted out, pieces may be fixed across it to prevent lengthwise movement (fig. 4.7e). The ends of the

4.6 *In bench construction the apron is dowelled below the top (a), the top rails tenon into the legs (b), which are cut back for the apron (c) or for the back piece (d). Alternatively, halve the parts (e).*

4.7 Lower bench rails enter the legs at different levels (a) or they are notched (b). The top is screwed (c), but the tool well rests on supports (d) and will lift out (e). Its ends are improved with sloping pieces (f). A tool rack can go at the back (g).

board should have pieces made up to the working height, preferably sloped (fig. 4.7f) for ease in cleaning and to act as rests for planes to keep their cutters clear of the wood surface.

If the back is to be made into a tool rack, you could fix a strip to it held off at intervals with spacers (fig. 4.7g). On a long bench you might have two parts with different width gaps; with this arrangement, saws, chisels and other thin tools can go in a narrow gap, while thicker things like hammer handles can have a wide one. However, it is a nuisance having to clear the racks to allow the wide boards to over-hang when you are working on them. So if there is a wall near, it is better to put there any tools that are not in the bench well.

There is a lot of spare space under a bench. Any boxing in to make drawers or cupboards is worth while, for the added stiffness as well as for added storage. The apron might be cut to admit a drawer, but one with a flush front. Closing in the back and ends under the bench with panels contributes to stiffness. If you are equipping a workshop from scratch it may be advisable to leave detailed bench storage until you are certain how it can most usefully be arranged.

4.8 A wooden vice usually has two screws.

VICE

The one vice, traditionally located near the left-hand end of the bench front, is the most important piece of bench equip-ment. This is something on which you should not comprom-ise. There may be other vices and holding devices, but it is at this vice that you will do much of your detailed and preci-sion work.

Some benches are sold ready equipped with wooden vices. A wood screw lacks precision and in such a vice there may have to be two of them to adjust (fig. 4.8), but the main drawback is in the way the front jaw can wobble out of true if the wood being held does not pass right through the vice. It is better to have a metal vice with wooden jaws, and to get one large enough to cope with your needs. There are some light versions that may suit modelmaking, but for

4.9 A metal vice has a single long screw and guides that go under the bench.

4.10 A metal vice should be fitted with wooden jaws (a). The vice has to be bolted through the bench top (b).

a

b

serious woodworking the vice should have jaws about 230 mm (9 in) wide, opening to 330 mm (13 in) (fig. 4.9).

The rear jaw is let into the front of the bench and most of the vice parts go under the bench-top. The front is attached to two slides and is worked in and out by a handle turning a substantial screw. A time-saver is a quick-release mechanism. By squeezing a lever near the handle you can free the vice to move in or out to any position, then releasing the lever re-engages the screw. If you expect to spend much time woodworking, this facility is worth the extra cost. Another feature available only on some makes of vice is a 'dog peg', which is a rectangular peg that can be raised on the moving jaw. With a stop on the bench-top, this can act as a cramping device.

The vice should be mounted so that there are wood faces on the jaws and on the upper surfaces, to prevent any metal from coming into contact with cutting tools (fig. 4.10a). The inner wood jaw has to be arranged flush with the front edge of the bench so that long boards are held level. A vice should be bolted to the top, but the heads of the bolts must be sunk below the surface and covered with wood plugs (fig. 4.10b). If coach bolts are used, their square necks pull into the wood to prevent turning. Use large washers under the nuts.

An apron must be cut away to admit the vice. That is best done before the apron is fitted, and the vice is most easily put in place before the top is attached to the underframing.

4.11 *Wood through the bench makes a good stop (a) and it may be locked with a wing nut (b). An iron casing for the bench stop may fit under the bench (c). A different type of stop fits into a recess in the bench top (d).*

BENCH STOPS

The bench-top should be uncluttered with projections, and if possible it is advisable to avoid metal on the surface. However, there are several additions worth having. Of most use is a bench stop, which is just a piece of wood projecting through a hole near the end of the bench. In its simplest form that is all it is – just a length of hardwood positioned so that its lower part comes against the bench leg (fig. 4.11a). It can be adjusted by tapping up or down.

For greater precision the lower part can be split, with a wing nut providing locking (fig. 4.11b). You can buy a cast iron casing to screw under the bench-top to give similar adjustment (fig. 4.11c). On a wide top there can be a second stop level wth the first, to give steadier support when plan-ing wide boards.

If the bench forms part of something longer or there is some other reason for not being able to arrange a stop through the top, a flush-mounted metal stop can be let into a recess in the top (fig. 4.11d). Height can be adjusted by means of a central screw, and the stop can be closed flush with the bench-top.

Old-time cabinetmakers made much use of a holdfast that could be pushed through a hole in the bench-top, where it was held by friction. The modern equivalent has a screw action and is valuable for holding wood down (fig. 4.12). A notched collar is let into the bench-top, then the rod fitted through it a suitable amount, so that tightening the screw forces the jaw on to the work. Collars can be put at several places on the bench-top, so that one or more holdfasts can be arranged to suit the work.

Holes may be drilled in the apron to take pegs for sup-porting long pieces when other parts of them are in the vice. The pegs can be simple roughly tapered pieces or parts turned like blackboard pegs. Cramps may also be used under or at the end of the apron.

If there is an end vice with a dog peg it is useful to have positions for other pegs, called 'bench dogs', further along the bench top. You can then use the vice as a cramp to bring parts tight for joining or working on. There are metal bench dogs (fig. 4.13) that need square holes, in which they are retained with springs. In a compact workshop you may want to mount a small machine on the bench, but it is advisable to arrange it with removable bolts, so that you can always re-vert to a flat top of maximum size. For the same reason, avoid any special attachments that could cause projections or unevenness.

4.12 *A bench holdfast presses down on wood on the bench top and holds with its stem fitted through one of the collars let into the bench top.*

4.13 *Wood may be held on the bench top by pressure from a vice against dogs fitted into holes in the bench. These dogs are metal with retaining springs.*

4.14 *Bench hooks may be narrow and used in pairs (a) or wider (b) and cut back on alternate sides for sawing (c). Cuts can be made as mitre sawing guides (d). The hook will act as a stop when planing end grain (e).*

Note: Measurements in millimetres are given in **bold type**; measurements in inches are given in normal type.

BENCH HOOK

The bench-top should be kept in good condition for as long as possible. Such work as chopping or vertical paring with a chisel should be done over scrap wood and not directly onto the bench. This also applies to sawing: the bench-top can soon become scored with saw marks from careless sawing. Freehand sawing can be done over scrap wood, but it is help in holding the wood to have one, or preferably two, bench hooks.

Older bench hooks were narrow and cut from solid wood (fig. 4.14a). They were used in pairs spaced as needed along the length of wood being worked on, but they did not protect the bench-top. It is better to make wider bench hooks, with crosspieces dowelled on. They should not be so long as to go over the edge at the tool well (fig. 4.14b), but a long bench hook is of more use than a short one.

A suitable width is 125 mm (5 in), with crosspieces high enough to prevent wood being pushed over the end. Join with dowels rather than screws, so that there is no metal for a saw to touch. Keep the crosspieces cut back, so that a saw breaks through on to the hook and not the bench. Most craftsman become ambidextrous with a tenon saw, so cut back one piece for sawing with the right hand and the other for turning over to use your left hand (fig. 4.14c).

If your work involves mitring small pieces, you could cut saw guides in a bench hook (fig. 4.14d). With a bench hook it is possible to use a block plane across end grain, so that the bench hook is functioning as a small shooting board (see below). For that to be most satisfactory, the board should be just thick enough for an average piece of wood being worked on to come near the centre of the plane sole (fig. 4.14e).

Bench hooks should be regarded as disposable. They take cuts that would otherwise fall on the bench, so be prepared to replace them occasionally.

SHOOTING BOARD

With power tools to help, getting edges straight and square is easy. A circular saw cuts straight and a planer makes the edge flat and square to the surface. However, there are occasions when an edge has to be straightened by hand. It can be done with the wood held on edge in the vice, but then you have to rely on testing with a straight-edge and square to get your freehand planing right.

4.15 *A shooting board is for holding wood being planed on its edge with a plane resting on its side.*

Note: Measurements in millimetres are given in **bold type**; measurements in inches are given in normal type.

A shooting board is a guide for a long-soled plane to get an edge true. The plane is used on its side so that the cutting edge is vertical against the wood being planed. The board should be long enough for preparing such things as small table-tops to be joined, so 600 mm (24 in) is a minimum.

Some craftsmen use a board on which the wood rests, attached to one on which the plane slides, with a stop to press the wood against (fig. 4.15). A piece 18 mm (¾ in) thick will lift it sufficiently to make sure that the centre of the cutting edge comes against wood of average thickness. The shooting board may be used on the bench-top and held with dogs, or it can have a strip attached underneath for gripping in the vice. As in the bench hook, it is better to make sure that no metal is involved, by assembling with dowels rather than with screws.

Another shooting board can be made for planing mitres (fig. 4.16). Sizes should be compared to the ordinary shooting board, to give the plane a long guide in either direction and certainly not less than 450 mm (18 in) overall. The mitre stops need not meet at a point. Their grain will be less likely to break out if a small thickness is left.

4.16 *A special shooting board can hold mitred pieces for planing.*

MITRE BOX

There are several devices available for cutting mitres, either with a separate backsaw or with one that is built in. If much mitring is to be done, one of these is worth having, particularly if it is a type that can also be used for cramping a corner joint.

Mitres on wider flat pieces are best marked with a mitre

square or an adjustable bevel, then sawn to the line; but, for small picture-frame moulding and similar sections, it is a help to use a guide for a fine saw. The simplest guide is a mitre block, which works in a similar way to the bench hook cut as suggested on p.67. Making the guiding parts deep and wide gives the best control over the saw. A piece can be set underneath, for gripping in a vice (fig. 4.17a). The cuts need not continue right through to the base of the block; a piece of scrap wood may be put under the work to make up the depth and prevent the block becoming marked.

Using a saw guide at one side only is more liable to lead to error due to saw wobble than if you use guides at both sides. With guides at both sides the tool becomes a mitre box (fig. 4.17b). Although you may not cut very wide pieces in this way, it helps if you spread the parts bearing on the saw by making the inside of the box 75mm (3in) or more wide. Extending one side of the box downwards allows it to be gripped in a vice while the main part is on the bench-top. Some mitre boxes are supplied with metal saw guides (fig. 4.17c).

4.17 *A mitre block is a saw guide for cutting mitres on narrow pieces (a). A mitre box gives better saw control on wide pieces (b), and some mitre boxes have metal saw guides (c).*

WINDING STRIPS

It is possible to test a board with a straight-edge and find it flat in the length and across at various places, yet the surface is twisted, or 'in winding'. This can be checked by sighting along the board, when one end will be seen to be twisted in relation to the other. Winding strips are used to extend the width and make the twist seem more pronounced. Basically,

4.18 *Winding strips aid in checking twist (a). Pieces of contrasting colour make the ends clearer (b). Dowels can hold the strips together for storage (c).*

they are two wood straight-edges thick enough to stand on the board, so you can look along and see if one is tilted relative to the other (fig. 4.18a).

Length should be about three times the width of the board to be tested, and the wood should be a stable hardwood. For better sighting, at the ends of one piece you can let in pieces of wood of a contrasting colour (fig. 4.18b). For storage, two short dowels fixed in one piece press into holes in the other piece to hold them together (fig. 4.18c) and a hole at the end of one piece can be used to hang the pair on a nail. If the winding strips are made of an attractive hardwood and polished, their quality encourages you to do good work. This applies to many things you use – a good tool or piece of equipment encourages you to take care and get better end results.

TRESTLE

4.19 *A trestle is used instead of a bench for holding work at a lower level (a). The legs are splayed (b) and notched and gussetted to the top (c). Mark the leg lengths parallel with the top after fitting to it (d). An extension can be used to support higher work (e) and a trough will hold parts that might slip off (f).*

Note: Measurements in millimetres are given in **bold type**; measurements in inches are given in normal type.

Not all work is most conveniently done at bench height. For some things, such as hand sawing downwards, it is better for the wood to be at about 450 mm (18 in) above the floor: sometimes old chairs can be pressed into use, or a *Workmate* can be set at a suitable height. For general workshop use it is worthwhile making two identical trestles of fairly substantial form, so that they are steady and will withstand hammering. Consider them as auxiliary benches. Much work can be done on one, but two will support long pieces of wood or provide a base for assembling a carcase or other framed work at a more convenient height than the floor or bench.

The standard trestle (fig. 4.19a) has four legs splayed outwards to points outside the plan of the top, so that the trestle will not tip over in normal use.

Metal parts are available for attaching the legs to the top. They give a rigid bolted assembly, and with some the trestle can be dismantled. Most trestles are made without such fittings.

The top of an all-wood trestle may be fairly wide (fig. 4.19b), to give a broad support to a board being worked on, or it can be narrower if you will normally use two trestles. The legs notch into it and there are gussets across the outsides of the legs (fig. 4.19c). Basic geometry will show that the legs should not be quite square on their corners, and the angles they make with the top should allow for the double slopes making the splay. In practice the differences in angles are slight and the parts can be positioned by trial and error: slight variations from the slopes originally drawn will not matter, provided that the result is symmetrical. And if two trestles are to be made, it is advisable to do all the stages in making them in step with each other, to get matching results. The legs should be left too long until after assembly. Then the ends are marked parallel with the top (fig. 4.19d) for cutting accurately.

Something similar to trestles could be made the same height as that of the circular saw table, to support long pieces of wood. Another way of dealing with this job is to make supports that can fit through holes in the ordinary trestle, either with permanent stops to set the height or – if you have more than one use for the extensions – with pegs to support work on several machines (fig. 4.19e). The top might be flat, or you could include a metal or rubber tube as a roller.

If you expect to work on chair seats or tackle upholstery, it is helpful to give the pair of trestles troughs to take two chair legs each. An upholsterer keeps trestles boxed round, but you can make troughs to slip into place and not affect the trestles for other uses (fig. 4.19f).

TOOL STORAGE

At one time any professional woodworker kept all his tools in a large chest that took at least two men to move, but in the usual workshop it is better to store tools around the place where they are accessible. If any have to be taken to outside jobs they can be carried in a smaller box: a rigid box can be fitted with drawers and racks, and – if made like an attache case with a partial door – it can open to show the contents in

4.20 *A portable tool box can be made to open at the front.*

an orderly manner (fig. 4.20). If the outside work regularly requires the same tools, it may be worth equipping the box with duplicate basic tools. Besides having the tools always ready to take out, this allows the shop tools to be kept in the finest condition while the others take any rough treatment that may occur on a building site or in any similar situation.

Plenty of thought should be given to the layout of permanent tool storage and you may want to try temporary arrangements first. Consider where a tool is most often needed. You do not want to cross the workshop to get it and to put it back. Much depends on available wall space. Hanging tools should not interfere with work in progress or be knocked out of their racks when you move a job around. Sharp tools should not have their edges exposed, where they could get damaged or cause an accident.

Bags

The alternative to a rigid container, for temporary storage, is a bag. We have tradition to guide us there. The older outdoor craftsman took his tools to the job in a stout half-moon canvas bag with two handles (fig. 4.21a). A hammer, or other long tool, was pushed through the handles so that the load could hang from it over his shoulder. These bags are still available. Some may have inside pockets, but otherwise all the contents come tightly together. Such things as nails and screws could be kept in small bags or boxes with lids. Chisels can be kept in canvas rolls with pockets for up to nine chisels, giving good protection to their cutting edges

4.21 *Traditionally, a carpenter carried his tools in a bag (a). Chisels may be protected in a canvas roll (b). Saws may fit into a canvas bag (c) or be protected by a strip over the teeth (d).*

(fig. 4.21b). Similar rolls are available for drill bits. The usual handsaw is too long to be enclosed in the bag and may be carried projecting each side of this type of bag, but its teeth should be covered. Canvas cases with perhaps two compartments are available (fig. 4.21c), but a simple way of protecting a saw is with a strip of wood cut along one edge, and with cords to tie it on (fig. 4.21d). In any case, this is the best treatment for a tenon saw carried in the bag.

If a box or traditional bag is not wanted there are other bags – like canvas shopping or sports bags – that will take most tools, leaving long things to be carried separately. Strap fastenings allow adjustment to suit the contents, but zip fasteners with a lock are more secure. For better bags, at a greater cost, leather may be substituted for canvas. It is unwise to keep tools for long periods in cloth or canvas containers, as the material attracts moisture and could encourage rust.

Racks

Tools that are in fairly frequent use may be kept in racks. If the workshop is left out of use for long periods, and if heating is only used occasionally, it is better to have the tools in wall cabinets or cupboards, preferably those that give similar access to racks when the doors are opened (fig. 4.22). Tools that are only occasionally needed are better enclosed, in any case. Many small items are better kept in drawers, preferably arranged as a block under a bench or other work surface, so that it is easy to reach down and open one when you are working at the bench.

In general it may not seem advisable just to put a lot of tools loosely together in a drawer or box, but that will almost certainly happen with some of them. Giving each tool a rack or compartment is desirable but no matter how compactly you make the stowage, the tools and their fittings will take up much more room than they would if they were packed together. Many things, other than edge tools, do not suffer if kept in contact with each other. Unless you have almost unlimited space for tool storage, you will have to decide which of your tools to give individual racks and which will have to be stored together in drawers or elsewhere. There are many small things, such as bits for ratchet screwdrivers and cutters of many widths for a plough plane, that only get occasional use and may be lost. They are best kept in their own small boxes, with divisions if necessary, in a drawer – rather than in racks, where such items would get dusty and rusty. Small drills of the metalworking type are a similar

4.22 A tool cabinet enclosed by doors protects tools fitted to racks inside.

problem. They will blunt each other if stored loose, so ought to be in individual holes and protected by a cover.

For hanging things, perforated hardboard is available, with a regular pattern of holes, and wire hooks of various sorts provided for insertion where needed. The idea is attractive, but there can be wear after much use and hardboard storage is not best in a workshop that will get long and heavy use. However, the material is comparatively cheap and it allows you to experiment with rack arrangements that might be converted eventually into something more permanent. The hardboard has to be held off from the wall with battens, to give the hooks space when they are inserted, and a panel can be made attractive by framing.

If something can hang from a nail, there is nothing wrong with using a nail, but it will look more business-like if you cut off and file the end round, then tilt it upwards (fig. 4.23a). A large screw hook might suit your needs better – the straight cup hook (fig. 4.23b) being more use for most tools than the commoner round hook.

Spring clips are sold as tool clips, sprung in two ways. With the simplest (fig. 4.23c) the tool to be held needs to be quite close to the size of the clip. With the other (fig. 4.23d) there is more tolerance for different sizes. In both cases the clips can be bought with plastic coatings and this is less likely to mark wooden tool handles. A row of clips on a batten will accommodate a range of tools, with the advantage that you can take the tool you want by just pulling it forward.

Many tools will fit through round holes. A long screwdriver will hang upright under its own weight through thin wood

4.23 *A tool may hang from a nail (a) or a hook (b). A simple spring tool clip (c) does not have as much tolerance as one with double bends (d). Some tools can hang through holes (e, f, g).*

(fig. 4.23c), but it is better to hang a more top-heavy tool, like a bradawl, in a hole made through thicker wood (fig. 4.23f). Countersink holes slightly below as well as above, to prevent the grain breaking out, and some tools may need a second hole lower down (fig. 4.23g).

Chisels and gouges are best kept in separate slots, but side by side they take up a lot of space (fig. 4.24a). If slotted across the grain they weaken it (fig. 4.24b), so a compromise diagonal stowage may be better (fig. 4.24c). A piece of rigid transparent plastic will protect the edges and let you see which is which. Longer chisels, such as lathe tools, may be kept in individual spaces with their blades pointing upwards, with a retaining strip at the bottom and another higher up. With these or similar racks, leave a gap at the bottom, otherwise sawdust will fill the space (fig. 4.24d).

Some tools are best hung in a notched strip where they can be removed by pulling foward, rather than lifting from holes or slots. The strip should slope up, so that vibration will not make a tool fall out (fig. 4.25a). It may help if you work a hollow along the strip before cutting the notches (fig. 4.25b).

It could be that you do not want the same tools always available. A general rack that will take different tools would then be more suitable. This could be a strip with many holes, but it is better if you provide it with one or more slots, similar to the arrangement described for the back of a bench. If the wall of the workshop is of stone or brick, put plywood behind the rack, then hold off battens with spacers at intervals (fig. 4.26a), making the rear one thick enough to hold tools and their handles clear of the wall. A wide slot behind a narrow one will cope with tools of different thicknesses, and the spacers between gaps stop tools falling over, particularly if many top-heavy ones are inserted together.

Having a number of racks for individual kinds of tool may use up more space than is available, and leave you with tools that have nowhere to go. But many ways can be found for storing different tools in the same rack. For instance, try-squares could go into slots on strips wide enough to have hooks or clips attached to the front (fig. 4.26b); or tools that fit into holes may be stored behind others that need clips or slots (fig. 4.26c).

4.24 *Tool slots in line (a) take up more room than those across (b); the weak cross grain thus caused can be reduced by having diagonal slots (c). Long chisels are best stood on end (d).*

4.25 *Tools fitted into notches will hold in place better if the strip slopes up (a). A hollow along the top also helps in retaining tools (b).*

4.26 *Parallel strips will hold some tools (a). One piece of wood can be arranged to support some tools in front of others (b). Holes for tools can go behind slots for others (c). Dowel rods into angled holes will support hammers and mallets (d). A saw fits conveniently inside a door (e).*

If there is wall space, saws can hang from nails or dowel rods. Similar dowel rods in pairs will take mallets and hammers, always arranged on a slight tilt (fig. 4.26d). If there is space from back to front – perhaps 200 mm (8 in) – such things as saws and try-squares can go edgewise into a slotted shelf. A stack of shelves can be made into multiple racks, with the whole thing enclosed to make a cabinet with doors: besides protection from damp and dust, doors can have racks inside for tools such as saws, which do not need much depth (fig. 4.26e). However, there must be enough space for the doors to swing fully open without interfering with other things on the wall. Sliding doors only let you get at half the interior at a time and are a nuisance. Doors can be made to lift off, if there is no room for them to swing open, but you then need somewhere to put them.

Planes are a special case. They could go on a shelf below

the bench, so that they are end-on and you can recognize their backs. If the end of the bench is accessible, a rod across allows them to be placed so that they are held by the wedges (fig. 4.27c), but make sure there is sufficient space to lift a long plane clear. Other tools could go through holes in a board that is also serving as a plane rack. Such a rack at the vice end of the bench is convenient, as you can reach over and get the tools most often in use.

For a wall rack the planes most needed could go upwards into compartments, either with retaining strips at different heights (fig. 4.27b) or with the bottoms raised to use one

4.27 *Planes can fit behind a bar at the end of a bench (a), or they can go upwards into compartments on the wall (b, c). Another wall rack (d) may hold them in a similar way to the one at the end of the bench.*

strip (fig. 4.27c). That gives space below the shorter planes for other tool racks. Another way is to provide a crossbar similar to that at the end of the bench, and put the planes downwards behind it (fig. 4.27d). The only snag with that is that, if it is placed high on a wall, the extra lift up to remove a heavy plane can be awkward.

Accessories and the tools to fit them to power tools should be kept near the machines, if possible, otherwise it is better to keep them in drawers with spare parts and accessories for hand tools. You will probably have some of these things that are rarely used, and can protect such tools from rust in storage by putting silica gel in the compartment. This, a chemical in crystal form that absorbs moisture, is supplied in two forms: sachets, or impregnated paper. In both cases you can dry out with warmth and use the sachet or paper again.

TIMBER STORAGE

As seen in the opening chapter, timber has to be looked after before use or it may suffer enough to make it useless for a particular project. Good wood is expensive and it is correct practice to store and use pieces down to quite small lengths and sections. Longer pieces should be kept straight. This means supporting at fairly close intervals and stacking boards neatly on each other, so that one does not get twisted in its length. This is particularly so with narrow battens, which may fall over and be left to take a distorted shape. Anything over about 1500 mm (6 ft) is better supported horizontally than stood on end, where it may bow between its top and bottom contacts.

Long pieces can often be put on crossbars high in the workshop, using space inside the roof or ceiling that would not otherwise be used. If the workshop has to double up with a garage, racks might go along one wall beside the car, with metal shelf brackets keeping obstruction to a minimum (fig. 4.28a). Part of the rack could be made into a shelf for shorter pieces of wood.

For pieces not long enough to store horizontally, a rack to take pieces on end is convenient (fig. 4.28b). Divisions can be made to prevent wood falling over when the rack is not full. Very small pieces still of useful size may be kept in a similar smaller rack, or on end in a box. If you have a circular saw, or a planer or a combination machine, small pieces of wood may be stored near or under it. With that equipment all sorts of oddments can be converted to sizes to suit the need of the moment.

Plywood, hardboard and similar sheet material is best

stored flat, but – with sheets of maximum size – that will probably involve more space than you can spare. If sheets are stored on edge for long, they should lean against battens to prevent them bowing. Thicker material, such as chipboard, will help to keep thinner materials flat.

4.28 *Long timber should be closely supported by racks (a). Shorter pieces may stand on end (b).*

Chapter 5
WOODWORKING TECHNIQUES

The difference between a craftsmanlike piece of work and one that is not as good as it should be can often be traced to the approach to the work. A good example of craftsmanship is probably the result of planning and an organized schedule as well as the ability to use tools. The work has been thought right through, and preparations for a later stage have been dealt with earlier before the assembly became more complicated. For instance, a beginner may put together a part of an assembly and discover that he should have cut mortises or ploughed grooves for a later part; they are now difficult, or impossible, to fashion cleanly and accurately. An experienced worker would have done all the work possible on each part in anticipation of later joints or other complications.

A drawing is always advisable, but it need not be a very full or detailed one, if you can visualize what you want to make. A scale drawing shows proportions, and may be the first indication that you have not got it quite right, so that you can correct sizes without wasting wood. The drawing gives you a chance to adapt sizes and design to suit available wood, or whatever sizes are more easily obtained.

There are a few design points to observe. This is not a book on design, but you can get more pleasing results if you understand a few principles. A rectangle, as part of a finished piece of furniture, is more pleasing to the eye than a square; so if you are planning some sort of a cabinet or table, try to avoid a square outline, no matter what angle it is viewed from. Part or the whole of an ellipse (fig. 5.1a shows a decorative cut under a rail) looks better than part of a circle (fig. 5.1b). An optical illusion makes lower heights look less than they are in relation to higher ones. So if you make a block of drawers all of the same depth, they will appear to get shallower towards the bottom (fig. 5.1c), and if you frame a door panel, it is usual to make the bottom rail noticeably wider (fig. 5.1d). Diagonal lines need care: they can be used, but sometimes they upset the overall appearance.

The drawing need not show the complete thing. If the finished article is to be symmetrical, half may be enough. For a table you can use drawings of half each of two elevations, and you may need a plan (fig. 5.2). From the drawing it always helps if you make a list of wood needed, showing widths and thicknesses, with a little extra added to each length. Remember to include enough for cutting joints. In the case of a table you can list the overall size of the top, but it may have to be made up from two or more narrower pieces ((fig. 5.3). The cutting list is a guide to what to cut from your own stock of wood, or it may be taken to your supplier so that he can select wood to suit.

5.1 An elliptical curve (a) looks better than a circular one (b). An even spacing appears to get narrower towards the bottom (c). Equal borders do not look as good as having the bottom one wider (d).

WOOD PREPARATION

There is a tendency with machined wood to assume that it is accurate, and to dispense with the traditional working from face side and edge, but for the best work this method should still be used. Look along the wood with one eye to sight for straightness. If necessary true one edge and face by hand planing. See that the edges are square to each other, then give them the traditional pencil marks (fig. 5.4a). If that is done on all pieces and you do your marking out from those

5.2 *Part views may show all you need to draw.*

4 LEGS 700 × 50 × 50
2 TOP RAILS 500 × 100 × 25
2 TOP RAILS 800 × 100 × 25
2 LOWER RAILS 500 × 75 × 25
2 LOWER RAILS 800 × 75 × 25
1 TOP 920 × 600 × 25

5.3 *A cutting list helps you pick from available wood or decide what to order.*

surfaces, vital outside surfaces will be level with each other, even if there are slight discrepancies on the inside when you cut joints. If you do not use the marks, and gauge a joint from one side of one piece and the other side of another piece with which it has to mate, there could be enough difference to spoil the fit. At this stage it will help to number the parts, or otherwise mark them, and also to put the numbers on the drawing.

In anything framed you cannot get the final assembly square in all directions if parts that ought to be the same length are not. A beginner may mark out each piece of wood separately, but a craftsman marks all pieces that have to be of identical lengths together, using a try-square across them all, with a knife where cuts must come and a sharp pencil elsewhere. In the case of the table shown being built here and on pages 170-1, the four legs are marked across with a little waste left at each end for trimming later (fig. 5.4b). All the rails going one way are similarly marked (fig. 5.4c) and all the rails the other way are marked together. In this case we assume dowel joints, but if tenons were used there would have to be allowance for them.

The marks on the face surface are squared round, on all four sides for the cut ends, and only to the surfaces necessary for joints. For each of these markings the stock of the try-square is put against the face side or edge. All the rails may be cut to length at the marked knife lines. Check that they match each way, and level anywhere necessary.

5.4 Work from a face edge and mark parts that are to be similar together.

DOWELS

The rails shown come level with the outsides of the legs (fig. 5.5a). This makes the use of a dowel drilling guide easier, but if the holes are to be drilled without it, mark across each rail end and its leg together (fig. 5.5b) and letter or number the parts that mate, so that you do not confuse them later. Gauge from the outside face surfaces (fig. 5.5c), and it is a help to push an awl into the crossings where the drill is to enter.

Drill squarely into each part. How far to take a dowel is a matter of experience, but about twice its diameter into each piece is usually enough. A dowel as it goes into a hole is something like a piston in a cylinder, and the wood could split if nothing is done to release surplus air and glue. You can buy dowels prepared with tapered ends and grooves (fig. 5.5d), but if you cut your own from rod, saw a shallow

Note: Measurements in millimetres are given in bold type; measurements in inches are given in normal type.

5.5 *For dowels to legs, mark rail and leg together. Grooved dowels allow air and surplus glue to escape.*

groove along each one (fig. 5.5e). Make the holes slightly deeper than you expect the dowel to go, so that there is no risk of the dowel bottoming and preventing the surfaces of the joint from meeting. In this example there are two dowels in each joint. There may be more in larger joints, but never come down to one in a small joint: it would be better in that case to change to two thinner dowels.

The solid wood of a table-top may expand and contract a little and that should be allowed for by using buttons. Plough grooves near the top edge of each top rail (fig. 5.6a). When you add the top later, screw buttons to the top with projecting pieces into the grooves (fig. 5.6b) so that they can slide if the top width varies.

5.6 *Buttons under a solid wood top allow it to expand and contract.*

5.7 *(Opposite) Drive and cramp joints tight (a, b), then sight across to check twist (c). Check squareness by comparing diagonals (d, e, f). A weighted board may be needed to hold the assembly true while glue sets (g).*

ASSEMBLY OF A FOUR-SIDED FRAMEWORK

Any four-sided framework is best assembled in two stages. In this case opposite long sides come first. Prepare the joints and their dowels with glue, then tap them together, using a mallet or hammer over scrap wood (fig. 5.7a). Remember to check that there is nothing on the bench that can mark the surface underneath. Move to bar cramps, if possible, with scrap pieces to take and spread the pressure (fig. 5.7b). Otherwise use wedges against blocks. Make sure the assembly is level and without twist by sighting across the rails (fig. 5.7c). You can partially check squareness with a try-square against a rail, but it is better to measure diagonals, preferably with a pencil and a light wood rod (fig. 5.7d). There is less risk of error with this than with a rule or tape measure.

Assemble the opposite side in the same way and check that the two assemblies match when brought together with their inner surfaces facing. When the glue has set, remove any surplus and cut the bottoms of the legs to length. The tops of the legs are better left until all the rails are attached and you can make the whole surface fit closely to the table top.

In the second stage, join the rails the other way. You have to square the assembly in two directions before the glue begins to set. Each new side must be checked by measuring diagonals (fig. 5.7e) and you must check squareness as viewed from above (fig. 5.7f). To guard against twist, have the assembly standing on a flat surface so that you can stand back and look at it in several directions. Check diagonals between legs at both rail levels, then sight across to see that rails are parallel with each other and all legs are upright. If there is any tendency to spring out of shape, you can put a board over the top with a weight on it (fig. 5.7g).

MAKING A TABLE-TOP

If the top has to be made up of boards joined together, there must be no risk of them separating later. With modern synthetic resin glues, a simple meeting of two true surfaces may be enough. If the edges are planed very slightly hollow in their lengths and a cramp is used across the centre, the ends will be brought together extra tight. It is at the ends that a joint may try to open after completion.

The edges could be dowelled (fig. 5.8a). Put dowels near the ends, but the others can be quite widely spaced. You could use tongue and groove joints (fig. 5.8b), but the appearance at the ends would not be acceptable for good quality furniture, although the joint is a good one for other applications.

A good way to strengthen the joint is by secret slot screwing, and this has the advantage of not needing cramps. At fairly wide intervals along the joint mark the edges as if for dowels (fig. 5.8c). On one edge make more marks 18 mm (¾ in) away (fig. 5.8d). Choose fairly stout steel screws – 10 gauge × 25 mm (1 in) should suit this joint. Drill for and drive

5.8 To make up width, boards may be dowelled (a) or tongued and grooved (b). Secret slot screwing will pull and hold parts together (c, d, e, f, g).

the screws into the centre of the edge with single markings, leaving about 6 mm to 9 mm of the screw standing above the surface of the wood (fig. 5.8e). In the other piece drill a hole large enough to clear the screw head at the offset position and the size of the screw neck at the other position, then cut a slot that width to the other hole (fig. 5.8f). Do all this deeper than the extension of the screw-head from the other piece.

Bring the boards together dry and knock one along the other so that the screw heads cut a way along the bottom of the slot (fig. 5.8g). If that is satisfactory, knock the boards back and separate them. Give each screw one-quarter turn. Put glue on the surfaces and knock the boards back together again to complete the joint.

The table-top could have square edges. They could be curved, but a partial curve (fig. 5.9a) looks better than a semi-circle (fig. 5.9b). There could be a graduated curve (fig. 5.9c). If you want the top to look lighter, that curve might be turned over (fig. 5.9d). Various mouldings are possible around the edge, either worked with appropriate planes or with a cutter in a router. A simple step down with a curve (fig. 5.9e) may be all that is needed. If your tool kit is limited, this has the advantage of being possible to cut by first making a rabbet and then rounding with a plane and glasspaper.

5.9 Edges may be curved to improve the appearance of a table top.

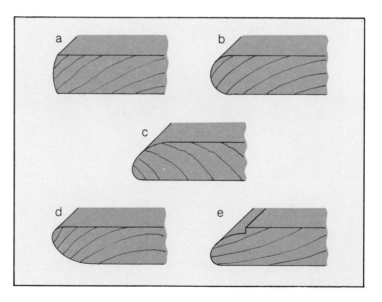

Make a trial assembly of the top to the framework, but it is easier to clean up the wood and finish with stain and polish or varnish if the top is removed until the framework has been completed.

MORTISE AND TENON JOINTS

The most widely used traditional joint is the mortise and tenon, in several variations to suit applications. Some parts that were joined with tenons are now dowelled, but any competent craftsman should be able to cut good mortise and tenon joints. They provide a good glue area and are mechanically strong.

The table with an enclosed shelf and diagonal lower rails (fig. 5.10) shows some applications of the joint. Cut and mark out the parts from the drawing and cutting list. The plywood

5.10 A table with a shelf and rails uses several versions of the mortise and tenon joint.

Note: Measurements in millimetres are given in **bold type**; measurements in inches are given in normal type.

CUTTING LIST FOR TABLE SHOWN ON P.91

4 legs	**600 × 45 × 45**	24 × 1¾ × 1¾
4 rails	**700 × 35 × 25**	28 × 1⅜ × 1
4 rails	**400 × 35 × 25**	16 × 1⅜ × 1
2 bottom rails	**850 × 35 × 18**	34 × 1⅜ × ¾
2 top frames	**800 × 65 × 18**	32 × 2⅝ × ¾
2 top frames	**475 × 65 × 18**	19 × 2⅝ × ¾
1 top panel (plywood)	**725 × 400 × 9**	29 × 16 × ⅜
1 shelf (plywood)	**750 × 425 × 6**	30 × 17 × ¼
2 fillets	**700 × 12 × 12**	28 × ½ × ½
2 fillets	**400 × 12 × 12**	16 × ½ × ½

panels are let into grooves in the rails and the tops of the legs, so plough them to suit. Cut back the legs to the bottoms of the grooves (fig. 5.11a) and mark on them the positions of the rails.

It is customary to make tenons one-third of the thickness of the wood if the parts are both the same thickness, but where the rails are narrower than the legs the tenons are stronger if thicker than one-third of the rail thickness. Cut back to the bottoms of the grooves those parts of the rails that will make tenons, and gauge both these pieces (fig. 5.11b) and the legs for the joints. The bottom shelf rails have tenons full depth (fig. 5.11c). At the top, joints cut to full depth would have weak mortises open to the tops of the legs. Instead, the tenons are haunched (fig. 5.11d). For this, the excess length first left on the leg provides a buffer to the risk of the end grain breaking out when the mortise is being cut.

Cut all the upper rails, their joints and the panels. But a trial assembly might wear the wood and loosen the joint. A craftsman does not usually make this sort of trial with mortise and tenon joints, trusting his workmanship.

Check actual sizes in relation to your drawing. Make a full-size plan view of the leg positions and mark on it the diagonal lower rails. This will give you rail lengths and angles. At each leg, cut away to the size of a rail (fig. 5.11e) so that the tenon shoulders will fit against it and the tenons go into the leg (fig. 5.11f).

HALVING JOINTS

Where the diagonal rails cross there must be a halving or half lap joint to keep them at the same level. This is a joint used in many places where parts cross and may even be used at a corner instead of a mortise and tenon in less-important work. Here the parts cross diagonally, so you have to mark with an adjustable bevel on the surface and square down to lines gauged from the top face edge of both pieces (fig. 5.11g). A common fault in a halving joint is to cut out too much in width or depth. Mark with a knife and cut inside the lines. Pare the bottoms with the chisel sloping upwards a little from each side (fig. 5.11h), and only level the bottom when you are down to the line each side.

The shelf could be rabbeted into the rails, but it is simpler to support the plywood on fillets glued inside the rails (fig.

5.11 *These table legs have thicker grooved tops (a). Tenons are cut in stages (b, c, d). Rail to leg joints are diagonal (e, f).*

5.12 *The shelf rests on fillets (a), glued and pinned (b). A nail from inside will hold a tenon after a cramp has been removed and while the glue sets.*

5.12a). This makes accurate fitting of the shelf easier after the other parts are assembled. Glue the fillets to the rails before assembly. They could also be screwed, but it should be sufficient to use a few panel pins to keep the strips in place (fig. 5.12b).

Assemble the back and front independently. The plywood panels need only have a small amount of glue near the bottoms of the grooves, so avoiding the problem of cleaning off excess. Cut the plywood to a size that makes an easy fit – it need not fit tightly against the bottoms of the grooves. With mortise and tenon joints you can manage with fewer cramps. When a rail is tight into its leg, drive a thin nail into it from the inside, where it will not show (fig. 5.12c). That will hold the joint close while the glue sets after you have removed the cramp.

When you assemble square parts like this, the diagonal rails have to be brought in at the same time as the two parts come together. The panels will help in squaring. Be careful that the widths across the legs at the bottoms are the same as at the tops. If you have to use a bar cramp across the diagonals, pad outside the legs to avoid damage to the corners.

MITRE JOINTS

The top, in this case, has a frame around a plywood centre. The width of the frame should extend past the inside of the rails (fig. 5.13a). Rabbet the strips, keeping them overlong at this stage. Leave the outside edges square, even if they will eventually be rounded or moulded. This is better for cramping. Mark opposite sides to length together, marking the corners with a mitre square. Something has to be done to hold these wide mitres together, although once the table-top is in position the framework will reinforce the joints.

Dowels could be set across (fig. 5.13b), but that brings problems of cramping. The cramping problem is eased if the dowels are parallel with one edge (fig. 5.13b), but that brings problems of cramping. The cramping problem is eased if the dowels are parallel with one edge (fig. 5.13c), but it is difficult to drill without slipping. Another way is to let in a piece of wood across the joint on the underside (fig. 5.13d), preferably while the joint is held close in a mitre cramp. Similar to this is the use of a corrugated fastener on the underside (fig. 5.13e). These fasteners are normally only associated with the crudest woodwork, but in this case they are justified, as they will not show.

With the frame assembled, carefully cut the plywood panel, which may be faced with a matching veneer. As you plane the panel near the size, make its edge slightly tapered (fig. 5.13f), so that it makes a very close fit as it is pressed in.

5.13 *The top frame comes over the rails and legs (a) and may be strengthened with dowels (b, c) or fasteners below (d, e). Tapering the panel edge makes a close fit (f).*

5.14 *The top may be dowelled (a) to the rails, or pockets for screws upwards may be cut (b).*

Use strips of wood along the joints as you press them tight with 'G' cramps.

As there is no problem of expansion and contraction with this type of table-top, it can be fixed down rigidly. You could fix a few dowels along each rail to supplement glue (fig. 5.14a). Another way would be to use pocket screws driven upwards from inside the rails (fig. 5.14b). Drill diagonally downwards into the rails, then chop out enough wood on the inside to admit the screw head. This is a good method of fitting a table or stool top, but as in this case the shelf makes access difficult – except with a short screwdriver – dowels are preferable.

HOUSING OR DADO JOINTS

The common application of a housing joint is in fitting a shelf to the side of a bookcase or something similar. It takes a load across the joint, but the basic form does not offer much resistance to pulling apart. A simple example is a wall bracket to support a vase of flowers (fig. 5.15). The back and shelf could be shaped or decorated in many ways, but this description is mainly concerned with the joints.

The shelf goes into a notch across the back and that is a simple housing joint. Except for cutting its end squarely, there is no special preparation of the shelf. Care is needed to avoid marking or cutting the notch too wide. It may go half through the back, although if that is thick the groove may be comparatively shallower. Use a knife to draw across the surface, and gauge the depth (fig. 5.16a). For hand cutting use a fine backsaw over a bench hook and keep the kerf inside the line. It helps to bevel across the deeply cut knife line with a paring chisel (fig. 5.16b) to keep the saw in position. The waste may be removed entirely with a chisel, but this is the place to use a little hand router to level the

5.15 *A shelf bracket is an example of the use of a housing joint.*

bottom. Use a straight-edge to check that the bottom is level. If it has any high spots away from the edges, the shelf will not bed down tightly.

As the back of the bracket will not show, a few screws can be driven into the shelf end (fig. 5.16c). The support can also be screwed through from the back without notching it in, but there may be a stopped housing joint under the shelf (fig. 5.16d). Its forward end is notched into a groove that does not extend across the full width. For hand cutting, the dado is marked out and the closed end of the groove chopped out with chisels, for a distance of about 25 mm (1 in), but with a

5.16 *Mark a groove across the grain with a knife (a). Paring against the cut forms saw guides (b). Screw the shelf joint from the rear (c). For the stopped housing joint (d), cut the closed end with a chisel to permit saw movement.*

little waste left at the extreme end (fig. 5.16e). This allows you to saw the sides of the groove, using a limited movement of the saw within the cut-out, and then removing the waste as in the simple housing joint. Finally, the end, which has taken knocks from the saw, may be trimmed to size. The support is glued into the groove without screws.

Through housing joints can be cut with a fine radial arm saw or with a circular saw set to a small projection, but the most convenient power tool is a router with a plain cutter, not necessarily as wide as the intended groove. With a piece of wood cramped across as a guide, a groove may be cut either through or stopped. If the cutter is narrower than the final groove you can use a second setting to make up the full width. With a stopped housing joint a chisel must follow the router to square off the end of the groove, or the piece fitting in can be rounded to suit.

Housing joints are used in a block of hanging shelves (fig. 5.17a), which are stiffened by a piece fixed across the top. The layout and assembly are straightforward. The narrower top shelf goes fully into a stopped groove (fig. 5.17b). The other shelves are notched to bring their fronts level with the uprights (fig. 5.17c).

5.17 *A block of shelves (a) has two forms of housing joints (b, c), which can be strengthened with screws or nails from below (d).*

5.18 *Dovetailing (a, b) strengthens a housing joint. Tapering (c, d) makes a tight fit.*

The grooves cannot be very deep, so they do not provide much area for glue, and the strength of the joint is reduced by end grain meeting side grain. The best glued joints come between side grain surfaces: there is not such a good bond between end and side grain, so this housed joint needs the added strength of screws or nails. Driven from outside, they would spoil the appearance of the sides. Instead, thin screws or nails can be driven diagonally upwards from the inside. Two in each joint should be sufficient. If the fastenings are kept close into the angle between the shelf and the side, they will not show much, if at all (fig. 5.17d). The angle of driving should be judged to bring the point out of the end of the shelf at about the centre of the thickness of the side.

Another way of increasing the mechanical strength of the joint is to cut it with a dovetail section, on top and bottom (fig. 5.18a) or on one side only – usually underneath (fig. 5.18b). The shelf must then be slid in from the back. The angle need only be quite slight and can be pared across with a chisel on the shelf, while the groove is angled by tilting the saw or by using a suitable router cutter.

If the shelf is wide, it is difficult to cut a dovetail-shaped housing so that the shelf slides in satisfactorily. Assembly is eased and tightness is ensured if the dovetailed part is tapered (fig. 5.18c). Marking out and cutting must be carefully done, but this makes a very secure joint. With a very wide shelf, getting an even taper is difficult: the dovetail part can be made parallel for perhaps half the width – measuring from the back – and the taper taken forward from there (fig. 5.18d).

5.19 *Hand-cut dovetails may have wide or narrow pins (a, b). Machine-cut dovetails may have pins and tails the same width (c). The dovetail slope can be drawn (d) for setting an adjustable bevel. There could be either a pin (e) or half a tail (f) at an edge.*

DOVETAIL JOINTS

Carefully-fitted dovetail joints are often regarded as the mark of a craftsman, although there are plenty of other woodworking processes at least equally difficult. Dovetails provide a resistance to pulling apart in one direction and a good strength the other way, due to the ample side grain glue area. Handcut dovetails usually have the tails much wider than the pins between them (fig. 5.19a). At one time cabinetmakers were proud of making joints with exceptionally thin pins (fig. 5.19b), but – except as a display of the craftsman's skill – such joints have no advantages. Dovetails can be cut by machine, but these are mostly stopped and can be recognized by their having the pins and tails the same width (fig. 5.19c). Dovetails are often cut with too great a slope on their sides. About 1 in 7 is reasonable (fig. 5.19d), but the degree of taper may be varied according to the thickness and hardness of the wood, with a wider angle for softer woods.

Haphazard dovetails might be just as strong as evenly-spaced ones, but they look ugly. To avoid this, time has to be spent judging how the parts of a joint should be spaced. In normal construction there are pins at the edges (fig. 5.19e), but sometimes it is better to have half a tail at an edge (fig.

5.19f). There are no rules about proportions of dovetail joints, but having the tails about twice as wide as the thickness of the wood, with pins rather narrower than the thickness, gives reasonable proportions in normal work. There must be modifications, though, to get spacing of pins even within any particular overall width. Once a craftsman tried to hide dovetails, but now well-fitted through dovetails are regarded as decorative features.

A box is a typical example of through dovetailing. Its bottom is of solid wood screwed and glued on (fig. 5.20). The wood section may be about 100 mm (4 in) × 12 mm (½ in) and overall sizes can suit needs without affecting details of the

5.20 *Dovetails make strong box corners.*

joints. It is possible to make the parts with tails first or those with pins first. Either method can give good results, but making the tails first permits easier marking of one piece from the other.

The angles can be marked uniformly with a template. Several are on sale, but one can be made of bent metal (fig. 5.21a) or thin pieces of wood (fig. 5.21b). Mark the wood's thickness back from the ends of each piece. There can be a very small amount of excess wood at each end, but too much waste will interfere with cutting the joints. Space the dovetails on one end. Put two pieces together in a vice, and square across (fig. 5.21c), then saw down the sides of the tails and cut in at the sides. Reverse the second piece and use the first as a saw guide for cutting that. Do the same with the fourth end, so that you have cut all tails after marking them on one only, and they will all look the same. In larger work some of the waste can be cut out with a bandsaw. Even in small joints, some waste can be removed with a coping saw, but mainly it has to be chopped and pared out with a bevel-edge chisel, working from each side and always supporting on a flat piece of scrap wood. Careless work can cause the grain to break out. Be careful not to cut below the line and not to leave high spots in the thickness (fig. 5.21d).

5.21 *A gauge can be made to mark dovetail angles (a, b). Tails can be marked and cut together (c), then pins marked from them (d, e). Cut between the pins (f) and drive joints together with supporting blocks.*

The pins and sockets can be marked with a tail piece held in place while a thinly-pointed pencil or a fine awl is used (fig. 5.21e). Use the base of the cut between the tails as a guide against the other wood – not the outside edge. At this stage it is advisable to mark the two parts of each joint, so that they are kept together. It is very unlikely that you will produce joints that are interchangeable and there is no need for that degree of precision.

Cut down the pins with the saw on the waste sides of the lines you have marked. Some of the waste can be removed with a few diagonal cuts (fig. 5.21f), then the bottoms of the sockets are levelled with chisels. Remember the slopes and be careful not to cut into them when working from the wide sides. As with mortise and tenon joints, trust your workmanship and do not risk wear in the joints by making trial assemblies.

When you assemble, the tails should pull the joints tight in the direction they are cut, but you may have to use cramps squeezing on scrap pieces of wood just inside the actual joint area (fig. 5.21g). Check squareness. Let the glue set, then level the joints by planing outside. Have a sharp finely-set plane and hold it diagonally to the way it is pushed – never let it run out at an end grain corner.

DRAWER CONSTRUCTION

There are ways of making drawers without dovetails, mainly devised to suit mass-production, but all the best drawers have the fronts and sides dovetailed to each other, preferably by hand. As the joint details are not wanted visible on the front, the bottom is usually grooved into the sides and front and a part tail at the bottom can hide this (fig. 5.22a). The front is usually thicker than the sides, so that the tails can be of adequate length. When marking out a joint, avoid going too far into the front, as appearance could be spoiled if the covering wood over the tails gets pierced or cracked.

The front is grooved to take a plywood bottom. The sides can also be grooved (fig. 5.22b) or there may be a separate grooved piece inside (fig. 5.22c). If the drawer slides on a runner and guide in the traditional way, the separate piece gives a greater bearing area along the bottom.

5.22 *Stopped dovetails cover a drawer bottom (a, b, c) with a part tail (d, e). Remove waste with a drill, chisel and saw (f, g, h).*

Mark out in a similar way to the through dovetail, but allowing for the stop piece at the front (fig. 5.22d). Cut the tails in the same way as for a through dovetail joint. Mark the other piece from them and square on to the surface (fig. 5.22e). You can saw diagonally inside the marked lines (fig. 5.22f). The rest of the waste has to be removed with chisels, but the work can be eased and the risk of breaking through the front reduced if holes are drilled (fig. 5.22g). Use a depth stop. Hold the wood firmly on flat scrap wood on the bench top, and make cuts across the grain before lengthwise cuts into them. Although bevel-edge chisels will do most of the work, the extreme corners of the sockets are best cleared with a sharp pointed knife (fig. 5.22h), or the inner corners of the tails can be tapered so that they do not bind in these angles.

It is usual for the back of a drawer to reach down only as far as the upper surface of the bottom, which can then be slid into its grooves after the other parts are assembled and held with a few screws driven up into the back. Through dovetails are used at the back (fig. 5.23a), arranged so that

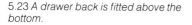
5.23 *A drawer back is fitted above the bottom.*

the back stops above the grooves – with its top often kept a little lower than the sides, and rounded (fig. 5.23b). If the drawer has to be adjusted inside the back of its casing, the tails may be left long and finally planed to stop the drawer at the right position. It is important that a drawer should be the same width at the back and front, and be made square, particularly when you check the sides in relation to the front. Any errors mean that the drawer will not run properly nor fit closely at the front.

Older drawers were always made to close flush with the front of their casing and any old furniture examined will be found arranged in this way. Much modern furniture has the drawer front overlapping so that it hides the gaps around the drawer. This greater tolerance is necessary if tedious hand

5.24 *An overlapping drawer front may be cut solid or a piece added.*

work is to be avoided in mass-production, but overlapping fronts are now accepted as features of modern design, so may be used in individual pieces of furniture.

The drawer front may be fairly thick and have a rabbet cut so that the joints are set back (fig. 5.24a). This makes a form of stopped dovetail, but because of the overhang, a saw cannot be used on the sockets. An alternative is to make the front in two thicknesses. This is simpler and allows of a neater fit than rabbets, as well as making it possible to use simple through dovetails (fig. 5.24b). The drawer can be made up completely without the false front, allowing any planing or other adjustment to get a good fit. The front can be added as a final step, with glue and screws from inside the drawer.

CHIPBOARD JOINTS

Although veneered chipboard can be treated as wood in many ways, its construction of wood chips in synthetic resin does not permit much detail work – such as the cutting of interlocking joints similar to those used in solid wood. In such uses there is a tendency for corners to break and particles to come away. Because of this and the widespread use of chipboard in mass-production, other techniques and joints have been developed, particularly where chipboard is almost the sole constructional material for a piece of furniture.

Chipboard can be cut to curves by hand or with a bandsaw, but the method of covering edges with self-adhesive strips of matching veneer cannot be relied on for very tight curves. If the curved edge is covered with solid wood, any shape is possible, but where it will be exposed there are limits to the amount of shaping. If specimens of mass-produced furniture are examined, nearly all will be seen to have been designed with far more square-ended parts than would be usual with solid wood. This is due to the need for convenience in manufacture and the limitations of the material for finishing curved edges. A maker of an individual piece of furniture can do better than the manufacturer in including some moderate curves, but edges have to be prepared square across and in a way that permits the use of a hot domestic iron for pressing the strip of veneer on. If the curve blends into straight edges, the strip can be in one piece that can be pulled along the straight parts as well as around the curve to get a close fit.

Probably the best joint for most parts of an individually-made assembly in chipboard uses dowels – 6 mm (¼ in) will suit. There are prepared dowels and drilling jigs available to suit the commonly used thickness of chipboard, but cut rod and measured positions may be preferred by a craftsman (fig. 5.25a).

It is not always easy to get close-fitting corners, so where the design permits one part may extend over another (fig. 5.25b). It may help if you cover the line where they meet with a strip of wood (fig. 5.25c). At a bottom a plinth effect can be made by letting the sides reach the floor and setting a front back a little (fig. 5.25d).

Chipboard will take screws, but a screw cannot be left to cut its own way for part of the depth, as is often done in wood (fig. 5.25e). If that was done in chipboard, the material would crack and expand to spoil the surface appearance. Instead, the core size hole should go further than the screw is expected to (fig. 5.25f). Although ordinary wood screws can be used, there are special screws for the material. They look like self-tapping screws intended for sheet metal, and have threads almost to the head (fig. 5.25g).

If screws have to be used through a surface that will show, they may be counterbored and the holes plugged. Instead of putting a wood plug in the hole, there are plastic plugs with shallow curved heads, supplied in colours to match the veneer, which can be glued in (fig. 5.25h).

Another way of joining chipboard parts is with strips of wood screwed both ways (fig. 5.25j). This is suitable for places where the strips will not show. Inside a cupboard or other places where they are hidden most of the time, they could be cut back a little and bevelled or rounded. Behind a plinth, or other place where they are out of sight, they can be fixed along all joints (fig. 5.25h). the same idea can be used to hold a plywood or hardboard back in a chipboard cabinet (fig. 5.25l).

There are plastic blocks for screwing in both directions in a similar way to the strips of wood, and others where two mating blocks can be fixed to the two parts and drawn together with a bolt. These are particularly suitable for furniture that has to be taken apart or is supplied in a knock-down form for the customer to put together. They have little value in the building of furniture that will never have to be dismantled.

5.25 *Dowelled joints (a, b) can be used with chipboard. Joints may be hidden with wood (c) or set back (d). Screw holes that need go only part way in wood (e) must be full depth in chipboard (f). Special chipboard screws (g) may be sunk and plugged (h). Wood strips can be used to join parts (j, k, l).*

WEDGES

A wedge can exert considerable power over a short distance. For a temporary cramp, blocks can be nailed or screwed to a stiff piece of wood, then a wedge driven against a block to tighten an assembly (fig. 5.26a). A single wedge has a tendency to push the parts to one side, but it is possible to give a parallel push with a pair of folding wedges (fig. 5.26b). Both wedges should be cut at the same angle. What the angle is may not be critical. A shallower angled wedge puts on more pressure, but can only move the part being pressed a small amount. With a steeper angle, the movement is more, but the available pressure is less – although it is usually more than enough. To reduce any tendency to move the work sideways, the wedges should be tapped in with alternate blows.

5.26 A wedge may be driven to apply pressure (a), but a pair of wedges (b) give a parallel action. Wedges may be driven outside a tenon (c), but are better arranged to spread it (d), particularly to give stiffness to a light assembly (see fig. 5.27). Wedges in a stub tenon (e) will spread it as it is driven in (f).

5.27 *A light clothes airer made with mortise and tenon joints.*

Before the days of reliable waterproof glues many joints were wedged to give them mechanical strength even if they were glued as well. Through tenons may have had wedges driven outside them (fig. 5.26c). This tightens by compressing the tenon, which is not as efficient as spreading it. A better way is to put one or two saw cuts across the end of the tenon before it is driven, with wedges driven into the saw cuts to spread the tenon. This is helped by making the mortise slightly tapered, so that the spread tenon widens and cannot pull out (fig. 5.26d). Even if the parts being assembled are softwood, it helps to use hardwood wedges, to get a better spread. Another way of increasing tightness is to thoroughly dry the wedges in an oven; then they may be expected to absorb moisture from the atmosphere and expand after driving. Have the wedges too long, so that they and the end of the tenon can be cut off and planed level after tightening.

That sort of joint is useful in outdoor carpentry, where the wedge joint stands a good chance of remaining tight whatever the weather does to the woodwork. It is also suitable for an assembly like a light clothes airer, where the wood is of comparatively light section and the maximum stiffness is needed in all the joints to keep the assembly in shape.

There is an ingenious method of spreading the end of a stub tenon with wedges, called 'fox wedging' or 'foxtail wedging'. A stub tenon is one that goes into a mortise that is not cut right through.

Make the joint with the tenon to fit the mortise, but the bottom of the mortise can be widened slightly to allow for the spread of the tenon (fig. 5.26e). Put two saw cuts in the end of the tenon. Make two small wedges of rather wider angles than would be used to spread a tenon in a through mortise. These go in the saw cuts as you assemble the joint, and press against the bottom of the mortise to spread the end of the tenon as the joint is drawn tight (fig. 5.26f). The skill comes in estimating the size of wedges that will give sufficient spread, yet not be so large as to prevent the tenon being pushed in fully.

A reminder of times when furniture often needed to be dismantled and re-assembled is the 'tusk tenon', which uses a wedge for tightening. This is seen in some chairs, but is best-known for the lower rail in refectory, or similar, tables (fig. 5.28). It looks best in oak of fairly stout sections, even if it

5.28 A refectory table shows a typical use of a wedged tusk tenon at the end of the lower rail.

is cut small as in a coffee table or for use in making a stool. The rail may go through the end either horizontally (fig. 5.29a) or on edge (fig. 5.29b), or for a larger table the shoulders may taper at the top and go into a step at the bottom (fig. 5.29d).

For tightening, the hole that takes the wedge is tapered to match the wedge, but it is cut back so that when the joint is driven tight there is still a gap behind the wedge, which is then levering against the table leg surface (fig. 5.29e). When making this joint it is advisable to start with a wedge longer than you expect to need, and then to make a trial assembly and trim the wedge so that it will extend approximately equal amounts above and below the tenon. The ends of the wedge can be decorated (fig. 5.29f).

The other joints in this sort of table could be dowelled, but traditionally they are mortise and tenons. At the tops and bottoms of the legs there are multiple tenons, with haunches between (fig. 5.30a). It is always easier to cut such joints before doing any shaping to the wood, so that you have flat rectangular stock to use on the bench-top or in a vice.

A central top rail could be fitted, but better support for the table-top would be provided by two rails (fig. 5.30b). A solid wood top should be held with buttons in slots, but for a framed top or one with the main area made of blockboard or plywood, and therefore not liable to expand or contract, dowels could be used.

Another way to tighten a mortise and tenon joint may not seem to be wedging at first glance. A peg or dowel inserted across the joint can be used to tighten it. This is called 'draw-pinning', and was used in timber-framed houses. It can be employed for any assembly in which there is no room for cramping – because of size or obstructions.

5.29 *Tusk tenons take several forms, but all go through to be tightened by wedging.*

5.30 *Multiple tenons are used on wide boards (a). Two rails come under a table top (b).*

A mortise and tenon is made in the usual way, then a hole for a peg is drilled across the mortise, preferably rather nearer where the tenon shoulder will be than the centre of the wood (fig. 5.31a). The tenon is put dry into the mortise, and the outline of the hole is marked through; then it is withdrawn. Instead of drilling a hole as marked, the drill is entered nearer the shoulder. How far depends on the hardness and strength of the wood and how much further in you want to pull the tenon. As an example, with 50 mm (2 in) square softwood, the hole could probably be moved 3 mm (⅛ in) in from the mark (fig. 5.31b).

Into this goes a peg of a diameter to suit the hole, but made too long and tapered for a short distance (fig. 5.31c). When it is driven in, it will pull the tenon tight into the mortise. The tapered part of the dowel goes right through, and the ends are cut off.

NAILED JOINTS

Most people claim to be able to drive nails, but there are differences between work done by an expert or by those of less experience. If wood has to be in a certain position, such as flush with a line, out of sight underneath a board into which you want to drive nails, other nails can be entered tilted along the line as a guide (fig. 5.32a) and withdrawn later. In a nailed joint, closer spacing of the nails is needed where the joint is most likely to be pulled open, or as the corner of a box (fig. 5.32b).

5.31 *A mortise and tenon joint can be pulled tight by draw pinning with a dowel through offset holes.*

A nail holds by squeezing the top piece of wood between its head and the friction of the nail in the lower piece. Tightness of the nail in the upper piece does nothing for strength in the joint, so if the wood is very hard or you are using large nails, a clearance hole in the top piece will aid driving and avoid the risk of a split near an edge.

A nail does not hold as well in end grain as it does when driven across the grain. You can get a better grip in that case by using dovetail nailing (fig. 5.32c).

If a row of nails is to be driven along a batten, there is a risk that if you keep them in a straight line cracks may develop – possibly some time after driving. The nail-heads could be staggered (fig. 5.32d), but the joint can be strengthened by sloping the nails towards the centre as they are driven – another version of dovetail nailing.

A problem when nailing thin parts together is that the lower piece will not take a sufficient length of nail to provide a sure grip, so the nails must be taken through and clenched. It may seem neatest to sink the nail end along the grain (fig. 5.32e), but there is a risk of splitting. It would be stronger to turn over the nail across the grain, but then it is difficult to drive it level and the exposed point could be dangerous. A better way is to bend the end so that you can drive it diagonal to the grain and bury the point. To do this

5.32 *Temporary nails locate the parts of a joint (a). Extra end nails (b) or dovetailed nails (c) give increased strength. Staggering nails (d) reduces the risk of splitting. Clenched nails (e, f, g, h) give the effect of rivets.*

drive the nail through, then support the head on an iron block. Hold the end of an awl or other spike against the nail end and hammer it over (fig. 5.32f). Remove the spike and hammer the point into the wood (fig. 5.32g).

Besides joining pieces, as in the overlapping planking of a clinker or clench-built boat, single nails can be used to make pivots in wood toys or at the laps of garden trelliswork (fig. 5.32h).

HINGES

There are now a very large number of ingenious hinges, mostly used for such things as kitchen equipment, with some designed particularly for chipboard. For most general cabinetwork and carpentry in solid wood, butt hinges are still the usual choice. They may be of steel or brass, and in sizes from those for tiny trinket boxes to some much larger than the everyday carpenter is likely to need. The ordinary type are intended to be let into the wood and it is in getting the hinges properly located that many workers go wrong.

A hinge swings on the pin through the knuckle. If there are two or more hinges, the knuckles must be in line. The knuckle must also be clear of the surface, so that the door or lid swings free. If the centre of the pin is below the surface of the wood the hinge is fixed to, the parts will bind on each other.

A butt hinge is made so that it closes with the flaps parallel, but not touching. If you let the flaps in that much, the door clearance will be the same (fig. 5.33a). You can let them in deeper if you want to reduce the clearance. If you cut too deeply the hinge can be packed out with paper or cardboard.

In most cases, it is best to cut the recesses to fit closely around the hinge flaps (fig. 5.33b). Keep them parallel. Hinges are supplied drilled and countersunk to suit a particular gauge of screw. If you do not drive a screw squarely, its head may project slightly above the surface of the flap and could bind against the one opposite – preventing the door

5.33 A hinge is made to give clearance when closed and let in (a, b, c). For chipboard there are thin hinges (d) that do not have to be let in.

from closing completely. One hinge flap can be let in at an angle to give better screw clearance (fig. 5.33c) without altering the position of the knuckle.

One modern version of the butt hinge was developed mainly for use with chipboard, where cutting recesses cleanly can be difficult. This is made of thin metal, with one flap folding into the other (fig. 5.33d) so that the total thickness is no more than the usual clearance between a cabinet door and its post. There is no cutting of the parts to be hinged, and the hinge can just be screwed straight on.

Gateleg and other tables with hinged flaps can present an ugly joint if a flap is cut square and is hanging down on ordinary hinges (fig. 5.34a). Better tables have rule joints, so named from the similarity of the section of the joint to those in the old two-fold carpenter's rule. For this to work properly special backflap hinges must be used. Most hinges do not open much more than 180°, but a backflap hinge goes back to a right-angle and its holes are countersunk on the outside (fig. 5.34b). The fixed table-top has a moulded edge over which a shaped edge on the flap goes, with the pivot coming within the thickness of the wood (fig. 5.34c and d).

To fit this sort of hinge, draw a side view and about this draw the thickness of the wood, with the hinge flaps let in

5.34 *A table flap on an ordinary hinge (a) falls to leave the joint open, but a backflap hinge (b) allows the flap edges to open with a moulded appearance (c, d, e).*

flush. The shaping of the section must be done with the compass point at the centre of the hinge knuckle (fig. 5.34e). Notice that the screw holes in one flap are kept far enough out to clear the hollowed edge of the flap.

Make the rounded edge of the fixed top first, by cutting a rabbet and rounding the part below. A card template of the shape, made from your drawing, is useful for putting over the wood and checking progress. Hollow the other part to match. In the finished joint the rounded fixed part will be visible. When you make trial assemblies, any adjustments should be made in the hollow part.

The outer edges of all parts of the table-top can be moulded in the same way as the flap joint, so that there is a uniform appearance whether the table is closed or open. There should be a hinge fairly close to the end of each joint and at least one elsewhere. If a flap warps, even slightly, the movement of the joint will be affected, but if it is fixed with enough hinges the wood will not warp so easily.

FRAMED DOORS

Besides solid doors, framed doors can be made with plywood or glass panels, and these make attractive fronts for cabinets. A plywood panel is usually let into a grooved frame (fig. 5.35a), but a glass panel is put in a rabbeted frame (fig. 5.35b), so it can be replaced - if it gets broken – by removing the fillets. Plywood is sometimes fitted in the same way. The frame is made with the sides carried through and the top and bottom rails tenoned into them, with the top

5.35 *A plywood panel may fit in a groove (a), but glass is better fitted in a rabbet (b). Corner joints must be cut back to allow for grooves (c).*

rail and the sides the same width and the bottom rail wider. Strength depends on the corner joints and these should be haunched mortise and tenons.

For a plywood panel in grooves, prepare the wood and keep the sides overlength. In most furniture doors the joints have stub tenons (those that do not go right through), but many room doors and others where appearance is less important may have the tenons taken through and wedged.

Mark out the sides with the positions of the rails and extra length left at each end. For the rails the important length to measure is between the shoulders, then allow more for the tenons and cut away the groove. Cut back the tenons to the bottoms of the grooves and gauge around the tenons and along the mortises – always working from the face sides, which will be at the front. Cut the waste from the sides of the tenons, which then have to be haunched (fig. 5.35c).

Make a haunch on the tenon as deep as the groove in the other piece and far enough from the edge to reduce the risk of the end grain beside the mortise breaking out, but not so far that the tenon is weakened by being made too narrow.

How far the tenon goes into the other piece depends on the wood sizes, but the deeper the tenon goes, the stronger it should be.

It is unwise to plan a mortise so deep that there is a risk of breaking through. About three-quarters of the thickness of the wood should be about right. Cut out the mortise and the socket for the haunch (fig. 5.35d).

The panel need not reach the bottoms of the grooves, but there should not be much clearance. Then, when you have squared up the assembly, the glued panel will help to keep it in shape. Join top and bottom rails to one side, then slide in the panel and add the second side. Cramp up and get the assembly square and without twist, then leave it for the glue to set. The horns projecting at the corners can be cut off if you are fitting the door soon, otherwise they offer protection if the door will be left about and could get knocked at the corners. House doors are often supplied with horns on for this reason.

For a glass panel in a rabbeted door, the construction is very similar except for the tenons having to be given stepped shoulders. Work to the front sizes, but then mark the depth of the rabbet for the shoulder at the back of each joint (fig. 5.36a). It is usual to arrange for the thickness of the mortise and tenon to come inside the rabbet, even if that puts them off centre. It is possible to cut into the front part, but it is easier to make the joint a neat one if it is set inside the rabbet.

There has to be a haunch, which could be the same as the sort described for the grooved frame, but it is possible to cut it sloping so that it does not show on the outside (fig. 5.36b). Assembly is the same as for the grooved frame, except that the glass panel does not go in until later. It may help to keep the frame square while the glue sets if a piece of scrap plywood or hardboard is fitted in temporarily.

When the glass is fitted, the fillets may have rectangular section and should come to the same level as the frame (fig. 5.36c). They could have their exposed edge rounded (fig. 5.36d). Where these pieces meet they should be mitred, but the first pieces put in could overlap instead. In any case, make the fillets full in the length so that they bow slightly and can be forced down as they are nailed. Use thin panel pins and have them driven already almost through the fillets before these are sprung in. It helps if you angle the pins slightly. Put a piece of stout cardboard against the glass and slide your hammer on it (fig. 5.36e). Only a few pins are needed. Too many may make it difficult to lever out the wood if you have to make a repair.

To avoid damaging the glass, cut the frame to size, prepare it for hinges and handles and make a trial assembly in its frame, all before putting in the glass. You may also find it

5.36 The shoulders of a tenon are stepped (a) over a rabbet. A haunch may be sloped (b). The fillet over glass may be flush or rounded (c, d). Card can be used to protect glass from the hammer when nailing (e).

worthwhile staining and polishing the wood first. To avoid reflections in the framing, the insides of the fillets and the rabbets could be stained or painted a flat black.

Corners of both sorts of door are sometimes dowelled, but this is not as strong as tenoning and is really an expedient for mass-production. A craftsman-made door should have mortise and tenon joints.

CLOSE CORNER JOINTS

There are many assemblies in which the corner post or leg is fairly thin in relation to the parts to be joined to it, meeting it from two directions. This means that joints of sufficient depth to be strong will overlap or meet. Care is needed to accommodate them so that the amount cut away does not weaken the corner piece too much.

An example is a stool frame intended for seating with rush or seagrass (fig. 5.37). The tops of the legs extend above the

5.37 *A stool frame intended to be covered with rush is an example of an assembly where rail joints have to meet inside each leg.*

top rails, so the tenons do not need to be haunched, but to ensure sufficient length in the tenons they are taken into the leg far enough to meet with a mitre (fig. 5.38a). Square the bottoms of the meeting mortises, but cut the ends of the tenons short so that they do not actually meet. There is no need for precision in cutting the mitres, but get them reasonably close to 45°.

At the lower rails there could be a similar joint, but it is usually possible to arrange the rail heights different in the two directions (fig. 5.38b). That allows the tenons to go further without mitres. You can deal with dowels or turned rods in a similar way, either mitring completely or partially (fig. 5.38c). If you use turned rails without shoulders, pencil on them where the leg surface should come in order to get the correct penetration. Otherwise you may find when you check that the legs are parallel with each other by measuring across at top and bottom, that much more of the rail goes in at one end than at the other.

There are ways of notching tenons into each other instead of mitring. Notches could be used with the stool rails (fig. 5.38d), but they are more appropriate to deeper rails, such as may be used for an upholstered stool or the top rails of a table. In that case part of the tenon is made like a haunch and the other part goes full depth. This cuts less out of the leg when mortising, so there is more solid wood left to provide strength than there would be if full tenons were mitred (fig. 5.38e).

5.38 *Rail tenons can meet with a mitre (a) if they cannot be arranged at different levels (b). Dowel ends may have to be mitred (c). Instead of a mitre, tenons can be cut to step over each other (d, e).*

5.39 *Rail edges may be fully shaped (a) or bevelled (b, c). Legs may be tapered (d).*

LEG AND RAIL SHAPES

In modern furniture there is less use of decoration than there was in years gone by. Some Victorian furniture is so covered with decoration that it seems the craftsman wanted to avoid leaving any plain wood visible. However, modern furniture benefits from some departure from straight lines and angular corners. The general effect, though, is of plainness: much of the beauty comes from the overall shape and the grain pattern.

The lower edges of top rails or other rails under shelves of a cabinet can be shaped. One way is to cut curves with a bandsaw and clean the edges with spokeshaves or *Surform* tools (fig. 5.39a). Another way is to leave the edge basically flat and straight, but work the curves diagonal to the edge (fig. 5.39b). If this is a part that comes below the normal sight line, the visual effect is as good as the cut right across and may be easier to work, if you do not have a bandsaw. In both cases the curves must be symmetrical and centrally located, so make a half template with card (fig. 5.39c) and turn it over.

If there is much extension of a leg below the lowest horizontal member, it looks better tapered. There could be a taper all round, down to a square on the end (fig. 5.39d). The taper might come only on the inner surfaces (fig. 5.39e), leaving the outer corner straight, and this appearance may be favoured. A slender taper looks graceful, but remember to leave enough bearing surface at the bottom – small ends may mark carpets.

Another method of lightening the appearance of a rail or leg is to use wagon bevelling, which gets its name from the practice of wheelwrights, who used their drawknife to make this form of decoration on nearly all otherwise square edges of wagon parts.

In its simplest form this is a stopped bevel or chamfer (fig. 5.40a). To mark it out use a notched piece of wood and a pencil (fig. 5.40b). Mark the ends on each surface at 45°. You can cut diagonally across with a saw at each end, but leave bevelling the ends until later, or they may become damaged. If you have to work by hand, pare with a chisel to the pencil lines. If the work is long enough, pare only towards the ends and get the middle to size with a plane (fig. 5.40c). You may want to level the bevel with abrasive paper wrapped around a block of wood, but be careful not to give it a round cross-section. When you are satisfied with the centre part, pare down the ends carefully (fig. 5.40d). The effect of wagon bevelling depends on clean accurate cuts.

If you have a router with a suitable 45° cutter the bevels can be cut accurately and quickly. That will leave rounded ends (fig. 5.40e), but you can convert them to the angled ends with a chisel.

On some legs the wagon bevelling may be at the outside corner only and carried to the floor (fig. 5.40f). On some tables it may be satisfactory to carry that outside bevel right through to the top, but it looks better in most cases if you leave something square above the bevel.

A long piece of wagon bevelling may be broken and a simple notch put between (fig. 5.40g). That can also be done at the end of any wagon bevelling and is effective on the lower edge of a rail, where the legs have wagon bevelling all round between upper and lower rails. Wagon bevels can be put all round square and rectangular lower rails but if the wood starts with a fairly small section already, be sure you are not weakening it too much. Remember that with a chair, stool or table, someone may push a foot hard against a rail,

plane off

or tilt the assembly on to two legs – putting a considerable load on the rails serving as bracing.

A simple alternative to basic wagon bevelling is to use curved hollows, which are much quicker to do and look quite effective when used, for example, to reduce a leg section between upper and lower rails (fig. 5.40h). With a little practice you can do the work between pencil marks without further marking out, using spokeshaves or curved *Surform* tools. Matching hollows may be worked along rail edges.

Cabriole Legs

In the eighteenth century there developed a fashion for cabriole legs on tables and chairs and the design is still used. The name refers to a leg with a pronounced knee and foot extending diagonally from the corner. In some antique examples there is elaborate carving in the length of the leg and many legs finish in the form of a claw holding a ball. In modern furniture it is more usual to use clean sweeps to the curves and finish the foot just as a rounded form. The design may be referred to as Queen Anne, but it was widely used during later reigns (fig. 5.41). In a chair, only the front legs are made in this way, while the rear legs curve to give support, but are otherwise plain.

Some cabriole legs extended outside the line of an imaginary containing square section, with the result that either much solid wood was cut to waste or pieces had to be glued on and shaped. But appearance may be spoiled by a glue

5.41 *Cabriole legs are a special form found in antique and reproduction furniture, as shown in this Queen Anne table.*

line and by the difference in grains. In a modern leg it is better to keep the curves moderate, so that they may be cut from solid wood, except for wings – which may be added at the top. The leg, wing and rail can then all make a matched system of outlines (fig. 5.42a).

The example shown is coffee-table size and the plan of the shaped part of a leg all comes within a square of about 70 mm (2¾ in) (fig. 5.42b). As there will be four legs to be marked with curves in both directions, start with a template of the outline. Use this to mark the shape on the wood (fig. 5.42c). Saw the outline in one direction (fig. 5.42d). This will remove some of the marking out in one direction, and – as you gain experience – you may omit the second marks until later. But if you are cutting with a handsaw it is helpful to put the scrap pieces back for the second cuts, to give you flat surfaces to work through the saw. They may be lightly nailed back or held with adhesive tape. This leaves you with a leg of rectangular section, but with the curves correctly outlined (fig. 5.42e). Make sure each leg finishes with the cuts as true as possible. Get the top part true and straight. It is advisable, if legs are to match, to do the same work to each leg in turn, before moving on to the next stage.

The rest of the shaping is mainly done by eye as you take off the angles with spokeshave, *Surform* tool, planes and abrasive paper. When sections are nearing completion you can make them even and remove tool marks by pulling a strip of abrasive paper or cloth around them, but you must finally get rid of the cross-wise scratches with lengthwise sanding. The foot should finish round in section, and this section continues up the slender part above the foot. But, as you shape progressively further up the leg, it should be allowed to get more angular and with rounded corners. This brings the shape to blend into the square top and leaves flat surfaces for the wings to be attached (fig. 5.42f).

Usually the rails have to be tenoned into the leg; then the wings blend into them (fig. 5.42g). If the wings are dowelled into the legs before assembly, they can be glued to the rails as they are fitted.

If the legs are to be used to make a coffee table, the top could be a plain rectangle with moulded edges, but to carry through the Queen Anne theme it should be scalloped or given a pie crust edge (fig. 5.42h). This needs careful marking out. You have to get the sets of curves to divide neatly into the length of the side both ways. You might make the curves slightly different one way from the other, but it helps if you start with the top design and modify it to take an exact number of curves each way, then make the other parts to

match, instead of trying to plan the edge-shape after making the underframing. Make a template of a series of curves and use that to move around and get the shapes matching. Moulding such a shape is difficult and tedious by hand. Once the outline has been cut truly, a moulding cutter in a router can quickly and accurately finish the edges.

There is an angular variation on the cabriole leg that has possibilities in small things, like footstools, but might not look satisfactory in larger assemblies. The effect is of a tapered leg with a foot, but with no curves (fig. 5.43a). Only the two outer surfaces are shaped. The inner corner remains square.

Start with a piece of square section, and mark the outline on one face (fig. 5.43b). Saw down into the angle and taper towards the cut. Bevel the bottom of the foot. Mark the shape the other way on what you have just cut (fig. 5.43c). This allows you to keep a flat surface downwards. Taper the other way, taking care to match the shapes. It is usual to do the shaping only below the rails, but you can include lower rails behind the tapered part, as the inner surfaces are flat. With these legs and the full cabriole ones, it is easier to cut most mortise and other joints while you are still handling a square section of wood, before you start shaping.

5.43 *A simplified version of a cabriole leg is suitable for stools.*

HANDLES

A vast range of handles, made of metal and plastic, is available for drawers and doors. If you are making reproduction furniture there are brass and other sets of handles, hinges, escutcheons and other things that will make your work look authentic. Of course, a plastic fitting would not be appropriate, although there are some with metallic finishes that would be difficult to identify.

It is easy to spoil the appearance of a piece of furniture with a wrong handle, but a safe choice in nearly all circumstances is a wooden handle. You could choose a handle made entirely of wood, or you might prefer one of wood mounted over a plastic or metal plate. Surfaces tend to get soiled round handles, so some sort of guard there may be a good thing. It could also show off the handle, which might not be very apparent otherwise.

Handles can often be worked in a strip, sufficiently long for all the handles needed. This also helps if you are planing the shape – it is easier to work accurately along a good length than to work on a short piece. It also helps if you make the handle on the edge of a wider piece of wood. That gives you something to grip in a vice and you can cut

5.44 *Drawer and door handles can be made from wood.*

through after you have made the section of handle. You could shape handles on opposite sides of the same piece.

A drawer handle needs a good lip to get your fingers under (fig. 5.44a). Its section can be made by hollowing, either with a router cutter or a plane. You can also get the shape by ploughing some of the waste away, following with coarse abrasive paper over a shaped wood block. The outside can be shaped with ordinary planes (fig. 5.44b).

A door handle may be made in a similar way (fig. 5.44c). Make two hollows in the sides to provide a grip, then round off the front surface before cutting it away from the wider piece (fig. 5.44d).

Handles of this sort would be cut to length and left with square ends in mass-production. For individual work we can improve the handles by rounding the ends. Both sorts of handles can be held with wood screws driven from the other side, but put the screws through large washers (fig. 5.44e). This is advisable even if you glue a handle on, as a pull sometimes puts on a considerable load.

A piece of metal or plastic may be sandwiched between the handle and the door or drawer (fig. 5.44f). Plated brass or translucent black plastic sheeting may be felt to give an air of quality with polished wood. In some cases the backing may be a piece of contrasting veneer stuck on. Even with a more utilitarian item, such as a workshop cabinet or outdoor furniture, a thin piece of wood or plywood can be fixed under a handle.

The two types of handle described are only examples. It is possible to spend considerable time shaping and carving handles to suit particular situations. Commercially-produced handles, often in plastic, can give you ideas for your own wooden ones.

Chapter 6
APPLYING TECHNIQUES

Carpentry, cabinetmaking, joinery, or whatever term is applied to any particular branch of woodworking, is concerned with making things. The work in producing the required results usually involves the application of many basic functions and techniques, which then have to be altered to match each other. Quite often adaptations have to be made, to suit the materials available, and sometimes one technique has to be worked in with another so that both differ a little from their basic form. It is in the combination of techniques that much of the interest and skill of woodworking comes in. Parts have to be joined so that joints have adequate strength, but these may have to be linked together and altered to suit circumstances.

With experience comes the ability to plan construction so that you know what stages are best made and assembled first. You learn to think ahead and do certain work in anticipation of a later need, at a point in your progress when the particular operation is more easily attended to. If, for example, a large number of holes have to be drilled, you mark them out and drill them all at one stage, rather than deal with them only when other work shows that they are needed. Besides enabling you to do better work more efficiently, you will find this makes progress more rapid. If what you are making is for sale, this is an important consideration. Your time is usually the most expensive part of a project.

This thinking ahead is important. You should know the move after the next. Not only that, you should know the sequence of moves right through to the end. It can be very frustrating and time-wasting to reach a point where, for instance, you need screws of a particular size and discover you do not have them. This also applies to wood. For most things you should have all the wood you need before you start, otherwise you may tackle part of a job and then find you cannot get matching wood later, or the stock sizes available are not what you expected: you might have adapted the design to use what was in fact available if you had known when you started. If there are metal fittings involved, it helps to get them quite early in the project so that the wood can be prepared to suit.

For most things you make, it is easier to work on the bench on individual pieces of wood than to wait until later and try to do the same process on a part that has been fixed to other pieces to form part of an assembly. All the joints in a particular piece should be cut in the single piece of wood, recesses may be made for hinges, prefabricate every piece as far as it is possible to go before joining it to anything else. Sometimes you may not be able to cut a joint or do some other preparation until parts of the assembly have been brought together, but even then you can do some marking out and possibly some preliminary cuts that will simplify the work later. You may even sand some surfaces, that would be difficult to get at after assembly, but do not use abrasive until after you have done all the cutting, as minute particles of grit embedded in the wood will blunt cutting tools.

Before starting any new project, check over the wood you have. It is a natural material and is far from uniform, but most of it can be used. A piece with a knot or other flaw near an edge might be built in so that the imperfection is hidden. Mark such a piece and arrange its face side and edge accordingly. You may even be able to use a piece of which part is undersize, by keeping that part away from the visible surfaces and cutting adjoining parts to suit. You only need to get into the loft of an old house or turn over a piece of old furniture to see how pieces that did not quite come up to size or had irregular surfaces were used in ways that made these things unimportant. It is not suggested that wood should be deliberately used unprepared where it does not show. But it is possible to do perfectly good work, by arranging wood at the preliminary planning stage so that the less-perfect parts will be hidden – provided, of course, that they will still function adequately.

This is not a book of projects, but this chapter shows various things to make using the techniques already described. Their purpose is to illustrate constructional and other techniques, but it is hoped that the designs will also have some appeal. There are cutting lists and information on making the projects, as well as details of the special techniques involved, but most individual craftsmen tend to modify published designs to suit their own ideas – and this is normally satisfactory: that is what makes them individual craftsmen.

TWIN PEDESTAL COFFEE TABLE

As shown (fig. 6.1) this table has two turned pillars as legs. Turned parts always give a light appearance, but a similar table could be made with square legs, possibly with wagon bevelling or other edge decoration. The curved feet might then be changed to a more angular outline to be more in keeping with the angular decoration of the legs.

The sizes (fig. 6.2 and cutting list) specify a table for use beside an armchair, intended for one person. It would be possible to increase the top area, but be careful to keep the spread of the feet ends to somewhere near the same spacing as the corners of the top, for the sake of stability. The design might be adapted to be a stand for a pot plant, but if it is taken much higher be careful to give the feet sufficient spread to prevent tipping.

The table should be made of the same hardwood throughout, although it could have an interesting appearance with the pillars in a wood of very different colour to the other parts. Whether the top can be made in one piece, or must be made up by edge gluing, depends on the wood.

Prepare wood for the pillars truly square before turning. You should not need to do anything to their surfaces after turning. There are a great many possible designs to use for the turned parts. One is shown (fig. 6.3a). What is important is, having turned one pillar, to get the other one to match. Leave a little excess wood at the ends at this stage.

At the top of each pillar the joint is an open mortise and tenon, or 'bridle' (fig. 6.3b). Cut this to be a good push fit before shaping the tapered ends, and make sure it finishes squarely. There are at least two ways of joining the feet to the legs. They can be dowelled, or you can use a dovetailed housing joint. In both cases the joint should be cramped, yet the outside curves are unsuitable for normal cramping. To allow for this, projections are left to provide square cramping faces on each leg (fig. 6.3c); these are cut off later.

Make a hardboard template (fig. 6.3d), so that the legs can be marked identically. The alternative is to make one leg and use that as a template for the others, but a hardboard or thin plywood template is more convenient.

Draw the final shape across the projecting ends, and clean up the edges of the feet as far as possible before assembly. The feet will be strongest if their grain is diagonal (fig. 6.3e). In particular, see that the flat under the foot and the flat against the pillar are square to each other and square across.

For a dowelled joint, mark the feet and pillar together in

6.1 *A coffee table on twin turned legs has a light appearance.*

6.2 *Sizes of a twin pedestal coffee table.*

Note: Measurements in millimetres are given in **bold type**; measurements in inches are given in normal type.

CUTTING LIST FOR TWIN PEDESTAL COFFEE TABLE

2 pillars	**500** × **35** × **35**	20 × 1⅜ × 1⅜
4 feet	**230** × **80** × **18**	9 × 3⅛ × ¾
2 rails	**225** × **35** × **18**	8¾ × 1⅜ × ¾
1 top	**300** × **300** × **15**	12 × 12 × ⅝
2 rails	**275** × **35** × **18**	11 × 1⅜ × ¾

each position (fig. 6.3f). Cut the bottom and top of each pillar to length, then glue and cramp on the feet (fig. 6.3g). Check one assembly over the other. When this glue has set, glue in the top crossbars with cramps pinching the joints. Check that the two assemblies match as a pair. Cut off the projections on the feet and smooth the edges. Remove any surplus glue and sand the wood.

If the legs are to be housed, the joint can have a parallel

dovetail section or be tapered for pressing in from the bottom of the pillar (fig. 6.4a). To avoid a gap showing, the top of each leg joint is cut back to a shortened groove (fig. 6.4b). An accurately-cut joint should pull itself tight, but it is still advisable to cut the projections on the legs and use cramps until the glue has set.

The rails between the ends are the same, and dowelled (fig. 6.5a). There is little strain on the dowels, and it should be sufficient to bore holes for them less than halfway into the pillars. Check squareness when you assemble, particularly across the feet. Have the assembly standing on a level sur-

6.3 *Suggested shapes for legs (a), top (b) and feet (d). A temporary projection in each foot (c) allows the dowelled joints to be cramped (f,g).*

Note: Measurements in millimetres are given in **bold type**; measurements in inches are given in normal type.

6.4 *Feet could be housed to the legs.*

6.5 *Rails and top are dowelled.*

face. Stand back and look at it to see that it stands upright.

The top is straightforward and can have moulded edges. Put the inverted framework against the underside of the top and mark its outline when it is symmetrically positioned. Glue will hold the top on, but this may be supplemented with dowels – five should be enough (fig. 6.5b). They need be set only 6 mm (¼ in) or so into the top.

UPHOLSTERED STOOL

Stools of various sorts are always useful in the home. They are easier to make than chairs, but those of suitable height can be pressed into use at a table when there is a crowd for a meal. A stool is usually made with square corners, but a chair more often has very few right-angles in it. The seat of a stool or chair may be of plain wood, woven cane, rush or seagrass, but the most comfortable top is upholstered. At one time upholstery was rather complicated and something of a trade secret, but with modern materials a stool or chair is easily dealt with.

This stool (fig. 6.6) is of a size for general seating, or it could be used in front of a dressing table or at a piano. It is

6.6 *Sizes of an upholstered stool.*

Note: Measurements in millimetres are given in **bold type**; measurements in inches are given in normal type.

CUTTING LIST FOR UPHOLSTERED STOOL

4 legs	**450** × **35** × **35**	18 × 1⅜ × 1⅜
2 rails	**400** × **75** × **25**	16 × 3 × 1
2 rails	**300** × **75** × **25**	12 × 3 × 1
1 rail	**400** × **25** × **19**	16 × 1 × ¾
2 rails	**300** × **25** × **19**	12 × 1 × ¾
1 top (plywood)	**400** × **300** × **12**	16 × 12 × ½
4 brackets	**100** × **50** × **19**	4 × 2 × ¾

6.7 *Alternative ways of shaping stool legs and rails.*

always advisable to make a stool longer one way than the other. Anyone sitting will then choose the long way. You can then provide back-to-front stiffening with lower rails, but so that there is leg room you can put a single central rail across from side to side. If a stool is square, the sitter may use it either way and you need to put four rails lower down; they do not allow the sitter's legs to be swung under the seat. The top is made to lift out, so that it can be upholstered as a separate unit.

The stool shown has square legs. The part below the bottom rail could be tapered all round or just on the insides (fig. 6.7a), there could be wagon bevelling on the outer corners only or all round (fig. 6.7b). The parts of the legs between and below the rails could be turned (fig. 6.7c). If the legs are wagon bevelled, the lower outer edges of the top rails should be also (fig. 6.7d). In other cases they could be cut back (fig. 6.7e) or shaped.

Rabbet the top rails (fig. 6.8a). Their joints to the legs could be dowels (fig. 6.8b), but they would be stronger with mortise and tenon joints (fig. 6.8c). The rabbets keep the tenons far enough down the legs to make haunches at the top unnecessary. Even if dowels are used for the top rails, tenons should be used for the lower end rails as they are stronger, particularly if the user tries to tilt the stool onto two legs.

The bottom central rail can be joined to the end rails with a horizontal stub tenon (fig. 6.8d). Cut the mortise as deep as possible. Another way of getting adequate strength there is to take the tenon through, but to let it project with a rounded end (fig. 6.8e) as decoration, instead of planing it level. Cut the mortises in the end rails, but it may be advisable to leave cutting the central rail to length until after the end rails and legs are put together.

Make up the two ends as matching pairs. Leave some excess length on the tops of the legs, to be levelled off after complete assembly. If the bottoms are square, chamfer them slightly all round to reduce the area and harshness of marking of carpets.

Add the lengthwise rails, being careful to get the distances between the shoulders of the bottom rail correct, so that the whole assembly stands squarely. A thin screw can be driven upwards through each of the joints, if you think it necessary.

At the top, the brackets in the corners help to stiffen the stool as well as providing additional support for the upholstered top. Their sides should be square to each other, but do not make a close fit against the leg (fig. 6.8f). This allows you to put in screws square to the sloping edge, and they will pull the bracket towards the corner to make the fit as tight as possible. Arrange these corner brackets level with the rabbets.

6.8 *Rails may be dowelled or tenoned (a,b,c,d,e). Corner blocks provide stiffness (f).*

6.9 *The upholstered top is pulled over a wood base and the covering is tacked below.*

The top is a piece of plywood. Its overall size has to be made so that the finished seat will push into the rabbets. To allow for this, wrap the covering cloth over and try length and width with this additional thickness. If you find the plywood is finally too small, you can pack an edge with a strip of thin cardboard under the cloth. Take the sharpness off the plywood edges. Drill a few holes in the central area (fig. 6.9a). They are to let air in and out of the filling in use.

The padding is plastic or rubber foam. It should not be more than 50 mm (2 in) thick, and half that might be enough for comfort. Over this goes a piece of cloth, which may have to be chosen to match other furniture. Plastic-coated fabric can give a leatherlike look. That or closely-woven cloth can go directly over the foam, but with a more open weave it is better to put a piece of light loosely-woven plain cloth over the padding first. So that the foam will make rounded edges, cut it slightly bigger than the plywood and bevel its underside all round (fig. 6.9b). This can be done by slicing with a knife, a process which may be helped by lubricating with water.

Fix the cloth with 9 mm (⅜ in) tacks. Stretch the cloth over near the centre of each side at first (fig. 6.9c), then work along the sides from there, keeping the tacks in line and putting on an even tension. How far apart to space the tacks to get a neat effect depends on the cloth and the filling, but 25 mm (1 in) will probably be about right.

At each corner the cloth has to be pulled into the hollow to fit around the leg. Pull diagonally and tack there (fig. 6.9d), then fold any surplus cloth and tack that, if it is thin and flexible. Thicker covering may need darts cut out to let the underside settle flat. Trim surplus cloth evenly inside the lines of tacks all round.

That will probably be all you need to do, but for a neater underside a piece of plain cloth can be tacked on, with its edges turned in (fig. 6.9e). If you plan to do this, keep the first lines of tacks further in from the edge of the seat, so that there is room for another line through the underneath cloth, which is folded back on itself before tacking.

DINING CHAIR

A dining or side chair looks a simple thing until its shape and many angles are examined. It has developed from a stool with a back to something designed to provide support and comfort without being as form-fitting as an upholstered lounge chair. There are not many right-angles in it, and the joints are quite small in relation to the loads they have to carry, yet most of these chairs stand up to a considerable amount of use, and abuse, over quite a long period.

In front view it is usual for the legs to be square to the floor and the seat, with the back often continuing straight up above the back legs, but in side view the front legs may slope, the seat may not be parallel with the floor, and the back legs extend on the floor for stability, then continue in a curve to form the back. When viewed from above the seat is narrower at the back than at the front, and the cross-members of the back are curved. Lower rails may be arranged in several ways and are not always parallel with the floor. All of this makes chairmaking into something different from the usual run of cabinetmaking or carpentry, yet if it is tackled in steps there is no reason why the amateur with a reasonable amount of practical experience should not be able to make satisfactory chairs.

It is usual to consider making four or six chairs at a time, rather than a single piece. If all are tackled together, the total time expended may seem considerable – but it takes less time overall than if you made the chairs one at a time, and they are more likely to finish as exact matches.

The chair shown (fig. 6.10) has a hollowed lift-out uphol-

6.10 *A dining chair is an example of basic construction adapted to an assembly that has to provide comfort for the human body.*

stered seat, which is slightly higher at the front than at the back. The basic chair has a single central splat in the back, and square front legs (fig. 6.11). There could be a number of narrower splats, or the central one could be fretted or carved. The front legs might be carved, wagon bevelled or turned. The back legs are best left untreated. Much depends on the wood chosen. A hardwood with an interesting prominent grain pattern would suit a plain design, while a plainer wood could be turned or carved.

It will help if certain parts of the chair are drawn to full size. Draw half a plan view of the seat to give you the sizes and angles of the side rails and their joints. A side view will give the shape of a back leg, and the seat may come about 30 mm (⁹⁄₁₆ in) higher at the front than at the back. The front leg is square to it, so it slopes back from the floor.

Mark out the pair of back legs (fig. 6.12a) and cut the front curves, but leave the rear edges straight until after the joints have been cut. Prepare the front legs a little over-length. The two side seat rails have rabbets to support the seat (fig. 6.12b), but the front and back rails are without rabbets, although they are hollowed across (fig. 6.12c). Shape the front rail and use it to mark the curve on the shorter back

CUTTING LIST FOR DINING CHAIR

2 back legs	850 × 90 × 35	34 × 3½ × 1⅜
2 front legs	470 × 45 × 45	18½ × 1¾ × 1¾
2 seat rails	400 × 45 × 35	16 × 1¾ × 1⅜
1 front seat rail	470 × 75 × 25	18½ × 3 × 1
1 back seat rail	360 × 60 × 25	14⅛ × 2¼ × 1
1 back top rail	360 × 50 × 40	14⅛ × 2 × 1⁹⁄₁₆
1 back lower rail	360 × 40 × 40	14⅛ × 1⁹⁄₁₆ × 1⁹⁄₁₆
1 back splat	300 × 750 × 12	12 × 30 × ½
2 seat sides	380 × 40 × 25	15 × 1⁹⁄₁₆ × 1
1 seat back	330 × 40 × 35	13 × 1⁹⁄₁₆ × 1⅜
1 seat front	460 × 40 × 40	18⅛ × 1⁹⁄₁₆ × 1⁹⁄₁₆
4 corner blocks	75 × 50 × 20	3 × 2 × ¹³⁄₁₆
3 bottom rails	460 × 30 × 15	18⅛ × 1¼ × ⅝

6.11 *Suggested sizes for a dining chair.*

Note: Measurements in millimetres are given in **bold type**; measurements in inches are given in normal type.

6.12 *Sizes of the rear legs control most other dimensions (a). Rails are notched and shaped (b,c,d,e). A corner block makes a seat support (f).*

Note: Measurements in millimetres are given in **bold type**; measurements in inches are given in normal type.

rail. Tenon the back seat rail into the leg so that its inner surface is level with the leg surface (fig. 6.12d). At the front legs, allow for cutting in to take the seat (fig. 6.12e). The front legs are square to the crosswise rail, when viewed from above, so the shoulders of the tenons on the side rails must be cut across at a suitable slight angle.

Dowels are sometimes used for the rails around the seat, but tenons are stronger. When the chair is assembled, notch the tops of the front legs down to the size of the rabbets and screw in corner blocks level with the rabbets (fig. 6.12f). Where they meet the hollowed front and back rails, keep their surfaces parallel with the curved rails. The corner blocks act as seat supports as well as strengtheners.

6.13 *The chair back and seat parts are curved.*

The lower rails are tenoned to the legs. Their shoulders have to be angled a little in both directions if they are to make close fits. Mortises for the centre rail can be prepared, but it may be best to leave cutting the centre rail to length until you have made a trial assembly of the other parts.

At the back, the two rails are cut to curves about 12mm (½ in) deep. These curves and those of the seat rails could be drawn round a steel rule sprung to shape. The ends of the curved rails must be cut square for tenons (fig. 6.13a). The central splat goes into one of these and into the top of the rear seat rail. If barefaced tenons are used (fig. 6.13b), only the shoulder at the rear has to be cut to match the hollowed seat rail.

Assemble the back and front parts as units first, and let their glue set. When the side rails are added, have the chair standing on a flat surface and check symmetry as viewed from above. Compare diagonals. If the corner blocks are prepared to the angles from your full-size drawing, they will pull the chair into shape. Bring in the bottom crosswise rail at the same time as the other rails are put in, otherwise it cannot be added.

The seat frame is made up of pieces finished to about 75 mm (3 in) by 15 mm (⅝ in), but as the front and back are curved, they have to be cut from thicker wood. Joints at the corners may be halved (fig. 6.13c). The overall size of the seat frame must allow for upholstering and the thickness of the wrapped cloth, so that the seat fits tight in its frame.

6.14 *The chair seat is supported on webbing stretched across the frame.*

Thin plywood could be used, sprung to the curve of the seat, but it would be more comfortable to have webbing under the padding. Webbing is about 50 mm (2 in) wide and may be of cloth or reinforced rubber. Either can be used, arranged so that the gaps between strips are not as wide as the webbing. A pattern is made up with the webbing inter-woven (fig. 6.14a). Fix the webbing with tacks a short distance in from one side. Turn the end back on itself. Three tacks there will probably be enough. At the other side the webbing has to be strained. There are special webbing strainers, but you can use a short length of wood to lever against the frame (fig. 6.14b). Put in two or three tacks, then cut off the webbing with enough to turn back over and tack again. With rubber webbing you can tack without turning over either end. Try to get the same amount of tension on each piece of webbing. If you mark at the edge when the first piece is unstrained, then note how far the mark moves, that will give you a guide to the load to put on subsequent pieces.

From this point the fitting of padding and covering is the same as for the stool, except that the corners are not hollowed to allow for the legs, so they are easier to deal with.

BEDSIDE CABINET

This is an example of carcase construction (fig. 6.15), with a fitted drawer and a cupboard with a door. The main parts are intended to be made of solid wood, but it would be possible to frame plywood for the sides and make a top with plywood framed round in a similar way to that described on p.94 for a table-top. The sizes (fig. 6.16 and cutting list) will make a compact table. They could be increased, but if the

6.15 *A bedside cabinet is an example of carcase, door and drawer construction.*

CUTTING LIST FOR BEDSIDE CABINET

2 sides	**660 × 300 × 18**	26	× 12	×	¾		
1 top	**380 × 300 × 18**	15	× 12	×	¾		
5 rails	**380 × 40 × 18**	15	× 1⁹⁄₁₆	×	¾		
6 rails	**300 × 18 × 18**	12	× ¾	×	¾		
2 plinths	**380 × 75 × 18**	15	× 3	×	¾		
2 plinths	**300 × 75 × 18**	12	× 3	×	¾		
2 door frames	**430 × 50 × 25**	17	× 2	× 1			
2 door frames	**360 × 50 × 25**	14	× 2	× 1			
1 door panel (plywood)	**400 × 300 × 6**	16	× 12	×	¼		
1 bottom (plywood)	**360 × 300 × 6**	14⅛	× 12	×	¼		
2 handles	**150 × 25 × 18**	6	× 1	×	¾		
1 drawer front	**360 × 150 × 18**	14⅛	× 6	×	¾		
2 drawer sides	**300 × 150 × 12**	12	× 6	×	½		
1 drawer back	**360 × 150 × 12**	14⅛	× 6	×	½		
1 drawer bottom (plywood)	**360 × 300 × 6**	14⅛	× 12	×	¼		

Note: Measurements in millimetres are given in **bold type**; measurements in inches are given in normal type.

6.16 *Sizes of a bedside cabinet.*

Note: Measurements in millimetres are given in **bold type**; measurements in inches are given in normal type.

cabinet is made wider, be careful to avoid having a drawer very wide in relation to its back-to-front depth. That might cause sticking, due to its trying to wobble as it is moved out or in.

Make a pair of sides and mark on them where the other parts will come. At the top edge there are two rails across at back and front, and they should be dovetailed to the sides (fig. 6.17a). When the top of the cabinet is put on it will be set back about 3 mm (⅛ in) at sides and front, so keep the dovetail far enough back for its details to be covered. At the bottom, the main area inside is plywood, resting on rail at the back and rabbeted into a front rail, with strips set across underneath as side support (fig. 6.17b). The two rails may be dovetailed into sides, but the support strips can be screwed on.

Between the drawer and the cupboard comes a front

stretcher or rail, which can be housed into the sides (fig. 6.17c). Mark out all the crosspieces together so that the distances between shoulders are the same.

6.17 *Constructional details of the bedside cabinet.*

In the cabinet shown, the space between the drawer and the cupboard is open and there is no need for a rail across the back below the drawer. But if you prefer to close that space, there will have to be a rail at the back; then the parts are grooved to take a thin plywood panel.

The drawer bottom has to rest on runners. These are side strips which continue the level of the front stretcher and they may be glued and screwed on. So that they maintain the level without risk of movement, put small tenons at their end (fig. 6.17d). At the top, the drawer has to be prevented from tilting as it is pulled out, and the piece of wood that does this is called a kicker (fig. 6.17e). It will also be used to take screws driven upwards into the top.

The back can be of thin plywood set in side rabbets, made with the solid outside part thick enough for the back to be hidden by the top when it is fitted. The edges of the back piece will not show at top and bottom, so they can be glued and nailed or screwed in place as one of the last steps of assembly. You may be glad to leave the back off, so that you

6.18 *Details of the plinth for the bedside cabinet.*

can see internal parts better as you work on them.

With the sides and all the crosspieces prepared, assemble the carcase, but do not finally fit the bottom plywood, although it can be cut and tried. Square the assembly in the usual way. Pay particular attention to where the drawer will fit, checking that the parts are square and that the spaces between runners and kickers are parallel.

The plinth is made up as a separate assembly (fig. 6.18a). The front corners are mitred, but the back ones can be simple laps or rabbets, both with reinforcing blocks inside. Make the plinth level with the back, but set in 12mm (½in) at the sides and front. At the sides and back, attach it with screws set downwards (fig. 6.18b), but at the front – to avoid screw heads spoiling the appearance inside the cupboard – fix a strip underneath with screws pointing both ways (fig. 6.18c). Alternatively, you can glue in the plywood bottom.

The door is mortise and tenoned as already described on pp.117-20. The frame edges around the panel could have wagon bevels, stopped in the usual way, or you could take them to the corners with rounded ends (fig. 6.19a). This feature is particularly suitable for cutting the bevels with a router. Two 50mm (2in) hinges may be used, allowing the door to swing whichever way is most convenient for the user. The handle shown is a wooden one, screwed on from the back. It should be located above the middle of the door, so that it is easy to reach from the bed. A magnetic or spring catch would be better than any fastener that requires a hand

6.19 *Constructional details of door, shelf and drawer of the bedside cabinet.*

movement before it is released. The catch may act as a door stop, but if it does not small blocks can be fixed inside, either at side or at top and bottom.

There could be a shelf inside. As with any shelving, consider the sight line. You might get maximum capacity in the cupboard by making a shelf that came out as far as the door, but because you look downwards into the cupboard, almost everything below the shelf will be out of sight. You must consider whether that matters. If you want to pack in as much as possible, it may not. Otherwise, it is better to set the front edge back and accept a narrower shelf.

Usually it is an advantage to make the shelf removable. In its simplest form the shelf is a piece of solid wood resting on a support, which is set back a little (fig. 6.19b). The shelf can be prevented from sliding forwards by putting a lip on the supports (fig. 6.19c). You can economize on materials by making the shelf of plywood with a solid wood front (fig. 6.19d), with the support hidden. If you want to fix the shelf, it can be screwed to this.

The drawer is a straightforward assembly (fig. 6.19e), with stopped dovetails at the front and through dovetails at the back. You can make it reach almost to the back, but it would be unwise to rely on the back of the cabinet acting as a drawer stop. Instead, gauge back the thickness of the drawer front on the top of the stretcher and put two stops there (fig. 6.19f). You could use a long one, fixed right across the width, instead. But do not rely on just a small central one, as that would not be sufficiently positive and the drawer might settle slighty askew. Obviously, the stops must be thin enough not to show under the drawer bottom.

If you want to prevent the drawer being accidently pulled right out there can be a stop at the top, but you need to make the back of the drawer as deep as the sides, instead of cutting down, as is often done. Put a stop under the top rail, very similar to those on the stretcher, but arranged so that the drawer back meets it when still a little way inside the cabinet (fig. 6.19g). With the natural tendency of the drawer to fall as it is pulled out, this will restrict its movement just before it comes out, but if you want to remove the drawer, tilting it upwards should free it. You may have to round the undersides of the sides at the back of the stop to permit this, if the drawer is a very close fit.

When you polish or otherwise apply a finish to the cabinet, it is usual to leave most of the drawer parts untreated, polishing just the front and a short distance back along the sides. A new drawer often sticks. It needs lubrication, but do not use any form of oil. Instead, rub along the runners with beeswax or candlegrease, which gets results without being messy and without soaking into the wood and swelling it.

Make the top carefully to give a parallel and equal margin over the front and sides of the carcase. At the rear it covers the plywood back. Round its top edges slightly, and attach it with glue and screws set upwards (fig. 6.19h). Fit the back to complete assembly.

If the sides are to be framed plywood instead of solid wood, they could – like the door – have grooved parts (fig. 6.20a), or the plywood could be fixed flush with the frame in rabbets (fig. 6.20b). With synthetic resin glue and proper cramping, the plywood joint in that type of framing can be relied on without nails or screws through the plywood. With both types the main joints to other parts can be the same as for solid wood sides, but you have to allow for the recessed plywood where the drawer comes. At the drawer bottom level put a strip behind each runner to act as a side guide for the drawer (fig. 6.20c). At the top the frame will come low enough below the kicker to act as a guide there.

6.20 *If panelled sides are used, plywood may go in a groove (a) or a rabbet (b). Drawer runners will have to be packed out (c).*

6.21 A three-legged table will stand level on any surface.

THREE-LEGGED STAND

A tripod will stand firmly on almost any surface. Anything with four legs may rock if the floor is not level. That is the main reason why three-legged pieces of furniture are made, apart from the attraction of their appearance. Arranging three symmetrically-placed feet brings special problems of layout. There are also some problems of design. It does not look right to put a square top above three legs. The top should usually be hexagonal or round. A triangular top would have corners too acute for normal use. Three separate legs cannot conveniently have square tops if they are to have rails between them: it would be better to make them round or hexagonal, to take mortise and tenon joints. Even then there is difficulty in cutting joints that are strong enough. The alternative is a central pillar with three feet and a basic design is shown here (fig. 6.21), to be made without the use of a lathe. A turned version follows on pp. 157-61.

In laying out a three-legged design a plan view is most important (fig. 6.22). The three feet should extend outside the area of the top to ensure stability. How much they need to extend depends on the size and weight of the stand. A tall stand ought to have a greater spread of feet than a short stand. The feet are at 120° to each other – that being one-third of the 360° of a circle. The easiest way to set this out is by stepping off the radius around the circumference of a circle (fig. 6.23a) and then joining alternate points to the centre.

The first thing to make is the hexagonal pillar. To look right, all six faces must be exactly the same width. Draw a hexagon the size you want, and prepare a piece of wood with its thickness the distance across the flats and its width the distance across the points. On the end of this draw the hexagon and continue the corner lines along the wood. A notched block and a pencil (fig. 6.23b) will do this without leaving the scratches a gauge would. If you have a circular saw and a planer with tilting fences you make your cuts close to the lines, otherwise use a hand plane all the way. Check the widths of the faces and make any adjustments with a finely-set plane.

Make a template for the three feet (fig. 6.23c). Mark and cut them with a projection for cramping, to be cut off after gluing. The bottom of the pillar may be cut square or it could project a little to an obtuse point. Mark around for the dowel holes, with matching markings on the feet (fig. 6.23d). When you drill for the dowels into the pillar, let them run into each other, leaving room for maximum penetration of the dowels.

6.22 *Suggested sizes for a three-legged stand.*

Note: Measurements in millimetres are given in **bold type**; measurements in inches are given in normal type.

CUTTING LIST FOR THREE-LEGGED STAND WITH HEXAGONAL PILLAR

1 pillar	**425 × 50 × 45**	17 × 2 × 1¾
1 top	**300 × 300 × 17**	12 × 12 × ¹¹/₁₆
1 top	**190 × 190 × 17**	7½ × 7½ × ¹¹/₁₆
3 legs	**220 × 90 × 19**	8½ × 3½ × ¾

6.23 *Stepping off a radius will give equal spacing (a). Mark the pillar section (b) and attach the feet (c) to it with dowels (d).*

Bore the holes in the feet slightly too deep for their dowels. Then, when you assemble, get the dowels tightly into the pillar before pressing on the feet. It will be easier to glue and cramp the feet one at a time, but be careful that there is not a build-up of hardened glue in adjoining empty holes.

At the top there is a piece of solid wood, reinforced below by another with its grain set crosswise. Mark and cut both hexagons (fig. 6.24a). Thin edges of the top piece equally all round, by tapering from below (fig. 6.24b) and round the edge section. Some of these tables or stands have carved top surfaces, but if most of the top will be covered by a plant pot, there may not be much point in this. One simple decoration can be made with a carver's 'V' tool or 'veiner', following two concentric hexagons (fig. 6.24c) or two interlocked triangles (fig. 6.24d).

The block under the top provides attachment to the pillar.

a

300 12

190 7½

b

c

d

Find the centre of the end of the pillar by joining corners, then drill there for a dowel. Drill the centre of the top block in the same way. Join the parts by gluing in a dowel. Cut the top of the dowel level and invert the stand over the inverted top and glue it on, with three screws or dowels set upwards, if you think they are necessary.

Take care that the top is put on squarely to the pillar in all directions, then put the stand on a level surface and measure the height of the edges of the top all round. If necessary make adjustments by planing the bottom of a foot.

6.24 *The top rests on another piece below (a). Its edge may be thinned (b) and incised cuts used to decorate the surface (c,d).*

Note: Measurements in millimetres are given in **bold type**; measurements in inches are given in normal type.

TURNED THREE-LEGGED TABLE

Except for the feet, all the parts of this table or stand are made on a lathe (fig. 6.25). The suggested sizes (fig. 6.26) make a small table that can be put beside a chair, or used as a plant stand. There is a similarity in general form to the previous stand, but there are additional problems in arranging the three feet around the round pillar. Turn the pillar with a dowel at the top and a parallel part at the bottom, keeping that part as large a diameter as you reasonably can in relation to the proportions of the other parts, so as to leave ample wood for cutting joints (fig. 6.27a).

6.25 *This three-legged table has all parts except the feet turned on a lathe.*

6.26 *Sizes of a turned three-legged table.*

Note: Measurements in millimetres are given in **bold type**; measurements in inches are given in normal type.

CUTTING LIST FOR TURNED THREE-LEGGED TABLE

1 pillar	**630 or 430** × **75** × **75**	25 or 17 × 3 × 3
1 top	**350** × **350** × **20**	14 × 14 × $^{13}/_{16}$
1 support	**175** × **175** × **25**	7 × 7 × 1
3 legs	**175** × **60** × **19**	7 × 2¼ × ¾

630
or 430
25
or 17

90
3½

25 1
squares

As with the previous stand, make sure you give the feet a sufficient spread on the floor to provide stability. The feet could be generally similar to those of the other stand or you might include some additional shaping (fig. 6.27b). There could be dowels, but tapered dovetailed housings are what is suggested.

You can find where to place the feet on the parallel part of the pillar by drawing a circle of the same diameter as the pillar and stepping off the radius, so that you can project along the cylinder. Another practical way is to wrap a strip of paper around the cylinder so that it overlaps, then prick

6.27 *The pillar (a) can be divided into three for the feet (b) with a strip of paper (c,d,e).*

Note: Measurements in millimetres are given in **bold type**; measurements in inches are given in normal type.

through the two thicknesses (fig. 6.27c). Open the paper out. The distance between the pricked holes is the circumference. Divide this distance into three (fig. 6.27d). Put the paper back around the cylinder and mark through the three positions.

At the three positions cut flats the same widths as the thicknesses of the feet (fig. 6.27e). These are the places where you mark and cut the dovetailed housing joints. As with the previous dowelled joints, fit and cramp each foot separately, checking the symmetrical arrangement as you go.

The top shown is turned with a lip at the edge (fig. 6.28a). Its size and that of the whole table may be determined by the largest diameter that can be swung in your lathe or the size of an available piece of wood. Before you remove the top from the lathe, hold a pencil against the underside of the revolving wood to draw a circle of the size of the support piece, so as to indicate its location.

Turn the support piece with a taper towards its edge and with a central hole to suit the dowel on the pillar (fig. 6.28b). Cramp and glue the support piece to the top, with their grains crossing. Cut the dowel on the pillar so that it is slightly shorter than the depth of the hole, then glue the pillar to the top. Check squareness and see that the finished table stands upright. Turning ensures parallel and square parts. Where the pillar comes against the top support piece it helps in getting a close and true fit if the shoulder is slightly undercut towards the dowel (fig. 6.28c), so that its outside comes close to the underside of the support piece.

6.28 *The table top has a lip (a) and fits over a support (b) with a hole for a dowel with a slightly undercut shoulder (c). If a leather inlay is to be fitted, turn a suitable recess (d).*

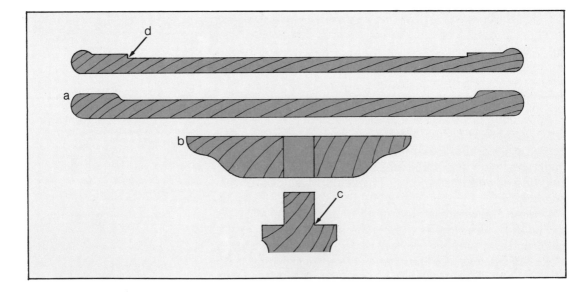

In its traditional form, this table had a piece of leather glued in the top. That is still possible, but it is probably better to use a plastic-coated fabric of the type that looks like leather, holding it down with a contact adhesive. To accommodate it, turn a recess of suitable depth (fig. 6.28d). Be careful that it is flat across, as unevenness will show through.

BUILT-IN TABLE

While most furniture is free-standing, some items can be built-in, with advantages of rigidity and economy of space. Furniture attached to a wall makes more use of available space and is firmly there with no risk of its being knocked over. Against this, it is necessary to be sure that what you are planning will suit your needs and not obstruct something else, as a piece of built-in furniture may be difficult to re-move without leaving marked or damaged walls.

It is possible to build comparatively narrow things, like bookshelves (which would be unstable if free-standing), up to the ceiling, with attachments to the wall. Corners and recesses do not normally get full use and something built-in will occupy them without interfering with other furniture or movement above a room. Shelves or tables can be fixed in such spaces.

Surprisingly, many houses are built with room corners not square and walls not upright. The errors may be slight and do not matter for normal purposes, but if you just make something to go in a corner and assume it is square both ways, you may be faced with gaps that should not be there.

Suppose you want to make a table top a close fit in the corner of a room. Mark the height it is to come on the walls. Measure two distances from the corner along these lines – not necessarily the final size of the table – then measure diagonally between the marked points (fig. 6.29a). You might measure with an expanding tape rule, but it is difficult to make such measurements accurate. It is better to mea-sure the diagonal with two overlapping pieces of wood, pre-ferably tapered at the ends (fig. 6.29b). You can pencil on them the positions of overlap or cramp them together to transfer the measurement.

Make similar measurements on your wood for the table-top, and you can draw a line to be cut that will match the room corner (fig. 6.29c). The front of the table should be parallel to the back and the end square to it. Never repeat an inaccurate angle away from the place where you have to fit to it. Anything built-in should be squared properly where

6.29 *For a corner table, check the angle and repeat it on the wood (a,b,c). In a recess, measure both ways (d).*

it is not in contact with the wall. For instance, you might have to cut an edge of an upright at an angle to suit an uneven wall in an old house, but the other side of the upright, which may be a doorway, should be vertical. It would be wrong to make a door out of square so that its post comes parallel with a sloping wall.

Another good place for a table-top is in a recess. Here you have the problem of checking two angles. With only one corner it is possible to fit by trial and error, but with an enclosed space your first fitting is probably the last. If the recess happens to be narrower at the front than the back, you cannot just put a squared piece of wood in and get it right. Instead you have to mark the height of the table-top on the walls and measure diagonals both ways (fig. 6.29d), then transfer the sizes to the wood.

Fortunately, floors are usually horizontal, even if wall corners are out of plumb or not square to each other, but it may be advisable to check with a spirit level that a line parallel with the floor is accurate (fig. 6.29e), before assuming you can use it as a datum.

Some prefabricated built-in furniture is sold almost like free-standing furniture, but if you are making a particular piece you can use the walls as supports and parts of the whole thing. There may be no need to include separate backs and sides. You then get the maximum capacity by going right to the walls. A simple example is a table-top in a recess, where there is no need for legs or framing, except at the front (fig. 6.30a).

Mark where the top is to come. It may be solid wood, or framed plywood, or it could be chipboard. Only the front edge needs a special finish. A plywood top might have a solid wood front edge, or if it is a kitchen working surface it could have one of the plastic or metal edgings intended for it – something that might not be acceptable in a desk or other table in a living room.

The front edge may need stiffening and some moulding could be attached (fig. 6.30c) to give an appearance of solidity. Screw supports to the walls, to be hidden by the front. There is no need for close fitting corners in the supports, but make sure that top surfaces are level with each other and that the opposite supports are trued with a spirit level – so that the top will not be forced into a twist.

Even with careful marking out, you may not get the top a very close fit at the edges, particularly if the plastering is

6.30 A table in a recess may be built up (a,b,c). Strips (d) protect the wall.

uneven, and it is worth putting strips around (fig. 6.30d). They should be mitred in the corners and rounded at the front. If the table will be used for things that might damage the wall covering, the strips could be quite deep.

A curtain rail could be mounted behind the front rail, so that a curtain can hide whatever is stored behind it. This is suitable for toys, vacuum cleaners and other things that have to be moved along the floor, as there is no step up – as there would be for a cupboard.

A corner table is simpler to fit, but you have to provide a leg (fig. 6.31a). Mark the table level on the wall and get the corner angle correct, as before. The table leg should get enough stiffness from the rails under the table-top. Lower rails would be inappropriate. Make the rails in the usual way, but it will add stability if you deepen their joints. So that there is enough knee room, the front rail should be cut away

6.31 A corner table needs a leg (a) strengthened with brackets (b) and secured to the floor with a cut-off screw (c).

and an additional small bracket could be included (fig. 6.31b), glued and dowelled to the rail and the leg. The end rail does not have to be cut away, but for the sake of appearance it could be treated in the same way.

The leg might be left square, tapered or turned, as you prefer or to match other furniture. It is liable to be kicked or knocked with other furniture. As the top is fixed to the walls, the leg might be fixed to the floor. An inconspicuous way of doing this is with a long screw driven partly into the bottom of the leg. Its head is cut off, and it acts like a thin metal dowel into a hole in the floor (fig. 6.31c).

A drawer might be a useful addition to either table. If the top is made without a front rail, the drawer could hang from it. It might be made like other drawers already described, or a simple one could be a tray with a hollowed front to provide a grip (fig. 6.32a). This would be suitable for tools, so

6.32 A drawer (a) may hang on runners (b,c) or it can go through a rail (d) with a frame behind (e,f).

that the whole thing could be lifted on to the work surface. For hanging, square strips are fixed to the top edges of the sides, then combined runners and guides put under the top. These could be rabbeted solid pieces (fig. 6.32b) or built up (fig. 6.32c).

If there is a front rail, it may be deepened so that it can be cut out for the drawers (fig. 6.32d). Strips have to be fixed under the top to carry runners (fig. 6.32e). They need not be solid wood, and it may be better to use thin plywood with strips attached to screw into the top and the rail. If the top is very wide you may not want the drawer to reach fully to the back, so the sides need not go all the way. So that they do not twist at the back, put a strip across below (fig. 6.32f). The drawer could be made in the usual way and may have a false front to overlap the opening in the rail: the front then acts as a stop. Otherwise you must put blocks on the runners to stop the back of the drawer.

CORNER FITMENTS

A table, cupboard or other fitment across a corner will use space that is not otherwise occupied in many rooms. However, a simple triangle does not produce as much useful space as you may need (fig. 6.33a), so it can be increased by squaring from the wall at each side (fig. 6.33b). A simple corner table or shelf made in this way is often used to support a television set. The direction of viewing should be considered. The shelf does not have to be at 45° but can be cut to suit (fig. 6.33c).

6.33 *In a corner a triangle (a) can have its area increased (b) and need not be symmetrical (c). Support rails can be straight (d) or follow the outline (e).*

If the angled corners do not project much, the supporting rail can go straight across underneath (fig. 6.33d), but otherwise the rail can follow the outline with mitred joints (fig. 6.33e) and possibly a curtain hanging underneath. The lower part could be made into a cupboard in a similar way to the hanging cupboard described below.

A corner cupboard shows how the triangulated shape can be dealt with. The example (fig. 6.34) could be made with a glass front as a display cabinet or with a closed front as a medicine cabinet in a bathroom. A larger version might be built over a lower cupboard, the two reaching almost from floor to ceiling. There are some attractive antique cabinets of this type, but their basic construction is the same.

The shape of top and bottom controls the other sizes. Check the angle of the corner of the room with an adjustable bevel and use that, rather than a try-square, to mark out the shape; make a full-size drawing of this (fig. 6.35a).

Make the two sides, which should be of similar shape and size, except that one overlaps the other in the corner (fig. 6.35b). In the corner they will be screwed and glued, but they will probably have to be rounded to suit the plaster on the wall. Top and bottom go into housings or dados cut right across the wood, but the shelf is set in stopped grooves. The top and bottom pieces should have their grain parallel with the front. Make them to fit into the grooves, but with the fronts extending enough to cover the upright pieces and allow a little overhang (fig. 6.35c).

If the door is hinged directly to one of the upright pieces at the side, this must be cut to an acute angle and this does not allow very long screws in the hinges (fig. 6.35d). It is better to mitre narrow pieces inside them, so that the door meets a square edge (fig. 6.35e). Glue these pieces together and glue the uprights to the sides when you assemble. If you think something more than glue is necessary you could use secret slot screws or a tongue and grooved joint (fig. 6.35f).

6.34 *A corner cupboard shows how a basically triangular shape can be made more roomy.*

CUTTING LIST FOR CORNER CUPBOARD

2 backs	**650 × 300 × 12**	26 × 12	× ½
1 top	**500 × 350 × 15**	20 × 14	× ⅝
1 bottom	**500 × 350 × 15**	20 × 14	× ⅝
2 sides	**500 × 110 × 15**	20 × 4½	× ⅝
2 door posts	**500 × 30 × 15**	20 × 1¼	× ⅝
1 shelf	**300 × 300 × 12**	12 × 12	× ½
2 door sides	**500 × 40 × 15**	20 × 1⁹⁄₁₆	× ⅝
1 door rail	**250 × 40 × 15**	10 × 1⁹⁄₁₆	× ⅝
1 door rail	**250 × 50 × 15**	10 × 2	× ⅝

Note: Measurements in millimetres are given in **bold type**; measurements in inches are given in normal type.

6.35 *Constructional details of a corner cupboard.*

Note: Measurements in millimetres are given in **bold type**; measurements in inches are given in normal type.

The shelf may be cut with its front straight across, or be shaped in a similar way to the top, but cut back far enough to clear the door (fig. 6.35g). If you are to stand plates or other things on edge, you might want to cut grooves parallel with the sides (fig. 6.35h). In any case, a lip on the shelf may be desirable (fig. 6.35j).

Assemble the cupboard before making the door. The shelf must go in before joining the sides. It can be screwed from behind as the screw heads will not show. If the sides are made first, they set the shape before sliding in top and bottom, which can be adjusted, if necessary. The general assembly should come square automatically, but check that the door opening is parallel.

Make the door with a plywood panel set in grooves or a glass panel in a rabbet. The inner front edges may be chamfered to lighten appearance and reduce any tendency to catch dust on the bottom edge. Hinge to whichever side will be most convenient. The door stop could be a small block on the edge of the shelf, if that comes near the door, or you could fix blocks inside top and bottom. If the door is to be locked, the key may serve also as a handle for pulling the door open. Otherwise, fit a small knob or handle, with a spring or magnetic catch.

MAGAZINE TABLE

A fairly light table with storage below its top can be moved about singlehanded and can be used for sewing equipment, as a coffee table, or something to be taken outdoors as a chairside tea table. But its basic use will probably be as a small side table with storage space for magazines and

6.36 *A magazine table has storage below and the many parts all contribute to the strength of the whole assembly.*

books. The table shown is of a moderate size, but the method of construction can be used for tables smaller or much larger (fig. 6.36). The dimensions shown (fig. 6.37) give a proportion that looks right. If they are altered, be careful to avoid too square an outline. The sloping legs look best with a table that is much longer than it is wide.

Make the underframing first, but decide on the type of top you will fix to it as you have to prepare for fitting. There are some suggestions later. Construction is a mixture of bridle, housing and dowelled joints. The bottom shelf is shown as made up of a number of slats set across the width. This is

6.37 *Sizes of a magazine table.*

Note: Measurements in millimetres are given in **bold type**; measurements in inches are given in normal type.

CUTTING LIST FOR MAGAZINE TABLE

1 top	**1000** × **400** × **20**	40 × 12 × ¾
4 legs	**500** × **75** × **30**	20 × 3 × 1¼
2 top rails	**1000** × **75** × **20**	40 × 3 × ¾
2 top rails	**400** × **75** × **20**	16 × 3 × ¾
2 bottom rails	**1000** × **50** × **20**	40 × 2 × ¾
2 bottom rails	**400** × **50** × **20**	16 × 2 × ¾
9 slats	**400** × **50** × **20**	16 × 2 × ¾

easy to clean and looks smart. Alternatively, you could have a plywood bottom let into grooves in the rails. The first assemblies are the two long sides, which are then joined with the shorter crosspieces, with the top being added last.

There is no need to draw the table to full size, except for one end elevation, to show the slope of the leg (fig. 6.38a). Although the legs taper, the part that forms the joint with the top rail must have parallel sides (fig. 6.38b). If the taper was allowed to follow through, the joint could not be pushed together. The outer edge of each leg is straight, but the top of the other edge is cut parallel to it. Cut all four legs to shape, leaving a little excess length at the top.

Make the two long rails, but cut their joints before trimming the ends to shape (fig. 6.38c). The table looks best if the undersides of these rails have a hollow ending a short distance in from the legs. About 12 mm (½ in) of hollow should be enough, and you can draw this by springing a lath so that it passes through the points and getting a helper to mark round it with a pencil (fig. 6.38d).

Your full-size drawing of an end will show you the angle for cutting the lower rail joints and this will provide a guide to length in relation to the top rail. But it is advisable to mark the joints on the legs and rail, then make a trial assembly of the top bridle joints and check the lower rail lengths before cutting them and their joints. The tenons fitted into the legs can be quite short (fig. 6.38e), otherwise you will have difficulty springing them in. Hollows on the lower edges of the top rail and similar hollows on the top edges of the lower

6.38 *Constructional details of a magazine table.*

Note: Measurements in millimetres are given in **bold type**; measurements in inches are given in normal type.

rails, with rounded edges on all hollowed parts, will prevent anyone reaching in from touching a sharp edge.

If the tray bottom is to be plywood, plough a groove to suit in the lower rails (fig. 6.38f). The simplest way to deal with a slat bottom would be to use a long groove and space the slats in it, but that would leave sections of groove showing between the slats. It would look better to cut out only where the slats come (fig. 6.38g). If you have a drill press, much of the waste can be removed with a drill, leaving only a little cleaning out to be done with chisels, or the slats can be rounded to match.

The crosswise rails at the bottom have dowelled joints into the legs (fig. 6.38h). Set the dowels as deep as possible into the legs without risking breaking through. They provide crosswise stiffness in the assembly. The slats are cut to come level with the bottoms of the long rails and their ends have barefaced tenons into the slots (fig. 6.38j). If the tray is to have a plywood bottom, groove the end rails and notch across the corners of the legs to join the grooves when the plywood is put in.

When you assemble the pair of long sides, the bridle joints can be reinforced with screws driven from the inside (fig. 6.38k) where they will not show. Leave marking and drilling the legs for dowels until after assembly.

The simplest top is a single piece of solid wood (fig. 6.39a) held with buttons in grooved rails. You may have to make up the width with two or three pieces glued together. A development of this is making the top of laminations of quite narrow pieces to form what may be called 'butcher-block' furniture. The strips should be square, or not much wider than they are deep (fig. 6.39b). With a good synthetic resin glue there should be no need for dowels or secret screws in the joints, but there may be difficulty in getting the whole top assembly true and flat if you try to glue all pieces at the same time. It is better to glue pieces in pairs or groups of three. When that glue has set, join further in pairs of groups until you have the full width made up. If you pull the parts together with sash or bar cramps, put weights on scrap wood over newspaper on top to prevent the parts bowing upwards under pressure. Newspaper prevents the wood on top sticking and can be easily scraped off afterwards.

The top could be framed plywood, but looks better and is more suitable for assembly to the framing if the end pieces are wide enough to come over the rails and the mitres are cut to suit (fig. 6.39c). As that top will not expand and contract it can be attached with dowels or pocket screws.

The top could be faced thick plywood or chipboard with

the edges covered with solid wood glued on with tongue and groove joints (fig. 6.39d). This could be an occasion when you veneer a pattern on the surface yourself. It is possible to buy panels already veneered in a decorative pattern, but then the standard panel will settle the size you make the rest of the table.

6.39 *The table top may be solid wood (a), strips glued (b), framed plywood (c), or chipboard or thick plywood (d).*

PARK BENCH

Outdoor furniture varies from the crudest hammer and nail construction with natural logs and branches, to things made with joints comparable to indoor furniture, using planed wood of good quality. Between these extremes are assemblies made from slabs of sawn wood joined with tusk tenons and wedges, with other parts nailed on, but without planing or much attempt at a quality finish. Much depends on the purpose of the furniture, but for good quality garden furniture that is to stay outside all through the year and is expected to have a long life, it pays to choose a durable wood and unite the parts with suitable joints. The ideal wood is teak. Oak is almost as durable. But both woods are expensive, and it is possible to use softwood that has been im-

6.40 *A park or garden bench shows how a properly-jointed construction can make a strong and attractive piece of outdoor furniture.*

6.41 *Overall sizes of a park bench.*

Note: Measurements in millimetres are given in **bold type**; measurements in inches are given in normal type.

pregnated with preservative. Almost any available wood might be used, if the furniture is moved under cover in bad weather.

Most outdoor furniture is for sitting on. It may be separate seats, just a form or something more elaborate with arms and a back. The most popular arrangement is a bench, and the example (fig. 6.40) is shaped to give reasonable comfort without padding for up to three people (fig. 6.41). The seat is made of slats arranged on a curve and the back is inclined.

The front legs are 45 mm (1¾ in) square (fig. 6.42a) and the back legs match with a bent section cut from a wider piece (fig. 6.42b), so that their lower parts are upright and the upper parts give the slope of the back. The bend comes just above seat level and should include a light curve. Mark the front legs together to get the seat and bottom rail joints level. Do the same with the back legs.

Stub tenons are used for nearly all joints (fig. 6.42c). They might be just glued, but it is better to drill across for dowels through them, with the holes offset for draw-pinning (see p.111) if you are unable to cramp any parts.

Mark the seat and lower rails together, so that the distances between the tenon shoulders are the same (fig. 6.42d). The top of the seat rails should be hollowed to about 50 mm (2 in) thick with smooth matching curves. When the two intermediate supports are made they should have matching curves. Cut the mortise for the bottom and seat rails at each end.

Make the arm rests (fig. 6.42e). For most of their length their sides are parallel to each other, except for tapering to the rear legs, where they are tenoned. At the front there is not much thickness for tenons. You could dowel or screw down into the leg tops. If tenons are used, it is better to use twin ones to get maximum glue area (fig. 6.42f).

Prepare the lengthwise parts, making sure that all the

CUTTING LIST FOR PARK BENCH

2 front legs	600 × 45 × 45	24 × 1¾ × 1¾
2 rear legs	875 × 90 × 45	35 × 3½ × 1¾
2 bottom rails	525 × 45 × 18	21 × 1¾ × ¾
4 seat rails	525 × 75 × 22	21 × 3 × ⅞
2 arms	600 × 90 × 22	24 × 3½ × ⅞
2 seat rails	1600 × 75 × 30	63 × 3 × 1¼
2 bottom rails	1600 × 45 × 22	63 × 1¾ × ⅞
2 back rails	1600 × 75 × 22	63 × 3 × ⅞
11 back slats	350 × 50 × 12	14 × 2 × ½
5 seat slats	1600 × 50 × 19	63 × 2 × ¾

Note: Measurements in millimetres are given in **bold type**; measurements in inches are given in normal type.

6.42 *Sizes of parts of a park bench.*

Note: Measurements in millimetres are given in **bold type**; measurements in inches are given in normal type.

distances between shoulders are the same (fig. 6.43a). The front seat rail comes almost level with the front of the legs. It can have a barefaced tenon, and its front edges can be curved for comfort (fig. 6.43b). The seat back rail also comes near the fronts of the rear legs, but it does not have to be rounded. It has to take the ends of the intermediate seat supports.

Make the top and bottom back rails the same, with tenons set into the upper parts of the back legs (fig. 6.43c). Space the slats evenly along the back. Put the mortises centrally in the rails, but shoulder the tenons on the thin slats on one side only (fig. 6.43d). Make up the back assembly, checking that it is square by measuring diagonals. This assembly settles the squareness of the whole bench.

Make up the pair of ends squarely, ensuring that they match each other. The arms and the seat should finish parallel with the floor and square to the legs. Use a single dowel through joints or two smaller ones set diagonally (fig. 6.43e). Assemble the lengthwise parts to the ends with the legs standing on a level surface. Make sure the assembly is square when viewed from above.

The seat slats go through the end frames for a short distance, and they need two intermediate supports. Make the supports to fit between back and front rails, where they can be screwed (fig. 6.43f). You could tenon or dowel them during earlier assembly, but screws should be enough. Notice that the intermediate supports come below the front rail edge, as that must line up with the tops of the slats. Use a long straight edged piece of wood to check that the hollows of the ends and the supports are level.

Well round the top edges of the slats. Space them evenly, with a central screw at each crossing, with the space between the front rail and the next slat about the same as the space between the other slats.

Take the sharpness off exposed edges that come near sitters. The bottoms of the legs have end grain exposed and they could absorb water. The ends could be sealed with waterproof glue, or you could nail on squares of wood about 25 mm (1 in) thick to overlap a little all round to form feet.

6.43 *Rails and seat parts of a park bench.*

Note: Measurements in millimetres are given in **bold type**; measurements in inches are given in normal type.

Chapter 7
FINISHING

Most things made of wood have to be given a protective coating that may also improve appearance. Leaving many woods bare would result in them deteriorating, becoming worn, and absorbing dirt or moisture. A few woods can be left untreated. Teak and oak are sometimes left bare in exterior work. Some of the resinous softwoods will stand up to the weather without protection. For most purposes, particularly for indoor furniture, some sort of applied finish should be regarded as normal. Besides the protective coat the wood may also be altered in colour by staining. Most finishes are sufficiently transparent for details of the wood to show through. If an opaque finish is required the wood may be painted.

The quality of any finish depends to a large extent on the state of the wood surface underneath. You cannot expect an applied finish to hide a surface that is rough or contains flaws. The finish follows whatever is underneath and may even make it look worse. Consequently, you have to consider the final appearance while still working on the wood.

The first step towards the finish is planing. If the wood has been machine-planed, you should follow with hand planing to remove the ridges across the grain left from the rotating cutters. Sanding would not have the same effect. Power planing tends to bend up minute ends of wood fibres and sanding may do the same, while hand planing should cut them off – assuming that the plane is sharp. In many hardwoods the grain, which is one of the attractions, does not plane smoothly in any direction. In that case, follow the plane with a cabinet scraper. Scrape all over, as well as over the uneven part, so as to maintain a flat surface.

Follow by sanding. Do not use a disc sander and limit the use of a belt sander to narrow parts. An orbital sander may be used on broader surfaces. But if planing and scraping have been thorough, you can go straight on to hand sanding. In any case it is best to do the final sanding by hand.

There are several abrasive papers available, but for wood the usual ones are glass or garnet, with the particles held to the backing with glue. Some glues used are not waterproof and they absorb moisture from the atmosphere. This weakens them, so that the grit comes away rapidly. It helps if you heat the paper before use, to drive off moisture, in order to get longer use from it. There are different systems of grading abrasive papers. Sometimes there is a number indicating the size of grit, but the usual method of grading papers uses 'F2' (fine 2), 'M2' (middle 2) and 'S2' (strong 2) for average general-purpose papers. A woodworker should not need anything coarser than that, but finer grades go down to 1½, 1, 0 and many further 0s, such as 3/0 (sometimes referred to as 'three nought').

Abrasive paper comes in sheets that can conveniently be torn into four (fig. 7.1a) and then wrapped round a block (fig. 7.1b). Cork is the traditional sanding block material, but wood faced with rubber or plastic is just as good.

If you need to sand across the grain, make sure further rubbing with the grain removes any of those scratches. A clear finish tends to emphasize scratches that might not have been obvious in the bare wood. It is unlikely that you will need to use paper coarser than F2 and that may be all that is needed, but if you follow with one or more finer ones, brush off any loose particles of the coarser grit before following with finer paper, otherwise you may drag it along and spoil the surface.

With some woods, particularly the open-grained types, there will be some tiny bent fibres left after sanding. When you apply a liquid finish they will stand up and leave a roughness on the surface. You can reduce this problem by wetting the wood after sanding. This lifts any small fibres. Let the wood dry and sand again to remove them.

Consider finishing as you approach assembly. Some parts, such as lower chair and table rails, will be easier to sand before assembly, provided that you are careful not to damage them or get excess glue on them later.

7.1 *Abrasive paper may be torn into convenient sizes (a). For flat surfaces it is wrapped around a block (b).*

FLAWS

Ideally, all the wood you use is perfect, but wood is a natural material and you may have to accept some slight flaws. Some irregularities of grain may be regarded as decorative.

A knot breaking the surface in softwood may exude resin for some time after the wood is cut, and that would cause unevenness and softness of any finish applied over it. Brush one or two coats of shellac in methylated spirits over the knot. Shellac can be bought ready made up as French polish, but a thicker mixture is preferable. This treatment is important under paint. Some clear finishes may act as their own sealers.

Cracks and holes, or even badly-fitting joints, can be disguised with stopping. There are prepared putty-like stoppings to press in with a knife. Some are coloured and intended to be used before staining. Not all stoppings will take stain and finish the same colour as the surrounding wood. Leave a stopping slightly above the hole, so that you can sand it level when it has hardened.

Plastic wood is rather more than a stopping. To a limited extent you can use it to build up something like a part that has splintered away and work it to shape to match the wood.

Do not be tempted to fill a flaw with glue. In anything much wider than close contact, the hardened glue crazes as it hardens, becoming full of tiny cracks that remove its strength. If you want to provide strength as well as filling, mix sawdust with glue to make quite a dense putty – which you press into the hole. The sawdust prevents crazing. However, such a mixture – or plain glue – will not take stain.

FILLERS

All wood is porous, but in most cases the tiny cells cannot normally be seen. In other woods the effect is to make gaps between the grain lines. The most obvious example is oak. A liquid finish sinks into these gaps and even after many coats there is still a mass of hollows. Such wood needs filling before finishing, but how much is needed varies according to the wood.

Fillers are related to stoppings. Some are fairly thick pastes, others are softer, while others are quite liquid. As a guide to the need for fillers: oak, chestnut, elm and ash all need a paste, rubbed hard across the grain to make it penetrate, and then the cloth is rubbed along the grain and the surface left for a day before sanding lightly. Mahogany varies, but most of it and walnut and sapele need a medium filler. The closer-grained hardwoods, such as beech, sycamore and birch can have a liquid filler brushed on. Some specimens of those, together with ebony, holly and many of the pines and spruces do not need filling. Hardboard is very absorbent and needs its own liquid filler.

STAINING

Most furniture is stained, but it does not have to be. Many woods are attractive if left in their natural colours. Some woods are so regularly stained that many users regard the stained finish as natural. Oak is usually made browner. Mahogany has its redness intensified. It is possible to stain one wood to look the same colour as another, but the grain pattern will not be changed, so it is still obvious to anyone who knows grain that the basic wood is not genuine. However, you may have to mix woods in a piece of furniture, and staining will match them. A plywood panel can be matched to the surrounding wood with stain.

A stain changes the colour of wood without obscuring the grain. Paint hides the grain details. A stain penetrates the wood. Paint remains on the surface. Varnish and other clear finishes remain mostly on the surface, like paint. There are varnish stains, where the colour is in the varnish. They are best avoided. If the surface wears, the colour as well as the gloss goes. With separate stain the colour is retained in the wood.

A stain consists of a pigment in a solvent. The solvent may be water, oil or spirit (alcohol or methylated spirit). The solvent affects drying time. Spirit stains are quickest to dry, water stains are slowest to dry – and cheapest – but oil stains will go on evenly and are most popular. A quick-drying stain is difficult to apply evenly. So spirit should be used only for narrow parts or touching up damaged wood.

Oil stains are sometimes sold as wood dyes and are available in a large range of shades, mostly browns and red/ browns or combinations, and given names that bear little relation to the woods they are used on. Brush oil stain all over a surface quickly, getting a good coverage. It should soak in evenly without brush marks. Any excess can be wiped off with a cloth. With any staining, start at the least important parts. This usually means the underneath, turning the work about until you finish with the top. Face towards a light. Look for runs from one surface on to another. Wipe them off. End grain soaks up more than surface grain. Wipe end grain with a cloth before it gets darker than the surface grain. Very open end grain may be partially sealed with thin glue sanded level, but that is not easy to get right.

Wood with an oil stain that has dried will look darker than when it was first applied. You can put on a second coat if you want a darker effect, but do this with care as there is no satisfactory way of lightening wood that has come out too dark.

Water stain usually comes as a powder to be dissolved in hot water. You can make up a concentrated solution and thin it as needed. You get a more even effect by brushing on two thin coats than by applying one thick coat. Go all over a piece of furniture with one application, so that it is all wet at once – splashes of stain on a dry surface are difficult to remove. Water stain tends to lift the grain, so feel for roughness after one coat. You may have to sand lightly before a second coat.

Oil and water do not mix, so do not try to mix stains. You might use an oil stain after a water stain that has thoroughly dried, but you cannot use water stain over an oil stain. Water stain is not always effective on oily or resinous wood. Try some on a scrap piece.

Spirit stain may come in liquid form or it may be a coloured powder to dissolve in methylated spirit. Besides the usual wood colours, also obtainable in the other stains, there are brighter colours, such as red, yellow and green, that may have uses for colouring veneers for marquetry. Spirit stain can be sprayed to give an even effect, but it is very difficult to brush over a large area smoothly. The stain dries very rapidly, but you should always try to add new stain against a wet edge. Bringing it against a dry stain will leave a line, so spirit stain is more successful on a strip narrower than the brush width, which can be covered in one stroke.

In repair work spirit stain may sometimes be used, even where there is polish or other finish over the original stain, as it can penetrate some of them.

There are some chemical treatments of wood that you should know about, but are unlikely to use. Much older oak furniture was 'fumed' – meaning exposed to ammonia fumes in a cabinet. This makes a rich dark brown colour different from anything that can be obtained with stains. Permanganate of potash is a chemical bought as crystals, to be dissolved in water. When brushed on many woods it turns them brown. This is a safe chemical to handle, but you need to experiment with scrap pieces of wood to see the effect on them. For most staining needs today it is best to use oil stain or wood dye.

POLISHES

There are several ways of putting a protective film over wood. Most finishes have a gloss, which may be quite high or anything less – down to a matt surface. Some gloss is usually desirable. The film has to stand up to wear in normal use, so it has to be fairly hard. A snag with a very hard film is that it is also brittle and may crack. The wood base on which the finish is put is also liable to expand and contract slightly, so there should be some flexibility in the film.

It is often desirable that a finish should withstand heat and moisture. Many of the traditional finishes will not, but there have been many developments in recent years, so synthetic finishes can be obtained with very good resistance to liquids of all sorts, as well as to heat and abrasion. Not all of these treatments are suitable for household furniture, where some traditional finishes still have a place.

Some of the finish on much old furniture is the patina of age. Animal or vegetable fats may have been rubbed in, and there may have been later polishing with oil or wax, but the quality of the present finish is mainly due to handling. Natural fats from the skin and the rubbing of clothing all helped to produce the finish. Obviously getting a finish in that way is no use today. The nearest similar modern treatment uses oil or wax polishes, either directly on the bare wood or over another finish used as a base.

Oil and wax polishes

Polishing with linseed oil is a slow process. Close-grained hardwoods, such as mahogany, respond better than oak and elm or other open-grained woods. However, these coarser woods are oil-polished. Much old oak church furniture has not had any treatment except oil. Linseed oil can be thinned with a little turpentine. Heat it by standing it in a container of hot water. Direct heating would burn the oil.

Put plenty of oil onto the wood, and let it soak in. Rub it hard with a cloth so that oil fills the grain. Wipe off any surplus. After a few days, do this again. To produce a lustre, rub the surface hard with a piece of coarse cloth, such as sacking. It is the heat generated by friction that produces the shine. It helps to wrap the cloth around a brick when working on a flat surface. Leave the work for a few days and do it again, and repeat for as long as necessary to get the desired results.

That is how it was done in more leisurely days. You can speed the process by mixing a little varnish with the linseed oil and turpentine mixture. As much as half varnish may be used for the first two coats. They will seal the wood and prevent too much oil soaking in. Later coats should have less varnish. No oil finish lasts indefinitely and you must be prepared to give further treatments at intervals, which may be quite long ones.

A modern varnish and oil mixture is sold as teak oil or tung oil. Follow the maker's instructions, but it is normally applied and rubbed in the way just described. If what you are making is a reproduction of something that was oil polished, you must use a similar treatment. If not, one of the other finishes may be preferable.

Treating with linseed oil is a good way of protecting outside woodwork. Thinned warm oil will soak in. There is no need to attempt to shine the finish. If time can be spared to treat wood in this way then let it dry, coats of varnish can then be applied. Much outdoor varnished wood deteriorates after long exposure to the weather and the finish becomes white, due to moisture soaking into the wood below the varnish. Oil in the wood prevents or delays this and helps the varnish to keep its appearance longer.

Wax polishing is probably at least as old as oil polishing. The original wax may have been beeswax, but that is rather soft and most modern wax polishes are mixtures. Many paste polishes sold for reviving the finish on furniture are basically wax. Carnauba is the hardest wax used – it is always mixed with beeswax, paraffin wax and ceresine, using turpentine as a solvent. It would be unwise to attempt to mix your own wax polish. It is better to buy prepared furniture wax polishes.

Wax polishing could start from the bare wood in the same way as oil polishing, but it would be at least as long a process. Part of the oil treatment involves forcing oil into the pores of the wood, but wax polishing keeps more to the surface; so it helps if you seal the wood first. The grain should be filled, then the wood given one or two coats of varnish, which can be lightly sanded smooth before a wax finish is added.

You have to build up wax on the wood before you can polish it, so at first you concentrate on making a layer of hardened wax. It can be lightly rubbed on with a cloth, working in a circular manner and then along the grain. Leave it for ten minutes or so, then rub lightly with a cloth again. Leave it for at least an hour, then go through the process again. You will probably have to repeat the action many more times before you finally achieve that mellow shine associated with wax. Further polishing may be done at longer intervals – say several weeks – as the sheen builds up and becomes more permanent.

Power cannot really take the place of hard work. You can use a powered buffing head driven by an electric drill, but keep it moving and experiment with the amount of pressure. Too enthusiastic power buffing may lift off the wax. Hand work will be needed to get an even shine.

Today, wax is probably best regarded as something for reviving other polished finishes rather than as a first polish in its own right. You can get a good finish by giving wood several coats of varnish, which is then rubbed matt and finished with wax. An alternative to abrasive paper is pumice powder on a cloth, used in a similar way to applying polish. Some so-called non-scratch domestic scouring powders can be used in this way. If you use powder, make sure it is all removed before polishing. A vacuum cleaner is better than a brush. A tack rag (from a varnish shop) will lift dust as it is wiped over a surface.

Not all furniture revivers are wax. Some may be suitable for use over an existing synthetic finish, as applied by spray to mass-production furniture, but they are not always suitable for more traditional finishes. Read the instructions. Some floor polishes are unsuitable for furniture.

French Polish

Since the days of Chippendale and the great cabinetmakers, much furniture has been French polished. It is a smooth finish with a high sheen, which has been considered superior to any other gloss finish. It is a technique involving a fair amount of effort and it requires skill. You have to be patient. The finish is not very durable. Many liquids, including water, will harm it. A hot cup stood on it will leave a ring. Consequently, care has to be taken with French polished furniture, using mats and other protections. Older pianos are examples of the high polish obtainable with this method of finishing.

French polishing is done with shellac dissolved in methylated spirit. Shellac comes from India in the form of flakes. You can dissolve your own or buy French polish already prepared. If you can buy it concentrated, you may thin it with more spirit, as you need it, but most suppliers only have the one concentration ready for use.

Normal shellac has a transparent orange colour, which is suitable for all woods except those of very light colour. If light woods are to be kept as light as possible, bleached or white shellac may be used. Bleached shellac does not have a very long life in store. It has even less resistance to dampness than orange shellac. Some methylated spirit contains resin, which makes it unsuitable for use in French polish, so it is usually better to buy the mixture described as French polish than to mix your own with spirit you are uncertain of.

Shellac *can* be brushed on like paint or varnish, but with spirit as a solvent it dries quickly and it is difficult to get an even result, with the same problem as spirit stains. An advantage of quick-drying is that you can put on coats at fairly close intervals, probably five or more in a day. For the best brushed result, sand lightly between coats. Hard shellac sands as a white powder. If it does not, you are sanding

7.2 The rubber for French polishing is made with a pad of cottonwool and a piece of cotton cloth (a), wrapped and squeezed to force out polish (b). Straight strokes on the surface (c) are followed by circular ones (d).

too soon. Besides abrasive paper you can use fine steel wool or pumice powder on a cloth. In all cases, make sure there are no particles left when you put on another coat.

Brushed shellac may be the treatment chosen for the inside of a cabinet when the outside is French polished, but brushed shellac is not as good as modern varnish for normal appearance and protection of the outsides of furniture. It is no use for exterior purposes, as damp weather will be certain to destroy it.

French polishing is a rubbing process with a pad that lets out small quantities of polish. The pad should be of cotton wool, wrapped in a piece of old cotton cloth. This must be old cloth, so that it is free of fluff and lint. The size of the pad should be comfortable to grip, possibly 75mm (3in) across, wrapped in a piece of cloth about 200mm (8in) square (fig. 7.2a). To make the pad, draw the cloth up around the cotton wool and twist it (fig. 7.2b). The pad will be soaked in polish, which will harden if left to dry, and then have to be discarded, but it can be made to last some time if it is kept in an airtight jar.

It is important that the wood surface is as near perfect as possible. More than any other method of finishing, French polish shows up flaws and minor imperfections. The three stages in polishing are called bodying-in, building-up and spiriting out. Bodying-in is the process of putting a coating of shellac on the wood, to be brought to a gloss later. The final polish is dependent on there being a good layer of shellac to work on.

Sprinkle shellac mixture on the pad and wrap the cloth round it so that the liquid oozes through. Rub across the grain and then with it (fig. 7.2c). Cover every part of the surface, including the corners, and keep the pad moving – never lift off the pad from the surface being polished, only raise it as it goes over an edge. Change to a circular or figure-eight action (fig. 7.2d) and continue rubbing lightly until all the polish in the pad has been used up. Let the surface harden – it does not take long – then repeat the bodying-in process with a newly-charged pad.

In all the polishing stages concentrate on the edges and particularly the corners. The body of the panel will then probably be taken care of in the process. Look at the surface and check that it has an even coating of dry shellac. Use more polish on the pad as often as necessary to body-in to a regular overall protective coat. Do not worry about the shine, or lack of it, at this stage. Leave the work for a day. For all polishing it is best to be in a room that is as dust-free as possible. Store the work in the same room. It helps if the work can be done in a comfortable temperature. You cannot polish successfully in cold conditions.

After the day's break, you can start the building-up process. Examine the surface in a good light and use fine abrasive to remove any unevenness, but avoid taking off too much shellac. Make sure there is no dust left, then recharge the pad with shellac mixture and go over the surface again. If the pad tends to stick, put one, or no more than two drops of linseed oil on the outside of the pad. At this stage there should not be very much polish on the pad. If the pad leaves an obviously wet streak across the wood as it is used, it has too much polish. If a shiny streak is showing you may have put on too much oil, which can only be removed by further polishing. You can test the pad on a piece of paper. If you press the pad onto it, any oil will make a mark. If there is no mark, you can add another drop of oil to the outside of the pad. Continue rubbing in the same way, with a fully-charged pad and occasional drops of linseed oil.

Work evenly all over and be particularly careful not to lift the pad anywhere except after it has cleared an edge. Similarly, make sure the pad is in motion when you bring it into contact with the surface. Never just put it down at the centre of the work before starting to move it. In this way you build up a good layer of shellac. Pause between coats. Finally, as a further treatment, go all over with the pad charged with polish diluted with about an equal amount of spirit, then leave the work for half a day, at least. You may see smears, but they do not matter at this stage.

For spiriting-out, use a new pad with a double thickness of cloth. Dampen this with a little spirit and leave it in an airtight container for a short time so that the pad becomes equally soaked. Go over the surface with quite light strokes to remove smears. Do not press hard or use too much spirit, as that may dissolve the surface shellac. Change to another dry pad and go over the surface with a circular motion and then in straight lines along the grain to burnish the wood. Leave it for a few days for the polish to harden fully.

French polishing is obviously a method for dealing with fairly large areas. You might deal with mouldings and narrow strips by working lengthwise, but for many parts that are shaped or pierced the polish must be brushed on. You must judge the amount of polish put on to be about the same as that applied with a pad to adjoining flat parts and be careful to avoid letting brushed polish make marks on pad-polished areas.

As can be seen, French polishing is a lengthy and tedious process – and so not very well suited to modern needs – but it has long been the established method of finishing good furniture and may still be employed on individual pieces of furniture to distinguish them from the products of factories, where this labour-intensive technique would not be economic.

PAINT

Most people are familiar with using paint. For carpentry it is only used on a small amount of furniture. It may be better if some items intended for children are brightly painted, but in most other cases it is more satisfying to let the wood show through.

Paint has uses in structural woodwork, on boats and on much exterior construction. Paints have changed considerably in recent years. Most of the important constituents are synthetic, giving much better all-round qualitities than some of the natural materials previously used. Modern paints are easier to apply and should retain their colour better. Not all makes of paint are the same, and some may not be compatible with others, so it is advisable to buy paint of one make for the various coats to be applied to a new job.

There is available a kind of paint that dries with a very hard waterproof coat. It comes in two parts, to be mixed just before use. In practice it is not a good choice for general woodworking, although it has uses – for example, on boats. For most things it is better to use the normal single-part paints.

Wood should be prepared for paint in the same way as for other finishes, except that you do not need to bother much about colour: a stopping in a crack or hole may be a different colour from the wood. What is important is that the surface is level. Paint makers supply comprehensive instructions for using their products. Follow them, but in general there are three stages when you start from bare wood; priming, undercoat and topcoat.

The primer may not be the same colour as the other coats. It is a thin paint that penetrates the wood to provide a grip in the pores and a surface that other coats will bond to. If the first coat does not disguise the grain marking adequately, you may need to apply two coats of primer.

Undercoat provides the body in the paint. It is in a colour compatible with the final coat, but probably a different shade. It dries with a matt surface. If you want to build up more paint skin, this is the stage where you do it, not at the top coat stage. Sand the undercoat if necessary, preferably using 'wet-and-dry' abrasive paper. This is like glasspaper, but the grit is bonded with a waterproof glue and you can use it wet to pick up particles of dust. Get the final undercoat as free of flaws as possible. You cannot level out ridges at the top coat stage.

The top coat is usually, but not necessarily, glossy. One coat over the base provided by the undercoats produces the final finish. Glossy paint tends to be more durable than most paints made with a matt or semi-glossy finish, so if there is no special reason for choosing anything else, choose glossy paint.

Use a good brush. The best are described as 'varnish' brushes, although they are just as much used for paint. Your brush should be as wide as can be comfortably employed on the surfaces. Check whether the paint makers advise stirring. Some must not be stirred as this causes bubbles that dry as marks on the surface. Spread the paint well. On a broad surface you can work across to get an even distribution, then finish with strokes along the grain. When you recharge the brush, spread the paint again, then make your final strokes along the grain back towards the previously painted part and lift the brush as it goes over the edge. In that way you can avoid brush marks.

So far as possible work on a horizontal surface. Turn the work around to bring each surface to the top. If it is a structure that cannot be moved, vertical brush strokes on upright parts will give a smoother result than horizontal ones, finishing off with upward strokes over wet paint above. If you have to brush across a vertical surface, make sure the paint is spread well or you will get 'curtains', which are runs due to too much paint forming ridges as it dries. The only treatment if this happens is to let the curtain fully harden, then sand it level and paint again.

Varnish

Varnish can be thought of as a clear paint. It is used in a very similar way and is always brushed. Varnishes have been used for a very long time to give wood a clear glossy surface. For nearly all that time they have been made from natural resins and lacs mixed with oil and other liquids that serve as thinners and driers. Some of these traditional varnishes are still available, but most varnishes now offered are partly or completely synthetic – and superior in many ways.

Natural varnishes needed precise conditions to be maintained during application. They had to be applied in the warm, and the atmosphere needed to be dry. Cold and damp would stop the varnish drying fully. They took a long time to set, during which they would often collect dust. Temperature and dampness are not quite as critical with most modern varnishes, and they dry in about four hours, becoming dust-free in a much shorter time. Old varnishes dried only by evaporation. Synthetic varnish uses chemical reaction as well as evaporation to provide the setting action.

There are two-part varnishes that make a very hard skin – so hard that some abrasives will not touch it. This is waterproof and resistant to many liquids. Besides its use on boats, this varnish gives protection to bar tops and similar surfaces, but for general use the one-part varnishes are easier to apply and their slight flexibility when set allows for movement in the wood below. A hard two-part varnish might crack with wood movement.

Carefully brushed varnish can give a good finish to furniture. Its resistance to abrasion, heat and moisture is much better than that of most other finishes. The best grade of varnish is sold as 'boat varnish'. Use that for furniture and anything else important. It has a slight orange colour. All layers of varnish are the same: you do not have to buy the equivalent of primer, undercoat and top coat. It may help if you thin the first coat, for better penetration. The maker's instructions tell you what thinner to use.

The number of coats applied depends on the quality of finish wanted. For normal work the first coat soaks in, the next coat forms a protective layer with a slight gloss, then a third coat finishes with a reasonable gloss that may be acceptable for some things. However, it is possible to sand each coat and continue sanding a great many coats. Some coachbuilders want up to eighteen coats or more to get a brilliant smooth high gloss. For furniture, three or four coats should be enough. A good finish can be obtained if the top coat is lightly sanded and then wax polish is applied.

Although synthetic varnish is more tolerant, it is still advisable to observe some of the conditions applicable to natural varnishes if you are to get the best results. Vacuum clean the room as dust-free as possible. Avoid draughts. The wood and the varnish should be over 18 °C (65 °F), so do not move the work in from the cold just before varnishing. Do not stir modern varnish or the resulting bubbles will dry on the surface as rough spots. It usually helps if you make the varnish more fluid by standing the can in hot water. Do not heat it excessively. Be careful of grease on the wood. Sweaty hands may mark the surface enough to affect the varnish finish.

A varnish brush should never be used for anything other than applying varnish. It may be stored in solvent between coats, but it is better to suspend it in varnish, ideally in a sealed container (fig. 7.3). With an open container a skin may form on the varnish. After use clean brushes thoroughly. For varnishing you must have very flexible bristles. An old brush with partly hardened varnish trapped will mark the surface. With good varnish and a soft brush it is easy to put on a coat that dries without brush marks.

Read the maker's instructions about brushing. Some varnish may be spread and worked out like paint, but others have to be 'flowed on' – that is, applied with the minimum of brushing. Spread with the grain and do not go back over for further spreading. Lift the brush off before it has become exhausted. Going over a part too often may suddenly lift the varnish and leave a rough surface. If that happens you must let it dry, then sand it smooth and varnish again.

The makers will indicate drying times. The surface must be hard before you rub down with steel wool, pumice powder or abrasive paper. Get each coat smooth before applying the next. With some synthetic varnish the makers specify a maximum as well as a minium period between coats. These are not sanded and are really intended for protection of boats and exterior woodwork, where the finest finish is not so important. They are not for use on furniture.

7.3 Cold varnish may be made more fluid by standing the can in hot water (a). Brushes should be stored in solvent or varnish (b).

Spraying

You will have to decide if spraying is the right finish for an individual piece of craftwork. It is the method used today in mass-production where large quantities of furniture can be dealt with as a batch. Spraying suits those circumstances, but might be regarded as unsuitable for a single piece, where there would be much time spent in setting up and clearing away after the job. Of course, spray equipment was not available when much of the earlier fine furniture was made, but there is still a feeling that good cabinetmaking is better finished in other ways.

Some traditional finishes may be thinned and sprayed, but most furniture manufactured today is finished with a special lacquer that leaves a glossy surface not very different from French polish or varnish. The solvent in some lacquers will attack other finishes, so do not use such sprays over or near them.

Spraying requires practice. Runs and curtains can occur and you may not get an even finish. It is unwise to try to spray furniture with the simple equipment sold for amateur touching up of cars. Efficient spraying equipment for furniture is fairly bulky.

SPECIAL EFFECTS

There was once a fashion for limed oak furniture. This used a white deposit in the open grain of the wood. Lime was probably never used, but there are special white pastes for filling the grain. Thick flat white paint can be used. Brush or wipe the material across the grain in all directions and remove the surplus. When it has dried, any surplus is better scraped away than sanded, as that would blur the edges of the filler. You can then apply bleached shellac or pale varnish, so that the filler still looks nearly white.

Furniture is sometimes antiqued by shading its stain to give the effect of wear. This can be done at the staining stage, especially with oil stain. Immediately after applying the stain, wipe parts that are to be lighter. High spots and open areas are normally lighter. You might want the framing of a panel dark and the edges of the panel itself graduated towards a lighter centre. Do not aim at geometric precision. Although the centre lightening may be elliptical, let there be some unevenness as it blends into the darker parts.

In good individual work it is advisable to avoid some of the things used in mass-production furniture, such as 'carvings' that are embossed, flock spraying and special paint effects. The beauty of an individual piece of furniture is in the display of mainly hand craftsmanship, followed by a finish that emphasizes it.

Chapter 8
MAINTENANCE

Much of the quality of work produced by a craftsman is due to the efficient maintenance of his equipment – in particular the sharpness of his cutting tools. Too often, a less-experienced worker puts off sharpening a tool until its bluntness is very obvious. Meanwhile the quality of his work has deteriorated, as a blunt tool tears the surface of the wood instead of cutting it. An experienced craftsman does not begrudge time spent on sharpening. He knows that frequent touching-up of edges will ensure the best possible cuts, and that getting accurate results quickly will be that much easier. There is also the question of safety – there is more risk of hurting yourself while forcing a blunt cutting tool than in handling a sharp one.

Besides tools that need sharpening, there are others that may function in almost any state, but there is a psychological effect to consider. You will feel more inclined to make your best efforts with, for instance, a try square that is clean and polished than with one that is rusty and covered with blobs of glue. Where there are calibrations to consider, as on a steel rule, the risk of error will be reduced if the steel is kept clean. Fortunately, the arrival of good stainless steel has made it easier to keep such tools clean. Where you have to deal with rust or discolouring, fine emery cloth and oil will clean the tool and leave a surface that will remain clean a reasonable length of time. There are not so many wooden tools in use today. At one time a new wooden plane had its mouth sealed with putty and linseed oil poured in and replenished until it exuded from the end grain. We can learn from that. If you are putting a wooden tool away for a period, coat it with linseed oil so that some of it soaks in. A wooden-soled plane soaked in linseed oil certainly performed very well.

SHARPENING EDGE TOOLS
A cutting edge is really a wedge section. The more acute the angle the sharper can be the edge. The edge of a razor is an example of an extremely fine-angled wedge, but it has

little strength. If you tried to work wood with a razor, it would not last long. The angle has to be increased to provide strength. How much depends on the purpose. An axe needs a less acute angle than a chisel. For the majority of wood-working bench tools, the cutting angle is between 25° and 35°· It is the angle between the faces meeting at the edge that counts. The surfaces of a knife blade may be parallel with each other, or nearly so, but the angle at the edge, where its sides meet, should be around 25° for woodworking (fig. 8.1a). It might be finer for cutting paper or other light work.

A plane iron (still called 'iron' although made completely of steel) is fairly thin in modern metal planes and the cutting angle is constant right across its full width (fig. 8.1b). Older plane irons and most chisels are thicker, and it is more convenient to remove much of the metal by grinding at an acute angle and then putting on the sharpening bevel (fig. 8.1c).

An edge is sharp if there is no thickness between the two surfaces when they meet. Perfection may be impossible, but when sharpening try to get as close to it as possible. Apart from knowing that an edge is blunt from the difficulty of cutting with it, you can often see the bluntness as a reflecting line if you look across a blade with a light at the far side. Whenever you sharpen, you briefly rub one or both faces until they meet again.

Sharpening is done with an abrasive stone lubricated with oil, although some workers outside England use water stones. The oil should be quite thin, or it will hold the steel

8.1 *A knife blade has bevels both sides (a). A plane iron or chisel has bevels on only one side (b,c). Most sharpening is done on an oilstone (d).*

off the stone and prevent sharpening. Light lubricating oil or paraffin will do. For plane irons and chisels the tool is rubbed on the stone, so there is an advantage in having fairly large stones – 200 mm (8 in) × 50 mm (2 in) × 25 mm (1 in) is satisfactory. Each should be mounted in a box or a hollowed block of wood (fig. 8.1d), preferably with a cover.

There are manufactured stones made of grits in various sizes, and a number of types of natural stone, which are all fairly fine. In the manufactured stones the grit size can be chosen, so varying degrees of coarseness are possible. But no manufactured stone can be as fine as the finest natural ones. It is possible to get manufactured stones fine on one side and coarse on the other. One of those is a good buy, otherwise you should have a moderately coarse stone for quick removal of metal and a fine one for finishing.

Most cutting edges have two existing bevels – one for grinding and a more obtuse one for sharpening. There is no need to measure exact angles when sharpening. A degree or so either way will not matter, but you should give – say – a paring chisel a finer angle than would be right for one to be used with a mallet. There are devices to attach to a tool that hold it at the correct angle in relation to the surface of the stone, usually with a roller on an arm that cramps on. However, most craftsmen rely on holding the tool freehand. What needs practice is keeping the tool at the same angle for the whole length of the stone. There is a tendency to drop your hands at the far end.

One hand grips the handle or the top of a plane iron and maintains the angle and thrust, while the fingers of the other hand provide pressure just above the edge being sharpened (fig. 8.2a). Besides wearing the steel away, the surface of the stone wears away. To keep this wear as even as possible, move a tool about on the stone as you rub it. A narrow chisel may take a figure-eight course (fig. 8.2b) and even a plane iron wider than the stone should be moved about.

With a chisel or plane iron continue rubbing on the bevelled side until you judge the edge to be sharp. Wipe off the oil with a cloth and feel with your finger on the flat side towards the edge. If you have made the surfaces meet there will be roughness at the edge. That is a 'wire edge', which is the ragged sliver of steel that was rubbed away as the surfaces met, clinging loosely to the edge. You can loosen or remove it by rubbing the other side of the tool flat on the stone with a circular action (fig. 8.2c). A slice across the edge of a piece of scrap wood will make sure it has gone.

8.2 Press and move a chisel about the stone (a,b) and finish by rubbing the other side flat (c). Plane iron edges may be rounded (d) or the corners taken off (e). Spread pressure when sharpening a knife (f).

The edge is now as sharp as that stone will get it. If the edge is examined under a microscope it will be found to be jagged like a saw edge, with the spacing of the teeth the same as the size of grit in the stone. If you were sharpening with a coarse stone, continue sharpening on a finer stone just long enough to remove the gaps left by the coarse grit and replace them with finer ones. Rub flat again and remove the new finer wire edge, then the tool is ready for use. For delicate work you may want to go to an even finer stone. This is particularly so for carving tools, although it may also be worthwhile for a smoothing plane that is to be used on wild-grained hardwood.

Chisels are sharpened straight across and should be kept absolutely flat on one side. Exceptions are carving chisels where a slight bevel may be put on the otherwise flat side. Block planes, rebate planes and ploughs should also have their irons sharpened straight across, but with the corners rounded to prevent them causing ridges (fig. 8.2d and e). The thinner steel of a modern plane iron has the one bevel for the whole thickness instead of a grinding and a sharpening bevel.

Knives are best dealt with by rubbing equally on each

side. You can find the angle by first laying the blade flat on the stone and then lifting it until its edge just touches the surface. A hand on the handle maintains the angle, while the spread fingers of the other hand apply pressure (fig. 8.2f). Move the blade about on the stone to sharpen all parts equally. Do not turn over until you have rubbed many times on one side and can see the bevel there, then aim to get the same amount of bevel on the second side.

When the sharpening bevel of a chisel or plane iron with two bevels is getting wide, the other bevel should be re-ground, so that you can start again on the oil-stone with a narrow sharpening bevel.

A gouge sharpened on the outside can be dealt with on a flat stone by moving the edge about and rolling the blade (fig. 8.3a), although there are some hollow stones available. Continue sharpening until you can feel the wire edge inside. That has to be removed with an oil slip, which is a small oil stone with curved edges (fig. 8.3b). Use the slip like a file to rub inside, moving it about to all parts of the edge. Twist the edge on the surface of a piece of scrap wood, to make sure the wire edge has gone.

If the gouge is sharpened inside (called 'in-cannelled') sharpen with the slip, moved about the bevel equally (fig. 8.3c), then remove the wire edge by rolling the gouge while resting it flat on the main oil stone, before twisting it on a piece of scrap wood.

Turning tools are sharpened in a similar way, except the chisels are bevelled equally on both sides. Some turners

8.3 *Roll a gouge as it is sharpened (a), then remove any wire edge inside with a slip stone (b). If the bevel is inside, sharpen with a slip stone (c).*

8.4 *A cabinet scraper uses a burred edge for cutting (a). To sharpen, its edge may be squared on a stone (b), then burrs turned with a burnisher (c).*

prefer to blend the sharpening bevels into the grinding bevels. Others maintain separate bevels for sharpening and grinding.

Spokeshaves are sharpened like plane irons, but you may have to turn the stone on edge in order to sharpen the type with projecting tangs.

There is a type of scraper with a replaceable hook blade, which may be sharpened with a fine file or a stone used as a file, but not many sharpenings are possible before the hook has to be replaced. A cabinet scraper is sharpened in a different way, as what makes it cut is a turned-over burr on the edge (fig. 8.4a). The scraper is tilted and pushed or pulled over the surface to take off very fine shavings.

The edge can be filed true, if necessary, and then it is rubbed on an oil stone to make the edge square and true. The flat sides can also be rubbed, followed by more rubs along the edge (fig. 8.4b). A hard steel burnisher is rubbed on the edge, first tilted slightly to one side and then to the other to turn over the cutting burr (fig. 8.4c). A gouge or chisel could be used as a burnisher. Use will turn the burr back, but the edge can be restored several times with the burnisher, before it is necessary to return to the oil-stone.

SAW SHARPENING

On a new saw the teeth are cut and sharpened by machine, so they are all the same. It is difficult to achieve the same precision by hand. Although it is possible to restore the teeth of many saws yourself, it is advisable at longer intervals to have the saw dealt with professionally, so that you start again with perfectly even teeth. Handsaws are made of a tool steel that can be filed. Some circular saws are of the same steel, but many now have tips of harder material. They go much longer before needing sharpening, but when that is due they must be dealt with by an expert with special equipment. Bandsaw blades are not resharpened, but are replaced when they are worn. It is handsaws that are normally sharpened by the owner.

Three things have to be considered. There is the set of the teeth: they are bent alternate ways to cut a kerf wider than the thickness of the blade, so that the saw does not bend in a deep cut. There is the shape of the teeth, which distinguishes a saw meant for cutting along the grain from one intended primarily for work across the grain. There is the angle given to the cutting edges of the teeth. Teeth must all finish level.

In side view, the teeth of general-purpose saws have their forward cutting edges sloping so as to sever the wood fibres (fig. 8.5a). A rip saw has the leading edge upright, or nearly so, the teeth acting more like plane irons – curling up the fibres before breaking (fig. 8.5b). In both cases the included angle is 60° (fig. 8.5c), so it is possible to file across both edges with a normal triangular file (often called a 'three-square' file). Saw files are made with fine teeth and may be reversible in their handles to give a double life. Do not use an ordinary coarser triangular file.

The first need will be touching up a saw that has got blunt for the first time. The tips of the teeth will be seen to have rounded and you have to take off enough metal to restore them to points. The saw has to be clamped with not much more than the teeth exposed and pointing upwards. There are special saw vices, but you can use two stiff pieces of wood in the normal vice (fig. 8.5d). The grip must be tight to prevent vibration, which is noisy and affects the accuracy of filing.

It is usual to sharpen fronts of the teeth set towards you, then to turn the saw round so that the alternate teeth can be sharpened in the same manner. You must guard against taking off too much from the teeth one way, which might happen if you sharpened without turning the saw round. Check the level of the tips of the teeth. If there is much unevenness use a large flat fine file to rub along a few times, but do not take off any more than absolutely necessary. If the teeth are fairly even you can omit this stage.

Look at the teeth pointing towards you. The forward cutting edges in a cross-cut saw will be seen to slope. Put the

8.5 Cross-cut saws sever fibres with a knife action (a). A rip saw cuts more like a plane (b). The included angle matches the section of a file used in sharpening (c,d,e,f). Circular saw teeth may be of a different form (g).

file in a gap and move it until it matches that angle (fig. 8.5e). The other side of the gap will automatically be matched. Go on, using the file at the same angle in alternate gaps all along the saw edge. Have one hand on each end of the file and use steady level strokes each time. File guides that maintain the angle are obtainable. How many strokes depends on the size of the teeth and amount of wear to be corrected, but do not file any more than necessary. Go all the way along, usually starting at the tip end. Be careful not to drop the file into any wrong gaps or you will spoil the saw by bevelling some teeth the wrong way. Turn the saw round and file the alternate teeth the same, but now the file will be angled the other way. After a few teeth examine what you have done and see that the height of all the teeth filed is reasonably even.

After filing, the teeth may be very spiky. Try the saw

across a piece of wood. You may be satisfied with it as it is, but if it tends to dig in at some stages of the cut, there may be one or two high teeth. You can use a fine flat file very lightly along the teeth to remove high spots, but keep this to a minimum.

To sharpen a rip saw, file straight across the teeth pointed towards you (fig. 8.5f). Turn the saw round and do the same with the alternate teeth. You may need to lightly rub the tops and sides of the rip teeth with a flat file if it seems spiky during first cuts.

Circular saw teeth are in many forms. Some are like hand-saw teeth and may be sharpened in the same way. You can make up a vice with a curved end and a bolt for the saw blade (fig. 8.5g).

You may file teeth perhaps two or three times, but this will reduce the amount of set each time, so the kerf cut will become so slight that there is no clearance on the blade. You then have to set the teeth again. This needs control in bending or you can break a tooth off. Do not try to bend at the base of the tooth; it is only the top half that has to be bent, and that not very much (fig. 8.6a). Setting should be done before sharpening, otherwise the action of setting may blunt the teeth.

There are now several types of plier-action saw sets (sometimes spelled 'setts'). They bend the teeth one at a time as you squeeze the handles. The amount of bend and the distance from the tip is controlled by stops (fig. 8.7). The most basic type is like open pliers with stops. There are older type sets with notched edges in a plate, but their only

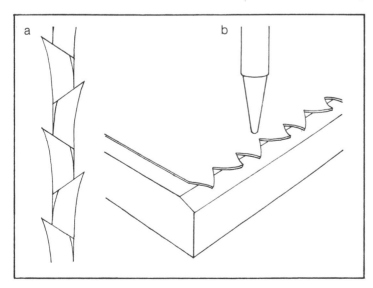

8.6 Saw teeth are set alternate ways (a). Large teeth may be bent with a punch (b).

8.7 A saw set uses a plier action to set saw teeth and has adjustable stops to suit the size of teeth.

use today is for the very large teeth of cross-cut saws used for logs. Bending is then done by eye.

The small teeth of tenon and dovetail saws should only be set with a plier-type tool. Teeth of hand saws at 4 or 6 per 25mm (1in) might be set by careful use of a punch and hammer over the edge of an iron block (fig. 8.6b), but it would be unwise for a beginner to try this method on small teeth. Too much set makes hard work of sawing. You have to judge it so that it is just enough.

POWER PLANER MAINTENANCE

A planer or jointer has a cylindrical block carrying two, three or four cutters or knives, each as long as the width of the table, the number depending on the capacity of the machine. The cutters are rotated at a very high speed. In ideal circumstances each cutting edge projects the same amount, is straight and exactly in line with the take-off table; then you get a smooth cut of even depth. A common arrangement turns the block so as to give 12 000 cuts per minute. If one blade is higher that one does most of the work at a fraction of the efficient speed, and the quality of finish suffers. Check that all blades are the same height and that this is the same over the width of the machine.

Knives are mounted in the cutter block in different ways, but in all machines there is provision for raising and lowering them, usually after slackening screws. The height of the rear table should be adjusted to the height of a blade when it is vertical and this can be checked with a straight strip of wood (fig. 8.8a). Try this at each end of the blade. Lock the knife blade at that positon and do the same with the others. With the motor disconnected, turn the block with your hand at one end, while holding the straight piece of wood in place. You will see if one edge is higher than the others as it tries to move the wood along. Ideally, at any position the cutting edges should just skim the wood. Checking may be easier if you accept a slight movement. By marking the wood opposite the edge of the rear table and putting another mark about 3mm (⅛in) beyond it (fig. 8.8b), you can try the wood in several positions while you turn the cutter block by hand and see if movement is nearly the same everywhere.

One way of lifting each knife level with the rear table is to use a powerful U-shaped magnet, to draw and hold up the blade while you tighten its screws (fig. 8.8c). With a broad spread it should be able to hold up both ends of the blade level at the same time.

It is important that the cutting edges should be absolutely straight. The ordinary woodworking shop does not usually have facilities for grinding such edges straight and it would be unwise to attempt freehand grinding. What is needed is a means of holding the knife at the correct angle and moving it under a flat grinding surface. It might be possible to arrange something with a grinder in a drill press (fig. 8.8d), but if the knives reach a stage when they should be reground, it is better to return them to the makers or to another grinder with suitable equipment. However, it is possible to sharpen many times without removing the knives from the machine,

8.8 *Power plane blade movement and setting may be tested with a strip of wood (a,b). A magnet will hold a blade level (c). Edges must be ground straight (d), then set level with the feed table (e).*

provided that you do not have to remove deep knicks due to hitting nails or pieces of grit.

To sharpen in the machine, have the motor and belt disconnected, then lower the feed table so that its surface comes in line with the bevel on a knife (fig. 8.8e). Have a flat fairly coarse oil-stone and wrap much of its length in paper. With one hand on the pulley keep the cutter edge in position and rub the oil-stone on it, with the paper sliding on the table (fig. 8.8f). Use plenty of oil and pressure. Wipe off the oil from time to time and check that you are not taking more off one place than another. Deal with all edges in the same way, then clean off any surplus oil and test the action of the machine.

If the planer can be used for cutting rabbets at one side and you are replacing or moving knives, make sure the knives project slightly an equal amount from the cutter block at the rabbeting end.

ROUTER AND MOULDING CUTTERS

There is not much you can do to a blunted rotary cutter. Most are made of special alloy steel or are tipped, and neither will sharpen easily by hand methods. If you attempt to sharpen, only the leading face of the cutter when it is rotating should be touched. Any wearing away of the outside surface would affect the profile the tool can produce. A slim round oil slip might have some effect. A file would probably not be hard enough.

If you want to sharpen the end of a square mortise chisel, there is a special tool (usually available from the stockist who supplied the mortise chisel) something like a countersink bit with a pilot, and matched to the size of the square. When that is turned with a brace it will remove metal at the edge. To get a fine edge you can follow with a stone that has a curved cross section.

DRILL SHARPENING

To a certain extent the various woodworking boring bits have to be regarded as disposable. A limited amount of sharpening is possible, but a stage may be reached where no more can be taken off if the bit is to work. The steel of most bits is tempered soft enough for a file to cut it, but sharpening is often better done with a small oil slip, used like a file.

In many bits there is an outer spur that cuts the circle (fig. 8.9a). It must not be sharpened on the outside, or the size of the circle it cuts will be reduced and the rest of the bit may not follow into a deep hole. Sharpen inside to get a knife effect in the direction of rotation. You may have to remove a wire edge outside, but do not rub off any solid metal there. Try not to reduce the length of the spur. If there are two spurs deal with them evenly.

Inside is a lip, or a pair of lips. They are there to remove waste outlined by the spur. Their action is more wedge-like, so a very sharp edge is not so important. There must be a slight angle on the underside (fig. 8.9b) to scoop into the wood. What is important is keeping the edge of the lip higher than the cutting edge of the spur (fig. 8.9c). It is the spur that needs most sharpening, and when that gets back to the depth of the lip, the bit may have to be discarded. You can file the underside of the lip, but you should not reduce its depth very much.

Twist bits, whether for hand or power drilling, are made and sharpened in the same way. Power-drilling spade bits have a different form. It is the broad cutting edges that need attention (fig. 8.9d), but it is their outer corners that wear. If they are rounded, file the whole width of each edge until they are restored to sharpness and will cut a clean circle. Do not sharpen outside. Countersink bits go a long time without needing sharpening, but if they do you need a file with a knife edge (to get inside a rose bit) or a small round file for a snail countersink. In both cases, file the leading edges and not the outsides.

Metalworking bits, such as are used for screw holes in wood, are difficult to sharpen freehand. There are jigs for

8.9 *The spur (a) of a twist bit cuts the circle of a hole, while the lip (b) removes waste, so the spur must project further (c). A power drill spade bit is sharpened with a file (d). Cutting angles of a metalworking bit are important (e).*

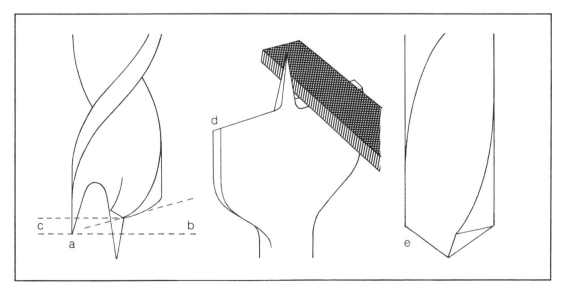

use on bench grinding wheels, but these are unsuitable for diameters of anything less than about 3mm (⅛in) – the assumption being that anything smaller than that will be discarded rather than resharpened.' However, for wood-working we do not need the precision of cutting edge angles that are necessary for metal, and it is possible to restore a reasonable edge by hand grinding.

Your best guide is a larger drill fresh from the makers. If you look at the end of a drill at least 6mm (¼in) diameter, you can see the angle between the two sides and the way the underside is backed off from the cutting edge (fig. 8.9e). Without this the drill would merely slide round and not pull itself into the wood or metal. What you have to do on any size drill, down to the tiniest, is to reproduce this end. Have a high speed dry grinding wheel and touch the drill on it very lightly. A common mistake with small drills is to press hard and take off too much. If you are sharpening a broken drill, first grind the end square across, then slope each side and finally back off the edges as shown.

SERVICING OIL-STONES

Oil on a stone attracts dirt. A stone should be wiped clean after use, but if you are using a stone frequently sound prac-tice tends to get neglected. Its case should have a cover to keep out dirt. Even if you have kept a stone clean it will gradually clog with particles of steel mixed with oil. A dirty stone does not sharpen properly.

You can soak the dirt out of a stone with paraffin. Leave it in a can of paraffin for a day or so, if possible. A scrubbing brush will remove loose dirt and you may have to change the paraffin before you complete the job. Newspaper will soak up surplus oil. What remains in the stone will help in later sharpening.

A stone regularly used for chisels and plane irons will get worn out of true. Hollow in the length is not so serious as hollow in the width, which makes it difficult to sharpen tools straight across. Spreading the points of contact when sharpening can delay hollowing, but the corners will always remain high.

To grind a stone level you need a piece of plate glass and some abrasive powder in oil, such as is sold as valve grind-ing compound at car supply stores. Spread the grinding compound on the glass and rub the stone on it with plenty of pressure, working with a mainly circular action. This is a slow process. You can rub two stones together to get a similar result, but the harder one will wear away the other.

Information

NAILS

Nails are produced in a large range of sizes and types. Most are made of iron, which may be coated with zinc or other metal to protect against rust, or made of brass, bronze or other alloy with a good resistance to corrosion. Brass is preferable to iron for furniture. Diameters are described by a gauge number, different from that for screws, but usually only one diameter is available for each length. Large heads provide the strongest grip, but small heads can be driven flush or sunk for a better appearance.

Note: Measurements in millimetres are given in **bold type**; measurements in inches are given in normal type.

TYPE		USUAL AVAILABLE LENGTHS		USE AND CHARACTERISTICS
Round wire nail		**20–150**	¾–6	General-purpose. Fairly large head.
Oval wire nail		**12–150**	½–6	Head buries, and shape reduces risk of splitting.
Cut floor nail		**12–150**	½–6	Flat, with hooked head that buries.
Clout nail		**12– 50**	½–2	Large head, for gripping roofing felt.
Panel pin		**12– 50**	½–2	Fine, with small head to punch into wood.
Hardboard pin		**9– 50**	⅜–2	Very fine, for fixing hardboard.
Tack		**6– 30**	¼–1¼	Large head, for fixing fabrics.
Sprig or glazier's point		**12 or 20**	½ or ¾	Headless, to bury under putty when fixing glass.
Annular or barbed ring nail		**20– 75**	¾–3	For boat building; teeth resist withdrawal.
Roofing or screw nail		**65**	2½	Large head and twisted body, for fixing corrugated sheets.

SCREWS

Choose wood screws, as distinct from metal-thread screws, which have threads for nuts. Wood screws are made in many lengths, from 6 mm (¼ in) up to 150 mm (6 in) and more, and diameters, indicated by a gauge number different from that used for nails, from about 2 mm (³⁄₃₂ in) to 7 mm (⁹⁄₃₂ in) and larger. The combinations of gauges and lengths shown below should suit most purposes and are normally available.

Most screws are of mild steel, but brass, stainless steel or other metals, plated or coloured, are available. Screws are boxed in 100s, but available in smaller quantities. Raised heads may only come in a few sizes.

Suggested sizes for holes suit hardwoods, and the pilot holes could be smaller in softwood and made with a bradawl for small screws.

GAUGE NUMBER(a)	COMMON LENGTHS(b)		CLEARANCE HOLE(c)		PILOT HOLE(d)	
2	6	¼	2.5	³⁄₃₂	1.5	¹⁄₁₆
3	9.5	⅜	3	⁷⁄₆₄	1.5	¹⁄₁₆
4	9.5 – 19	⅜ – ¾	3.2	⅛	2	⁵⁄₆₄
5	12.5 – 19	½ – ¾	3.2	⅛	2	⁵⁄₆₄
6	12.5 – 38	½ – 1½	4	⁵⁄₃₂	2	⁵⁄₆₄
8	19 – 76	¾ – 3	5	³⁄₁₆	2.5	³⁄₃₂
10	25 – 76	1 – 3	5.5	⁷⁄₃₂	3.2	⅛
12	51 – 76	2 – 3	6	¼	3.2	⅛
14	64 – 76	2½ – 3	7	⁹⁄₃₂	5	³⁄₁₆

Note: Measurements in millimetres are given in **bold type**; measurements in inches are given in normal type.

ABRASIVES

Many grits are used for abrasives and may come loose, on paper or on cloth in sheet, disc, strip or endless bands. Most sheets are 280 mm (11 in) by 230 mm (9 in). Glass and garnet coating sheets for wood may not be fixed with waterproof glue. Most other abrasive materials are. Abrasive sheets described as 'wet and dry' have waterproof glues. Emery is only used on metal. Several grit classifications are used. The best refers to the fineness of the grit (used for manufactured grits and given in the first column), but other classifications are used and are listed for comparison. Steel wool for wood finishing is available in three grades, approximately comparable to abrasive grits as shown.

GRIT	GLASS OR GARNET PAPER	TRADITIONAL GRADE	EMERY CLOTH	STEEL WOOL	USE
400	–	10/0 ('ten nought')	–	–	Very fine finish
320	–	9/0	–	–	
280	–	8/0	–	–	Flatting polish
240	–	7/0	–	–	
220	–	6/0	–	–	
180	00 (flour)	5/0	0	–	Finest normally used on bare wood
150	0	4/0	FF	00	
120	1	3/0	F	–	Medium sanding
100	1½	2/0	1	1	
80	F2 (fine 2)	0	1½	–	Usual first sanding
60	M2 (middle 2)	½	2	3	
50	S2 (strong 2)	1	3	–	Rough sanding
40	2½	1½	4	–	
36	3	2	–	–	Coarse stock removal

GLUES

Many different adhesives are available, but any described as suitable for paper or card as well as wood should be avoided as not strong enough for constructional joints.

TYPE	APPLICATION	COMMENTS
Animal or fish	Heat, then rub and cramp.	Traditional type. Non-waterproof.
Casein	Mix powder with water. The joint should be cramped.	Derived from milk. Moderate damp resistance.
Cellulose	Apply and hand hold briefly.	Little strength but quick-acting and waterproof. For fixing small parts only.
Contact cement	Allow to become tacky then postion parts exactly.	For fixing plastic laminates to wood. Immediate adhesion.
Epoxy	Two-part (resin and hardener supplied separate). Apply and cramp for two days.	Strongest waterproof glue. Sticks most most materials to themselves as well as to wood. Quicker-acting type available, but not as strong.
PVA	One-part. Cramp briefly.	Non-waterproof. Dries clear. Suitable for furniture and indoor use.
Resorcinol formaldehyde	Two-part. Cramp closely.	Strong and waterproof. Red glue line. For boat building.
Urea	Two-part. Cramp closely.	Strong with good water resistance. For furniture and small boats.

FILLERS

Prepared fillers are supplied as paste to be applied with a knife, or as liquid to be brushed on, with another semi-liquid medium grade between these two extremes.

PASTE FILLER	MEDIUM FILLER	LIQUID FILLER	NO FILLER
Ash	Mahogany	Bass	Cypress
Chestnut	Rosewood	Beech	Ebony
Elm	Sapele	Birch	Gaboon
Hickory	Walnut	Cedar	Hemlock
Oak		Fir	Holly
Padouk		Maple	Pine
Teak		Sycamore	Spruce

STAINS

Stains alter the colour of wood without hiding details of grain. They are used before applying a protective finish.

TYPE	COLOURS	AS SUPPLIED	CHARACTERISTICS
Oil	Mostly to deepen natural wood tone	Liquid, ready for use	Even spread and deeper penetration than other stains.
Water	Wood shades and a few other colours	Crystals to dissolve in water	Colours not as intense as oil. Can be mixed. Little penetration. Better spread with several coats.
Spirit	Wood shades and some bright colours	Powder to dissolve in methylated spirit	Quick drying. Good penetration. Unsuitable for large areas. For small parts or touching-up.
Permanganate of potash	Colourless, but turns many woods brown	Crystals to dissolve in water	Chemical actions, so check effect on similar scrap wood to see resulting colour.

FINISHES

A finish is applied to improve appearance and to protect the wood from abrasion and the penetration of dirt and liquids. A clear finish shows grain and stain. An opaque finish hides wood detail and may be any colour.

TYPE		COMMENTS
Clear finishes	Varnish	Made from natural or synthetic lacs. Slight golden tinge. Applied by brush. Several coats needed.
	Varnish stain	Varnish with stain included, so that colour is in the finish and does not enter the grain.
	Shellac	Flakes dissolved in methylated spirit. May be brushed, but more often used as French polish.
	French polish	System of pad polishing using shellac. Ordinary polish has slight golden tinge, but bleached polish is almost clear.
	Lacquer	Synthetic sprayed finish. Clear with any degree of gloss.
	Oil polish	Pad polish with linseed oil. Slow to dry.
	Teak oil	Oil and varnish pad polish, much quicker to dry than oil only.
	Wax polish	Mixture of waxes for pad polishing. Slow to apply if used as sole finish, but may follow varnish or other finish.
Opaque finishes	Oil paint	Traditional type mostly superseded by synthetic. All colours available. Several coats needed. Gloss or matt or intermediate surface.
	Emulsion paint	Water-based paint. Not a wood finish, but may be used to seal hardboard before application of ordinary paint.

Glossary

Adam A period of furniture building and decoration. Ascribed to Robert and James Adam.

Adze A tool like an axe with the blade set at right angles to the haft, used to level surfaces.

Alburnum The botanical name of sapwood.

Annual rings The concentric rings that form the grain of a tree. One ring is added each year.

Annulet A turned raised bead around a cylindrical part.

Antiquing A finish that makes modern furniture look old.

Apron A wide shaped rail in cabinetwork. Projecting ornament on a door lock rail.

Arbor A temporary tapered turned piece to hold a hollow article being turned. Also a fitment for an electric drill.

Arch back An armchair where the arms continue at the back to make an arch (as in a Windsor chair).

Architrave Outer molding around a door.

Arris The line or sharp edge between two flat or plane surfaces.

Astragal A raised moulding or bead on a flat surface.

Auger A long drill, with its own handle, for deep drilling.

Autumn growth Part of an annual ring in a tree. It is formed by the descending sap.

Awl A pointed tool for making holes.

Axis An imaginary line about which a body can be assumed to revolve. The centre-line of a solid object.

Backboard The piece of wood closing the back of a cabinet.

Back-flap hinge A hinge designed to swing back further than a normal hinge. It is often used under a drop leaf on a table.

Back iron Cap on plane iron to stiffen it and break shavings.

Badger Large rabbet plane.

Ball-foot A turned round or elliptical ball on the bottom of a leg.

Balluster (baluster) Pillar to support a rail.

Banding A strip of inlay laid around and usually parallel with edges of panels, such as drawer fronts, table-tops and cabinet parts.

Bar Intermediate member dividing a window into smaller parts.

Bar cramp Alternative name for a sash cramp.

Barefaced tenon A tenon shouldered on one side only.

Adze

Annulet

Arris

Auger

Base The foundation of anything or the main bottom portion in an architectural or other assembly.

Basil Grinding angle of a cutting tool.

Batten Any narrow strip of wood. A strip fitted across boards to join them, cover a gap or prevent warping.

Baulk (balk) Timber roughly squared before cutting into boards.

Beam Strong horizontal timber, load-bearing and supported by a wall or other means.

Beam compass Two points or a point and pencil adjustable along a wooden rod.

Beaumontage Wood stopping like sealing wax to melt into holes.

Bench stop A wood or metal stop on a bench top. Wood is pressed against it when planing its surface.

Bevel An angle or chamfer planed on an edge. Also the name of an adjustable tool for testing angles.

Bezel Ring around glass over the face of a clock or other instrument.

Bill hook Chopping knife used by woodcutters.

Blind Not right through. A stopped hole for a dowel or a mortise for a short tenon.

Blind nailing or screwing Using the fastener in a rabbet or elsewhere that will be covered by another part so that the head is not visible in the finished work.

Bolster A pad to withstand a thrust.

Bonnet Decorative shaping and moulding or carving at the top of any piece of cabinetwork, but particularly on a clock.

Book matched Veneers cut next to each other and laid together so that one is a mirror image of the other.

Bow back A chair back with a curved bow and spindles enclosed in it, but not necessarily an arched back.

Bowing Warping in the length only.

Bracket An angular support used particularly to support a shelf or flap.

Brad Nail cut from sheet metal, parallel in thickness and tapered in width.

Bridle joint The reverse of a mortise and tenon joint, with two ends extending at either side of a central web.

Bull-nose plane A plane with its cutting edge very close to the front of the body. Usually the edge is the full width of the body, for getting close into the end of a stopped rabbet.

Bureau A writing desk, with a closing front and storage places inside.

Burr (burl) An outgrowth on a tree. It can be cut across to

Ballusters

Barefaced tenon

Blind nailing

Bill hook

Bolster

Capping rail

Cock beads

Cross banding

Dentils

show a very twisted grain that is valued for its decoration when cut into veneers.

Cable moulding Moulding with a rounded part carved diagonally to look like stranded rope or cable.

Cabriole leg Leg given a flourish so that it curves out from a corner in a stylized form of an animal's leg. Usually it finishes in a ball foot.

Capping The top moulding on a pedestal or post.

Capping rail Rail over top of fence or gate.

Carcase The main assembly parts that make up the skeleton of a piece of furniture, such as the framework of a table, cabinet or chest of drawers.

Casement Hinged sash window.

Cast Twisting of a surface that should be flat.

Caul Part of press for holding glued veneers.

Chaise longue Long low chair for reclining.

Chamfer An angle or bevel planed on an edge.

Cleat A small piece joining other parts together or an alternative name for a wood clamp.

Cock bead A bead standing above the surface of the wood.

Coniferous A cone-bearing sort of tree, the main source of softwoods.

Conversion The process of cutting logs into boards.

Comb An undulating edge that is found particularly on a chair back.

Core Base wood on which veneer is laid.

Cornice A moulding above eye level that projects around the top of a cabinet.

Cramp (clamp) Tool for holding parts together, particularly when gluing. Batten fixed across other boards.

Cross banding Decorative veneering that uses narrow strips cut across the grain.

Crook (crotch) Wood cut from the point where a branch leaves the tree. Cut to take advantage of the curved grain in order to get maximum strength in a shaped part or for decoration.

Cup shake Defect in lumber. A crack around the lines of annual rings.

Dado A groove in wood.

Dead pin A wedge.

Dentil Rectangular ornaments on cornice mouldings.

Distressing Intentionally damaging furniture to make it look old.

Doatiness Speckled marking in wood indicating the start of decay.

Donkey A quick-action vice used for holding work during the cutting of marquetry designs.

Dowel A cylindrical piece of wood that is particularly used as a peg in holes for making joints.

Dovetail The fan-shaped piece that projects between pins in the other part in a dovetail joint.

Dressing Planing and finishing wood.

Drift Large punch, tapered to pull holes into line.

Draw bore or draw pin A tapered peg or dowel through staggered holes in a mortise and tenon joint, to draw the parts together.

Drop leaf A flap that swings down at the edge of a table and can be supported when raised to enlarge the table-top.

Ellipse The inclined transverse section of a cylinder or cone.

Escutcheon A keyhole, or the plate covering and surrounding it.

Face marks Marks put on the first planed side and edge to indicate that further measuring and marking should be made from them.

Fall front A flap that lets down to be supported in a horizontal position. An example is the writing surface of a bureau.

Fastenings (fasteners) Anything, such as nails and screws, used for joining.

Fiddle back Grain pattern shown when wood is quarter-sawn, particularly in mahogany as used in violin backs, but also seen in sycamore, maple and some other woods.

Figure Decorative grain pattern and particularly that shown when the medullary rays are prominent in quarter-sawn wood. Especially seen in oak.

Fillet A narrow strip of wood used to fill or support a part.

Finial A turned end to a post.

Fish plates Strips of wood or metal each side of an end-to-end joint.

Flour paper Very fine glasspaper.

Flush bead moulding A bead worked into a surface, instead of standing above it, as in an astragal.

Fluting Rounded grooves that are the reverse of beads.

Folding wedges Two similar wedges used overlapping each other to provide parallel pressure.

Foxiness Reddish colour in wood indicating the onset of rot.

Foxtail wedging Using wedges driven into the end of a tenon so that they spread the wood and make it grip when it is driven into a blind mortise.

Framed construction In which the carcase is formed of strips of wood, with the spaces filled by panels.

Drift

Face marks

Finial

Fluting

Fish plates

Gussets

Haunch

Fretwork Pierced work done with a very fine fretsaw.

Furniture Besides its usual meaning, this also applies to iron-mongery for doors, windows etc.

Gate leg table A table with drop leaves that can be held up by swinging legs like gates.

Gauge A marking tool or a means of testing. A definition of size. The thickness of sheet metal or the diameters of wires or screws.

Glaziers' points Small steel triangles used like headless nails to hold glass in a frame.

Groundwork The base surface to which veneer is applied.

Groove Any slot in wood such as a dado. Less commonly a rabbet.

Growth rings See annual rings.

Gunstock stile Sort of upright at the side of a panelled door, wider beside the lower panel than beside the upper one.

Gusset Piece over frame joints to strengthen and stiffen.

Haft The handle of a tool.

Halved joint Two pieces of wood notched to fit into each other where they meet or cross.

Hand screw A wooden cramp.

Heartwood The mature wood nearer the centre of the tree.

Handed Made in pairs.

Hanging stile The stile on which the hinges of a door are attached.

Haunch A short part of a tenon in a corner joint.

Horse Trestle. Temporary strut.

Impact adhesive Alternative name for contact adhesive.

Incising Carving below the surface.

Inlaying Setting one piece of wood in another, either in solid pieces of wood or as a veneer.

In the white Furniture completely made and ready for stain-ing and polishing.

Jamb Vertical side of a window- or door-frame.

Jig Guide for shaping.

Joggle Protection on the end, particularly beyond a mortise. A double bend.

Joist Wood to support a floor or ceiling.

Jury Anything temporary, e.g. jury strut.

Kerf The slot made by a saw.

Keying Fitting pieces of veneer into kerfs. Used particularly to strengthen a mitre joint.

Joggles →

Knee Shaped bracket or brace.
Knot A flaw in wood caused where a branch left the tree.
Knuckle The pivot part of a hinge.

Lac Resinous substance secreted in trees by insects.
Lacquer A transparent varnish. Traditionally a brushed finish on gilded work, but now more often a sprayed finish.
Ladder back A chair back with several cross members between uprights.
Laminating Constructing in layers with several pieces of wood. Used particularly in curved work.
Lath Strip of wood of smaller section than a batten.
Lattice work Pierced strapwork.
Laying out Setting out the details of design and construction.
Lineal Specified by length only. Sometimes used when pricing quantities of wood.
Lumber American term for converted wood.

Marking out Marking ends and positions on wood before cutting shaping and drilling.
Marquetry A system of inlaying that uses many woods to produce a pattern or picture using solid wood or veneers.
Matched boarding Joining boards edge to edge with matching tongues and grooves.
Medullary rays Radiating lines from the center of a log, which can be seen in some woods radially cut but are invisible in others.
Mill work Manufacture of joinery mainly by machine.
Mitre A joint where the angle of meeting is bisected as in the corner of a picture frame.
Moulded plywood Double curvature laminates built up in layers with strips of veneer.
Moulding Decorative edge or border which may be a simple rounding or an intricate section of curves and quirks. Many are of named classical form, used in architecture and cabinetwork.
Mullet A grooved block used for testing the thickness of the edge of a panel or drawer bottom that will have to fit in a groove.
Muntin An internal rail in a framed assembly as between the panels in a window frame.
Mullion Vertical division of a window.

Necking Turned bead on the upper part of a pillar, pedestal or finial.
Newel Post carrying the hand rail to a flight of stairs.

Knee

Matched boarding

Mullet

Nosing

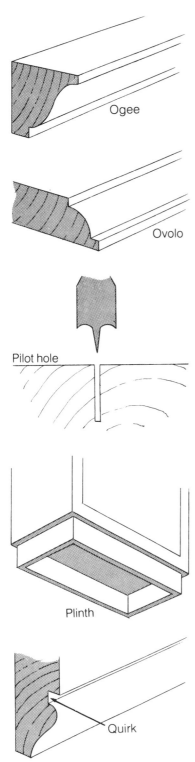

Ogee

Ovolo

Pilot hole

Plinth

Quirk

Nosing Semi-circular moulding.

Ogee moulding A moulding with a convex curve above a concave one. It is named for its likeness to a combination of the letters O and G.

Onion foot A squat version of a ball foot.

Ovolo Classic quarter circle or ellipse moulding.

Parquetry Wood-block flooring laid in geometric designs. Not to be confused with marquetry.

Patina Surfaced texture that is due particularly to old age.

Pedestal A supporting post.

Pediment A top shaped and moulded or carved. Larger than a bonnet.

Pegging Dowels or wooden pegs through joints.

Pendant, pendil, pennant A hanging turned or carved decoration. The reverse of a finial.

Piercing Decoration made by cutting through the wood, in the splat of a chair back for example. Similar to fretwork, but more robust.

Pilaster A decorative half column fitted on a flat surface.

Pilot-hole A small hole drilled as a guide before using a larger drill.

Pintle A dowel or peg on which parts pivot – the name taken from the pivotal point of a boat's rudder.

Planted Applied instead of cut in the solid. Moulding attached to a surface is planted. If it is cut in the solid wood it is stuck.

Plastic glues General name for resin-bonded adhesives.

Plinth The base part around the bottom of a piece of furniture.

Plumb Vertical.

Plywood Board made with veneers glued together with the grain of alternate layers at right angles.

Pokerwork Designs formed with red hot point. Pyrography.

Pollarding Continued lopping of the top of a tree. This produces decorative burrs in the wood.

Proud Standing above a surface, not flush with it.

Punchwork Background to carving made with punches having patterned ends.

Purlins Horizontal beams in a roof carried on the principal rafters.

Pyrography Pokerwork.

Quarter-sawn Boards cut radially from a log to minimize warping and shrinking or to show the medullary rays as 'figure' in oak and some other woods.

Quatre-foil A tracery detail based on four interlocking circles.

Quirk A narrow or V-shaped groove beside a bead, or the whole bead when worked to form part of a cover or disguise for a joint. A raised part between patterns in turned work.

Rabbet

Rabbet (rebate) Angular cut-out in section, as in the back of a picture frame.

Racking Out of square.

Rail A horizontal member in framing.

Rake Incline to horizontal.

Rank set Having the cap iron of a plane well back from the cutting edge.

Rat rail Small round file.

Reeds Series of beads sunk on a surface.

Relief Cut back, usually to gain emphasis in appearance.

Riser Vertical front of a step.

Rive (riven) Split boards from a log instead of sawing them.

Rod back A type of Windsor chair that has many spindles, with the arms joined to spindles forming the back.

Rolled arm The arm of a chair shaped for comfort and the front finished in a scroll.

Rule joint Moulded joint used between a table-top and its drop flap used with a back-flap hinge. Named for its similarity in section to the joint of a two-fold rule.

Run In an unbroken length. Timber can be quoted as 'so many feet run'.

Reeds

Rolled arm

Rule joint

Saddle back Part curved both ways.

Saddling Scooping a chair seat to a comfortable shape.

Sandpaper Common, and incorrect collective name for abrasive papers.

Sapwood The wood nearer the outside of a log. Not as strong or durable as the heartwood in most trees.

Scant Slightly undersize, sometimes applied to sawn wood.

Scantlings Wood of small sections and various lengths.

Scratch moulding Small moulding cut with a scratch stock, which has a cutter sharpened like a scraper.

Scribing Cutting a joint with one part of moulding fitted into the other, instead of mitring.

Scroll Carved shape like end view of loosely rolled paper.

Seasoning Drying wood to an acceptable moisture content.

Second growth Natural growth, often from stumps, after first trees are cleared.

Segments Curved pieces of wood used to build up table rails and similar things of curved form.

Scratch moulding

Shot joint

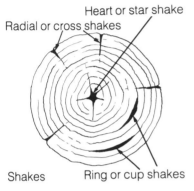

Heart or star shake
Radial or cross shakes

Shakes   Ring or cup shakes

Spiling

Spline

Set To punch a nail below the surface, or the tool with which this is done. The bending of saw teeth in alternate directions to produce a kerf wider than the thickness of the saw metal.

Setting out Laying out details of the whole furniture or a particular part of it.

Shooting board Device for holding wood when trimming its edge with a plane.

Shot joint Planed edges glued together.

Shoulder piece An extra bracket at the top of a leg extending under the rail or framing.

Shake A defect or crack that occurs in the growing tree, but might not be found until after conversion.

Skew Out of square or twisted.

Slabbing Squaring a log.

Slip Oil-stone with shaped sections, for sharpening inside hollow tools such as gouges.

Soffit The underside of a window or door opening.

Spandrel A shaped rail between the upright parts of a piece of furniture.

Spiling Copying a shape by using a pointed stick over a board at many positions, with the stick pencilled around and the positions repeated to transfer the shape.

Spindle Rounded slender part, usually vertical, as in a chair back.

Splat Central upright member in a chair back. Usually decorated by shaping, piercing or carving.

Splay To spread out.

Spline A narrow strip of wood fitting into grooves and strengthening two meeting faces that are glued.

Split turning A piece with semicircular section made by turning two pieces of wood glued together and separating them so that the half turning can be glued to a flat surface.

Spud A dowel at the bottom of a doorpost. A tool for removing bark.

Square turning Wood of square section, but with lengthwise shaping similar to a turned outline.

Star shake A defect in a tree shown as star lines radiating from the centre of a log.

Sticking Making moulding.

Stile The vertical part at edge of furniture framing to which rails are attached.

Stopped Not carried through, as in a stopped chamfer or rabbet.

Strap hinge Hinge with long narrow arms.

Strap work Carving that looks like interwoven crossing straps.

Stretcher A lengthwise rail between the lower parts of a chair or table.

Stuck moulding Moulding made in the solid wood, not planted.

Stud Vertical member in a partition or wall.

Surbase moulding A moulding placed between the cornice and plinth, on – for example – the table part of a bureau bookcase.

Swag Carved ornamental detail in the form of flowers or material suspended.

Strap hinge

Tang Pointed end of tool to fit in handle.

Tester The roof over a four-poster bed.

Thread escutcheon A metal liner for a keyhole.

Throating Groove under a projecting sill or similar member to prevent water running back.

Tote A handle (particularly on a plane).

Tread The horizontal part of a stair.

Trunnel (treenail) Peg or dowel driven through a joint.

Twist turning Spiral turning. Characteristic of Jacobean furniture.

Throating

Undercutting In carving, cutting under the design to give it emphasis due to the better shadow.

Upset Cross fracture in wood. May be natural or occur in felling.

Veneer A thin piece of wood that is usually of a decorative type and intended to be glued to a backing. If very thin and cut from a rotating log, it is cut with a knife. If it is not so thin it is cut with a saw.

Veneer pin Very fine nail with a small head.

Volute A spiral scroll in carving.

Twist turning

Wainscot This term means the panelling around a room, but it is also applied to quarter-sawn wood, such as oak, that shows figuring.

Waney edge The edge of a board that still has bark on it or is still in the pattern of the outside of the log.

Warping Distortion of a board by twisting or curving because of unequal shrinkage as moisture dries out.

Winding A board or assembled frame is said to be in winding when it is not flat and a twist can be seen when sighting from one end.

Working drawing The drawing showing elevation (side or end view), plan (view from above), sections and details from which measurements can be taken.

Part 2: HOME MAINTENANCE

Robert Tattersall

Chapter 1
ROOFS

Steeply sloping roofs – 'pitched' roofs – are the type from which rainwater drains most easily. They also cause snow to slide off before it overloads the structure. Pitched roofs, however, are expensive to construct, so it is standard practice on outbuildings such as home extensions to fit flat roofs; and even flat roofs are made to slope slightly, so that water can drain off.

Major roofing repairs are beyond the scope of the do-it-yourselfer, not least because of the hazards of working at heights. There are, however, many minor jobs that can be done safely.

GETTING UP THERE

Roofing work is not particularly difficult or skilled, but working high above ground can be extremely hazardous so do be cautious if you ever climb up to a roof.

Confidence comes only from working with the right tools and knowing exactly what you are doing. This applies equally to all types of job – not just those carried out at heights. If you are unsure of your competence, then opt out and employ a professional.

Provided you are careful, however, you should be safe. The appliances for access to a roof are: ladders, roof ladders, and access towers or proper scaffolding.

Ladders

Ladders made of aluminium are preferable to the traditional wooden ones. Aluminium ladders do not rot (unlike wooden ladders), so there is less risk of a rung collapsing under your weight. Even so, you should always examine a ladder before use to make sure it is sound. Aluminium ladders are also lighter, so are easier to carry around and less likely to topple as you position them.

When carrying a ladder, keep it vertical and securely supported by your body. Raising a ladder from the horizontal is easier if someone helps you. Ask your helper to place a foot on the bottom rung. Then, after lifting the other end,

1.1 *Jam a ladder under the sill of a door when you want to raise it.*

1.2 *The safe way to carry a ladder*

1.3 *At its foot, lash it to stakes in the ground.*

walk towards the helper, raising the ladder over your head as you go until it is vertical. If you have no one to help you raise it, jam the foot of the ladder against a wall, or under the sill of a door (Fig. 1:1). Lower a raised ladder in the reverse order.

Most right-handed people will find it easier to support a vertical ladder on their left side. To do this, extend your right arm to hold the rung just above your head, and curl your left arm round the other side to hold a rung just below waist level. If you find it easier to support the ladder on your right side, put the left hand above the head and the right hand below the waist (Fig. 1:2).

When positioning the ladder, make sure its distance from the bottom of the wall is at least a quarter of its height up the wall. If the ladder is extendable, stand on the ground, not on the ladder, while you extend it in two or three stages. Between stages, rest the hooks attached to the bottom of the upper section on to a rung of the lower section. Watch out that the top of the ladder does not hit any obstructions as you raise it. If you need to go higher than you can extend the ladder while standing on the ground, extend the ladder before raising it.

A rope-operated ladder can be extended fully while it is leaning against the wall. Grasp a rung of the lower section just above your head and pull the top of the ladder away from the wall. At the same time pull on the rope with the other hand. Some extending ladders have wheels at the top to make it easier to raise them when they are against a wall.

You must always raise a ladder sufficiently high to allow you to work in safety. It is dangerous to stand on the uppermost rungs, for you need something to hold on to. The fourth rung from the top is about as far as you should safely go. Also do not extend an extendable ladder too far. Allow at least a two-rung overlap on a 4 m (13 ft) ladder; three rungs on a 5 m (16 ft) one. If the ladder you own is not tall enough for the job in hand, hire one that is rather than risk serious injury just to save yourself a hire fee.

For access on to the roof, the ladder should extend beyond the eaves. Provided that they are sound, cast iron gutters will support a ladder, but in general plastic ones will not. In any event, a ladder can easily slip along a wet gutter, so the safest course is to fit ladder stays. These are metal or wooden brackets near the top of the ladder to support it on the wall away from the eaves.

Make sure the ladder is secure at the bottom. Ask a helper to keep it steady with a foot firmly placed on the bottom rung. If you do not have a helper, lash it to stakes driven into the ground (Fig. 1:3). If you are working near a front door you can pass rope through a letter box and tie it to a stick that cannot be pulled through (Fig. 1:4). On concrete, place sacking under the base of a ladder that does not have rubber feet or tie it to a heavy object; on soft ground, stand it on a board so that it cannot sink – otherwise there is a danger that one stile might sink farther than the other. Do not tie the ladder to the base of a drain pipe, which may not be fixed securely enough, and always make sure the ladder is standing evenly. On uneven ground, place a wedge under one foot.

1.4 *A ladder tied to a stick on the other side of the letter opening...*

Lash the ladder at the top, too. It is a good idea to fix stout, rust-proof ring bolts permanently just below the eaves (Fig. 1:5). Where a window has two opening sashes side by side you can tie a ladder to the transom (Fig 1:6).

To climb the ladder, hold the stiles not the rungs. Wear stout shoes with a good instep to support your weight and prevent you tiring quickly. If you have to carry only one or two small tools, wear overalls with pockets in which to put them, leaving your hands free to climb and work. But never put in your pockets sharp tools that could cause injury if you fell. Sharp tools or large numbers of items should be placed in a bag or bucket, which you hold well clear of the ladder in one hand, while gripping a stile with the other. Hook the bag or bucket, or a paint can, on to a rung while you work.

Never be tempted to lean out that little bit farther just to save yourself the trouble of climbing down and moving the ladder along: it is too dangerous.

1.5 *...to a ring bolt fixed permanently at the eaves...*

When you come down an extending ladder, be prepared for the misalignment of the rungs of the upper and lower sections, which can cause you to miss a rung and be thrown off balance.

Roof Ladders

To climb from the eaves and up the slope of a pitched roof you need a roof ladder. It is dangerous to dispense with this and walk across the roof, because you risk breaking the roof tiles and slipping off.

It is not easy to manoeuvre a roof ladder up from the ground. Probably the best way is to tie a rope to it, climb up the ordinary ladder, then, with a helper down below to guide it, haul it up. Aluminium roof ladders are easier to handle.

A roof ladder has wheels at one end, so you can push it across the tiles to the ridge. When it is there, you turn it over, and it hooks on to the ridge. You can also lash it at the base – to the top of the ordinary ladder, for instance, which must in turn be lashed securely. If you have any doubts about the security of the fixing of your roof ladder, do not climb it, but seek the advice of a professional.

1.6 *...and round the transom of a window frame.*

1.7 It is easier, safer and less tiring to work from an access tower.

Access Towers

Working from an access tower (Fig. 1:7) is much easier, safer and less tiring than from a ladder. It is, however, expensive to buy or hire an access tower, but the expense is easily justified for some jobs – when you wish to finish a job quickly in bad weather, for example, or to support large quantities of heavy material, such as bricks and mortar for a chimney stack.

Access towers are delivered as metal frames, which you lock together, without nuts and bolts, to form a rigid structure. A platform of boards is fitted, and toe boards should be used, too, so that tools and materials cannot fall over the sides. Various types of feet are available for the bottom frame. For example, you can have metal plates for grass or soft ground; or castors for easy mobility over firm ground; and for uneven ground, the feet can be adjusted to different lengths.

Before buying or hiring an access tower, ensure that it is tall enough for your use. In general, the maximum height available is only about 4.9 m (16 ft), although outriggers can be added to raise it to 6.1 m (20 ft). That gives a reach of about 8 m (26 ft). To the tower can be fitted a ladder with which you can climb on to a roof, and some can be built cantilevered, for instance, over an extension.

Some precautions are necessary when you work from a tower. If the base of the tower is of the usual size – 1.2 m (4 ft) square, and the tower is taller than 3.7 m (12 ft), it must be lashed to the house at the top. If the base is only 1.2 × 0.6 m (4 × 2 ft) the tower should be lashed in place when it reaches a height of 2.4 m (8 ft). Ensure that the tower is level and sits squarely on the ground. If it has castors, ensure that these are locked before you climb up. Never move a tower on which there are people or tools and materials.

Scaffolding

For some types of job there is no satisfactory alternative to scaffolding. Typical examples of such jobs are the renewal of a section of the roof, and the repair of a chimney stack high up on a gable wall. The need to erect scaffolding appears to place most roofing work out of the scope of the do-it-yourselfer.

In fact, if you have a relatively minor job to do that nonetheless requires scaffolding, it is probably better to employ professionals. If there is a large and costly job, which you think you have the skills to carry out competently and safely yourself, you might consider having the scaffolding erected professionally.

PITCHED ROOFS

Pitched roofs are normally clad with slates or tiles. Such roofs have to be strongly constructed to support the immense load of the slates or tiles as well as any snow that settles. Moreover, the roof is exposed to the wind, which can exert a large force in exposed areas.

1.8 *Types of roof: two-way pitched*

How they are built

There are two common shapes for a pitched roof. If the roof has just a simple slope on each side, meeting in a ridge like a tent, it is said to be two-way pitched (Fig. 1:8). The walls at the ends of a two-way pitched roof are the gable walls, and are often triangular in shape at the top. It is usual for the roof to project slightly beyond, and be supported by, the gable wall. The end of the roof is concealed behind bargeboards, which are nailed to the end rafters. The roof projection beyond the gable is the verge which shields the top of the wall from the rain.

1.9 *Hipped roof*

On some houses, the gable wall extends higher than the ridge. In such cases the gable is square at the top, capped off with a stone coping or rendering. This type of wall, against which a roof abuts, is an abutment wall. The other common type of roof shape is called a hipped roof (Fig. 1:9). It is formed when the roof has a third slope, rising from the end walls to the top like the side of a pyramid.

Some houses have both types of roof joined in one: for instance a house that is L-shaped in plan may have a two-way roof on one leg of the L, but a hipped roof on the other; a T-shaped house, too, may have hips at the two ends of the roof covering the top cross-member, but a two-way pitch at the end of the main T-section (Fig. 1:10); a hipped roof may have a dormer window with a two-way pitched roof; and there are other variations.

1.10 *Roof combining both types: two-way pitched and hipped*

Another type of pitched roof you may see occasionally is the mansard (Fig. 1:11). In this the pitch is at two angles – a gentle one at the top and a steeper one below, nearer the outer wall. Often, these roofs were designed to allow a room in the attic. They were, in fact, a cheap way of getting an extra storey, for the lower parts of such a roof are more easily and cheaply built than a brick wall.

Lean-to buildings, verandahs and porches often have a single-sloped roof covered by tiles and slates. These are known as mono-pitch roofs (Fig. 1:12).

1.11 *Mansard roof*

Traditionally, the frame for a pitched roof was built up on site by skilled joiners (Fig. 1:13). On pitched-roof houses built since about 1950, however, the triangular frame is of a trussed rafter construction. With these, the triangular frames are constructed as a whole in a factory, and brought to the

1.12 *Mono-pitch roof*

site looking much like giant coat hangers (Fig. 1:14). They are strengthened by lengths of timber known as trusses. The difference between a trussed frame and the traditional type is crucial if you ever think of building a loft extension. It is impossible to erect a room in an attic formed by trussed frames, for you cannot remove any of the middle trusses to clear a space for a loft conversion without seriously weakening the whole structure. It is possible, however, to remove sections from an older-style roof, provided that compensating support is added elsewhere. But the subject of loft conversions is complicated and you should never attempt it without expert advice.

Whichever construction method has been used, the frames are broadly similar. The lower member of the triangle is the joist, to the underside of which the ceilings of upstairs rooms are fixed. These joists are fixed to wall plates at the top of the main walls of the house. The two sides of the triangle are the rafters, and these are joined both to the wall plates and to the sides of the joists. At the top end, the rafters are joined to a horizontal length of timber known as the

1.13 *Traditional method of roof construction*

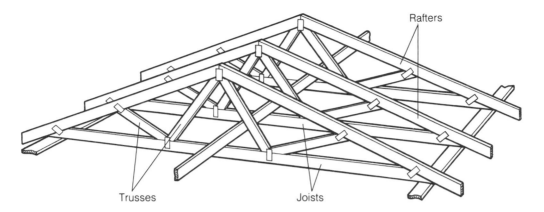

Rafters

Trusses

Joists

1.14 *Trussed rafter roof*

ridge board. Intermediate support for the rafters is provided by purlins, which are usually braced. Two methods of bracing are used. There may be struts supported on an internal load-bearing wall, or hangers fixed vertically to the joists and further strengthened by runners extending vertically between the hangers. The purlins may be notched into the rafters, or just bevelled to suit the angle at which they meet. (For general construction of a pitched roof, see Fig 1:13.)

The rafters project well beyond the eaves and are finished off by two lengths of timber. The one underneath the rafters is the soffit board, and the other – to which the gutters are fixed – is the fascia. Sometimes the eaves are left open. Never block off open eaves as a draught-proofing or insulation measure. They are left open to keep the loft well-ventilated and dry. Blocking off might encourage condensation, which will dampen and rot the roof timbers and saturate any loft insulation, rendering it ineffective. Houses built with blocked off eaves have compensating ventilation elsewhere.

Older houses often have a front external wall extended to form a parapet. This is sometimes topped with a stone coping. The parapet has a damp-proof course (see Chapter 3) two or three courses from the top to stop moisture being conducted from the parapet to the main walls of the house. In such instances, a gutter as such is not installed; gutter boards are used to form one artificially.

A parapet wall hides the roof from view. Often the roof behind it consists of two small pitched roofs which are joined to form a valley (Fig. 1:15), which serves as a gutter to collect water from the two inner pitches. The two parts of a valley roof do not need to be as high as would a single, pitched roof covering a house of the same size. This, with the fact that they are concealed behind a parapet, ensures that they are sheltered from some of the effects of the weather. An unfortunate consequence of the lower height, however,

1.15 *A valley roof*

is that there is not much headroom beneath them should you ever have to do work up there.

Slates and tiles

The slates and tiles on a pitched roof are fixed to a series of battens that extend across the rafters. It is good practice to fit felt underneath the slates, and this, too, extends lengthwise across the rafters. The felt is there to catch any moisture that gets through gaps in the tiles, and to prevent it from falling into the attic. It should sag slightly between the rafters to form a small shallow channel into which the water can collect and run away. The felt is held in place by the tiling battens, and where an overlap is required, it should be at least 75 mm (3 in) wide with the layer nearest the ridge covering the one on its eaves side. At the eaves, the felt should project beyond the tiles so that water running down it will be carried clear of the roof and into the gutter. Extra layers of felt are sometimes fitted into valleys and eaves.

For a very strong, waterproof construction the rafters may have first been covered with boards, either tongued and grooved or square edged. The felt is nailed to the boards, and tiling battens are fitted as usual on top of the felt. The expense of this type of construction makes it rare.

The tiles or slates overlap each other by an amount determined by the space between the battens. This spacing is a crucial part of the building design, so do not increase it for any reason. Usually the overlap is between 60 and 90 mm (2½-3½ in).

Slates are secured by nails, which should be of copper, aluminium or a non-corroding alloy, such as bronze. Never use ferrous nails; they are sure to rust. Two nails per slate should be used, preferably in the middle of the slate, so they are less likely to be levéred up and broken by the wind (Fig. 1:16). Moreover, it is easier to replace a centre-nailed slate if it does break, than one nailed at the top edge.

Nails are also used in fixing tiles, but there is no need to nail every one. Tiles have nibs that locate on the battens, and the weight also helps to keep them in place (Fig. 1:17). It is usual to nail only every fourth or fifth row.

It was once customary to fix slates and tiles to the battens by mortar, which also helped to seal the gaps between them. This process is known as torching, but it is now obsolete. You may, however, still see it on older houses. Never apply torching to a roof in which it is not already used.

Tilers usually start work at the eaves, where they lay two rows one on top of the other because this is where water is most likely to penetrate the roof. The double course projects well into the gutter, and it is lifted up either by the fascia board, or by a small triangular batten known as a tilting fillet,

1.16 *Slates are nailed to the roofing battens.*

1.17 *Tiles have nibs that locate on the battens.*

so that the tiles bed properly on the nails. Similarly a double course is laid on gable wall verges. Often the bottom tiles are bedded in mortar, and the gap between them and the wall is pointed so that high winds cannot get through and dislodge the tiles.

Ridges are usually finished off with V-shaped tiles, bedded in mortar, although dry fixing systems, which make use of metal clips and sealing strips, are being introduced. Sometimes a lead joint is applied. Similar tiles are used at hips. A piece of metal known as a hip iron (Fig. 1:18) is fitted to stop the tiles from sliding down the hip before the mortar has set. Valleys are lined with lead or zinc, or shaped tiles are fitted.

1.18 A string line from the hip iron to the ridge acts as a guide when you are fixing hip tiles.

Simple repairs to pitched roofs

As roofs are often out of view, we tend to think of them only when some defect shows, but you should check up on your roof from time to time. Perhaps you can get a good view of it from a neighbour's window or even from your garden or the road. Use a pair of binoculars to help you make a closer inspection. When you decorate the exterior of the house or maintain the gutter, take the opportunity to inspect the roof. Look for missing or cracked roofing tiles and slates, damage to the ridge or hip tiles and defects on the chimney stack. There might be some flaw letting in damp – which, though not showing through in the house below, is nevertheless attacking the structural timbers of the roof and attic, and could be causing rot that will lead to extensive (and expensive) repairs. Occasionally also you should look through the trap door to the attic for defects to the roof visible from the underside.

The roofs on some older houses are in such bad condition that re-roofing has become a major industry. Some slated and clay-tiled roofs built before 1939 are nearing the end of their period of usefulness. Many of the clay tiles with which houses in the 1930s were roofed are crumbling, due to weathering by water and frosts. Some slates too have started to delaminate. Many roofs were built with ungalvanized ferrous nails, which have started to corrode; the roofs are then suffering from what builders call nail fatigue.

When a roof deteriorates badly, complete renewal is the only option. Old slates can be replaced with new or second-hand slates, and clay tiles with new clay tiles. Concrete tiles are less expensive so they are more popular. A wide selection is available and you should be able to choose a style that suits your house. Re-roofing, however, is not a job for the do-it-yourselfer. You should employ a roofing contractor, having obtained at least three different estimates before placing your order.

1st coat

Membrane

2nd coat

3rd coat

1.19 *Sealing a leaky roof: (a) Brush on a waterproofing liquid then (b) bed the membrane firmly in it.*

There remain, however, many minor repairs that you can tackle. Often a damp patch on the ceiling is the first sign of trouble. Should this occur, inspect the roof both from above and from the attic to pinpoint the source of the leak. Remember that the position of the patch is only a rough guide, because the water might have seeped across the inner surface of the roof or along the top of a ceiling after dripping through the roof itself.

Sealing a leaky roof does not need to be an extensive or an expensive job. In some instances it can be achieved by brushing on a waterproofing liquid. In others a reinforcing membrane is bonded to the roof (Fig. 1:19). These systems are supplied by firms that specialize in damp repellents, and are stocked at DIY stores and builders' merchants. Usually full instructions are provided with the product.

These systems provide an effective barrier against porosity and can be useful in an emergency to provide a temporary seal. Against major defects such as corroded nails, or rot in the timber structure, however, they are ineffective. Even when they do seal a leak, they have the disadvantage that they are noticeable, and draw attention to the fact that you have a problem roof, which could be a drawback should you want to sell the house. Nevertheless when funds are tight and a roof is leaking, they can be a solution, although perhaps only a temporary one until you can afford a new roof.

Replacing a broken slate can be a straightforward DIY job. First remove the existing slate. It may be so loose that you can merely pull it away. If it is still held by nails, remove them with a slater's ripper (Fig 1:20). This is a long flat blade with a handle at one end and one or two hooks at the other.

Ripper

1.20 *Removing a broken slate with a slater's ripper*

Push the blade up under the slate and engage a nail with the hook. Give a short sharp tug, and the nail will break. Repeat the process for the other nail, if there is one, then you should be able to pull the broken slate clear.

You cannot nail the new slate into place, because the batten into which the nails should be driven is hidden under neighbouring slates. Secure the slate instead with a small clip, which you can make from a strip of lead, aluminium or copper about 225 × 25 mm (9 × 1 in). In the first instance, bend just one end of the metal, slip this end on the batten and fix it by driving a galvanized nail through it and into the batten below (Fig. 1:21). Take the new slate and ease it into place keeping it flat. When you are satisfied with its position, bend the end of the clip up and over it to hold it securely in place.

Metal strip

1.21 *First stage in forming the clip that will hold a replacement slate in place*

Replacing a broken tile is simple once you realize that roof tiles are held by slots or nibs in the tile which engage on the roof batten. Only every fourth or fifth row is nailed. If the tile to be replaced is not nailed, remove it by pushing a trowel underneath it, and lifting its nibs clear of the batten. Push the new tile into place under the surrounding tiles, engaging its nibs on the batten. Should it be nailed, loosen it with a tiler's ripper, as described above for slates.

Fitting underfelt

Many older houses do not have felt under the tiles or slates, so there is no second barrier to water or draughts that might penetrate the gaps between the slates or tiles. There is an improvised method for adding felt to the roof. It will not offer as good a protection as felt fixed before the slates were laid but it is well worth doing.

The method involves cutting strips of felt to go from ridge to eaves between the rafters. The strips should be just wider than the space between the rafters so there is a slight sag in the middle down which any moisture that collects can run. They should also project under the eaves so the moisture can drain into the gutter.

To fix the strips, nail or staple them to small-section battens, and screw the battens to the sides of the rafters. Use non-rusting materials throughout. If you cannot make up the strips from one length, so must use two pieces, allow a generous overlap of 150 mm (6 in) or more. The ends nearest to the ridge should be on top in the overlap!

Replacing ridge tiles

If a ridge tile becomes loose, it might slip out of place. Loosening can result if the mortar holding the tile has cracked, perhaps because of slight settlement of the roof, and water has got into the joint. Repairs should be carried out as soon as possible because the tile could slip further, or even be blown off in a high wind.

You can merely replace a loose or missing tile, but it is best to remove all the tiles and reset them. If one of the ridge tiles has been forced loose, there is a good chance that the mortar holding the others is weak. Since you have gone to the trouble of climbing up on the roof, taking tools and materials, you might as well do the job properly.

Using a hammer and cold chisel, chip away at the mortar holding the tiles. Remove the tiles and chip off the bedding mortar. Any tiles that are broken or cracked should be discarded. Shop around for second-hand tiles to match these and any that happen to be missing. If matching tiles are not available, it is probably as well to replace all the tiles. The appearance of the house is marred if all the ridge tiles do not match, because they are such a noticeable feature.

The tiles are bedded in mortar of three parts sharp sand to one part cement. Before laying the tiles, soak them in water so they will not absorb the moisture from the mortar and cause it to dry out too quickly with the consequent risk of shrinkage and cracking. Spread the mortar along the ridge, place each tile in position, and press it down on the mortar with a small trowel. Point the joins.

Some ridge tiles – the traditional pantiles, for instance – have an unusually large cavity. Do not fill this with mortar, because such a large amount of mortar might shrink and crack. Instead, fill the gap by mortaring in dentil slips, available at builders' merchants (tradesmen often use bits of broken tile for this purpose). Dentil slips should also be included in tiles at the verge.

Replacing hip tiles

The join where two pitches of a roof meet – the hip – is covered with hip tiles, which are similar to ridge tiles, and fixed in the same way. Any that are defective should be replaced as described for ridge tiles. The bottom tile, however, has to be cut at an angle on both sides to follow the line of the eaves, and is held in place by a hip iron. Make sure there is one on your roof, especially before you carry out repairs to the hip tiles. If not, replace it. It is screwed into the end of the hip rafter.

When replacing all the tiles on a hip, cut and fix the bottom tile first. Then stretch a string line from it to the ridge, so that all the tiles will be aligned (see Fig. 1:18). On a hip, just as on a ridge, deep profile tiles should be packed out with dentil slips.

Sealing verges

The mortar in the verge at the top of a gable wall can deteriorate and allow moisture to penetrate the roof. Fine cracks can be sealed with a mastic – the sort you squeeze out of a gun, for instance. If the mortar has deteriorated badly, chip it out and re-point. For repointing see Chapter 3.

Leaks in the valley

Leaks can develop in the valley – the internal angle where two roofs meet. The zinc or lead of which these are traditionally made can become porous or cracked. Seal cracks with a proprietary bituminous mastic, which is sold at DIY centres and builders' merchants. Spread the mastic to a thickness of 1.5 mm (¹⁄₁₆ in) and about 50 mm (2 in) beyond the crack on all sides. Cover the mastic with metal foil or thin roofing felt. Ensure the edges are well bedded-down in the mastic, and sealed by it. Cover with a further 1.5 mm (¹⁄₁₆ in) layer of mastic.

To make sure that no fine cracks have gone unnoticed, coat the whole length of the valley with a bitumen-based damp-proofing liquid, sold widely for such a purpose in builders' merchants and home improvement centres. A valley that is leaking because it is porous, but in which there are no cracks, should be treated with such a liquid.

If the valley has deteriorated beyond repair, replacement is a major job, probably best left to a professional. It involves stripping off the tiles or slates on each side, and taking out the old gutter. The timber supports underneath should be checked for signs of rotting and replaced as necessary, and any rusty nails should be replaced. Then the new valley is fixed in position.

A valley may also be formed from tiles, and these may need replacing from time to time. New valley systems, for professional installation, are also available from manufacturers.

Woodworm and rot

The cold, moist atmosphere of an attic is ideal for woodworm, which can infest the timber of the roof. Make periodic checks for signs of infestation. In particular, always treat any new timber you install with preservative.

Rot is usually more of a problem in the lower regions of the house, which are likely to be damper and less well ventilated. Should any of the roof timbers get wet, however, there is a risk of rot developing. Keep the roof in a good state of repair and well ventilated so the attic remains dry.

Wood that is badly damaged by worm or rot needs to be replaced, but beware of cutting out any of the structural

1.22 *Prise away the damaged fascia.*

1.23 *Offer up a new soffit board and mark where it should be fixed to the bearer.*

1.24 *Nail the new one in place.*

members of a roof without expert supervision. Techniques for dealing with woodworm and rot are discussed in Chapter 5.

Repairs to fascias and soffits

Just as with any other exterior woodwork, the fascias and soffits are likely to rot if they are not well maintained. Remove small areas of rot by chopping them out with a hammer and chisel, then fill them with an exterior-quality filler. Sand the filler when hard. Repaint the whole board, so the repair will not be noticeable.

If the fascia and soffits are in bad condition, they should be replaced. This involves removing the gutters, so a good time to do the work is when you intend to install new gutters and downpipes (see Chapter 2). You will need a helper, and scaffolding, which you can hire from a plant contractor.

The fascia and soffits (which often come in more than one length of board) are nailed into place. To remove them, prise them free with a lever, such as a crowbar or cold chisel (Fig. 1:22). Then remove the nails with a claw hammer or pincers.

If the joist and rafter ends and the soffit brackets are rotten, cut them back to sound wood and replace with new, otherwise you will not be able to get a firm fixing. Good timber need only be cleaned up, any old nails removed, and the holes filled with exterior-quality filler. Treat both old and new timber with preservative, then paint.

Cut the new soffit board to length and prepare it, then fix it in place with nails driven into the soffit brackets.

Where a run has to be made up from more than one length of board, you get a neater result if you use a mitre rather than a butt joint. Offer the board up into place, and mark on it the centre of the bearer to which it will be fixed (Fig. 1:23). Cut a mitre at this mark and in the next length of board so that the half-way point of the joint is at the centre of the bracket (Fig. 1:24).

The boards that make up the fascia are fixed next. As before, use mitred rather than butt joints where more than one length is needed. The fascia is fixed by being nailed to the rafter and the soffit (Fig. 1:25).

Punch home all nail heads, fill, then paint. The painting should consist of knotting, primer, undercoat, then two top coats. Parts that will be inaccessible once they are in place should be painted before they are fixed.

Bargeboards

Bargeboards that have deteriorated are replaced in the same way as fascias. The job is not so cumbersome, because there are no gutters to be removed and replaced.

Notice that the bargeboards are shaped at both ends – where they meet at the ridge and where they fit round the eaves. Use the old board as a template for marking out the new.

At the lower end of the bargeboard a shaped piece of timber is fitted. This is known as the tail piece. Use the old as a template for marking out the new, then fix with glue and screws or dowels.

1.25 A mitred end gives a neater fixing.

CHIMNEY STACKS

A chimney stack is installed to carry the flue from the fireplace well clear of the roof, so that the flue gases cannot be sucked back into the house. The flue lining continues up the stack and ends in a chimney pot, set in a bed of mortar, which is known as the flaunching. The chimney pot may be fitted with a cowl, which is necessary to prevent some types of chimney from smoking.

The stack could need re-pointing, which can be done as for other external walls (see Chapter 3). Just as any other wall that butts up against a roof, the chimney stack has flashing, which can be renewed as described later in this chapter. There are two defects, however, that are specific to a chimney: the flaunching might become badly cracked and chipped, causing damp to enter the structure; and the pot might become damaged.

Repairs to the flaunching

Chip off the old flaunching with a hammer and cold chisel. Make sure you remove all loose material – it often helps to brush the top of the stack with a wire brush. Take care, though, that nothing goes down the flue – you can cover the top of it temporarily as a precaution. Place the debris in a bucket, and lower it on a rope to the ground. If the chimney pot is to be dispensed with, tie a rope round it and lower it to the ground. Take care as you do this – the pot is heavier and much bigger than it appears from the ground. In fact, throughout this job it would definitely be desirable to have a helper on the ground to untie buckets and pots as they are lowered, to tie a new pot to the rope and to mix cement for you and shovel it into a bucket so you can haul it up.

Place the new or existing pot in position over the top of the flue, and brush water round its base so that it will not absorb moisture from the flaunching. The mortar should be a mix of 1 part of cement to 3 parts of sharp sand. Apply it with a trowel, building up from the edge to a depth of about 75 mm (3 in) round the pot. The flaunching should be smooth and shaped so that rainwater will drain away and not llodge there. Clean off any mortar that has stuck to the pot.

1.26

1.27
Slate bedded on mortar

1.26 *Lay a band of mortar round the top of the flue.*
1.27 *Cover the top of the stack with mortar, sloping it downwards from a high mid-point.*

Blocking off a chimney

If you are certain never to use the flue again, the top of a chimney can be blocked off. If you choose to do this instead of renewing defective flaunching or a pot, remove the flaunching and pot as already described. Clean up and dampen the brickwork at the top of the stack. Lay a 25 mm (1 in) thick band of mortar round the top of the flue (Fig. 1:26), and bed on it a slate big enough to cover the flue mouth. Now cover the whole top of the stack with mortar, sloping it from a high point in the middle down to the edges, so that water will run off (Fig. 1:27). Alternatively, fit a capping pot (available from builders' merchants).

A blocked-off flue requires ventilation at fireplace level, to prevent condensation forming inside and passing through the chimney breast to affect the decoration of the room. If the fireplace is left intact, it will give all the ventilation required. But should you decide to remove the fireplace and block off the opening, you must incorporate a ventilation grille.

FLASHINGS

The line where a roof meets a vertical surface, such as a wall or chimney stack, is a vulnerable spot and needs to be well sealed off to stop rainwater getting through. The usual method of doing this is with flashing. Lead is ideal because it is impervious to water yet easy to shape and bend. Recently, however, it has become expensive, so bituminous felt is often substituted.

The lead or bitumen is dressed into a mortar joint, and bent down to cover the tiles, the felt being sealed on to the tiles with mastic.

Repairs to flashings

The flashings for the main roof are intricate. Where a two-way roof meets an end wall, for instance, a stepped flashing is required to follow the slope of the roof. Much more complicated is the arrangement round a chimney stack, with an apron flashing on the lower side, stepped flashing on perhaps two others, a back gutter, and perhaps even soakers – small pieces of lead, copper, zinc, or bituminous felt used to weatherproof the joints between these or bituminous felt.

Given all these complications, and considering the difficulty of access, it is perhaps better to employ a professional when renewal is necessary, although you might feel confident about tackling the minor repairs. Renewing a straight, horizontal flashing, however, especially on the roof of a small lean-to building where access would be easy, is certainly much simpler.

For the new flashing you could use lead, but bituminous felt is less expensive. Remove the old flashing (Fig. 1:28), and rake out the mortar joint to a depth of about 25 mm (1 in) (Fig. 1:29). Clean the brickwork and tiles – a wire brush is suitable for this. If there is a small mortar fillet where roof and wall meet, inspect it for damage, and repair it if necessary, as described in the next section. Bend the flashing over then push it into the join and wedge it there (Fig. 1:30). Next bend it over the tiles, sealing it with mastic to stop it from curling. Then repoint the mortar joint.

You may prefer to use a proprietary flashing, which is sold in home improvement stores and builders' merchants. The method of applying such flashing strips varies, so always follow the manufacturer's instructions. These strips usually have a backing tape, which you peel off to reveal an adhesive. Some are in grey plastic, to simulate lead; others have an aluminium foil covering.

The fault in a flashing may not be so drastic as to call for complete renewal. For instance, the flashing itself may be sound, but the mortar in the joint might have deteriorated, causing the flashing to fall away. In that case, rake out the joint, put the flashing back into place, and re-point.

Cracks in an old flashing can be sealed with bituminous mastic. The method for doing this is as for dealing with cracks in a valley (see page 19).

Mortar Fillets

A mortar fillet is sometimes used instead of flashing, particularly where a party wall in a row of terraced houses extends beyond the roof line to form an abutment wall. The effect of the weather and perhaps settlement of the roof may weaken

1.28 *To renew defective flashing first take out the old.*

1.29 *Rake out the mortar joints.*

1.30 *Finally, fit the new.*

this fillet and cause it to crack or fall away from the wall. If
the fillet is in a bad state just here and there, repair it as
necessary with new mortar. Usually, however, the fact that it
has deteriorated in one place can be taken as a sign that the
whole lot may be ready to crumble. The best thing to do is
chip it all away with a bolster chisel and club hammer, and
renew it. Use a mix of three parts of cement to one of sharp
sand, and apply it with a small pointing trowel, or filler knife.
It is not easy to make the fillet as neat as the original builders
left it, but it is worth the effort to try.

The line between a wall and a new or old fillet can be
sealed with mastic applied with a gun.

INSULATING PITCHED ROOFS

About 20 per cent of the heat lost from the average house
goes through the roof. So while you are considering your
roof you should ponder on how well your loft is insulated. To
minimize heat loss, a thickness of 100 mm (4 in) or even
125 mm (5 in) of insulation in centrally-heated homes is today
more desirable than the mere 25 mm (1 in) that was recommended previously. If you insulate your loft or top up the
insulation already there you should recover your outlay, by
way of reduced fuel bills, in about a couple of years.
Although it is an unpleasant task carried out in cramped
conditions, doing it yourself will guarantee that the work has
not been skimped.

Loft insulation is available either in the form of a blanket
that is rolled out between the joists or a loose-fill material,
that you pour from a sack. Both types are equally effective,
but in an odd shaped loft with lots of nooks and crannies, it
can be quicker and easier to pour out a loose material than
to fit blanket. If you are starting from scratch use whichever
you wish. When topping-up, it is better to use the type you
already have.

Take care not to place any load – even a foot – on the
ceiling while you are in the loft, or it might break through. It
is a good idea to take a plank with you and stand on that.

Opinions vary about the clothes you should wear. Some
people believe that if you wear as little as possible, you can
take a shower afterwards and quickly wash away all the
scratchy fibres. Others say you should protect yourself with
long-sleeved shirts buttoned at the collar, trousers tucked
into socks and sleeves into gloves. In any event, you should
protect your hands with gloves, and wear a cap or something to cover your head.

Roll out the blanket, making sure it is well tucked down at
the eaves so that wind cannot blow underneath it. If you use
loose-fill, simply pour it into place. It is, however, surprising-

ly easy to misjudge the depth to which you have filled a gap, so make a gauge from a length of wood with a notch cut out of each end of the lower edge to form a T with a short stubby descender. The depth of this descender should equal the distance from the top of the joists to the required top of the insulation. Rest the cross-piece of the T on top of the joists, and drag it along to spread the granules to the correct depth.

A well-insulated loft is cold, so make sure the water pipes and tanks are well protected, either with lagging or, if the pipes are low enough, by laying the blanket over them and draping it on top of the tank. Leave the space under the tank clear, however, so that warmth can penetrate up to it from the rooms below, as a further aid to stop it from freezing.

One problem with attic insulation is that it can make the loft so cold that condensation develops and soaks the insulation, rendering it ineffective. Most lofts have sufficient ventilation to stop this from happening. If not, lay polythene under the insulation as a vapour barrier, or install ventilating grilles.

FLAT ROOFS

Flat roofs are usually covered with two or three layers of roofing felt. The top layer has embedded on it a covering of stone chippings, which may be added either at manufacture or during installation. The chippings reflect ultraviolet rays, which could damage the felt. Usually the first layer of the three layers of felt is laid lengthwise in the direction of the slope. The second layer is laid across, and the final one in the direction of the first. Some experts say it is better for all three layers to run lengthwise, provided the joins do not coincide (Fig. 1:31). To ensure that they do not, the roofer begins laying at one edge and works across to the other, where the final piece is cut to width. The second layer begins at this edge with a full-width roll until the first edge is reached, where the last piece will once again have to be cut to width. The third layer begins at the initial first edge, so the joins in this are kept apart from those of the first and second.

In two-layer coverings, the first usually goes across the slope of the roof, and the other one lengthwise. Alternatively, both can be laid lengthwise, using the method already described to ensure that the joins do not coincide.

The felt is laid on some form of decking, which can be made up of either planks (tongued and grooved or square-edged), exterior-grade plywood or chipboard, compressed strawboard, or a concrete screed on top of some other form of board. The decking is supported on rafters at centres

1st layer

2nd layer

3rd layer

Wall plate   Rafter   Decking

1.31 *Construction of a flat roof*

between 400 and 450 mm (16-18 in). Lengths of tapering small-section timber, called firring, are fixed to the top of the rafters to ensure the slope needed to allow the roof to shed rainwater. Insulation and a vapour barrier are incorporated in modern constructions. For general construction of a flat roof, see Fig. 1:31.

The rafters may be fixed in one of several ways. They can rest on, and be skew-nailed to, timber wall plates on the top of the external walls. Where the rafters meet a parapet wall, or where the walls of a lean-to join up with the house wall, the rafters can be fixed to a wall plate resting on a brick-work corbelled out of the main wall. They can be supported on a joist hanger, or let into a socket formed by the omission of bricks here and there. On extra-lightweight structures, such as garages and conservatories, they may merely be supported by wall plates bolted to the wall. As with pitched roofs, the ceiling is fixed to the underside of the joists.

Access to flat roofs

Flat roofs are often used on single-storey buildings. Reaching them is not much of a problem, and does not re-quire such equipment as access to a pitched roof. For in-stance, you might climb on top of a single-storey extension from a large stepladder. Nevertheless, where appropriate, all the safety precautions outlined at the start of this chapter should be observed strictly. The flat roof of, say, a modern town house may not seem as daunting as the slate-covered pitched roof of, for example, a turn-of-the century building, but do not be lulled into a false sense of complacency: a fall from a flat roof can be just as serious.

The equipment for reaching the flat roof of a house is the same as for a pitched roof: extending ladder or access tower. Roof ladders are not required, however, and complex scaffolding is seldom necessary, but you will need sturdy boards across the roof.

Mending flat roofs

Most repairs to flat roofs should pose few difficulties, but the complete re-felting of the main roof of a house is a big job and not one to be undertaken lightly.

1.32 To repair a bubble in felt, first make two cuts across it.

Just as with pitched roofs, you cannot assume that the source of a leak in a flat roof is immediately above a damp patch on a ceiling. Water can run a long way on top of the ceiling before finding a way down. Climb on to the roof to inspect it. The fault might be a local one. For instance, you could discover one or more thin cracks. Seal these with mastic sold for such a purpose at builders' merchants. If you notice bubbles, these are caused when moisture has penetrated underneath the felt and is warmed by sunshine. The moisture expands, and forces the felt upwards, forming the bubble. To remove a bubble, make two cuts across each other (Fig. 1:32), and peel back the four sections formed. Leave them for a short while to make sure all the moisture has evaporated, so this job should be done during warm weather. Bed the felt back in place in a bitumastic compound (Fig. 1:33). Press the cut felt down well, apply more compound on top, then sprinkle on a few chippings.

1.33 Peel back the triangles thus formed and bed them back in mastic.

Holes in the felt can be repaired, provided that you can get hold of offcuts of felt – by no means easy, because it is sold by the roll. Cut a piece of felt about 50 mm (2 in) bigger all round than the hole. Bed it in bitumastic compound, apply more compound on top, and add a few chippings (Fig. 1:34).

Leaky felt may bear no obvious signs of damage. In old faded felt, the likely cause of leakage is porosity which requires waterproofing. At its simplest this consists of the application of a waterproofing liquid, of the type supplied by the companies that specialize in damp-repellents. A more thorough treatment involves bedding a reinforcing membrane in the liquid. These materials are sold at builders' merchants and DIY stores.

1.34 To repair a hole in felt, cover with a felt patch, and bed it down in bitumastic compound.

Clean the roof thoroughly with a stiff brush. If there is any moss or lichen present, scrape it off and apply a fungicide. Ensure that no debris falls into a downpipe, for it might cause a blockage: to be sure, bung up the top of the pipes. Give the roof a close inspection for small cracks. If you spot any, treat them as already described, then carry out the waterproofing.

Re-felting a flat roof

To make sure you comply with local bye-laws, find out from your local authority what type of felt you should use and the fixing method (there are fire precautions as well as water-proofing considerations to take into account). Generally the procedure is to buy the felt in advance, cut it to size with a sharp knife, and let it lie flat for a day or two to uncurl. If you have the most common type of flat roof, one with a decking of planks, the old felt will be fixed with nails. Removing this will be a dirty job, so beware blocking the downpipes. Prise up the top layers of felt with a tough paint scraper, an old chisel, or a long-bladed knife. If you have any trouble, try a garden spade. Its sharp blade will probe under the layers, and the long handle gives plenty of leverage. The bottom layer is almost certain to be fixed with clout nails. Remove these with a claw hammer or a tack lifter (a tool that looks like a screwdriver, but with a V-shape cut in its blade) (Fig. 1:35). Once the nails have been removed, you should be able to lift the felt clear.

Inspect the timber decking for faults. You may have to replace missing nails – there should be two per board, per rafter. All heads, on old or new nails, should be punched well home.

Some of the boards may have swelled slightly, because water finding its way through the defective felt has soaked into them. If the swelling is slight, plane the board down flat. Where it is severe, the board may have to be replaced. Any boards that are damaged, or any areas affected by rot, should be removed and replaced. Treatments for rot are described in Chapter 5.

New wood should be treated with preservative; old wood may need this too. Do not use creosote, because this reacts adversely with the bitumen that is used both for the manufacture and the bonding of the felt.

On a flat-roofed lean-to, look at the flashing. If it is sound, roll it back carefully so that it can be re-positioned once the job is done. Should it be defective, remove it and install a new piece after the felt is in place.

The first layer of felt is fixed with galvanized clout nails (Fig. 1:36). Use 20 mm (¾ in) extra large-headed nails, spaced at 150 mm (6 in) centres. Begin nailing in the centre of each sheet and work outwards, to make sure that it lies completely flat and there are no air pockets, otherwise bubbling might occur later. Overlaps should be at least 50 mm (2 in) wide and here the nailing should be at 50 mm (2 in) centres.

Subsequent layers of felt are bonded in place. Professionals use a hot bonding method, but a do-it-yourselfer might

1.35 *Prise off top layers of felt with a paint scraper. Remove nails with a clout hammer or a tack lifter (inset).*
1.36 *Fix the first layer of felt with clout nails.*
1.37 *Apply the mastic to the roof, and roll felt on to it.*
1.38, 1.39 *Finish off the edges with welted aprons.*

Clout nail

prefer a cold bonding method, using a suitable mastic adhesive sold at builders' merchants. Each length is stuck down in two halves. With the length laid flat in position on the roof, take one end, and roll half back on the other half. Apply the mastic to the roof, and roll the felt back, carefully bedding it into position (Fig. 1:37). Work from the centre outwards to all edges to make sure no air pockets are trapped underneath. Now roll the second half back on this first one, apply adhesive to the roof and stick the felt down in position, using the same method. Carry on in this way with subsequent lengths, until the roof is covered.

The cap sheet, as roofers call the top felt, is fixed similarly. Make sure, though, that the joins do not coincide, as described in the introduction to this section.

The edges are finished off with welted aprons (Figs 1:38, 1:39). The apron at the eaves needs to project well into the gutter so that rainwater will be thrown well clear of the structure.

Do not try to economize by cutting these aprons across the width of a roll. Cut along the length so that the material folds easily.

Finish off by bonding chippings at the rate of 100 kg per 5 sq. m (122 lb per 9 sq. ft) of roof. The chippings should be about 13 mm (½ in) across and can be of limestone, granite, gravel, or calcinated flint. Do not skimp on these, for the sun will damage the felt if you do.

Other deckings may have been used on a recently built flat roof. Plywood or chipboard is treated in the same way as planks. Where other materials are used, however, some points are worth noting.

Joints between sheets of compressed strawboard need to be sealed by tape. If, when you remove the felt, you find that the tape has been damaged, you should renew it. The tape, which is 100 mm (4 in) wide, is sold at builders' merchants.

The surface of the board should be clean, dry and free from dust. Seal it with a special primer; do not fix this board with clout nails. Instead, nail the first layer with aluminium serrated nails; or bond it in the way described for the top two sheets on a plank decking. Top layers are bonded in this way.

A concrete decking needs a thorough brushing to remove any bits that are loose, and any holes or depressions should be filled. For this you can use an exterior-grade filler, or a sand and cement mix. The concrete should then be treated with a primer, which will be sold at the outlet where you buy the roofing felt. This seals the surface and ensures good adhesion. When the primer is dry, you can fix all the layers of felt by the cold bonding method already described.

Insulating flat roofs

Insulating flat roofs can present a problem if the insulation provided by the original builder is no longer satisfactory. It is difficult to remedy the situation because, unlike pitched roofs, flat roofs have no accessible loft you can insulate.

You can fix tiles to the ceiling, but these have only a limited effect. In severe cases the only course of action is to construct a false ceiling below the present one (see Chapter 8) and pack insulation between the two.

Should it ever be necessary to carry out major repairs that involve the lifting of decking, you should take advantage of the opportunity to insulate between the rafters.

GLASS AND PLASTIC ROOFS

Besides the materials already discussed in connection with pitched and flat roofs, there are various kinds of glass and plastic roofs.

Conservatories, verandas and many types of lean-to often have glass roofs. For purposes of repair and maintenance, these are generally treated as though they were horizontal or sloping windows. Such roofs are prone to excessive heat loss, and they promote condensation. In fact, the condensation can be so severe – with water dripping down continually – that it is sometimes difficult to distinguish between condensation and a leak. The best way to be sure is to observe when it happens. Leaks will occur only during rain; condensation can happen during cold, dry, as well as wet, weather. To carry out a diagnosis in warm, dry weather pour a little water on the suspect spot and see if it comes through.

Besides replacing the roof, there is little that can be done about the condensation, or the lack of insulation. In any event, such glass structures have undoubted advantages, and are part of the period charm of older houses.

Leaks can be cured. Keep the putty in good condition. It and the glazing bars should be well painted. Make sure the paint goes beyond the putty and on to the glass by 3 mm (⅛ in) in a neat line all round to effect a good seal. If leaks persist, a tape is available to seal off the joins between glass and frames.

Be wary of climbing on to a glass roof. Usually the glazing bars are simply not strong enough to support a person's weight. Place scaffold boards, which you can hire, across the roof so that they rest on the wall of the structure at each end. If the strength of the wall is in doubt, the scaffold board should rest on a large stepladder at each end. Take care not to overbalance, or step off the plank.

Even if the roof is strong enough to support you, do not put your weight on the panes of glass.

Corrugated plastic

The roofs of many home extensions designed as sun rooms and conservatories, but not intended as habitable rooms, are covered with corrugated plastic. This is a long-lasting material, but leaks can develop.

1.40 *Fixing corrugated plastic*

Physical damage to the plastic can be caused by heavy objects being thrown or blown on the roof during a gale. A heavy fall of snow cascading from the main roof could also cause cracks. If this occurs, take off the damaged sheet and replace it with a new one. Take a little of the old sheet with you when you go shopping to make sure the profiles match exactly. When fitting the new sheet, remember that each should overlap its neighbour by two corrugations, and that overlaps between the ends of sheets should be at least 150 mm (6 in) (Fig. 1:40).

Sealing washers may be defective. The sheets are fixed to wooden rafters with screws or nails, or to iron rafters with clips. Such fixtures should have a nail cap and a rubber or plastic washer between the head of each nail and the sheet, to stop the rain getting through (Fig. 1:41). These may have deteriorated, or might never have been fixed in the first place. Replace any defective washers; install them where

1.41 *Fixing nail, with cap and washer*

they are missing. You can buy replacement caps and washers, as well as nails if these need renewing.

The flashing may have come adrift from the wall, or be defective. You may be able to re-fix loose flashing back in the mortar joint as described in this chapter. If the flashing is defective, buy and fit a replacement. Flashing specifically for corrugated materials is available.

Support for the sheets may be insufficient, in which case they can buckle, causing gaps through which rainwater can penetrate. The only remedy is to provide extra support, and replace the affected sheets.

Chapter 2
GUTTERS AND DOWNPIPES

Gutters and downpipes, known collectively as 'rainwater goods' (Fig. 2:1), need to be kept sound and free of obstructions, otherwise house walls can become soaked and the structure damp. The ground can become waterlogged, leading to damp in the foundations as well.

MATERIALS

Traditionally rainwater goods have been made of cast iron, which is a strong, tough material. It is also durable if its tendency to rust is checked. Unfortunately, frequent preparation and repainting is tedious and expensive. In any event, you cannot paint the insides of downpipes, which are just as liable to rust as the outsides, and eventually, cast iron rainwater goods disintegrate under the attack of corrosion. Cast iron has the added disadvantage of being heavy and awkward to handle during installation. In the 1940s asbestos was sometimes used, but proved impractical. Today, rainwater goods are invariably made of plastic.

Plastic rainwater goods are made from upvc (unplasticized polyvinyl chloride). The material is light and easy to handle. It does not corrode or deteriorate from weathering, and it requires very little maintenance – you can choose whether or not to paint it. In fact, provided upvc goods are not damaged physically they are virtually everlasting.

MAINTENANCE

Cast iron rainwater goods should be kept well painted to contain corrosion. Remove rust by rubbing with emery paper or a wire brush (a wire brush on an electric drill is a useful aid). Another method is to apply a proprietary chemical rust remover.

Loose or flaking paint should also be removed by scraping or wire-brushing, or with a chemical stripper. Never use a blowlamp on metal – the heat will force it to expand and damage could easily result. If you are working on a bare metal surface, the first coat put on after cleaning should be a

Union seal   Gutter

Outlet union

Swan's neck

Gutter bracket   Union clip

Downpipe bracket   Hopper head

Angle piece

Downpipe   Downpipe clip

Bend

Branch   Stop end

Shoe

2.1 *Components of a typical gutter and downpipe system*

metal primer. On previously painted cast iron, spot prime any bare patches. Then follow with an undercoat, and two coats of top-quality gloss. Do not neglect the inside of the gutters – the part of the system most at risk. Clean out thoroughly, remove any rust, then treat with a bituminous sealer.

There is a tendency to skimp on painting the back of drainpipes. These areas are out of sight, hard to get at, and difficult to treat without getting paint on the house wall. Do not just ignore the problem, however, for the backs of pipes are just as likely to corrode as the fronts. To avoid defacing the wall, protect it with a small sheet of hardboard or card while you paint.

If yours is one of the rare houses with asbestos rainwater goods, then take care because the material is a health hazard. I suggest that you contact your local council's Building Control Department for advice.

Plastic rainwater goods require little maintenance. If you wish to paint previously unpainted ones, apply an all-surface primer, followed by an undercoat, then one or two top coats of gloss. If they are already painted and are in good condition, one or two coats of gloss will do. Flaking paint can be removed with a chemical stripper. Never use a blowlamp on plastic goods.

CURING FAULTS

Various problems can develop with a rainwater disposal system. These are the more common ones.

Overflowing gutters

One of the commonest reasons a gutter overflows is that it has become blocked, perhaps by dirt, leaves (in the autumn) or a bird's nest (in spring). The solution is straight-forward – look for and clear the blockages. If the gutter is of cast iron, clear it with a garden trowel – its rounded shape will fit the inside of the gutters better than a bricklayer's trowel. For plastic gutters, make a half-round scoop in hard-board. If you are working near the outlet to a downpipe, block it off with a rag bung to prevent debris falling down to cause a blockage there. Scoop out the blockage from the gutter, and shovel it into a bucket suspended from one of your ladder rungs.

Flush the system through with buckets of cold water, and then clean out the insides of the gutters with an old brush or a cloth.

There is not much you can do to prevent a recurrence of the trouble. Atmospheric dirt will fall on the roof and, during a downpour, wash down into the gutters. If the house is surrounded by trees, however, it might be worth fitting net-ting on top of the gutters, to keep out falling leaves.

Another possible cause of an overflow is that a section of the gutter may have sagged, making it lower than the top of the downpipe, so that water cannot flow away. A pool of water in the gutter at one place is often a sign that the gutter is sagging there. On iron gutters, try to bend the brackets upwards to restore the correct slope. Otherwise drive small wooden wedges between the bracket and the guttering to achieve the same effect (Fig 2:2). Fill the gap with the aid of a glass fibre repair kit if you wish. Take care not to flex cast-iron guttering by more than about 25 mm (1 in), or you risk breaking the seal at the joints.

With plastic guttering, it is usually better to re-fix the brackets slightly higher up. Make sure you plug up the old screw holes to stop moisture entering the wood.

In either case, a new bracket might be necessary.

Leaking joints

Water may be escaping where two lengths of guttering join. Sections of cast-iron guttering overlap each other slightly, and are fastened together by a nut and bolt, the joint being sealed by a waterproof mastic. The joint can deteriorate because of age or movement. If it has, it will have to be re-made from scratch. Begin by unfastening the nut and bolt.

2.2 Wedging up a sagging gutter

2.3 *To repair a leaky joint in cast iron gutters, first remove the bolt (e.g. by sawing) that holds the sections together.*

2.4 *Scrape away the old sealant.*

2.5 *Apply new sealant and fit a new nut and bolt with washers.*

That will not be easy because they would have corroded. Try to free them with penetrating oil, but usually you will have to cut through the bolt with a hacksaw, and perhaps drill out the remains of it (Fig. 2:3). Sometimes you can knock out the stub of the bolt with a hammer, but be careful not to strike the iron with too much force, for it can shatter dangerously. Lever the two sections apart, using an old chisel or screwdriver, and scrape away all the old sealant (Fig. 2:4), cleaning up finally with a wire brush. Apply a bed of sealant to the lower of the two overlaps, bring both together and fit a new nut and bolt, with a washer on each side (Fig. 2:5). Wipe up any sealant that oozes out. Treat the inside of the joint, or even a longer stretch of the gutter if need be, with a bituminous sealer.

Plastic sections lock together in various ways, according to brand. Some have a self-locking seal; others are welded together by solvents. Examine their joint to determine the method of sealing. Renew a failed seal with non-setting mastic, or apply fresh solvent to a loose, welded joint.

Leaks in gutters

The middle of a section of plastic gutter is unlikely to leak unless it has been damaged physically. Mid-section leaks usually occur on cast iron when the metal has rusted through. What you do about it depends on the extent of the damage. Repairs can be carried out with waterproof tape, or even a glass fibre repair kit. Such a leak, however, might indicate extensive rusting and that complete replacement of the section is required.

Damaged guttering can be replaced with a plastic section, even if the existing gutters are of cast iron.

Remove the defective section of guttering by dismantling the joints as explained above. If it is cast iron, take care how you get it to the ground. It can easily shatter, causing dangerous fragments to fly everywhere. Either fasten a rope to it and lower it gently, or carry it down. Always keep children and pets well out of the way when you are taking down old cast-iron rainwater goods. New plastic guttering can be cut to the correct length, if necessary, using a sharp fine-toothed saw, such as a hacksaw or carpenter's panel saw.

Adapter joints can be bought to connect plastic to cast-iron guttering. Since your present gutter is defective, it is likely that the brackets need replacing too. Buy new ones and fix them at the spacings recommended by the manufacturer. Your supplier should have leaflets giving such information. More detailed instructions on fitting new guttering are given later in this chapter.

Blocked downpipes

The dirt and debris that causes trouble in the guttering can also block downpipes. You will know there is a blockage when you see water standing in the gutter near the top of an outlet to a downpipe, or leaking from a joint between sections of downpipe.

To clear a blockage, push it through with a long stick or cane. In stubborn cases, tie a wad of rags to the end of the cane to make a sort of plunger.

On simple, straight runs of downpipe (such as on a garden shed or garage, or even a simple one-storey home extension) that end in an open gully, push the cane through while the pipe is still fixed to the wall. Make sure you cover the gully so that the blockage is not pushed there to cause more trouble.

Downpipe runs on houses tend to be more complicated. For instance, there are offsets – or 'swan's necks' – that take the pipes under the eaves of the house and there are bends and curves elsewhere. To clear curved pipes, you will have to dismantle them, but that does not mean taking down the whole pipe. The joins between sections of downpipe are unsealed so that you can tell at a glance in which section a blockage has occured. If rainwater pours out of a joint, then it is certain that a blockage lies below the joint.

Even a straight run may end in a sealed connection, and a blockage pushed down it would enter the drains, perhaps causing a blockage there, where it would be more tiresome to clear; so these pipes, too, should be dismantled for clearing. Remove the section of pipe from the two clips or brackets holding it in place. It should then be easy to poke through the stick or cane to remove the debris. Clean the pipe thoroughly by pulling through a rag wad tied to the end of a length of rope. To prevent further blockages cover the top of the pipe with a wire dome.

Leaks in downpipes

Small cracks or holes can appear in cast-iron downpipes because of rust. They can be repaired with waterproof tape, or a glass fibre repair kit. Holes in plastic goods should come about only because of damage, and they can be mended in much the same way. A section of downpipe – or indeed the whole run – may be so badly damaged, however, that replacement is the only course.

Damaged downpipes should be replaced with plastic. You should have little difficulty in joining up the new pipe to the existing outlet from the gutters. Take down the existing pipes from the bottom, working upwards, and fit the new ones from the top, working downwards. Details for installing new rainwater goods are given later in this chapter.

FITTING A NEW SYSTEM

Eventually, a cast-iron rainwater disposal system can become so corroded that the only course is to remove it completely and fit a new one. Installing a new system is not beyond the scope of a competent handyman. Try to finish the job as quickly as possible because, for a time, your home will be without the protection of gutters and downpipes. The work might take a do-it-yourselfer a few days.

Planning the new system

Plan the new system before ordering materials, and have all the components you will need to hand before taking down the old system. Study the instructions, both those given in this chapter and those in the manufacturer's manual. This way you will minimize the time when the house is without the protection of a rainwater disposal system.

Decide on the shape of the new rainwater goods. Plastic ones are available in the normal half-round, as well as square (although it is not exactly so) and ogee profiles. There is also a semi-elliptical shape that is deeper and more efficient than the half-round (Fig. 2:6).

Adaptors are available for connecting new plastic to neighbouring old cast-iron gutters if necessary. Should your system be on the point of collapse, then it is likely that your neighbour's is in a similar condition. Two or more of you might get together to renew a joint system at the same time. This would speed up the whole process, and reduce its cost.

Next, you must determine the size of the gutter from lip to lip. Three common ones are 75 mm (3 in), for extensions and outbuildings; 100 mm (4 in) for normal ,sized houses; and 150 mm (6 in) for larger house roofs. Ensure you buy the right size: too small, and it will not carry the rainwater away properly; too large, and you have spent more money than necessary.

Working out the amount of rainwater that will fall on a roof of a given size, and from that determining the size of gutter required to carry it away, requires the skill of an architect or surveyor. You can, however, simply specify the same size as the present one (assuming that it performs satisfactorily).

Finally, determine what components you need. Choose a brand that can be bought from a store near your home. Bearing in mind what your chosen manufacturer can supply, inspect the present system and try to buy a plastic equivalent. The guttering consists of one or more openings – called outlets – to connect up to the downpipes; a stop at the end of the run (if necessary); angles to take the guttering round corners; joints; support brackets; and the guttering itself, which will probably come in standard lengths.

Choose downpipes that are the same brand as the gutters,

2.6 *Possible profiles for new gutters*

and be sure to use a matching size. Besides the pipes there are the clips; the brackets; the offset, or 'swan's neck', that takes the pipe under the eaves or under or round some other obstruction; and some means of feeding the water into the drain – a shoe for an open gully, an adaptor for the connection to a closed drain. There may also be a hopper head if waste pipes in an upstairs room – the bathroom, for instance – discharge into a pipe.

Removing the old system

Dismantling the old system might take longer than you had imagined, so allow ample time when you plan the work.

Begin by removing the downpipes – start at the bottom and work upwards. The pipes should be in sections, joined by clips or brackets and screwed to plugs in the wall or the mortar joints. At the bottom will be a shoe or adaptor for directing the water into the drain. Pull out the pipes, and remove the brackets. If these are so corroded that you cannot move their fixing screws, cut through them with a hacksaw then prise out any short stubs left in the wall. Do not worry about damaging the metal, because it is only fit for scrap. Take care, though, not to damage the walls.

Most older houses, other than those with a single-stack plumbing system, have a soil pipe to carry waste from the lavatory. Do not confuse this with the rainwater downpipes. It should be dealt with entirely separately (see Chapter 11). To distinguish between the two notice that a soil pipe projects much higher than the gutters so noxious fumes and smells are carried well away from the house, and the joins between sections are sealed for the same reason. Moreover, you should be able to see where the outlet from the lavatory connects with the soil pipe.

Dismantle and remove the drainpipe in sections. Remove the fixing brackets next. Usually, these are screwed to the fascia, but occasionally you may come across gutters held in brackets fixed to the rafters of the roof. In either case, withdraw the screws with a screwdriver. It is likely that the screws have corroded, so removal is not easy. In that case, one of the methods suggested (on page 83) for loosening screws in door hinges may work. As a last resort, cut away as much as possible with a hacksaw, and prise out, with pincers or a claw hammer, any piece that remains in the timber, taking care to cause as little damage as possible.

This is a good opportunity to examine the fascia, for any signs of damage, and to carry out any repairs. You might be surprised to discover how much of the wood you have missed when painting behind the gutter. Take this chance to repaint thoroughly. Brush away all dirt and cobwebs and fill all holes and cracks through which damp might enter the wood. Remove any loose or damaged paint, wash down and rinse; then brush a primer over bare spots. Cover knots and other resinous areas with knotting, followed by an undercoat and two top coats of gloss.

Installing a system

A manual containing detailed instructions for installation can be obtained from a supplier or manufacturer. The general procedure is to install the gutters first – all else will be governed by the position of the outlets to the downpipes. To pinpoint this position, drop a plumb line from the gutter to the drain outlet at ground level. Then mark on the fascia the centre of the position for the outlet.

At the end of the run, fix a bracket to support the guttering as close as possible to the underside of the felt projecting from beneath the tiles or, if felt is not fitted, as close to the tiles as possible. Tie string to this bracket and stretch it taut to the position of the outlet. Use a spirit level to ensure that the string is level, then slant the string to give the correct fall (Fig. 2:7). This will be specified by the manufacturer, but it should be about 5 mm ($\frac{1}{5}$ in) for every metre (40 in) of gutter run. Mark the position and fit the brackets to support the outlet. Now fit all the other brackets in that run. Two brackets are usually needed for the outlet, plus one at each join and at the spacing recommended by the manufacturer, which is likely to be one bracket about every metre (40 in). Use the string, tied taut to a bracket at each end of the run, as a guide to setting all the intermediate brackets at the correct height, and mark the positions at the correct spacing on the fascia. Use non-rusting screws for the fixings. The brackets are normally screwed to the fascia, but if there is none, brackets for screwing to rafters can be bought.

Now fit the gutter to the brackets. Use a sharp, fine-toothed saw (a hack saw or a carpenter's panel saw) to cut standard lengths to size. The gutter should be cut squarely across its length. To ensure this, place it upside down on the bench and drape a sheet of newspaper over it. Bring the two edges of the newpaper together, and use the side of it as a guide for the saw (Fig. 2:8), or draw a guide line next to the newspaper. Remove the swarf with a medium-grade file. Fit the gutter to the stop end and outlet. On some brands this is done with clips; others use a sealing device, or solvent welding. If two lengths are to be joined to make a run of suitable length, follow the manufacturer's instructions. Leave gaps within the joints to allow for expansion or contraction during hot or cold weather.

When all the gutters are in position, install the downpipes. These are usually assembled from one or more standard lengths and are cut to size. As with the gutters leave expan-

Detail of downpipe clip

sion gaps. The pipes are held to the wall by clips (Fig. 2:9). Place a clip at each join, where provision will be made for the expansion gap, and at intervals as recommended by the manufacturer – probably every 2 m (6 ft or so). There is no need to drill into brickwork to make the fixings. The weight they carry is minimal, so fixings into mortar joints are adequate. Cut the pipes to lengths that allow such a fixing. Cut the pipes as described for gutters. Do not seal the joints: should a blockage occur later, water issuing from a joint helps to detect its position.

To take the pipes under the eaves, you need an offset or 'swan's neck'. Either buy one or make it from an offcut of pipe, an offset socket and an offset spigot. Seal also the joint between the gutter outlet and the offset socket, but not that between the spigot and the rest of the downpipe. Joints in pipes that are not vertical should be sealed, otherwise water will pour out of them regardless of whether there is a blockage farther along.

Position the fixing clips so that the main runs of the pipe are vertical. When the clip holding the offset spigot is in place, drop a plumb line from it to help you mark on the wall an accurate position for the clips lower down.

2.7 *Use a spirit level and string to get the correct fall between brackets.*
2.8 *Use a sheet of newspaper as a cutting guide.*
2.9 *Downpipes are held to the wall by clips.*

If the downpipes discharge into an open gully, install a shoe at the bottom (a clip will be needed here, too) pointing away from the house wall and no higher that 50 mm (2 in) above the grating of the gully. This ensures that water will enter the shoe and not splash up against the house wall. If an adaptor is needed for a direct connection to the drain, buy one from a supplier's catalogue.

As a final check, pour a bucket or two of water in the gutters at the highest point to make sure everything is functioning correctly.

Chapter 3
EXTERNAL WALLS

CONSTRUCTION

External walls can be of cavity or solid construction. Cavity construction is by far the better of the two in that it ensures a warmer, drier building. All homes built before 1914, and many built between 1914 and 1945, have solid walls, however. The only way to determine which type a house has is to measure the thickness of its walls at window or door openings, for the dimensions of cavity and solid walls are different. In taking such measurements, always remember to allow for the thickness of the internal plaster or any other internal or external wall cladding.

The foundations

The exact nature of the foundations will depend on the size and construction of the building, and the nature of the sub-soil. The most common type for small buildings is known as the strip foundation, which is used where the soil is firm. It consists of a trench all round the perimeter of the house, filled with concrete in the case of modern homes, or with bricks or stone in older houses. The trench serves as a 'footing' on which the external walls rest. In older houses the walls may be thicker, or stepped at their base.

Similar, though less substantial, foundations are also constructed to support internal walls and the 'sleeper' walls – brick walls or piers only a few courses high – that provide intermediate support for the joists of a suspended timber floor.

On soft, sandy soil the foundation may be one large concrete raft, with an extra-deep perimeter and a central spine or spines to support internal walls. Such a raft may also be placed inside strip foundations to support internal and sleeper walls.

The substructure of a house needs to be extremely well ventilated to keep it dry and free from rot. For this reason air bricks are placed low down in external walls; below the ground floor, and internal and sleeper walls are built honeycomb fashion – bricks are left out here and there – so that air can circulate freely. It is most important that the

ventilation holes are not blocked, otherwise you risk introducing damp into the foundations. If you see airbricks covered – either accidentally by, for instance, garden rubbish,
or deliberately in a misguided attempt to stop draughts –
unblock them immediately.

Cavity walls

A cavity wall consists of two separate walls, or leaves, each
the width of a single brick, with a 50 mm (2 in) space in
between. A leaf built today would be 100 mm (4 in) thick,
whereas one built before metrication would be 113 mm
(4½ in). The gap not only stops rainwater that might penetrate the outer leaf from soaking through to the inner one,
but also provides a cushion of air that acts as an insulating
material (Fig. 3:1). When cavity wall insulation is installed, it
is this gap that is filled.

To make the whole construction stronger, the two leaves
are held together by wall ties, which are bedded into the
mortar on both sides. The ties are galvanized so they do not
rust, and may be of wire, or of flat metal twisted so that any
moisture collecting on them will be thrown off and not carried across the cavity.

When carrying out any work on a cavity wall that involves
drilling or cutting through one of the leaves, it is essential not
to allow any debris to fall into the cavity. It might lodge on
one of the wall ties and collect in a pile, where it could cause
a bridge that might introduce damp into the inner leaf. This
is often the cause of a puzzling case of damp in the upper
parts of a cavity wall.

Lightweight aerated concrete blocks, and building blocks
made from clinker or clay, are used increasingly for the
inner leaf. These are cheaper and better at conserving heat.

3.1 *How a cavity wall is built*

Solid walls

Solid walls are usually as thick as the length of a brick, about 230 mm (9 in), although some houses have what are known as 'brick-and-a-half' walls, giving a thickness of about 345 mm (13½ in). In three- or four-storey houses, the lower floors may be 'brick-and-a-half' and the upper ones single brick.

A solid brick wall offers only limited protection against the weather, because rainwater can soak through it to the plaster and the decorations. It is also a poor insulator, but can be improved by a cladding of tiles or timber.

If your home has solid walls without cladding it is a worthwhile addition - for insulation and appearance. To add tiles, fit horizontal battens by screwing them into wall plugs, using brass or other non-rusting screws (Fig. 3:2). Then fix the tiles to the battens with galvanized nails. The battens should be spaced to allow a generous overlap on the tiles.

Timber cladding is fixed in a similar manner, but needs fewer fixing points – battens spaced at about 900 mm (3 ft) would be adequate. Both battens and cladding should be treated with a preservative.

REPAIRS TO BRICK WALLS

Many homes have bare brick walls, in which various faults can develop.

Efflorescence

Efflorescence is the name given to a white powdery substance that can appear on the surface of a wall. In modern homes it is nothing to worry about: it is simply caused by the

3.2 *Tiles cladding an external wall:*
(a) The tiles are nailed to battens.
(b) Detail, where the tiles meet the top of a window opening (c) Plan view showing how tiles meet the side of an opening.

salts in the brickwork drying out and crystallizing as they come to the surface. Eventually it will go away of its own accord, but if its appearance bothers you, remove it with a stiff brush. On no account use water, for that will only make matters worse by slowing up the crystallizing process.

On old walls, an outbreak of efflorescence could mean that the wall has suddenly become damp, so look for and remedy the cause.

Crumbling bricks

On a house built of soft brickwork, the face or edges of some bricks can begin to crumble. This is caused when moisture in the brickwork freezes and expands, shattering the substance of the brick. The condition is known as spalling. The best way to deal with a badly affected brick is to remove it, and replace it with a matching one.

Use a long, thin cold chisel and a hammer to cut away the mortar all round, then lever the brick away. Wet the surrounding brickwork thoroughly to make sure it will not soak up moisture from the new mortar. Place mortar on the bottom and sides of the opening and on top of the replacement brick, then lay it into place, cleaning up any mortar that oozes out. If a matching brick proves impossible to locate, you can always turn the damaged brick round, cleaning up the face now on view.

Repointing

The mortar in brick walls can become affected by the action of wind and rain. It may become loose and crumbling or be worn down below the level of the brickwork. Repointing is then called for.

Repointing consists of applying new mortar on top of the old to bring it to the correct level. It is not a difficult job, and requires only a few specialist tools, but if you are going to tackle any high places, get a good strong ladder or a scaffold tower.

You will also need: an old chisel or screwdriver for raking out loose or crumbling material, and perhaps a hammer to help dislodge difficult pieces; a hawk, which you can buy from a builders' merchant, or make yourself from a small square piece of board and a short length of dowel or broom handle; a small pointing trowel; a straight-edge; an old painting brush; a bucket; and a 'frenchman', which you can fashion from an old kitchen knife sharpened to a point and bent at right angles at the end.

Work on a small area of the wall at a time: you will probably find a square metre (10 sq. ft) about the right size. Begin by raking out the old mortar to a depth of 13 mm (½ in), then brush out any loose material. Use the brush to wet the brickwork thoroughly with water from the bucket, so that it will not draw out the moisture from the new mortar.

The mortar should consist of 1 part cement to 4 of sharp sand, and be mixed to a stiff consistency. Place some mortar on the hawk, and smooth it into a pat. Holding the hawk close to the wall, pick up some mortar on the back of the trowel and push the trowel forwards, tilting the front of the hawk upwards at the same time so that the mortar is lifted clear.

Point the vertical joints first, holding the trowel at a slight angle to press the mortar well into the joints. Using the frenchman with the straight edge, chop off the thick surplus at the outside of each joint when a section of verticals is finished.

Next, point the horizontal joints. Use a similar technique to fill each one roughly, then draw the trowel across it to form a smooth continuous band of mortar. Cut off the thick surplus at the bottom with the frenchman.

The horizontal joints must be formed so that rainwater will not lodge in them; there are several ways to do this (Fig. 3:3).

3.3 *Steps in repointing a brick wall: (a) Two of the tools – a pointing trowel and a hawk. (b) Point the vertical joints first, pushing the mortar well into the joints. (c) Chop off large amounts of excess mortar with the trowel. (d) Use a straight edge and a 'frenchman' to remove the surplus at the bottom edge. (e) Three ways of finishing the joints so that rainwater will not lodge: flush, keyed, and weathered.*

Painting bricks

Many householders, when faced with bricks that are past their best (dirty, slightly porous, perhaps crumbling a little), decide on painting as the cheapest, easiest way of covering up the defects. Certainly bricks are a suitable surface to receive masonry paints, but this is a solution to be adopted only as a last resort. Once you start painting bricks, you have to repaint them every five years or so, perhaps more frequently in exposed areas. Bricks are porous and the paint will soak into them so that it can never be removed. In any event, bricks are a beautiful building material in their own right, so cover them up only if the wall is a problem.

RENDERED WALLS

Rendering is a mix of cement, lime and sand (or other aggregate) that is applied to external walls to make them more weatherproof or to cover up poor quality materials. It is found mainly on solid walls, but modern homes, built of cavity construction, may also be rendered, either for protection or for decoration. Stucco, a form of rendering, was very often applied to houses in the eighteenth and nineteenth centuries as decoration.

The main problems with a rendered surface are that all sand and cement mixes shrink, and that all buildings move, even if only slightly. As a result, cracks can develop in the rendering. Rainwater can penetrate even the smallest cracks and work under the surface of the rendering, weakening the bond of the sand and cement to the bricks, and causing blisters of loose material or even patches of the surface to fall away. The damage can be especially severe if the water under the surface freezes.

Protecting the rendering

The main task is to make the surface waterproof, so that rainwater cannot penetrate. Top-quality exterior wall paints provide such protection, and cover hairline cracks too. They can also improve the appearance of the house. Alternatively, apply a coat or two of a clear silicone water repellent. This will not make the house look any better, nor will it disguise repairs, but it is easier to apply than paint, and much less preparation is required when you have to re-treat the wall.

Repairing cracks

Paint will not bridge cracks greater than, say, 1.5 mm (1/16 in), so any larger cracks will need to be filled. You can use an exterior-grade decorators' filler for this, but if the cracks are wide, a sand-and-cement mix would be better and more economical. Small packs of ready-mixed mortar to which you merely add water are available for such repairs. If you mix the mortar yourself, use 1 part cement to 3 of sharp sand.

Clean out the crack with the point of a trowel or filling knife, and remove loose material. Then push home the filler – in more than one application if the crack is big – and smooth it off flush with the surrounding surface.

Repairing patches

If a patch of rendering becomes loose and falls away, or a blister of loose rendering develops, repair it immediately, because the rendering is usually part of the weatherproofing of your home.

With a bolster chisel and hammer, hack away the loose, crumbling material back to the brickwork. Begin in the centre of the blister and work outwards towards the edges, until you come to sound material. Similarly, with a bare patch, hack away all round the edge of the hole until you reach sound rendering.

Make your own mortar for the repair – 1 part of cement to 5 or 6 of sharp sand with a proprietary plasticizer added is a suitable mix – or buy a bag of ready-mix and add water. In either case the mortar should be of a stiff consistency.

First, treat the bare bricks with a pva building adhesive, mixed and used according to the manufacturer's instructions. Apply the mortar in two stages. Place some on a hawk, hold it close to the wall and push the mortar into the damaged area with a steel float (Fig. 3:4). Just before this first application hardens, scratch its surface in a criss-cross pattern with a knife or the point of a trowel – builders call it the 'scratch coat' (Fig. 3:5).

Leave for 24 hours, then apply the finishing coat, making it as similar as possible to the finish of the rest of the wall. For instance, if the wall is smooth, spread out the top coat until it

Patching-up damage to rendering:
3.4 Apply the first coat with a steel float.
3.5 Scratch it with the point of a trowel.
3.6 Remove surplus mortar from the final coat with a batten.

is slightly higher than the surrounding area. Then draw a batten across the surface of the patch in a sawing motion to remove surplus mortar (Fig. 3:6). Leave it for about an hour to dry, then dampen it with water – you can apply this with an old paint brush – and smooth it off with the steel float.

The other finishes you can achieve, which are listed below, should be worked while the finishing coat is still soft, a few hours after it has been applied.

Roughcast has a proportion of coarse aggregate in the final coat, which is thrown (literally) on to the wall as a wet mix, and left untrowelled.

Scraped finish is achieved by leaving the final coat to harden for several hours, then scraping it with a tool, such as an old saw blade.

Textured finish has the final coat worked with a trowel or even an old banister brush.

Stippled effect, too, is created with a soft banister or dustpan brush.

Wavy effect is produced with a piece of ribbed rubber.

Bold texture is achieved by dabbing with a fabric pad.

Pebbledash

Small cracks in pebbledash (a rendering containing small pebbles) should be treated with mortar just as those in the smoother forms of rendering. However, you will need to add pebbles to larger patches in order to keep the texture of the surface uniform throughout.

The pebbles can be mixed with the final coat, or added after it has been applied. In the latter case, carry out the repair as already detailed for smooth rendering. Then place the pebbles on a container, such as a small shovel, throw them on to the wet mortar, and press them into place with a wooden float.

New rendering

Defective walls, especially solid ones, are often rendered to make them more weatherproof, or to cover up faults in the brickwork. This job requires a high degree of skill, and is carried out by plasterers. It also demands a detailed knowledge of the sub-surfaces in order to decide on the preparatory work and the exact type of mortar mix needed. Without this skill and knowledge, the rendering simply will not adhere properly to the wall, and faults will develop quickly. So if you want a whole wall rendered, employ a professional.

DAMP IN WALLS

Damp is one of the worst defects that can affect a house. Even in its milder forms it is unpleasant, but a serious outbreak will first destroy the decorations, then in time attack the woodwork, and eventually strike at the fabric of the building; it will make the place dank and unhealthy.

There are three types of damp, each with its own causes and cures. Rising damp, as its name suggests, is damp rising up into the structure from the ground. Penetrating damp, caused by rainwater (or occasionally by water from a plumbing mishap), enters through defects in the shell of the building. The third type of damp is condensation, which originates inside the house.

It is not always easy to decide which type of damp your home is suffering from. In extreme cases it will take an expert to give a correct diagnosis. However, there are some general pointers. For instance, if the damp occurs low down on the wall near floor level, you can suspect rising damp. In, say, a bathroom that is prone to severe condensation, the paint can be lifted away from the wall by damp near the skirting, which is a symptom of rising damp, but the cause could equally be condensation streaming down to the bottom of the wall.

The effects of condensation can also appear misleadingly on many parts of the walls and ceiling, but this type of damp is usually easy to recognize. It occurs when most of the windows are closed (which reduces ventilation) and after water vapour has been released into the air by cooking, washing clothes, or bathing.

Rising damp

There is always moisture in the ground, even during dry spells, and it can find its way up walls like paraffin rising up the wick of an oil lamp unless there is something (such as a damp-proof course) there to stop it.

All modern buildings are built with a damp-proof course (dpc). It is near ground level and looks like an especially thick horizontal mortar course, with a thin, usually black line in it, going all the way round the house. In older homes the dpc might be of slate, lead, mastic, asphalt or bituminous felt; pvc is often used in modern buildings. Substitutes for a dpc include chemicals injected into the brickwork, or ceramic tubes drilled into the walls low down at regular intervals.

A dpc that is in good condition should keep rising damp at bay. If rising damp is evident despite a dpc, one of two things must be wrong.

First, something might be creating a bypass to the dpc

and introducing damp into the walls above it. The cause might be garden soil piled up against the wall, or a bulk delivery of builders' sand or coarse aggregate for concrete work. A garden wall meeting the house walls without a damp barrier in between could bridge the dpc, as could a porch or lean-to unless precautions were taken. Some wall claddings – tiles or timber – and rendering can have the same effect if not applied correctly.

The second possible cause is that there may have been a failure in the dpc. Settlement of the structure, for example, can fracture it. If you get rising damp in a home with a dpc, carry out a thorough inspection looking for a likely bridge. Should you find a simple bridge, such as garden soil, get rid of it immediately. A more complex bridge – a garden wall, or porch, for example – presents greater difficulties. Although a dpc for dealing with such situations can be bought at builders' merchants, inserting it once the construction is finished is a major task; you might have to demolish the offending structure – at least in part. If no bridge is apparent, seek expert help, as vetting and repairing a dpc is not work for the do-it-yourselfer.

Inserting a proper dpc in a house that does not have one is a job for trained operators. However, there are several methods of keeping damp at bay that can be employed by the practical do-it-yourselfer.

You can inject into the walls a silicone-based water repellent normally applied to the surface of exterior walls. To do this, bore a series of 16-19 mm ($\frac{5}{8}$-$\frac{3}{4}$ in) holes into the middle of the bricks in two courses immediately above the floor or dpc level. Such large holes might overload an ordinary DIY electric drill, so it might be worth hiring an industrial drill and bit for a day. Slope holes downwards at an angle of about 15° and stop them about 20 mm ($\frac{3}{4}$ in) from the other side of the wall (stick a strip of tape round the drill bit as an improvised depth gauge). In solid walls – the kind most likely to be affected by rising damp – bore the holes from inside the house. Treat each leaf of a cavity wall separately, boring holes from both inside and out.

Bung up each hole with a cork or rubber bung that has a hole in the centre: corks of this type are used in home brewing and can be bought at chemists or home-brew shops. You now need a garden pressure spray fitted with a lance. Fill it with water-repellent liquid and push the end of the lance through the hole in the bung. Operate the spray so that the liquid is forced into the hole. Continue until the liquid comes to the surface of the wall round the hole – it will look as though the wall is sweating – which will take from two to five minutes depending on the porosity of the brickwork. Treat each hole in the same way.

You might be able to hire an electric pressure pump, which would be better than a garden spray, speeding up the work, and forcing the liquid farther into the brickwork.

As soon as the treatment is finished fill the holes with a sand-and-cement mortar, and leave for 24 hours. Then brush the area round the holes with more water-repellent liquid. Leave for at least a week before replacing plaster and skirting boards, then redecorate.

Another method is to buy an interior damp barrier kit. This does not form a damp-proof course, but provides a barrier that stops damp in the wall from getting through to the inside and damaging the decorations. Normal paint and wallpaper decorations can be applied on top of it.

The kit consists of a waterproof laminate, a primer and an adhesive. Remove any wallpaper and loose or flaking paint, and take down the skirting board. Treat the wall with the primer, then fix the laminate in place.

A third method is to brush a water repellent made for interior application on to the wall. It will not last as long as the laminate barrier, but will give some protection.

Damp can also rise through solid floors (see Chapter 9). Treatments carried out on the walls should be continued on to any membrane fitted to a floor.

Penetrating damp

Penetrating damp is caused by water entering through defects in the structure of the house. The way to prevent and cure it is through a high standard of house maintenance. Keep the roof sound, and maintain the walls as described in this chapter. Repoint when it becomes necessary, and remedy any defects in rendered walls. Seal any gaps between window and door frames and the walls with a proprietary sealant; keep gutters and downpipes clear of blockages; deal immediately with any plumbing mishaps that soak a wall; and apply an exterior-grade silicone-based water repellent to porous walls.

3.7 *One way of keeping damp at bay in basements: nail bitumen lath to the walls.*

Damp in basements is common because they are below ground level and are surrounded by soil, in which damp is present. There is no practical way to eliminate damp from basement walls, but you can keep the damp at bay.

Prepare the walls by fixing a polythene sheet to them or by applying a damp-repellent liquid. Then fix bitumen lath to the walls with galvanized clout nails (Fig. 3:7). Bitumen lath is a pitch-impregnated corrugated fibre. The corrugations create channels on both sides of the material: those on the wall side form ventilation corridors in which the dampness can evaporate. Those on the room side provide a key to recieve plaster (Fig. 3:8). Plasterboard can be used by do-it-yourselfers instead of plaster.

3.8 *The lath's corrugations act as a key to receive plaster.*

Another possibility is to build a partition wall clad with plasterboard close to but not touching the main wall of the basement, creating in effect a cavity wall. Normally the framework for a plasterboard partition is screwed to the wall, but for damp-proofing it should be fixed to the ceiling and floor, in the way outlined on page 126 for constructing a non-load-bearing partition. It is a good idea to fit insulation blanket (of the kind used to line a loft) behind the plasterboard, so that the basement will be warm as well as dry.

The floor of the basement will also need a damp-proof membrane (such as clear polythene) to stop damp from rising through the floor. Overlap the membrane and the damp-proof treatment on the walls.

Condensation

Whereas rising and penetrating damp are becoming more and more easy to control, the problem of condensation is probably getting worse. Certain steps may be taken to ease the problems of condensation, but there is no lasting cure.

The trouble arises from the simple fact that the warmer air is, the more moisture it can hold. As air in a room is warmed, it absorbs extra moisture, and in some parts of the home – the kitchen, with cooking, washing-up and laundry going on, and the bathroom, when people take a bath or shower – there is a lot of moisture to be picked up.

Warming a room also causes the air in it to move. As it does so, it meets cold surfaces – glass, tiles, or plaster walls. Immediately it touches them, the water-laden air cools, shedding some of its moisture.

There are two ways in which you can combat condensation. The first is to reduce the amount of moisture in the air. Ventilation lets in more air and thus brings the humidity indoors into line with that outside, where there is much less moisture in the atmosphere. Leave a window open whenever the outside temperature permits. Where the problem is severe, have an extractor fan fitted. In kitchens, fit a cooker hood with a fan, ducted to the outside.

The second method is to turn cool surfaces into warm ones. Cork and timber cladding on floors and walls are warm. Soft, dull paints such as emulsions are better than the hard, brittle surface of gloss, and wallpaper is better than either, especially if it has expanded polystyrene beneath it. The more effective of these materials are, of course; the more expensive, but where the problem is severe it will be worth considering them, if only for the coldest parts of a room, which are the external walls. As a last resort you might install a de-humidifier – an electric device that removes moisture from the air.

Chapter 4
WINDOWS

Windows are not the only means of ventilation. This can also be provided by an air-conditioning system or an air brick. Some bathrooms and lavatories, especially in modern flats and conversions, have a fan instead of a window, but cellars and foundations have air bricks.

The minimum amount of ventilation required in a room is specified by the regulations. The rules governing ventilation would affect a planned conversion only if it would result in a room having smaller windows. For example, if you plan to enlarge a room by knocking down a wall, there should be no objection if the resulting room would have windows at both ends. If, however, there is a windowless adjoinment – such as a store room on one side of the wall – then you might not be allowed to make the alteration.

Your main concern with windows will be to see that day light and ventilation are all that they let in.

The windows are among the most vulnerable parts of a house – not only to the weather but also to intruders. Most burglars break into houses through the windows. They do not like to break the glass, because of the noise it makes, so usually they force the catch, then climb inside.

Window catches are, in fact, the easiest to open. Fit security devices to them, and particularly to those that are out of sight yet easily reached, such as ground-floor windows and those accessible from a drainpipe, extension or lean-to. Do not think that a small window is secure against burglars – they can usually find a way through.

There is a great diversity of window locks. For casement windows, there are lockable catches and lockable devices that fit on to the window stays. For vertical sliding sashes, there are devices that lock the window either when closed or slightly open – to air the room while keeping out thieves. In extreme circumstances, there are iron bars, or security grilles fixed on a sliding track so they can be opened or closed.

FRAME STYLES

Glass cannot be connected directly to masonry. It needs to be housed in a frame, which is fixed to the wall, with an arrangement for opening to give ventilation. Over the years a wide variety of styles of window frame has evolved.

Casement Windows

Casement windows are the most common type (Fig. 4:1). The frame is made up of vertical sides (jambs), tenoned into a horizontal top (the head) and a sill at the bottom. Larger windows have intermediate vertical members (mullions) and subsidiary horizontal ones (transoms). The mullions and transoms are also fixed by means of tenons. The panes of glass are held in small sub-frames, or sashes. The word sash is used for a style of window fitted commonly in Georgian and Victorian houses. In fact a sash is any frame that holds a pane of glass.

The sashes in a casement window may be fixed or opening. Opening sashes are hinged either on the side or the top. Sashes with hinges at the top are called top-hung vents. Usually sashes open outwards, because that makes for a good weather seal when they are closed. Where a window is divided into several small panes, the glass is housed in a framework of small glazing bars. These bars may be joined by means of halving joints, or mortise and tenons.

Besides reglazing (dealt with later in this chapter) the maintenance of casement windows is as for doors. Opening sashes that stick should be dealt with as sticking doors. Hinges and sections of rotten frame should be repaired as rotten door hinges and frames. The similarity between

4.1 A typical casement window

opening sashes and doors extends even to the naming of the parts. The two sides of a sash are known as stiles, and the top and bottom are called rails. Should the join between the stile and rail become loose, repair it with dowels, as described for doors. Alternatively, use brackets or repair plates. Chisel out a groove in both stile and rail, then sink the bracket or plate in it and screw it into place. Fill the hole and re-paint.

If the window is badly rotted, replace it completely (see pages 77-9).

Vertical sliding sash windows

The correct term for the type of window referred to popularly as 'sash windows' is 'vertical sliding sash windows'. They consist of two sashes which might be sub-divided into small panes. Both sashes can be opened by sliding them up or down in grooves within the frame. When they are closed, the outer sash should be at the top. The sashes are kept closed by a catch.

The sashes can be left open in any position, because they are counterbalanced by weights attached by cords. They slide in channels formed by three sets of beading. From the outside inwards, these are termed the 'outer', 'parting' and 'staff' beads. Staff beads are sometimes called inner beads. The staff beads are fixed to the top and bottom of the window opening as well as to the sides, but usually a parting bead is placed only on the sides. The outer bead is usually part of the profile of the window frame, but the others are separate pieces nailed in place. The staff bead lies flat on the frame, but the parting bead is fixed on edge – usually lying in a small groove in the side of the frame, formed there as an aid to the correct positioning of the bead.

Each set of windows has four weights – one for each side of each sash. The weights are within a weight compartment on each side of the window and are attached to the sashes by cords nailed to the sides of the sash. The cords pass over pulleys in the weight compartment. Each compartment is divided in two by a parting slip, which keeps the two weights apart.

Sashes that rattle are too loose within the channel formed by the beads. A temporary remedy is to place rubber or plastic wedges (sold for just this purpose) between a sash and the beads. The wedges are inconvenient, however, because they drop out whenever a sash is opened.

To effect a permanent repair, prise away the staff bead (if the inner sash rattles), the parting bead (if the outer sash is at fault) or both beads (if both sashes are loose). Insert a screwdriver, chisel or paint scraper between bead and window frame to prise the bead away. Then re-fix the bead slightly closer to the sash, but not so close that it prevents free movement.

Repositioning the beading will damage the paintwork, so the job is best done just before you intend to decorate.

Sashes that stick may have absorbed moisture and become too thick for the channel, causing the beads to hold the sash in a vice-like grip. The immediate remedy is to prise away the affected bead, as explained above, and reposition it. Be careful, however, not to place it so far away from the sash as to cause rattles. Should the sash shrink and begin to rattle, it should be weather-proofed and the bead repositioned.

The other probable cause of sticking sashes is a build-up of paint. If you apply coat upon coat of paint each time you redecorate, the channel will eventually be narrowed sufficiently to stop the smooth running of the sashes. The only remedy is to scrape off, or sand down, the paint to an acceptable thickness, then re-paint.

Pulleys that squeak as the cords pass over them should be oiled. Apply the oil sparingly to prevent it soiling the panes and curtains.

Draughtproofing is one of the major problems with sliding sashes. A channel that is wide enough to let a sash slide will also cause air to enter. The only way to draughtproof them is to double glaze them by installing a secondary pane on the room side of the window. This solution is expensive, but it will make the house more comfortable. You may prefer instead to hang heavy curtains in front of the window.

Renewing the cords is necessary when one has frayed and broken (Fig. 4:2). When a cord breaks, renew all four, because if one has failed, it is a safe assumption that the others are beginning to weaken too. Aim to do the job when the weather is warm and dry.

First prise off the staff bead from both sides of the window – there is no need to bother about those at the top and bottom. Swing the inner sash clear. Cut the cords if they are still intact, but not so that the weight crashes to the bottom of its compartment. Remove any remnants of cord still clinging to the sash. Now place the sash away securely, so the panes do not get broken. Next prise away the parting bead, then free the outer sash as before, cutting any cord still intact. Remove any bits nailed to the sash and put the sash out of harm's way.

Renew each cord in turn, beginning with those on the outer sash. Each is dealt with in exactly the same way. First, retrieve the weight from the bottom of its compartment. Access to it is through a pocket piece – a piece of wood cut out of the side of the frame. Usually there is one piece covering two weights. The pocket piece may be held by a small retaining screw, but usually it is a push-fit in the

Sash

frame. Lift it out by pushing a thin-bladed knife down its side and prising it away. Lift out the weight and untie the cord. The weights are not painted, but it is not a bad idea to wire brush them to remove rust. Remove dust from the bottom of the compartment with a vacuum cleaner.

Pass a length of new cord over one of the outer pulleys at the top of the frame. The cord will probably not drop down under its own weight so improvise a 'mouse'; a small weight tied to the end of a length of string. The weight should be small enough to pass over the top of the pulley, yet sufficiently heavy to drop down into the compartment. Trades-

4.2 Renewing sash cords: (a) Prise off the staff bead so that the inner sash can be lifted clear. (b) Prise off the parting bead to release the outer sash. (c) Drop a noose into the weight compartment to pull through the new cord. (d) Fasten cord to weight and tie knot at other end (inset) so it cannot be dragged over pulley. (e) Nail cord to groove in side of sash. The arrangement is shown in close-up (top/right).

men use a small piece of lead, which they tap with a hammer round the end of the string. Drop the mouse down into one of the outer weight compartments and tie the free end of its string to one end of the new cord. Pull on the mouse to pull the new cord through, then fasten the end of the cord to the weight in this compartment. Cut the cord to length at the pulley end. To determine the correct length, pull on the cord until the weight is just clear of the bottom of the compartment. Cut it about 150 mm (6 in) from the top of the pulley. Tie a knot at the top of the cord to prevent it slipping through the pulley.

Deal with the outer weight on the other side in just the same manner.

Bring back the top sash to the window opening. Draw the knotted end of one cord clear of the pulley to give yourself a comfortable length on which to work. Untie the knot and fix this free end to the top of the side of the sash. The length of cord should be such that, when the sash is fully closed, the weight is just clear of the bottom of the compartment. There is usually a small groove to accommodate the cord, and it is fixed in place by small galvanized clout nails. Do not fix the cord right to the top of the sash, otherwise it will not close properly: the top fixing nail should be slightly farther from the top of the sash than the distance between the top of the pulley and the top of the window opening. Fix the cord on the other side in just the same manner, and put the sash carefully in place in the window opening.

Renew the cords on the inner sash in just the same way, then replace the pocket piece. Fix the beadings back in position.

Fixing new beads may be necessary either because of wear and tear over the years, or because they might have been broken during the repairs described in this section. The parting bead is a plain length of timber. Usually it is fixed only to the sides, so there is no need to match it. The staff bead is ornate and, since it is fixed to the top and bottom of the opening as well as to the sides, any new lengths will have to match those already there. If you cannot buy matching timber, replace all four lengths of this beading – it is neither expensive nor difficult to fix. The lengths of staff bead should be mitred at the corners, but the parting bead is cut square.

All the beadings are simply pinned in place. Do not use glue, otherwise it will be impossible to renew the sash cords without causing extensive damage to the frame. The beadings are fragile – especially the parting bead – so drill pilot holes for the fixing pins, to prevent the timber from splitting.

Horizontal sliding sashes require no balancing weights to keep them in a chosen position. Usually the frames are made of aluminium with very few mullions or transoms, so they admit a large amount of daylight. They are popular as one form of double glazing.

French windows and patio doors

French windows and patio doors give easy access to a garden or terrace. French windows are hinged and door-height. Patio doors are tall horizontal sliding windows. They are more convenient than French windows because they do not blow about in a wind and space need not be allowed on the patio or balcony for them to open. They are also much easier to operate than French windows. They usually have slender frames (nearly always in aluminium) with few, if any, mullions or transoms and no glazing bars, so they offer an uninterrupted view. As with all sliding doors or windows, however, one sash slides behind the other when they open, so they do not offer such easy access to the outside.

If patio doors have not been built into the existing structure, installation may involve cutting a new opening in an external wall. So that the structure of the house is not weakened, a lintel must be fitted before the opening is cut. The work is beyond all but the most adventurous of do-it-yourselfers.

For most home-improvers, installing patio doors will be a case of fitting them as replacement windows. Often they take the place of existing French windows, in which case installation is comparatively easy. They can also be fitted in locations where there is just a conventional window with its cill well above the floor, because chopping out the brickwork to extend a window opening downwards presents no difficulty. Widening an opening, however, is an entirely different proposition, for that involves removing the existing lintel, and installing a longer one in its place. If French windows have a conventional window on one or both sides, these, too, can be extended downwards, because a single lintel would have been used to cover all the openings.

There are several points to consider in deciding whether to have the doors installed professionally, or to fit them yourself.

First, many companies offering such doors give you no choice – they operate on a supply-and-fit basis only. Others install them for you or let you do the work yourself or have it carried out by a local builder.

Second, if you shop around, it is possible to buy doors and have them installed for only slightly more than it would cost if you install them yourself.

Third, the work of installing patio doors, even as a replacement for French windows – the simplest of all the jobs – means that there will be a gaping hole in the wall of your house during installation. The sooner the gap is plugged, the better. Preferably, the work ought to be finished in a day. (If it takes a weekend or more, cover the opening each night with, say, a sheet of polythene.) A professional could work quicker than a do-it-yourselfer, and the installation would be finished in a much shorter time.

Whatever you do, remember that the installation of patio doors has become popular and has attracted many firms into the business. Make sure you deal only with a reputable one. Study the advertisements and get quotes from a least three firms. Some will try to rush you into ordering by offering a discount if you sign on the spot: do not fall for that one. If eventually you decide to buy from a firm offering such a discount, give the order on condition of that discount.

Most patio doors are framed in aluminium, which has many advantages over wood. It is immensely strong, so the frame members can be of small sections, allowing larger areas of glass for more light and a better view of the outdoors. It is durable, does not twist, warp or rust, requires no maintenance, and comes in a range of anodized coloured finishes. There is, however, one big disadvantage. It is a good conductor of heat, so will carry the heat of the room to the outside rapidly, making the metal almost as cold inside as it is outside. Inside the room, warm air condenses on the cold frame and might even set up slight downdraughts. The way around this problem is to choose a brand that incorporates an insulation barrier inside the frame.

The doors run in a track set in a timber surround, which can be of either hardwood or softwood. Hardwood is more durable than softwood, and is usually sealed or varnished, requiring much less effort than the frequent painting required by softwood.

Patio door frames made from wood will not get as cold as aluminium, so condensation is not the same problem. Rot and woodworm might affect the wood, and the timber will require maintenance – painting if it is softwood, varnishing or sealing if it is hardwood. Hardwood patio doors, however, are expensive.

A recent innovation is plastic patio door frames. These, too, are durable, rust free and require no maintenance (they probably keep their looks better than aluminium). The only drawbacks are that the frames are bulky, and they come only in white.

Most patio doors are double glazed – a sealed unit is set into the frames. The few that have just a single pane are intended for indoor use. Never be tempted to install a single-glazed door on an outdoor wall: they are only slightly cheaper, and will make the room colder by setting up downdraughts.

Doors can be supplied with safety glass, which is highly advisable, especially where young children might bump into the glass as they play or hit a ball against it.

Normally two doors are needed to cover the window, but three or even four are better on a larger opening. The doors can all be sliding, or you may decide to have one fixed. On a two-door unit, for example, if both doors slide, one must in any event go behind the other, so only half the opening can be used at any one time. It might not, therefore, be worth paying the extra to have the choice as to which half opens. If you choose one fixed door, give some thought to how it will be used before deciding which door it would be more convenient to have as the opening one.

Sliding patio doors used to be a burglar's delight, because they were insecure. Some could be lifted out of their tracks from the outside, and that left no problem about wrenching the rest open. Modern designs have no such faults. High security locks are usually standard fittings and bolts can be ordered as an extra or fitted later.

Patio doors are an excellent means of supplying ventilation to a room during hot sunny weather. When the temperature is cooler, however, for instance during the evening after a warm day, ventilation through a patio door (even if it is slightly closed) can be too much. A better arrangement is to incorporate top-hung vents over the main doors.

Most patio doors are built to standard sizes. If the opening at your home is not of standard size, the doors will have to be made specifically to fit, and will be more expensive.

Installing patio doors yourself requires only a brief outline as manufacturers give full instructions.

Accurate measurements are the most important part of the job. In fact, even if you are doing the installation yourself, it is not a bad idea to let a company representative take the measurements, so that the company are responsible for any mistakes. However, if you take the measurements yourself take both width and length measurements at several points. If they vary, supply the smallest dimensions. Measure the actual opening – not the window frames you have at present, and take the measurements on the outside of the house, for you need to know the spacings between brickwork, not plastered walls indoors.

To carry out the installation remove the existing windows, then carry out any planned enlargement downwards. Install the new timber frame, and fix the sliding channel to it. Hang the doors into place, adjusting as necessary, then seal the gap between timber sub-frames and wall with mastic.

To make sure that the job is carried out as quickly as possible, read the maker's instructions thoroughly and make sure you understand them fully before you start. Assemble all the tools and materials that will be needed. If any cutting of the various members to size – or any removal of the projecting horns from a sub-frame – will be required, do this in advance. Make an early start on the morning that work begins.

Windows that increase room size

Bay windows can be installed to add a little more floor area to a room at minimal extra cost, either just on the ground floor or on the floor above as well. They also give a room wider windows than could be fitted flush with the existing external wall. The cost is less than for a full extension, because the bay does not usually extend the full length of the external wall, and it does not reach the full height of the ceiling – except where it is the lower window of a two-storey bay. In plan view, bays come in a wide range of shapes, including square, rectangular and semicircular. The roof can be either pitched or flat to match the style of the main roof.

Bow windows are a sort of bay, but in plan they form the shape of an archer's bow.

Dormer windows project from a pitched roof, but the panes – unlike those of a roof window (see below) – are vertical.

Oriel Windows are a form of bay on an upper floor that does not extend down to ground level. They are usually quite small, but are not generally found in modern homes.

Other types

Pivot-hung windows open on a central pivot, so that the face usually turned outwards can be cleaned from inside. Some windows pivot horizontally, and others vertically. The problem of cleaning is particularly acute in high-rise flats, but in any event it is something to be considered even on two-storey houses.

Louvred windows consist of narrow lengths of glass, held in a metal frame (usually aluminium) that allows them to be tilted open, similar to the wooden slats of a louvred door. At one time they were popular, especially in kitchens and bathrooms, because it is possible at a touch to increase the ventilation they provide – to expel steam and cooking smells, for instance. They are, however, draughty and the louvres tend to rattle in the wind. Worse still, they are the easiest windows for burglars to break into. As a result they have fallen out of favour.

Roof windows are fitted into the slope of the roof, instead of a section of slates or tiles. They give light and ventilation into a loft area and can be installed by any competent do-it-yourselfer. Various proprietary kinds are available – follow the maker's instructions for installation.

MATERIALS

Frames

Most window frames are of wood. Steel frames were once popular, until it was realized that protection from rust would be a problem. Aluminium has also been used – especially for patio door frames. Increasing use is being made of plastic.

Wooden window frames The timber used is usually softwood, which has to be painted, although in a few expensive houses hardwood may have been used, and the frames sealed or varnished. Even softwood frames, however, often have a sill made of hardwood – such as oak – which is extremely durable.

Window frames are not square in section, but consist of several mouldings. For instance, there is a rebate to receive the glass and to ensure that opening sashes fit snugly when closed. The top rail head has a shaped piece (a drip bead) to throw off rainwater, and there are 'anti-capillary grooves' within the frame and opening sashes to prevent water creeping through. The sill is sloping so that rainwater runs off it, and there are (or should be) drip channels underneath it to stop water running back and on to the house wall.

On the inside, keep the frames well painted or varnished. If you are starting from bare softwood timber, treat knots and other resinous areas with knotting. Prime the whole frame, then apply an undercoat and two top coats of gloss. If you paint regularly, and the top surfaces are in good condition, you can make do with just a couple of top coats – provided that you wash down and rinse the frames, then allow them to dry first. Beware, however, of a build-up of paint on the edges of opening hinged sashes, the rebates into which they close, and the grooves of vertical sliding sashes. If they are painted too thickly, they will not work properly. Hardwood frames should be sealed or varnished regularly.

Steel frames (consisting of sections of mild steel welded together) were very popular in the 1930s and just after the last war. Then it was thought that they had several advantages over timber frames – that they would not be affected by woodworm or rot, and they would not shrink or warp. In fact, experience showed that they are subject to something that is probably as bad, and may be worse – rust. They are no longer popular, but many are in use. The tendency to rust is especially noticeable in the earlier frames, which were protected only by painting. Later frames were hot-dip galvanized at the factory.

The frames are fixed by means of screws driven through pre-bored countersunk holes. Originally the fixing was direct to the brickwork, but later it became the practice to set the frames in a wooden surround.

Rust can eat right through steel frames. It can also cause them to twist so that gaps develop between fixed casements and the surrounding brickwork or timber, and opening casements will not work properly.

Regular re-painting of treated frames is most important. Provided that physical damage does not remove any of the coating it is possible to keep rust well under control. The problem is not so easy with untreated frames. Remove all rust before you paint, either with a wire brush or abrasive paper. (Use a power tool to make the work quicker and easier) or apply a chemical rust remover. Next apply a metal primer, followed by an undercoat and a couple of top coats. On no account should you remove paint from a metal frame with a blowlamp. Besides the hazard of the glass being broken, the heat could twist the frame out of shape. Besides re-painting, the only other maintenance required for steel frames is the occasional oiling of the hinges.

A steel frame that twists out of true needs to be repaired by an expert. Consult the manufacturer. If, however, the frame becomes so badly damaged that complete replacement is necessary, it can be removed simply, especially if it is set in a wooden surround. The fixing screws are probably jammed by corrosion, or so covered with paint that they will not turn. The procedure explained in the later section on removing old doors will work here – see page 83. Almost anything can be freed if you apply a little heat to the screw head – do not worry about damaging a frame that is to be replaced.

There should not be too much difficulty in finding a replacement steel frame of the right size. In any event, minor adjustments can be made to the thickness of the existing timber surround, if there is one, or a surround can be inserted where there is none.

The timber surround will be fixed by one of the methods described on page 67 for fixing timber frames. If this surround has to be removed, it should be taken out as described for such frames.

Aluminium frames are used for many modern windows – especially sliding ones. Aluminium does not rot or rust. It needs no painting, but should be kept clean and polished to prevent the surface tarnishing and becoming pitted.

Plastic frames are, as yet, rare and expensive, but keeping a house in good repair will be easier when these become universal. They do not deteriorate from rot or rust, will not warp or twist and need no maintenance.

The hole in the wall

The frame of a window fits an opening in an exterior wall, without supporting the wall above. Support is given by either an arch or a lintel, and sometimes a combination of both. In old houses, the lintel might be of stone, or it could be of timber and covered with bricks. Timber lintels might need to be replaced after many years but the work affects the structure of the house and should not be attempted by the do-it-yourselfer.

Modern buildings have reinforced concrete lintels. These may be visible on the outside of the wall, or they could be set back and hidden behind brickwork. They are either pre-cast, brought to the site and hoisted up into position, or they are cast *in situ*, with concrete poured into a framework. If an *in situ* lintel is faced with bricks, wall ties are usually inserted in the mortar courses, and these project into the concrete.

A damp-proof course (dpc) has to be fitted above a lintel, and it should project slightly so that any moisture collecting on the inner surface of a cavity wall will run clear to the outside. A dpc is also required across the cavity before a sill is fitted, to stop moisture crossing from the outside leaf to the inside.

In modern houses, the gap at the side of the opening between the two leaves of a cavity wall is bricked up; slate may have been used in older houses.

The wooden sill of the frame may rest on a stone lintel in older houses or on a reinforced concrete one in modern houses. A tile sill, resting on concrete, is also often found.

There are various ways in which a frame can be fixed to the brickwork round its opening. For instance, the frame will probably be delivered with the top rail projecting (just as a door frame) to form a horn on each side to offer protection during transit and on site. These horns may be embedded in the brickwork during installation or they may be sawn off. Lower down, screws or nails can be driven through the frame and into wooden plugs cemented into the mortar courses, or the screws can go into wall plugs inserted in the brickwork. Alternatively, fixing cramps – a sort of angle bracket – can be screwed to the side of the frame, and embedded into the mortar courses.

On the inside, the join between frame and wall is plastered over, and in addition may be neatened by some form of moulding. Outside, it can be pointed with mortar, or a non-setting mastic. Sometimes mortar is used to within 13 mm (½ in) of the surface, and the rest topped off with mastic.

This pointing needs to be well maintained to keep the

house weatherproof. Should it get worn down, repoint it with mastic – the type squeezed out of a tube is the most convenient.

Reglazing wooden windows

A broken window pane should be replaced as soon as possible to keep out the weather and prevent injury. Even if the glass is merely cracked it can fall out of a frame unexpectedly.

If the damage occurs after the glass merchant has closed, tack polythene sheet over the window to give overnight protection against the weather. Fix the sheet to the frame with drawing pins, then nail small battens around the polythene to complete the seal.

A new pane should be about 3 mm (⅛ in) all round smaller than the opening to give the glass room to expand or contract in hot or cold weather. The window frame may not be truly square, so measure the opening on each side and at the top and bottom. Order the glass to the smaller measurement.

You also need to specify the thickness of glass, although your supplier will advise you. For windows of up to 1 sq. m (about 10 sq. ft) use 3 mm thick glass. If the window is larger,

4.3 Reglazing wooden window frames: (a) Tap out the broken pane with a hammer. (b) Scrape out the old putty. (c) Work the new putty into the rebate. (d) Tap in the new glazing sprigs with the edge of a chisel. (e) Smooth the putty. (f) A detail of how the glass is held by putty and sprigs.

Score line

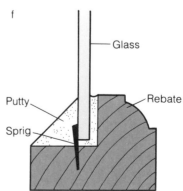

Glass

Putty

Sprig

Rebate

use thicker glass. For very large picture windows, you need glass twice as thick, but such a job is beyond the scope of do-it-yourselfers.

To carry out the repair (Fig. 4:3), remove the damaged glass. Always wear protective gloves. One of the safest ways of taking out the old pane is to score it with a glass-cutter on all four sides about 25 mm (1 in) away from the edge. If the window is hinged, open it fully and tap out the broken bits from one side with a hammer, pulling them away with gloved hands on the other. If the window is fixed, work from the inside, tapping out the glass, but trying to hold it so that it doesn't fall away dangerously. This is particularly important on an upstairs window.

Score the border of glass that remains, then tap it to break out the sections. Lever out the short stubs of glass that are left. With an old chisel, scrape out the putty from the rebate, then use pincers to remove the glazing sprigs. Dust out the rebate, and coat with a wood priming paint.

Take a handful of putty and knead it into a pliable ball, then work it into the rebate with your thumb. Place the glass in the rebate, and press it gently into position. To prevent the glass from breaking, press it at the edges, never in the centre. Fix glazing sprigs to hold the glass into place. Tap them into the wood with the side of the chisel, taking care not to damage the glass. Press putty on the outside of the glass and smooth it down with a putty knife. Make sure the line where the putty meets the glass lies slightly below the level of the rebate, so that the putty will not be visible from inside. Mitre the corners neatly. On the inside of the room, trim off any surplus putty.

Seal off all round the putty outside by brushing it gently with a damp brush. Clean the pane. The putty should take about a week to harden, then it can be painted. The paint should stray on to the glass by about 3 mm (⅛ in) to weatherproof the putty.

Reglazing metal windows

The technique is similar to the method for wooden ones, except that wire clips are used to retain the glass instead of glazing sprigs (Fig. 4:4). It is important to use a putty that is suitable for the frame. Ordinary putty is based on linseed oil, and it dries out and hardens as the oil is absorbed into the timbers. Metal frames cannot absorb moisture, so the putty must be self-hardening. Dual-purpose putty (suitable for either wood or metal) is available.

The wire clips are fitted into holes in the metal frame. There is no need to insert a clip into every hole – three or four on each edge are usually adequate. The clips are available from glass merchants.

4.4 *Wire clips used in glazing metal frames*

4.5 Reglazing leaded lights: (a) Make a pattern of the shape of the panes. (b) Tap open the frame. (c) Close the beading with a lead boat.

Reglazing leaded lights

Leaded lights require great care, because they are delicate and can easily be damaged. As a precatuion, cut a sheet of hardboard or thin plywood, and ask a helper to hold it against the back of the window while you work on it. An opening window should be taken down, and placed on a workbench. Support the back of the window with blocks of wood.

If the panes are not a regular shape, give the glazier a pattern with your order. To make this, place a sheet of paper flat over the broken piece, and take a rubbing of the lead pattern. Have the new glass ready before proceeding further (Fig. 4:5).

Gently tap open the mitred corners of the lead framing, with a putty knife or old chisel. Lever open the rest of the beading, using the broken pieces of glass still in it. Clean out the old putty.

The new pane should have its sharp corners nipped off – something the glazier might do for you. If not, remove them with the tip of a pair of pliers. Nip small pieces only so you do not break the pane. Close the beading so that it is parallel to the glass, but not touching. Glaziers use a wooden tool, called a lead boat (because at one end it is shaped like the bow of a boat) but you can make do with a scrap of wood. Take some putty suitable for metal, darkening it if possible with black lead powder. Push it into the gap between beading and glass on both sides, smoothing it off neatly.

The sill

Wooden window sills are among the parts of a house most vulnerable to the weather. If they are not well protected with paint or varnish they will rot. Small patches of rot are easy to repair. Deal with them instantly to prevent them spreading. Test for rot by pushing a sharp knife or other tool into the sill. The tool will meet resistance in sound timber, but pass easily through rotted wood.

Dowel

Repair strip

Dowel

Metal repair strip

Wedge shaped repair piece

Corner repair piece

4.6 *Fixing new timber to a damaged sill in the middle and at the corner.*

· Begin by cutting out the rotted section. Cut well into sound wood on each side to form a wedge-shaped section. Burn the rotted timbers. To repair modern sills, you may be able to buy a matching piece of standard sill moulding. For older sills, it might be necessary to plane down a piece of square timber to match. Remember that drip channels will need to be cut into the section (see below).

Brush wood preservative well into the cleaned edge of the sill and soak the replacement piece in it thoroughly.

Fix the new timber into place with dowels driven into the sill (Fig. 4:6). You need two dowels, no matter how small the repair, and extra dowels at 100 mm (4 in) intervals for longer pieces. To strengthen the repair, fix steel strips to the underneath of the sill. Corners can be repaired similarly.

Concrete sills can be repaired, too. Fill small cracks with a decorator's filler suitable for outdoor use. Paint the sill with either a masonry or gloss paint to conceal the repair.

Large holes and cracks should be filled with cement; buy a small bag from a DIY store. First, though, treat the crack with a pva building adhesive, and add some of the adhesive to the mortar to make it more workable, as recommended in the adhesive instructions.

A deep hole is best filled in two stages. Smooth the finishing coat down flush with the edge of the sill, then disguise the repair with paint.

A framework is required if a concrete sill needs extensive repair. Make it of stout timber at least 25 mm (1 in) thick. Hold the formwork in place by nailing it to blocks of wood fixed to the wall with masonry nails (Fig. 4:7).

Drip channels prevent rainwater from running over and under a sill back on to the wall under the window opening. The drenching that results could cause the foundations or

Formwork nailed to batten

6″ nails driven into window frame to reinforce concrete

Line of cord to provide drip groove

Wood batten nailed to wall

4.7 The formwork for extensive repairs to a damaged concrete sill

the interior of the house to become damp. Drenching is to be avoided especially under a window opening, where it could be conducted to the frames and eventually cause them to rot. One or more grooves formed, during manufacture, into the underside of a timber sill or moulded into a concrete one will prevent the rainwater reaching the wall, causing it to drip harmlessly off on to the ground instead.

It is important to keep drip channels clean, otherwise they will not function effectively. Dirt and spiders' webs tend to gather there, so scrape or brush them out regularly.

If there are no drip channels under your sill, it is worth fitting them. Using a router, you could cut out a couple of grooves in a timber sill while it is *in situ*. This, however, is not an easy task. An alternative that works just as well as a groove is to glue and pin a couple of lengths of half-round moulding underneath the sill (Fig. 4:8). A gap between the mouldings forms an effective groove. On concrete, merely glue the moulding into place.

DOUBLE GLAZING

The commonest reason for installing double glazing is as a means of insulation. The cost can be recouped in reduced fuel bills. The 'pay-back time' – the time taken for reduced fuel bills to equal the cost of the system – is complicated by inflation, but it can be reckoned in years, rather than months.

At its best, double glazing can reduce the amount of heat lost through windows by half. In most homes, with average-sized window panes, however, the amount of heat lost through the windows is significantly less than the amount that escapes through an uninsulated roof, say, or badly built

Sill

Pin

Half-round moulding

4.8 Half-round moulding forming a drip channel under a timber sill

walls. So, unless you live in a house with enormous windows, you are unlikely to save at best any more than ten per cent of your fuel costs. When compared with the cost of double glazing, a mere ten per cent of fuel bills seems a meagre saving, but sound-proofing and cost saving are not the only reasons for double glazing.

Double glazing can add to the comfort of your home by cutting out downdraughts. These are produced as air is warmed and rises towards the ceiling, then cools and falls back towards the floor. This movement will always occur when there are areas of air of different temperatures in a room. A pane of glass in a window is like a large cold panel in the room. It will cool the air around it and cause it to move. The cold air from the glass can have the same effect as draughts entering through gaps between the edges of the frame and walls. Double glazing, because it makes the windows warmer, helps to eliminate such draughts, and make agreeable parts of the room that hitherto were too cold.

How double glazing works

Glass is a good conductor of heat – it conducts warmth rapidly from inside your home to the outside. By installing thicker glass you would reduce the flow of heat only slightly, but double glazing is a better alternative. It consists of two panes of glass between which air is enclosed. The insulation is improved if the enclosed air is rarefied – forming a weak vacuum. The amount of air – the spacing between the two panes – is important. The ideal is 19 mm (¾ in). A smaller gap would allow even rarefied air to conduct the warmth away. You can increase the gap without causing too much loss of heat, but beyond a certain limit movement of air inside it will negate the insulating effect.

Types of double glazing

There are various ways, in domestic situations, of providing insulation with two panes of glass. A 'sealed unit' of insulating glass is made in a factory. It consists of two panes of glass sealed hermetically during manufacture, with a gap between them (Fig. 4:9). The gap between the two panes is formed by a strip of metal or plastic, or the pane may be fused together. The double pane of glass permits the heat from the sun to enter a room, but stops it from getting out. The unit takes the place of an ordinary pane of glass. If the rebate of an existing window frame is not deep enough to take a sealed unit, you can get a stepped unit, which is thinner at the edges.

Sealed-unit double glazing works extremely well, because there can be no movement of air between the glass. Moreover, it is never dismantled, so it involves no more

4.9

Sealed unit

4.10

Coupled sash

4.11

Secondary sash

4.9 – 4.11 *Types of double glazing.*

window cleaning than does a single pane. It is also virtually unnoticeable. Make sure, however, that any gaps between the frame and the surrounding wall are sealed, and that opening sashes fit well so that draughts are not admitted.

The overwhelming disadvantage of sealed-unit double glazing is its cost. If you are building a house – or even just an extension – then plan to have standard units to simplify the job. The greatest expense is incurred when you have to order non-standard sizes for an existing window opening. Sealed units are not suitable for certain types of period architecture.

In existing locations, it is usual to fix one of the other types of double glazing – 'coupled sash' or 'secondary sash'. These two are similar, and many people group them under the same general heading. The coupled sash (Fig. 4:10) consists of an extra pane attached to each of the sashes already in the window, which might be either fixed or opening. Secondary sash is a separate installation of windows just inside the existing ones (Fig. 4:11). The secondary sash can comprise both fixed or opening sashes, but usually it consists of a series of horizontal sliding sashes – much like small patio doors.

Aluminium or plastic strip is used to hold coupled sashes in place (they may be screwed, clipped or hinged to the main frame) and to form the frames of secondary sashes. There should be no gaps between the channel holding secondary sashes and the surrounding window opening.

Secondary sashes can block off any draughts coming through the gaps round opening sashes and between the wall and the frame of existing windows. Even so, such draughts would set up movement of air in the gap between the two panes, and reduce the effectiveness of the air as an insulator, so always eliminate draughts before you install double glazing, instead of expecting double glazing to block them off.

A disadvantage with both coupled and secondary sashes is that they increase the amount of window area to be cleaned.

Coupled and secondary sash double glazing can be bought from a company that supplies and fits them. They will send a representative to measure the opening and estimate the cost of the job. The sashes will then be assembled to fit the window, as with patio doors. Remember to investigate what several suppliers have to offer, and get two or three quotes. Some firms will make the sashes ready for you to install yourself.

The alternative method is to buy a DIY kit. This consists of lengths of aluminium or plastic that you cut to size and screw to the window to hold each pane in place. Although these units are not as sophisticated as manufactured ones they work well and are easy to fit; the overwhelming advantage is the cheapness.

Double glazing to keep out noise

As well as retaining heat in the home, double glazing can also be used to reduce the amount of noise that enters it – from aircraft or a motorway, for example. This is called acoustic insulation. To be effective, the gap between panes should be about 200 mm (8 in) – much wider than for thermal insulation. That, at any rate, is what contractors who build hotels on, for instance, the edge of airports or motorways aim for. In most homes such a dimension is impossible, because the spacing between glass and wall is usually only between 100 and 150 mm (4-6 in). Nevertheless, good acoustic installation can be achieved with a set of secondary sashes. Place the sash as close to the inner edge of the window reveal as possible, making sure there are no gaps between the track and the reveal. Line the inside of the reveal – the window cill as well as the sides and top – with acoustic tiles. Such an installation will also give some thermal insulation.

MODERNIZING

Window frames are part of the architectural style of a house. Many people modernizing a period house want to change them, but beware of altering the style of your home too much; you might destroy its character and ultimately its value. Many charming old houses have been ruined by the insertion of huge, gaping windows. Anyone who wants an ultra-modern home ought to buy one, rather than modernize an older one. Nevertheless, some changes are essential, but they should be carried out with discretion.

Larger panes

It is possible to replace some of the smaller panes in a window with one large sheet of glass (Fig. 4:12). First, you have to remove the individual sashes. If they are opening ones, withdraw the screws holding the hinges. The fixed sashes are nailed into place. Tap them out by using a hammer to hit one end of a stout piece of wood while the other end is on the sash.

Be mindful of safety: you might well break the glass, which could fall outside. Make sure there is no one there to get hurt.

With the sashes out, you will still be left with the transoms and mullions. Saw these out as closely as possible to the main frame, without causing any damage to the rebates. Remove short stubs with a chisel. Clean up with a rebate plane, then sand the surfaces thoroughly.

4.12 Adapting a casement window to take one large pane of glass: (a) Tap out a fixed sash. (b) Saw through a mullion. (c) Chop out the mullion stub so that the new pane (inset) can be fixed in the rebate.

Make sure the new pane of glass is sufficiently thick. A glazier will advise you, but here is a guide. For panes up to 3.5 sq. m (12 sq ft) with a maximum single dimension of 1300 mm (51 in) use 3 mm (24 oz) glass. For panes of between 3.5 sq. m and 8.5 sq. m (12 – 28 sq. ft) with a maximum single dimension of 2100 mm (84 in) use 4 mm (32 oz) glass. Larger windows are unlikely to figure in DIY work.

If some of the original sash designs are to remain in the window, then it is as well to make up a new sash, nail it in the frame and glaze it. This gives a uniform look.

Beware of disposing of too many opening sashes during a conversion both for your own comfort, and possibly to comply with local building regulations.

Converting fixed sashes

A fixed sash that is merely nailed into place can be converted into an opening one, although you risk breaking the pane in doing so. Gently tap out the sash from its transoms and mullions, as described above. Fit hinges to the sash and to the frame, as described in the next chapter.

New windows for old

The time may come when your window frames are so rotted that complete replacement is the only course. When this happens, take the opportunity to install your choice of window, but in keeping with your home's outside appearance. When starting from scratch like this, the possibilities are enormous. For instance, you could ensure that the new frames have rebates sufficiently deep to take sealed-unit double glazing. The extra cost would be moderate at this stage. You might like to have extra opening sashes or you could have pivoted, instead of hinged, sashes. At the back of the house, consider extending the opening to make patio doors.

You have also to decide whether to do the work yourself or not. Often the extra cost of having the work done for you, instead of buying the components and carrying out the work yourself, is small. Moreover, the work will probably be done more quickly – an important point with regard to security and sudden changes in the weather.

Should you decide to do the work yourself, make sure you measure up properly. Measure each dimension in at least two places and take the smallest. Have all the components to hand, and all preparatory work completed, before you take out the existing window.

Begin by removing the individual sashes. Saw out the transoms and mullions. Cut out any external rendering that will prevent the main frame from being moved easily (Fig. 4:13). Then saw through the jambs on each side near the cill and the head, and prise out the jambs. Next, saw through the window cill and board, and prise these out. Remove the remains of the jamb at the bottom. Lastly, prise out the frame head. To do this, you may have to remove the brickwork holding the horns in position. Or you can just saw them off,

4.13 *Replacing a damaged timber frame: (a) Chop a border of rendering from round the opening. (b) Saw through a jamb. (c) Prise out the jambs. (d) Remove sill and remains of jambs. (e) The frame head (f) The new frame in position.*

and leave them *in situ*. If the fixing was by means of nails driven into wooden plugs, examine the plugs to see if they are in good condition. If they are, use them for fixing the new frame. If they show signs of rot, pull them out and point the gap with mortar. Fix the new frame with screws driven into wall plugs.

Clean out the old opening, removing dirt and debris, then place the new frame in position to try it for size. Adjust it with a plane if it is too big. Apply a bed of mortar to the bottom of the opening, and sit the frame on this. Fix the frame into place by driving screws through pre-drilled holes in it and into the original wooden plugs or into new wall plugs. Seal the gap round the sides and on top with mastic applied from a gun. Replace any brick to cover the horns.

Chapter 5
JOINERY

'Joinery' describes all work carried out with wood. This includes large sections of the floor and roof structure, however, which are more conveniently dealt with elsewhere. In this chapter we shall be looking at the finishing wood touches on the walls – skirtings, doorways, picture rails – and the doors.

If you have an old house, it is all too easy to rip out the joinery and replace it with something new, with the aim of modernizing your home. Remember, however, that the joinery is an important factor in determining the atmosphere of a period home. If you remove it, you risk destroying the house's character. It is a fact that houses with period features intact or sympathetically restored are the ones that attract the highest prices on the housing market. So, if you are not careful, you could be lowering the value of your most precious asset. Nevertheless warehouses selling appropriate mouldings are becoming increasingly common.

DOORS

It is impossible to make a door from one single piece of timber. You cannot get wood of sufficient width to span a door opening, and even if you could, it would be intolerably heavy and expensive. The methods used to solve this problem can be seen in the various styles of door that have been fitted.

Panelled doors (Fig. 5:1) are the most decorative. They are made up of two outer vertical members known as stiles. Joining them are horizontal members called rails. Usually there are three of these – the top, bottom and middle (or lock) rails – although there may be more. Traditionally, the rails were mortised into the stiles, but nowadays it is usual for them to be joined by means of dowels. The spaces between the main members are filled with panels that may be solid or of glass. Previously, solid panels were of natural timber, but recently plywood is likely to have been used instead. Solid panels are usually fitted into grooves in the stiles and rails, and the join is neatened by moulding. Glass panels cannot be recessed into grooves, because re-glazing would then be impossible.

The size of panels used in glazed doors varies enormously. Some doors are almost entirely of glass, with just a stile at each side and rails at top and bottom. Others have a number of thin glazing bars dividing the glass into small panes.

Solid panel door have become popular again and it is now fashionable to fit panelled and other period-style doors, particularly as the front door.

External doors are not interchangeable with internal doors: they have totally different functions. An external door has to be made of weather-resistant materials and must be strong enough to resist burglars. Internal doors need to be of a fire-resistant construction. Internal doors are usually about 35 mm (1⅜ in) thick whereas external doors should be about 44 mm (1¾ in). Hardwood is usually used only for external doors, and softwood for room doors, but practice varies.

Flush doors (Fig.5:2) evolved as an alternative to panelled doors, because of the soaring price of timber. They consist of thin sheet material – hardboard or plywood – fixed to both sides of a timber framework. This framework consists of a stile on each side edge and a cross rail at the top and bottom. There may be other cross rails and diagonal braces. The facing is glued and pinned to the framework. Alternatively, instead of the intermediate support battens, there may be a honeycomb of toughened paper, or curls of wood shaving, glued to both facings. Blocks of wood (called lock blocks) are fitted on both sides to take handles and latches.

5.1 – 5.3 Three types of door.

5.1   Rails

Stile

Panels

Panelled

5.2

Flush

5.3

Ledged
and braced

Some doors are designed to be fitted on to either the left or the right edge, so they have only one lock block. If you buy a door, be aware of the choices.

On exterior flush doors, there will be provision, too, for fitting a letter flap. The edges of a well-made flush door will have thin lengths of timber (lipping) to give a neater finish and protect the edges of the facing. The lipping may be fixed by means of a tongue and groove, or it might be glued and pinned into place. Lipping is particularly important on an exterior door and usually matches the facing. A flush door can also be partly glazed – it may, for instance, have a glass panel at the top.

Ledged and braced doors (Fig. 5:3) are nowadays used mostly on outbuildings – garden sheds, for instance – or as a full-height garden gate. At one time they were used also as house doors, and examples of this can still be seen in many period cottages. This type of door is based on tongued and grooved timber, or matchboarding with a V-shaped groove between the boards, as in some wall cladding. Ledged and braced doors are invariably made of softwood.

The timber is joined together and nailed to horizontal members known as ledges. Usually, there are three ledges – one is placed some way from the top, another some way from the bottom, with a middle one usually half-way up the door. To strengthen the door and prevent it from sagging, diagonal timbers – the braces – are fitted between the ledges. The braces should always slope upwards from the hinged edge – so when buying such a door bear in mind that there is a left and right hand choice. These doors are stronger when the braces are jointed into the ledges.

Ledged and braced doors do not have thick edges so they cannot be fitted with mortise locks or be hung by means of hinges recessed into a stile. You must use surface fixed hinges, which can easily be removed with a screwdriver. As a result, such doors are not secure.

Framed ledged and braced doors are variants of ordinary ledged and braced doors. A frame is made, similar to that for a panelled door, with a stile on each edge and a top, bottom and middle rail. The rails take the place of the ledges but braces are fitted, and the door is clad with tongued and grooved cladding or matchboarding. This construction is much stronger than that of an ordinary ledged and braced door. Furthermore, it will take mortise locks, and butt hinges can be fitted to the edges, so it is suitable where greater security is required.

Glass doors without any timber framing whatsoever can be bought. The glass is opaque, to ensure some measure of privacy with the door closed, and is toughened, so there is no fear of breakage. Such doors are very useful as a means of letting light into dark rooms. They are, however, more expensive than a timber door with glass panels, and cannot be reduced in size if they are too big for the opening.

Louvred doors originated in Mediterranean countries, where there is a considerable need for ventilation. They have become popular in cooler climes, however, as a decorative feature. The main disadvantage is that they cannot serve as draught excluders if necessary. Moreover, dust can pass through them. The louvred door is made up of two stiles and two or more cross rails. The louvres – horizontal slats – are set at an angle and overlap each other, so that although spaces are left between the louvres, you cannot see through them. A door can be louvred from top to bottom, or it may have louvres just in the top half, and be a panelled or flush door lower down. Mock louvres are made up of triangular slats fixed to a hardboard or plywood background, or to moulded plastic. These look like the real thing, but there is no space for air to pass through.

Aluminium doors are also available, but they are expensive, and thus rarely found.

Buying a new door

New doors are widely stocked – at DIY shops, builders' merchants, home improvement centres and joinery suppliers. Some large firms specialize in doors, and produce lavish catalogues of what is available. Many of them make a speciality of supplying feature doors.

Before you go shopping, find out what size of replacement door you need. Measure the opening, rather than the existing door, which may have shrunk over the years. Doors and door openings are made to standard sizes, so you should be able to buy one to fit into a modern house. Older houses might have non-standard openings.

If you cannot find a door of the right dimensions, you might be able to cut one down to size, but this is difficult to do without weakening the door.

Panelled doors, because of their wide stiles and cross rails, can be slightly reduced – by up to 19 mm (¾ in) all round. Flush doors should not be pared down at all if you can possibly avoid it. Remember there is a lipping on the side edges, and the top and bottom cross rails are too small to stand much of a reduction. You can, however, plane a little off them to get a good fit.

You can also, of course, have doors made to size, but these are much more expensive than standard-sized doors.

The thickness of the door can be a problem too. You might be unable to find one to match the rebate in the frame. The problem is easily solved with an internal door, because the door stop is usually just nailed into place, and can be prised off and re-positioned. On an external frame the rebate is usually an integral part of the moulding. To increase it, trim some of the timber away, but not too much or it will be weakened. To reduce the rebate you might be able to glue and pin extra timber to the frame. If either of these methods fail, then order a made-to-measure door. Tell your supplier whether you want an external or internal door.

Removing an old door

It is always advisable to hang a new door with new hinges. Remove the old door by withdrawing the screws that hold the hinges to the frame, not those fixing them to the door. Try every screw on all the hinges to make sure that they can be turned – it is likely that some of them have become so clogged with paint, or affected by corrosion, that they are stuck firmly in place. There are several methods for loosening these.

First of all, ensure you use a large enough screwdriver. The width of the blade tip should be almost the length of the screw slot, and the blade should be of a thickness that fills the width of the slot. The blade should be in good condition, not worn at the edges. Scrape all paint from the screw slot and the top of the head, then place the screwdriver blade into the screw slot, and give the handle a short sharp blow with a hammer – this will not cause damage to a modern plastic-handled screwdriver, in the way it would to an old wooden one. The blow should be sufficient to dislodge the screw from the wood. If the screw still does not turn, use a screwdriver blade inserted in a carpentry brace to give you a better purchase.

If you still have no success, try applying mild heat, from a soldering iron or a pencil flame blowlamp for example. The heat causes both the screw and the surrounding woodwork to expand – but at different rates, because they are different materials. When they cool, they will revert to the former size, but should no longer be stuck together. You probably intend to re-decorate in any case, so the damage caused by the heat to the paintwork will not matter.

Once you are sure every screw is freed, start to withdraw them. Starting from the top, take out every screw but one from each of the hinges. Now either get a helper to hold the door or place wedges underneath it, so that it cannot fall away from the frame. Take out the remaining screws, then lift the door clear.

Fitting a new door

Fit the hinges (see later sections) to the door before raising it into position. It is convenient to carry out other work, such as adding locks and – in the case of front doors – letter flaps

5.4 *Hanging a new door: (a) Saw off the 'horns'. (b) The door is wedged in position. (c) Mark where door needs to be reduced. (d) Plane it down to size. (e) Mark a hinge recess on a frame. (f) Chop out the recess on the frame.*

before the door is hung. The striking plate, into which the lock, bolt or latch locates, cannot be fitted until the door is hung, however. If the door is to be glazed, wait until it is hung before doing so. Then there will be less risk of breakage.

A panelled door will be delivered with the stiles protruding top and bottom. These 'horns', as they are known, are there to protect the door during transport. Saw them off with a tenon saw, working from the outer edges inwards, to lessen the risk of splitting (Fig. 5:4). If you need to saw any timber off the height or width of a panelled door, do so at this stage. Note though that you cannot just saw the excess from one edge, because the door will appear unbalanced. Remove equal amounts from both top and bottom or from both sides.

With the door roughly to size, stand it in the opening, on small wedges. Note how the door fits, marking with a pencil where it needs to be reduced in size, then take it down and plane it as necessary. To avoid splitting the ends of the stiles, work from the outer edges inwards when planing the top and bottom of the door. On a flush door do not plane too much off the lipping.

Size the door so that there is a clearance of about 3 mm

(⅛ in) at the top and sides; slightly more at the bottom where it has to clear the floor covering. Stand it once again in the opening, on wedges, and mark on the side of the door the position of the hinge recesses on the frame. Fit the hinges at these spots and hang the door. Initially, fix only one screw per hinge. Now see if the door opens and closes properly. If it is binding in places, shave the edges where necessary. If the recesses in the frame are slightly too deep for the new hinges, pack the hinges out with card. When you are satisfied, fix all the remaining hinge screws.

Fitting butt hinges The position of the previous hinges on the door frame will determine exactly where the new ones should be fixed on the replacement door. Assuming that the old hinges worked satisfactorily, fit new ones of exactly the same size, so that they will fill the recess neatly. If, however, you have replaced the doorway lining of the door frame, or you are hanging the door in a new site, there will be no hinges to guide you. Note then that you need three 100 mm (4 in) butt hinges. The top one should be placed a distance of one and a half times its length from the top of the door. The bottom one should be one and a half times its length, plus 50 mm (2 in) from the bottom edge. If both hinges were sited at equal distance from the edges, the bottom one would appear to be lower down than it actually is. The middle hinge should be halfway between the top and bottom ones.

To cut a recess for a hinge, place the door on edge on the floor. Have it held steady, preferably using a vice. Determine the distance of the first hinge from the top or bottom of the door, and mark the spot on the door in pencil. At this point draw a line across the edge, using a try-square, so that it is truly square to the face of the door (Fig. 5:5). Draw a similar line, with the aid of the square, the length of the hinge away from the first. Now set a marking gauge to the width of one leaf of the hinge. Mark a line this distance away from the closing face of the door. The knuckle of the hinge,

5.5 *Fitting butt hinges: (a) Mark out the top and bottom of the hinge recess with a square. (b) Complete the outline with a marking gauge. (c) Chop out the recess.*

when closed, should be just clear of the door face. Next, set the gauge to the thickness of one leaf of the hinge, and mark this on the face of the door. Make a saw cut, using a small tenon or dovetail saw, along the top and bottom lines, down to the thickness line on the face.

Chop out the recess with a chisel and hammer. Make a series of chisel cuts, 3 mm ($\frac{1}{8}$ in) apart, to the depth of the line on the door face and parallel to the saw lines on the edge. Clean out the waste with the chisel, working from the front edge. Position the hinge leaf in the recess, to check that it is a good fit, and that it lies flat. The door will not close properly otherwise. Make any adjustments needed. If the hinge is proud of the recess, shave off a little more timber with the chisel. If it is sunk too deep, pack it out with card.

Drill pilot holes for the fixing screws, and screw the hinge into place, taking care to position it accurately. Some hinges are pre-packed complete with fixing screws. If yours are not, test the gauge of screw required by test-pushing a screw into the hole. Use 25 mm (1 in) screws. Fix the other hinges in the same way, then hang the door.

Recesses for a hinge in the frame are cut in much the same way. The work will be more difficult because of the awkward working position, so take extra care to ensure accuracy.

Fitting rising butts Unlike ordinary butt hinges, rising butts raise the door as it is opened, and lift it clear of any carpet. You can remove the existing hinges of an ordinary door, and fit rising butts in their place. A door fitted with rising butts also tends to be self-closing.

The leaves of a rising butt are not fixed together as are those of an ordinary butt. Instead, one leaf can be removed-from the hinge pin, which is fixed to the other leaf. The leaf with the pin is fitted to the frame and the other to the door. Provided you fix the pin leaf clear of the frame, the door can merely be lifted clear, should it ever be necessary to re-move it.

Rising butts are available in right or left hand sets, so note the side on which your door is hinged before ordering. They are fitted in much the same way as ordinary ones, but there are two points to note. First, the two parts must be positioned on both frame and door with extreme accuracy, otherwise only one will be seated properly, and too much of a strain would then be imposed on it. Second, the top of the door must be bevelled off towards the frame, so that it can open properly.

Fitting a letter plate A new front door will need a letter plate. Aim to position this at a height that will allow the postman to push letters through without having to stoop. On a panelled door, set the plate in the middle rail; never the bottom one.

5.6 *Fitting a weatherboard: (a) Trace its outline on a door stop. (b) Chop out its shape from the stop. (c) You can nail the weatherboard in place or fix it with screws driven from inside.*

On a glazed front door that has no middle rail, fit a vertical flap in the lock stile. Provision for a flap to be fitted is usually made in an external flush door. In that case the position is decided for you.

Letter plates are usually fixed by means of bolts that pass through the door, and are held in place by nuts on the inside.

Place the door flat on a bench, and position the plate accurately and squarely. Mark in pencil on the door the outline of the opening. Drill a large hole at each corner of the opening, and cut out the shape with a padsaw or powered jigsaw. Clean up the edges of the cut with glass-paper. Now place the plate back in position, and mark the position of the fixing bolts. Drill clearance holes for these bolts. Place the plate on the front of the door, push in the bolts, and on the other side fit and tighten the nuts on the bolts.

An internal flap can be added to eliminate draughts. Normally this is just screwed into place.

Fitting a weatherboard A weatherboard is a shaped piece of moulding fitted to the bottom of an external door to throw rainwater clear. It prevents the door from becoming soaked, and so makes it less likely to rot. Some have a flatback, and are held to the door by nails. Others have a tongue, and this locates in a groove that has to be ploughed in the door.

To fit a weatherboard (Fig. 5:6), first cut it to match the exact width of the door. Take an offcut from the moulding making sure both ends are square and hold it in place at the bottom of the door stops on each side of the opening. Trace in pencil the outline of the moulding on both stops. Chop out this shape from the stops so that the weatherboard will fit snugly into them when the door is closed.

Treat the bottom of the weatherboard with an exterior quality sealer and brush a gloss paint on the back. You can also paint the underneath. To help you grip the timber drive one or two nails into the front. While the paint is still wet, place the weatherboard on the door, and nail it in place. Punch home the nail heads, fill them, and paint over. Do not forget to treat the bare wood which you exposed on the frame.

Security

One of the most important functions of an external door is that it should keep out burglars. In fact, the most popular point of entry for housebreakers is through a window, but it is still good sense to make it as difficult as possible for them to walk through a door.

One of the most common security devices for external doors is a night latch. Most people would refer to it as a lock, but there is a difference: both locks and latches have a bolt, but a latch bolt is sprung so it closes automatically. To open the latch, you turn a handle inside or a key outside. A lock can be closed or opened only by a key. A lock or latch that is actually housed in a hole cut in the body of the door is known as a mortise lock or latch. If it is fitted on the surface of the door, it is called a rim lock, or latch. A night latch is a rim latch. It is fixed to the back of the door, and the keep into which its bolt locates is fitted to the back of the frame (Fig. 5:7).

This latch is the easiest of all security devices to force. Although it has a catch to prevent the bolt from moving, the only value of this is to stop the latch from closing and locking you out if, for instance, you go outside for a moment without your keys. It is useful to have a latch on an external door. When you are at home, it keeps the door closed without your having to lock it, but when you go out you need greater security.

5.7 *Security devices for a door*

Horizontal mortise lock

Rim lock

Mortise bolt

Barrel bolt

Staple

Mortise dead lock

Mortise latch

Hinge bolt

Some night latches can be deadlocked both from inside and out. These are more secure than the simple latch, but they are no substitute for a mortise lock on external doors. When you are out the only protection for the door by which you have left is the lock you close with a key as you go, so make sure it is a good one. Buy a good quality mortise lock, with five levers and steel roll bars inside the bolt, so that it cannot be sawn through.

If your home has two external doors, the back door can have bolts instead of, or in addition to, a mortise lock. If you fit it with both, it will be more secure than the front door. This can be an advantage because usually the back of a house is more vulnerable, as a burglar at work will be less visible there than at the front.

Cheap barrel bolts that have the staple (the part into which the bolt locates) fitted to the inside face of the frame are not very secure, for a door held by these can be pushed in. It is much safer to fit bolts with staples in a hole bored into the side of the frame. Better still, fit mortise bolts, which are like simplified mortise locks.

It is not just at the lock edge that a door needs protection. It is just as vulnerable to a determined thief along the hinge edge. If the hinges are weak, or not securely screwed in place, they can easily be broken off, if forced. So replace any that are in doubtful condition, and insert longer screws instead of the existing ones.

Another way to strengthen the hinge side of the door is to fit bolts there, making it less easy to force the hinges. These are variously known as hinge, stud, or dog bolts. They are fixed to the frame, and locate in holes bored in the door when it is closed.

You can also fit a spy hole as a means of checking on the identity of callers before you open the door. Alternatively, you can fit a door chain.

Another worthwhile device is some strong, wide metal trim around the letter plate, to prevent a determined thief from trying to saw the door in half.

Fitting a night latch

A night latch consists of a cylinder barrel, into which the key fits, and a latch case, mounted on a backplate on the inside of the door. To fit one of these latches you need to drill a hole through the door of sufficient diameter to take the cylinder barrel. Start drilling from the front of the door, using a brace and bit. The hole will probably need to be about 38 mm (1½ in) in diameter and should be positioned so that the connecting bar of the cylinder locates correctly into the latch case. The dimensions for aligning both parts of the lock are usually given with the fitting instructions. The connect-

5.8 *Fitting a night latch: (a) The cylinder passes through the latch pull. (b) The back plate is fixed to the inside of the door. (c) Fix the keep.*

ing bar will also have to be cut to a length to suit the thickness of the door.

The cylinder passes through the latch pull (Fig. 5:8), a surround that incorporates a small handle with which you can pull the door closed. Screw the back plate into place on the inside of the door, aligning the hole in the plate with the hole in the door. Cut the connecting bar so that it protrudes about 13 mm (½ in) on the inside of the door into the latch case. Screw the latch case to the cylinder. Shut the door and slide the keep on to the latch. Mark the position of the keep on to the frame, then chisel out a small recess so that the edge of the keep fits flush. Fix the keep with screws.

Fitting a mortise lock

A mortise lock should be fitted to an external door to make it more secure. If the lock is to be fitted on an existing door, there is no need to remove the door from its hinges. Should the door be new, however, fit the lock before hanging it. The striking plate, which receives the lock bolt, cannot be fitted to the frame until the door has been hung.

In a panelled door the lock is fitted at the level of the lock rail; in a flush door it goes into the lock block, which is usually higher than a lock rail. Determine the position of the lock, and hold the casing on the front edge of the door. Mark the top and bottom lines of the mortise to be cut for the lock (Fig. 5:9). Push a pencil through the keyhole of the lock, to mark on the face of the door where the keyhole of the door has to be cut. Using a try-square, draw a pencil line on the stile edge, at right angles to the edge of the door, to mark the top and bottom of the mortise. To ensure that the lock will be positioned centrally, measure the thickness of the door, and subtract from this the thickness of the lock. Set a marking gauge to half the remaining thickness, and use it to mark lines from both the inside and outside faces of the door to complete the outline of the mortise. The easiest way to cut out the mortise for the lock casing is to bore a series of holes with a brace and bit, the diameter of which equals the thickness of the lock. The depth of the holes should be the same as that of the lock casing. Make sure that the brace is held square to the work. Clean out the mortise with a chisel, and push the lock casing into it to test that it is a good fit. If the fit is bad, withdraw the casing and examine it. Scratches in its paintwork and paint marks on the inside of the mortise will show where the mortise needs to be eased off slightly.

Push the casing into the mortise once again, then draw a line on the door edge around the face plate. Using a chisel, pare out a recess in the edge to take the face plate and the cover plate. When fitted, the cover plate must be flush with the stile edge. Since the closing edge of the door is usually slightly bevelled off, to allow it to enter the frame more

5.9 *Fitting a mortise lock: (a) The parts of the lock (b) Hold the casing on the face of the door to mark out for the mortise. (c) Bore holes for the mortise. (d) Clean out the mortise. (e) Pare out for the cover plate. (f) Mark the position for the striking plate. (g) Mark for the hole to receive the bolt. (h) Fix the striking plate.*

snugly, the recess for the cover plate will need to be a little deeper along that edge.

Make the hole for the key; drill the top half, then complete the lower half with a padsaw. Neaten the keyhole by screwing an escutcheon plate (a small metal surround) on each side of the door. A small pivoted cover may be incorporated on both plates, or merely on the one intended for inside.

Now fit the striking plate to the door frame. To do this, close the door and turn the lock with the key. A slight force on the key will cause the position of the bolt to be imprinted on the door frame. If the mark is not clear, try pushing a sheet of carbon paper between door and frame, or smearing a little paint on the end of the lock bolt. Hold the striking plate on the frame, position its hole directly over the mark of the bolt, then draw on the frame the position of this hole and of the entire plate. Chisel out a mortise to take the bolt and a recess for the plate. Screw the plate into position.

Test that the lock works properly. If the bolt does not enter the hole in the striking plate easily, you might be able to enlarge the hole slightly with a metal file. Otherwise, the plate may have to be re-positioned. Marks on the sides, top or bottom of the bolt and hole will show where the bolt is binding.

Fitting a mortise latch

A mortise latch is fitted to a room door. It may, or may not, incorporate a lock. The catch is fitted in the same way as for a mortise lock, except that there is a handle on each side of the door. These locate on a spindle that passes through the door. A hole for the spindle is drilled through the door. When the latch case is in position in the mortise, the spindle is pushed through to engage in the hole for it in the case. The handles engage on the spindle.

The handles are merely screwed into place. When a combined lock and latch is fitted, there is no need to fit an escutcheon plate (to cover the keyhole) because this is incorporated into the handle.

Fitting a spy hole

A spy hole is a lens system in a solid door through which you can peer at callers before deciding whether you should open the door to them. The lens gives an exceptionally wide angle of view. The spy hole comes in two parts that screw together from opposite sides of the door. To fit it, bore a hole through the door (the instructions will tell you the correct diameter) at a convenient height for your eyes. Push the front half of the spy hole in from the outside of the door, and the back half from inside. Thread them together. There is a slot on the inside section to allow you to tighten it on the thread of the other half, so that the front portion cannot be extracted from the outside.

Faults with doors

One of the simplest faults that can develop in a door is that the hinges might start to squeak as the door is opened and closed. Apply a light oil sparingly to the top of the hinge pin, so that it will work its way down the knuckle. Applying it at any other part of the knuckle will be ineffective; and too much oil will merely drip onto the floor coverings.

Various faults can prevent the door from opening and closing properly.

The hinge may not be securely fixed to the frame. If this is the case, try fitting longer screws – the diameter of the hinge holes will prevent you from fitting thicker ones. Take out and replace only one screw at a time so that you do not disturb the door on the frame. If a new screw goes in too freely, remove it, then pack out the hole with a small dowel – tradesmen often use a matchstick or two. Then fit the screw again.

One or more of the hinges may be worn. Try rocking the door gently to see if there is play at the hinges. If so, fit new hinges. Fit the hinges one at a time, so that the door can remain hanging. If there are only two hinges, ask a helper to steady the door, or support it on wedges as you renew each hinge.

A door can be 'hinge bound' – a condition in which the door meets the hinge side of the frame before it is properly closed. One possible cause for this is that the hinge screws protrude, instead of fitting flush. If so, drive the screws fully home. A door can also be hinge bound if one or more of the hinges is recessed too deeply in either the door or the frame. If this is so, withdraw the screws holding the hinge, then place card or hardboard underneath it to pack it out level and flush with the surrounding timber.

An external door may become too tight to fit in its frame, particularly during rainy weather. This is a sign that damp is causing the door to swell – perhaps because it is not sufficiently protected against the elements. Wait until the door has dried out thoroughly, then paint or varnish it properly.

Binding or sticking can also be caused by a build-up of paint on the edges of a door. Open and close the door to see where it is binding. If the spot is not obvious, rub chalk on all the edges. The chalk will be removed where the door binds. Plane the door so that there is a clearance of about 3 mm (⅛ in) between the frame and the door when closed, then repaint. Do not take much off an external door in damp weather because when the door dries out the gap will be too much.

Dowel coated in glue

5.10 *Using a dowel to repair a loose joint between a stile and rail*

It is impossible to plane a door properly – especially at the top and bottom edges – while it is still hung. You will have to take it down, but before you do, make sure you know where it is binding. If the bottom binds, swing the door backwards and forwards several times over a sheet of coarse glasspaper placed on the floor. This might remove the cause of the trouble. Finish off with fine glasspaper so that there will be no rough edges to catch on any carpet.

If the door binds near the top of the lockstile and on the floor on the same side, the bottom hinge might be at fault, causing the door to sag. Pack the hinge out with card or board to bring the door upright, or fit a new hinge. If the binding is at the bottom of the stile and the top of the frame, look for the cause in the top hinge.

In both panelled and flush doors, the joint where the top or bottom rail meets the stile might work loose. You can often repair this by boring holes through both rails and stile, and inserting dowels on which you have smeared glue (Fig. 5:10).

A tongued and grooved door may sag because it is inadequately braced. In fact, although such doors are invariably described as being ledged and braced, there may be no braces – just ledges. Fit braces, after making sure the door is squared up properly.

Warped doors will not close properly, and if a lock is fitted it might not turn. Take the door off its hinges and remove all the door furniture. One way to cure the warping is to place the door flat on the ground with the bow uppermost, in an enclosure such as a garage or shed. Raise the door by sup-

Cures for warped doors: 5.11 A brace between a ceiling and the door 5.12 Force a door flat with a batten screwed to the floor.

5. 11

Brace between door and roof

Block of wood

Ground supports

5. 12

Batten screwed to floor

Blocks under corners that are true

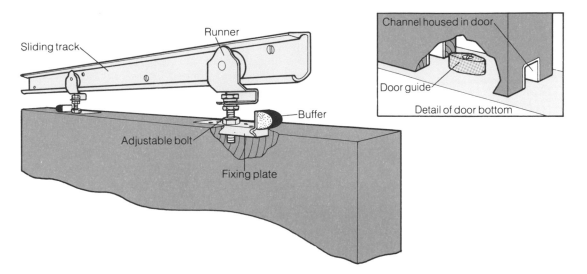

Sliding track

Runner

Buffer

Adjustable bolt

Fixing plate

Channel housed in door

Door guide

Detail of door bottom

5.13 *Typical sliding door gear*

porting it at each end, then put a brace between the roof or ceiling and the face of the door (Fig. 5:11). The aim is to distort the door as far the other way as it is warped on its face. Leave the brace in position for a few days.

Another method is to lay the door on a boarded floor with blocks the thickness of the distortion under the corners that are true (Fig. 5:12). Force the door flat with battens screwed to the floor.

Fitting sliding doors

To allow sufficient space for the average room door to open and close you have to leave clear at least a square metre (about 40 sq in), of floor space. This is a large area to take out of the small rooms of today. To give more space, you could convert your present hinged doors to sliding doors. The conversion is simple for most doors, and you can buy kits for this purpose.

The kits come with complete instructions, which you should follow carefully. Basically you have to prise off the architrave on one side of the opening, fit a track over the opening, and add wheels (which locate on the track) to the top of the door (Fig. 5:13). Hang the door by its wheels on the track. A channel at floor level makes the whole thing work smoothly, and there is a pelmet to hide the mechanism. A different type of handle is required – usually it comes with the kit – so the present latch and its striking plate on the frame will have to be removed and made good.

DOORWAYS

Doorways are lined with timber to neaten the opening, give a stop against which the door can close, and provide a fixing point for hinges, locks and latches.

External door frames are usually fitted into a recess in the brickwork. They consist of two upright side members (jambs) into which a rebate is machined at the factory to form a stop for the door to close against. The jambs are nailed to wooden plugs set into the wall while it is being built. The timber at the top of the opening is known as the head, which may project beyond the opening and be mortared into the brickwork. The projections are known as horns. The jambs are mortised into the head. Some doorways have no horns: instead the jambs are dowelled into the head, which may also be nailed to wooden plugs. At the bottom the jambs may be tenoned into a wooden cill. Alternatively, they may be fixed with rustproof dowels cemented into the step, and bedded on a layer of mastic to protect the end grain.

At the foot there is often a threshold, against which the door closes, to make the opening more weatherproof. Metal thresholds incorporate a strip of rubber or plastic that seals against the bottom of the door.

Internal door openings (Fig. 5:14) usually have a wooden door lining at both sides and at the top. The lining is nailed to timber plugs, and its width is the thickness of the wall with the masonry and plaster on both sides. Linings machined to fit various thicknesses of wall are available at wood yards.

A stop bead, against which the door closes, is fitted. It is formed either by a rebate or (more usually) by a separate length of timber nailed into place.

An ugly join line between the plaster and the edge of the door lining can be covered and neatened with lengths of moulded timber known as architrave. These are an important feature of the room, and can add as much to the period quality of the room as the skirting and picture rails. The architrave is usually mitred at the top corners.

Sometimes the plaster is taken up to the edge of the door lining, and the architrave nailed to the edge of the lining. In better quality work, however, a batten the thickness of the plaster is fixed to the face of the brickwork, butting up against the lining on both sides and at the top. Then the plaster is taken to the edge of the batten, and the architrave is nailed to this batten. No threshold is normally fitted to the foot of an internal door.

Lengths of timber machined to form lining, stop bead and plaster bed in one profile are sometimes installed.

Fanlights may be fitted above both external and internal a — Head — Horn — Stop bead — Jamb-lining — Plug and nail — Wooden sill — Mastic — Dowel into stone step

b — Wall — Plaster — Architrave — Stop bead — Door lining

c — Door — Plaster — Skirting — Wall — One piece timber lining

doors. On external doors – and occasionally on internal ones too – the fanlight can be opened for extra ventilation.

To accommodate a fanlight, the door opening is made extra tall, and jambs and head are installed in the normal way. A transom is fitted to form the bottom of the fanlight and the top of the door opening. In fixed fanlights over internal doors, the pane of glass is usually held merely by lengths of beading. On external and hinged fanlights putty is required, just as for any other window.

Doorway repairs

The jambs of an external door become exposed to the weather, particularly at the foot, when the step gets soaked. As a result they may rot. To repair them, cut out the damaged section, then beyond it into about 75 mm (3 in) of sound wood. If there is a wooden threshold, the jamb may be tenoned into it, and you will then have to cut through the tenon. Get a new piece of timber (it might be easier to use two pieces to form the rebate). Plane it down to size if necessary, apply preservative to the back, and fix it with screws. Join to the existing timber by means of a scarfe joint.

Shrinkage of the timber and settlement of the wall may cause gaps to develop between external door frames and

5.14 Construction of doorways: (a) How an external doorway is built up (b) How an internal doorway is formed with lining, stop bead and architrave (c) Plan sketch of an internal doorway

the wall. These can be filled with mastic – the type squeezed from a tube is easiest to apply. To save on the amount of mastic needed, a large gap can first be packed out with rags or rope.

The architrave is the part of an internal doorway most likely to suffer damage. It is virtually impossible to patch up a damaged architrave because of the difficulty of buying new mouldings to match the old. The only course is to remove it totally (on both sides and the top) by prising it off. Then buy new architrave from a timber merchant.

Stop beads, too, are easily damaged. These can be patched, in the manner described for external door jambs, or you can prise the whole length off and replace it. Since this is usually a straight piece of wood, and not moulded, matching up presents no problem. A damaged lining can be repaired or replaced similarly.

Jambs and lining may shake loose from the wall, even though the timber is sound. The traditional way to re-fix them is to remove them, cement new timber plugs into the wall, then nail the pieces back in position. Sometimes, however, it is possible to re-fix sound jambs or lining without removing them from the wall. Drill through the loose section and into the wall, using a masonry bit. Twist a plastic wall plug on to the end of a wood screw, and insert the wall plug into the hole. Tap the screw head with a hammer, and the plug should pass into the wall – you will feel when this has happened. Tighten the screw, cover its head with filler, and re-paint. Do this at sufficient spots on the frame to ensure a firm fixing.

Linings and jambs can become so damaged that they have to be renewed completely. If you attempt this job, make sure the sides are truly upright, and the opening square, otherwise it will be more difficult to fit the door and get it to work properly. It is difficult to make the sides vertical using the brickwork as a guide. A more reliable method is to drive extra long plugs into the wall, leaving them sticking out well proud. You can make the plugs from 50×25 mm (2×1 in) softwood. They should be propeller-shaped at the end so they lock into place when driven into the mortar. For extra security, place mortar into the hole before fitting the plugs. Now drop a plumb line from the top of the opening and saw the plugs level with the line. Screw the lining to the plugs and it will be vertical.

SKIRTING BOARDS

Skirting boards are lengths of decoratively shaped timber, fitted to neaten the gap between floor and wall. The plaster does not normally extend down to floor level. In period houses, skirtings can be as high as 300 mm (1 ft) or more – and moulded ornately. Today skirtings are much plainer and smaller – perhaps only 100 mm (4 in) in height.

Modern skirtings are usually fixed by means of cut nails driven through the timber and into timber plugs in the masonry. In period houses, where the skirting is deep and elaborately moulded, it is more likely to be nailed to wooden grounds fixed to wall plugs. Rarely, the skirting is of two sections; a bottom piece with a tongue located in a groove in the floorboards, and a top piece joined to the bottom, also by a tongue and groove.

Plugging the gaps

As the timber shrinks, gaps appear between skirting and wall at the top, and between skirting and floor at the bottom. Draughts can enter through these gaps, particularly the one at the bottom. In any event, gaps are unsightly, so it is as well to cover them. The gap where the skirting meets the wall can be stopped up with ordinary decorator's filler. It is quicker and easier to pin lengths of moulding to cover the gap between floor and skirting. Use either quarter-round or triangular-section mouldings (Fig. 5.15). The moulding should be pinned to the skirting (never the floor) to prevent it shaking loose by the vibration of the floor. Mitre the mouldings at the corners.

5.15 *Moulding pinned to skirting to keep out draughts*

Removing skirting board

Badly damaged skirting board should be completely re-placed. If you are fitting built-in floor-standing cupboards – kitchen cabinets, for instance – to a wall, it is often easier and quicker to remove the skirting, then cut it to length and refix it to any part of the bottom of the wall that remains on view, than to trim the cupboard base to fit round the skirting.

Prising off the skirting is easy. Take an old carpentry chisel, and wedge it behind the skirting, preferably near one of the fixing nails. It is worth scraping off the paint to locate one of these nails. Pull hard on the chisel handle and the skirting will start to come away. You can now push timber wedges behind it while you wrench away near the other nails to free the whole length of skirting.

Fitting new skirting

First get your skirting. Choose with care, because skirting contributes to a room's character.

5.16 *How skirtings are fitted:*
(a) Ornate skirting of a period house
(b) Modern skirting.

If you are fitting skirting to just one wall of a room, the problem will be to match it to the rest. This should present no difficulty in recent houses, for skirting with the right profile will be readily available. Older skirting, however, might have to be replaced completely, so that the entire room will look the same.

Modern skirting, as sold widely in timber yards, would not look out of place in a house built, say, since World War I, but it is worth trying to match the period appearance of skirting on buildings earlier than that.

Finding matching skirting need not be difficult now that the importance of period fittings is recognized. Many firms specialize in salvaging such fittings from buildings due for demolition, then offer it for sale. Ask around locally, or look at advertisements in local newspapers to find out if there are any near your home.

The other possibility is to buy separate pieces of small-section moulding, and join them together to form something that looks like your skirting.

Aim to buy skirting in lengths that will cover the whole wall in one span, because joins in the middle never look as neat. Fix the skirting by driving nails through it and into the plugs on the wall (Fig. 5:16). It is worth the effort to position the nails accurately enough to allow you to drive them into the original fixings. All you have to do is cut the skirting to length, then lay it flat on the floor in front of the wall where it will be fixed. Make pencil marks on its face where the nails should go. Drill clearance holes for these nails so that there is no chance of splitting the timber. This is particularly important if you have bought expensive period skirting, or are using lengths of thin moulding. Punch the nails home, cover the heads with filler, and paint the skirting.

Patches for skirting

Where a part of a length of skirting board is damaged, it may be possible to insert a patch. To repair damage in the middle of a length of skirting, begin by cutting out the defective portion. Cut at an angle so that the skirting is wider at the front than at the back. One method of cutting is to push wedges behind the damaged section to force it away from the wall (Fig. 5:17). Now set up a small, fine-toothed saw (preferably a dovetail) in front of the skirting, and in a mitre box. Saw through the skirting at an angle of 45°. This is difficult, because it requires many short movements with the saw, but it can be done. You may have to finish off with a thin bladed saw, such as a keyhole saw.

If you find this method too difficult, there is another, but it is not as neat. This involves making a series of holes with a drill (you will get greater accuracy with an electric one) from the front to the back of the skirting. As with the saw cuts, these should slope, but you do not have to aim for an accurate 45°. It is more important to make all the holes at exactly the same angle. Chop out the waste with a chisel.

5.17 Patching damaged skirting: (a) Cut through the damaged section with either a small saw and mitre box, or bore holes with an electric drill. (b) Mark the new skirting if you have cut out the old with a drill. (c) Make fixing points. (d) Nail the new skirting in place. (e) Deal with corners – external (bottom inset) and internal.

Scrap wood

Shaped interior angle

Mitred exterior angle

If you have sawn out the damaged timber with the aid of a mitre box, use this same guide to cut new timber at exactly the same angle. If you have used the second method, place a length of new moulding in front of the gap. Place a ruler on top of the existing skirting. Align the ruler accurately along the cut so that it overlaps the new skirting. Draw a pencil line along the ruler on top of the new moulding. Cut to this line and you should get a perfect fit.

To provide fixing points for the new mouldings, you need two pieces of scrap wood the same thickness as the plaster (you may have to plane them down to get an exact match) and the same height as the gap between floor and bottom of the plaster. Push these timber packing pieces behind each cut end of the existing skirting, and drive masonry nails through them and into the wall behind. Nail the new skirting to this timber.

Where the damaged portion is near the end of a run of skirting, such as in the corner of the room, you will need to cut through the skirting only once – on the side of the damaged portion furthest from the corner. Prise the damaged piece free. Cut the replacement so as to get a neat join at the corner as well as to fit the angle of the cut you have made. An external corner will probably be mitred – any variation from a 45° joint is due to inaccuracies in the angle of the wall. So, using a mitre box, saw at the angles that give an accurate fit.

At an internal angle, cut one length square to butt up against the wall. Shape the end of the other length to fit the contours of the first. It is much easier to do this before you cut the pieces finally to fit.

PICTURE RAILS

Besides providing an anchorage on which to hang pictures, picture rails provide an important visual break in the walls of high rooms. They are not usually fitted in modern rooms, which are rarely tall enough to take them, but they are widely found in older houses. Many such rails are beautiful additions to the charm of rooms built in a more graceful era, and to remove them would be an act of wanton destruction. Some picture rails, however, are not especially attractive, and even the best can become so badly damaged, or affected by woodworm or rot, that their removal becomes necessary.

Removing picture rails

Picture rails are fixed by means of cut nails driven through them into wooden plugs set into the masonry at centres varying from 450 to 600 mm (18 to 24 in). Prise them away as described for skirting boards, with either a claw hammer or an old chisel. Concentrate your efforts at the locations of the fixing nails. Once you start to lever, you will see their position at a glance. The wall will be damaged as you pull the rail away, but you can make good afterwards with plaster or decorator's filler.

If it is difficult to move the rail, perhaps because the nails have rusted, scrape off the paintwork until the nails are revealed, then punch them through the rail into the wall behind. The rail will then simply fall away. Or just split the rail along the line of the nails with a carpentry chisel, then lift it clear.

Whichever of these two methods you adopt, pull the nails out afterwards, otherwise they might rust and discolour any subsequent decorations. Take them out with a claw hammer, protecting the plaster by placing a small piece of thin waste wood on it. If the nail cannot be withdrawn, drive it well below the surface of the wall, so that it can later be covered with a thick layer of filler.

New picture rails

You may want to replace a damaged rail. Alternatively, you might like the elegance of a rail and the convenience it offers to hang pictures on the walls. Just as with skirting, it is often possible to buy old picture rails from firms that specialize in salvaging period timber from buildings about to be demolished. Otherwise new timber can be used.

If the rail is to replace a damaged one that has been removed, try to make use of the wooden plugs to which the original rail was fixed. Aim to get a rail long enough to cover a wall in one span, to avoid having untidy joins. Cut the rail to size. Hold it just below the plugs on the wall, and mark on the face of the rail where the fixing nails should go. Drill clearance holes for these, especially in old valuable timber, to lessen the risk of splitting the wood. Hold the rail in place, and hammer home the nails, taking care not to mark the face of the timber. Punch the nails home, and disguise the heads with filler.

If there are no timber plugs you can use, fix the rail with screws driven into plastic wall plugs. The heads of these will be more difficult to cover up on more intricate mouldings, but that cannot be helped.

To make your own picture rail, you can buy ornate modern moulding, or merely use a straight batten – timber 45 × 13 mm (1¾ × ½ in) is suitable. There needs to be a space behind the timber into which the hanging clips can locate. To provide such a space, glue small neatly-cut blocks to the back of the rail (Fig. 5:18). The blocks should be of the same size as the main rail and be placed at 900 mm (3 ft) intervals.

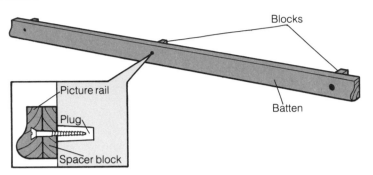

5.18 *Making a new picture rail by screwing a batten to spacer blocks.*

Fix the rail to the wall by means of screws driven through it and the spacer blocks into plastic plugs inserted in the wall. It is easy to paint such a rail without getting paint on the wall.

STAIRCASES

The type of staircase fitted will depend on the plan of the house. Simplest of all is a straight flight, which just goes up from ground to first floor in a single, straight run. Sometimes, however, the staircase changes direction. A half-landing may be fitted if the staircase doubles back on itself. There may be a quarter-landing when the turn is a right-angled one. As an alternative to a quarter landing, there may be angled steps, known as winders.

It is amazing how little appears to go wrong with most staircases when you consider the pounding they take from so many passing feet, and how comparatively slender their construction seems. It pays, though, to take care of staircases, and to rectify faults as soon as they appear, so that they can go on giving trouble-free service.

Avoid carrying out conversions to a staircase – for instance, to make an old-fashioned one look modern – because you might weaken the structure, besides the fact that you will destroy the character of your home.

How staircases are built

Traditionally, staircases were built on the spot by master carpenters working on the construction of the house. This practice has long been discontinued. Instead staircases are supplied to the site as factory-made units.

Usually the staircase is fitted in the hall, with one side against a wall and the other side open.

The part of the stair on which you actually walk is the tread, and the vertical timber that closes the gap between two treads is the riser. The riser is usually merely butted up to the treads and fixed by screws or nails. A better but rare practice, however, is for the riser to be joined by means of tongues and grooves. Sometimes, too, a length of moulding is fitted to the top of the riser, just underneath the projection of the tread, to mask any gap that may develop as the wood shrinks. The front edge of the tread – the nosing – is usually rounded off.

Some modern staircases are of an open-tread design – to make it seem less bulky in the confines of the hall of a small house. It is dangerous to attempt to convert a conventional staircase into an open-tread one, however, for structural reasons.

At each side of the staircase is a long length of timber, called a string. Two types of string are found – open and closed. An open string has a cut-out profile, into which the treads and risers are fitted. A closed string has straight edges, and the treads and risers fit into grooves cut into its side. Wedges are fitted to hold the tread and riser tightly in the groove. The two strings in a staircase need not necessarily be of the same type. It is not uncommon for the wall string (the one against a wall) to be closed, and the outer string (the one away from the wall) to be open.

A safety barrier or balustrade (also called a banister) is fitted to the open side (or sides) of a staircase. The length of timber which you hold as you climb a stairway is a baluster rail and the large upright members into which the baluster rail joins at each end are newel posts. The rail is supported by uprights known as balusters. Modern staircases have fewer balusters than older ones, but you should never alter the number of balusters, because you risk weakening the structure.

A balustrade can also be fitted to the landing, if required. When a staircase has a wall on both sides, there is no balustrade, but instead a handrail is fitted to the wall by means of metal brackets.

Underneath, the staircase is supported on lengths of timber on edge known as carriages. There may be just one central carriage, or there may be an additional two – one near each edge. Lengths of timber, called brackets or sometimes cleats, are fixed to the carriages, to give extra support to the treads. In addition, triangular pieces of wood, known as glue blocks, are fixed to strengthen the join between tread and riser. For the general structure of a staircase see Fig. 5:19.

In many small houses it is customary to have a cupboard under the stairs. In some instances, the underside of the staircase is in full view from within the cupboard. More usually, however, the underneath is covered with either plaster (plasterboard in modern homes, lath and plaster in older ones) or some form of board, such as hardboard.

General repairs to staircases

Major faults that develop in a staircase often require the services of a builder. There are, however, several types of maintenance that the do-it-yourselfer can carry out.

If the underside of the staircase is accessible, maintenance is easy, because you can see at a glance when anything is wrong. It pays to have a look at it from time to time to see that everything is all right. For instance, glue blocks may have fallen off. If so, fix them back with glue and nails. Similarly, a bracket may have worked loose, and should be properly fixed again. Any members that are damaged should be repaired. If the treads or risers are loose in the grooves in a string, make small timber wedges, smear glue on them, and drive them into the groove. You can also nail these wedges in position, using fine pins. Remedial work is much more difficult if the underside is covered. Do not remove the covering, except to repair a major fault.

Creaking stairs

One of the most common and irritating faults that can develop in staircases is creaking. The reason for this is that a tread or riser is not securely fixed and is flexing under the weight. If you can get at the underside, look to see if any blocks are missing, and re-fit them. The wedges holding the treads and risers in the grooves of the strings may have dropped out. Fit new ones if necessary (Fig. 5:19). If the whole staircase creaks, it may be well worth fixing an extra carriage. Indeed there may not be a carriage there at all, and in that case you should fit one.

It is not worth the bother of removing an understairs covering just to silence a few creaks, but makeshift remedies can be tried. Look if there is a gap between the noisy tread and the riser above or below it. If there is one, the simplest remedy could be to puff in a little talcum powder, which would act as a lubricant. Or you could squirt a little woodworking adhesive into the gap, then tap some thin nails down through the tread and into the riser below. Thin section moulding, fitted to both tread and riser just below the nosing of the tread (assuming that none is there already) might also stop the movement. You would, however, probably want to fit it to every riser to maintain continuity of appearance.

Worn nosing

The nosing on the front edge of a tread can become worn. Besides looking unsightly, this can be dangerous. To repair it, use a straight edge and pencil to draw a line on the tread parallel to the undamaged front of the nosing. Remove any

5.19 *How a staircase is built (a) and how to repair it: (b) New wedges stop creaks. (c) Mend worn nosing. (d) Re-fix a loose string. (e) To fit a new tread, remove the balusters so that you can free the damaged tread. (f) Make and fit a new riser. (g) Make a new tread, cutting out mortises to fit round the balusters. (h) Fit wedges, if needed, to hold the new tread in the string. (i) The mortises round the balusters should be closed off with moulding fitted after the balusters have been inserted.*

a

Glue block

Bracket

Carriage

Riser

Nosing

Tread

(Wall) closed string

Balusters

(Outer) open string

Newel post

c

Use batten
to draw line

d

Wooden
wedge

e

f

Nail driven through
riser into string groove

Wedge

g

Shape to original
nosing

Mitred end

h

i

moulding covering the join between tread and riser, then, with a hammer and broad chisel, chop along the pencil line to remove the nosing. Finish with a clean, straight line.

You should aim to have about 13 mm (½ in) of the edge of the riser exposed. If the tread and riser are joined by a tongue projecting from the riser into a groove in the tread, this tongue will have to be removed. Cut a length of softwood to match the width of the stair, and shape one edge to match the profile of the original nosing. You can do this shaping with a file, finishing off with glasspaper. Glue and screw this softwood to the front edge of the tread. Allow the glue to set, then, if necessary, plane the top of the new nosing down to the level of the tread. Replace any beading removed from the join between tread and riser.

Loose treads and risers

Settlement of the building may pull the string away from the treads and risers. Where the gap between the two is not large – up to, say, 19 mm (¾ in) – you could remedy the fault by driving wedges between the string and the wall, and these will force the string back on to the treads and risers. To do this, hack off plaster from the wall above the string near where the gap between string and tread has developed. Take a piece of timber about 300 mm (1 ft) long, 38 mm (1½ in) wide and 25 mm (1 in) thick. Taper one end to form a wedge, then tap it into the gap between the string and the wall as far as it will go. Fit as many wedges as are needed to reposition the string correctly. Saw off the protruding tops of the wedges so that they are flush with the string. Drive screws through the front of the string and into the wedge – you will need to drill pilot holes for the screws. Cover the screw heads with filler and paint. A wide gap – greater than 19 mm (¾ in) – indicates a more serious conditon, and you ought to call in a builder.

Loose balusters

Movement of the staircase can make a baluster loose at its joint with the string or the handrail. To wedge it back into place, smear matchstick-size pieces of timber with glue and push them into the enlarged hole. Top off with filler and paint.

Sometimes, too, a secure fixing can be obtained if you drill a pilot hole at an angle through the baluster and into the string below or rail above, then drive a nail through it.

New treads and risers

You may need to fit a new tread or riser, because one is damaged. Equally likely is that a gap larger than 19 mm (¾ in) may have developed between a tread or riser and the string so that a wider step is needed. If both strings are closed a repair will involve the virtual dismantling of the staircase and so should be left to a builder. If at least one string is open, however, it is possible for a skilled do-it-yourselfer to do the work. Remember, though, that a badly made staircase is a hazard, so if in doubt, leave the work to an expert.

Begin by removing the balusters from the affected tread. Tap them with a block of wood until any nails holding them in position are revealed. Remove the nails, then bend the balusters to spring them out. The tread will be joined to the riser above. Make a few test borings with a small drill bit to determine whether the joint is by means of a tongue and groove. If it is, saw through the tongue with a padsaw. If there is no tongue, the tread and riser will be joined with screws or nails. Saw through these with a hacksaw blade. Prise the tread from the string. Then prise out the riser, if it is to be removed. Cut a piece of softwood to size to make a new riser, and glue and nail it into place. If the joint between the riser and the string is mitred, then mitre the end of the new riser. In a closed string, the riser is held into the groove by means of a wedge.

Cut a tread to size, using the old one as a pattern, and shape the nosing. Cut out mortises in the balustrade edge to take the balusters. Pack the groove of a closed string with wedges if necessary, and fit glue blocks where the treads meet the riser below, then glue and nail the tread into place. Fit the balusters in the mortises, and close off the front of these with a piece of moulding.

A new staircase

The staircase may have so many faults that complete renewal is the only solution. If you have any doubts about your stairs, it is safest to seek the advice of a surveyor.

If a new staircase is to be fitted into an old house, it is unlikely that a factory-made replacement will be available, so a new one will have to be built on site. This is not a job for the do-it-yourselfer, because it requires expertise that only a craftsman has. If a staircase in a modern house is damaged, however, you may be able to buy a factory-built one to replace it yourself.

Spiral staircases

Spiral staircases are an old idea that has been revived for modern homes. All but the most minor repairs should be left to an expert. So if you spot any defects in a modern staircase, consult the supplier or manufacturer.

If you want to install a spiral staircase in an existing house, make sure that there is sufficient room for it. Contrary to popular belief, they do not require less space than conventional staircases; just space of a different shape. They also impose a heavy strain on the floor where the central pillar rests, and this area may need strengthening. Fitting a spiral staircase is a job for a specialist.

ENEMIES OF TIMBER

The joinery of your home, including timber floors, window frames and the wooden structural members of the roof and walls, is liable to be attacked by two main enemies – woodworm and rot. Whenever you are carrying out maintenance (lifting floorboards, for instance) or decorating, always look for signs of woodworm and rot. Indeed, it is a good idea to make periodic inspections to see if they are present anywhere. This is especially true of those parts of a house that are rarely seen – the loft, for instance, and any part of the foundations and underside of the floor that you can get at. If tackled early, an outbreak of woodworm or rot can be cured fairly easily, but if they are left to develop they can seriously damage the structure of your home.

Because it has become possible to calculate accurately the amount of stress that a piece of timber can withstand, modern buildings can be made from much less sturdy timber than previously. These calculations hold good so long as the structural timber is not weakened – and weakening is most likely to be caused by woodworm or rot.

Woodworm

Woodworm is not a worm at all, but a beetle that bores its way into timber, causing damage and unsightly holes. There are, in fact, several varieties of wood-boring insect, but the one commonly referred to as woodworm is *Anobium punctatum* – the common furniture beetle.

It is called the furniture beetle because at one time it attacked the traditional hardwoods from which furniture was made. It has now become more widespread and developed a taste for the structural softwoods used in house building. It used to be thought, too, that the furniture beetle went only for old timber, but in fact it attacks new wood as well.

The female beetle mates in the spring and early summer, then looks for a safe, hospitable place to lay her eggs. Holes or cracks in the wood, badly fitting joints, even stretches of especially rough timber, are all ideal. There she will leave as many as 60 eggs at a time.

The eggs hatch within a few weeks, and grubs emerge. It is these, in fact, that cause the damage. To feed on the wood, they bore into it and move in the direction of the grain. For two or more years they chew their way along the grain, leaving behind them what looks like brown sawdust. This debris (known as frass) consists of tiny pellets. Eventually, the grub prepares to enter the chrysalis or pupal stage. To do so, it scoops out a small chamber near the surface of the timber, where it lies for a few weeks, gradually turning into a beetle. When the change is complete it bites its way out, leaving behind one of those holes that are the principal sign of an attack of woodworm.

As soon as they emerge, the beetles mate, and the female lays her eggs – this time in old borings as well as in cracks and joints. So, once an infestation starts, there is a good chance that it will continue.

The adult beetle can fly, so they may have come into your home on the wing. In general, however, beetles do not move very far from their original flight holes, so it is more common for a ready-made infestation to be brought into a beetle-free home – perhaps in a piece of old furniture or a wooden box. A typical example occurs if there is woodworm in a loft; someone puts an old chest there; then you buy the chest, bring it home and the woodworm continues to breed.

There are several other wood-boring insects in addition to the furniture beetle, but it is this particular creature that causes most worry in the home.

Preventive measures: the most obvious way of keeping woodworm out of your home is to be wary of what you bring into it. By all means buy antiques and snap up bargains in second-hand furniture shops, but give them a thorough examination, and if you suspect the presence of worm carry out remedial treatment immediately.

In particular, be careful about what you store in the parts of your home that you seldom visit, such as lofts and cellars. Even though no sign of attack may be evident, eggs might have been laid there recently, and the grubs may be burrowing out of sight. The beetles like the glue used in old plywood, for instance, and many attacks can be traced to old tea chests pushed up into a loft and forgotten.

The beetles always seek bare wood on which to lay their eggs; they will not attack timber that is polished or treated with preservative, although the adult beetles will emerge through polished surfaces. They will not bite through paint, although paint is not a woodworm killer. The unfortunate aspect of this is that they might well emerge through the back of such parts of the joinery as a skirting board, so that there would be no outward signs of the infestation.

The beetles like wood that is slightly damp. They find decayed wood more nutritious than sound wood, so a dry home is less likely to attract them. The installation of central heating, with its warm pipes going under floorboards, is thought to discourage them.

If you ever introduce new structural timbers into your home, use only timber that has been factory-impregnated with preservative.

Looking for woodworm is not a pleasant task. Wood-boring beetles strike in the least accessible, dirtiest, coldest and most uncomfortable parts of the house – the loft and the cellar, for instance. However, it has to be done. Wear old clothes, and take a torch and a magnifying glass. Look at the roof joists, rafters and other timber in the loft. Do the same in the cellar. The most obvious signs of infestation are the flight holes left by the adult beetle. The may indicate an attack that is no longer active, however. Woodworm sometimes extract all the goodness they can from a length of timber, then abandon it – but do not rely on this. Signs of frass – which you would detect with a magnifying glass – are evidence that the attack is still active.

If you come across signs of infestation in the loft or under the floor of a terraced or semi-detached house, tell your neighbours. The worm might have strayed next door.

Getting rid of woodworm can be complicated by the difficulty of reaching likely sites of infestation. Modern woodworm killers are effective, and not particularly difficult to apply. The work, however, has to be done in some of the most uncomfortable parts of your home, and the disturbance to family life will be considerable. The furniture must be moved, floor coverings disturbed and floorboards lifted.

The advantage of calling in a specialist firm is that you can be sure they will be thorough, because they normally give a guarantee against re-infestation. They know exactly how much liquid to apply and where. They are trained to look for signs of attack, and know from experience exactly where the treatment ought to be carried out. They will finish the work more quickly than you, and will have less difficulty working under the eaves or down in the cellar. Moreover, a home-loan may depend on a certificate to show that eradication has been carried out by professionals, and loans to help pay for the work may be available. Make sure that any company with which you deal is reputable and is well-established. A guarantee from a company that is no longer trading is not worth having.

There is no doubt, however, that you can reduce the cost by doing the work yourself. For small, local attacks, the fluid can be applied to the wood by brush, and even injected in the holes by means of the small nozzle that can be fitted to the tins of the liquid. Where the infestation is on a large scale, the liquid must be sprayed on.

Suitable sprayers can be hired, but most types of garden spray will do provided they give a good pressure, and will hold a couple of litres (4 pints). You also need a nozzle that gives the correct type of spray. Ideally, you need a fairly coarse, fan-shaped spray. If the spray is too coarse, excess liquid will soil the plaster. If it is too fine, liquid will vapourize and pollute the air, making the work unpleasant. Furthermore, the spray should have a long lance – at least 600 mm (2 ft) – so that you can reach under the eaves and into the apex of the roof in the loft, and get a good distance under the floorboards.

Take care, too, about how you dress. Although you should wear old clothes that you do not mind getting dirty and stained, they should also offer you protection. Cover your arms with long sleeves and tuck your trousers into your socks. Wear gloves and goggles, and a light fume mask – sold at DIY shops and in some chemists – so that you will not inhale any vapour in a confined space. Do not smoke while spraying.

If you are going to work in a loft, lift up any insulation material to reveal the timbers. If your loft has no insulation, do the spraying just before you install it. The liquid cannot easily penetrate the layers of dust and cobwebs that will undoubtedly be lying on the timber, so clean the area. Use a vacuum cleaner, preferably a cylinder type with a hose. The heavy duty, industrial-style cleaners are ideal for this work – they can be hired.

If the cold water tank is insulated with expanded polystyrene lagging, this must be protected from the fluid, and in any event the tank itself must be covered so that no vapour from the spraying gets into the water. Look, too, at any wiring in the loft. If it is of the rubber-coated type, make sure no liquid gets on it. In any event, this type of cable is nearing or past the end of its useful life, so you ought to get it renewed. Even modern pvc-sheathed cable should be inspected for signs of wear. Fluid getting on to bare wire could cause a short circuit, but even more important is the fact that damaged cable is dangerous and should be replaced immediately.

When you start spraying, pay special attention to the affected areas, but treat all exposed timber. Apply sufficient fluid to wet all the surfaces thoroughly, but not so much that any runs through to stain the ceiling below. There will be a certain amount of fine spray falling as a mist as you work on the ceiling joists, and this should be sufficient to treat the laths on a lath-and-plaster ceiling.

When the floorboards and joists need treatment, lift up every fourth board, and clean the area below with a vacuum cleaner before spraying. Treat the area below the floor, not forgetting the undersides of the boards. When you have finished this, apply fluid to the undersides of the boards you have lifted, then replace them. Finally spray the top.

The floorboards will need at least six months to dry out thoroughly. While they are moist they could damage synthetic floor coverings, such as vinyls. In the meantime, use a temporary covering, or use a natural material such as cork, which would be immune to chemical attack. It has been suggested that lining a floor with hardboard will give sufficient protection, so you could lay any floor covering you like on top of it, but in fact the woodworm killer is so penetrative that it will work its way up through the nail holes and stain the top of the hardboard.

Rot

An occasional splashing, or even dousing, does no harm to timber, provided that it is allowed to dry out thoroughly. Timber that is continually and excessively moist, however, will eventually rot. Most people can recognize the signs of rotting wood. It warps and the surface starts to break up. Press it and it feels soft and spongy. By itself, the moisture in the timber does not cause rot. Rot is caused instead by fungi that are encouraged to grow in the dampness. A house that is well maintained, free from damp and well ventilated will not harbour rot.

Rot is usually classified into two types: wet rot and dry rot. Do not be misled by the name of the latter; it, too, is caused by damp. It gets it name because it reduces the timber it attacks to a dry powdery surface. Wet rot is much more common than dry rot, but fortunately is easier to cure. Both are serious conditions – much more so than woodworm. They can destroy the timbers of your home, reducing it to a dangerous, unhealthy and unsightly condition.

Identifying rot is not difficult. Dry rot causes a musty smell and a lot or rust-red dust. The dust is, in fact, spores from a fungus. In advanced cases, deep cracks will break up the surface of the wood into cubes, some of them quite large.

The surface of badly affected timber will be covered by a web of matted fungus. This web grows rapidly in humid conditions and generally looks like cotton wool. If it comes into contact with drier air, or is exposed to light, bright yellow patches appear. When the fungus is growing in damp conditions, globules of water-like drops are formed. The fungus also produces a thin, pancake-like fruit. The centre is ridged and rust red in colour, but the edges are white. The wood darkens in colour, is powdery when rubbed between the fingers and loses its resinous smell. If you pick it up, it feels much lighter than it should.

The most damaging parts of the fungus are the strands of the web. They spread, often unseen, and convey water to wood farther away that is dry and sound. Thus the condition spreads. Even if you remove defective wood, these strands could be left behind to continue spreading the fungus. As well as infecting the wood, they can pass through soft mortar and brickwork and find their way around stone and metal.

The fungal strands of wet rot are never as thick as those of dry rot, and they do not spread with the same ease. They cannot, for instance, penetrate brickwork. Moreover, they are dark brown in colour and, when growing over the surface of wood or damp plaster, form a sort of fern shape. A thin veneer of surface wood may conceal a soft dark mass of rot underneath.

Keeping rot at bay is better than treating it once it already has a hold. Rot is caused by damp. Dry rot cannot form in timber containing less than 25 per cent moisture, and wet rot requires a moisture content in the timber of between 50 and 60 per cent. To prevent rot, therefore, make sure your house is dry. If you suspect damp to be present anywhere, treat it as described earlier. Keep the gutters and downpipes in good order, so that the walls of the house do not become saturated.

Moreover, the fungi do not spread so easily when there is good ventilation. Check that air bricks and grilles are not blocked and keep the paintwork, especially that on outdoor timber, in good condition so that rainwater cannot penetrate it.

Getting rid of rot. Wet rot is the easiest to deal with. As soon as you remove the damp, it will die out. You are, however, left with the job of replacing all the damaged timber. If these are important structural members, then seek professional advice. Non-structural timbers, such as skirting, window frames, picture rails, door frames and floorboards can be replaced as described elsewhere in this book.

Prod the surface of the timber with a sharp instrument to determine the extent of the rot. Cut out and burn all affected wood, and remove all dust, dirt and debris. Make sure the new timber you use is sound, thoroughly dry and well seasoned. Also treat it, and the nearby timber, brick and concrete areas with dry rot fluid, to prevent that developing.

Dry rot is much more difficult to eradicate, and dealing with extensive attacks is beyond the scope of the average do-it-yourselfer. A thorough knowledge of building techniques is required, as well as a full acquaintance with the behaviour and symptoms of the fungus. Moreover, the disturbance caused can be tremendous and the house may be uninhabitable during the work. You can, perhaps, cope with small outbreaks yourself. As with wet rot, it is essential to remove the conditions that cause the fungus to develop in the first place: make sure the house is dry and well ventilated.

To tackle the infestation, inspect your home minutely for

evidence of the rot. Wherever you see any sign of attack, consider that point as being the centre of a sphere with a radius of 900 mm (3 ft) and make a close examination in every direction within that area. If you find any sign of decay, carry on with the sphere principle, until eventually you get to the limits of the attack.

Cut away affected timber to a point 900 mm (3 ft) beyond the visible limits of an attack. If this involves the structural timbers, seek expert advice.

The timber you cut out should be taken out of the house and burned. If strands have penetrated plaster, it must all be hacked off, taken outside in plastic bags and sprayed with dry rot fluid, before being taken away. Clean the whole area of the wall behind the plaster with a wire brush to make sure no strands are left. The debris from cleaning must also be taken outside in plastic bags and sprayed before disposal.

Where masonry has been affected, drill holes into the wall and fill them with dry rot fluid. The holes should be 13 mm (½ in) in diameter, 150 mm (6 in) deep, and at an angle of 45°. They should cover the contaminated area at 600 mm (2 ft) staggered intervals.

Working from the top downwards, spray all brick, block, concrete and earth surfaces until they are saturated, using a spray with a coarse nozzle. The precautions about clothing and a mask suggested in the section on woodworm should be observed. If the strands have gone through the brickwork, deal with both sides similarly.

Two coats of dry rot fluid must be applied to timber around the decayed timbers that have been cut away. The treatment should extend to a distance of 1500 mm (5 ft) from the last affected spot. Treat the new timber with a fungicidal wood preservative. Brush on liberal applications, and stand sawn ends in a pot of the liquid for a good five minutes.

Allow the wall to dry out properly before re-plastering and decorating. As an extra precaution, you may apply zinc oxycholoride plaster before the wall plaster.

The whole essence of the treatment of dry rot is thoroughness. Leave any of the strands behind, and it can go on spreading. So you must carry on looking for further signs of the attack, and be sure that you have removed every trace. It would be a pity to go to all that trouble, then find in a short while you are having to carry out the remedial treatment all over again. It is because of this – in addition to the scale of the work involved – that perhaps the work should be left to the experts, even though the cost of doing so can be high.

DECORATING THE JOINERY

The joinery discussed in this chapter needs to be well protected, both to keep it looking attractive, and to prevent it
from deteriorating. This is especially true of timber that
comes into contact with the weather outside. Doors, in particular, should be well cared for, since if they warp they will
not operate properly. Protection is particularly necessary to
keep rot at bay.

The best type of paint to use on joinery is a gloss. It is a
little more troublesome to apply – and cleaning the brushes
afterwards can be a chore – but it gives better protection. If
you are starting off with bare wood, treat all knots and resinous areas with knotting, to prevent the resin form "weeping" through and spoiling the finished result. Then apply a
wood primer. Follow this with an undercoat, then one or two
coats of gloss.

Paintwork that is in good condition need merely be
washed down, rinsed and allowed to dry, then have two
coats of gloss brushed on. If you are changing the colour
apply an undercoat.

Repainting should be carried out regularly – and ideally
just before it is necessary. It will then be a much easier job,
because less preparation will be required.

Chapter 6
INTERNAL WALLS

CONSTRUCTION

Some internal walls serve a structural function in that they actually help to support the house. These are called load-bearing walls. Others offer no support; they merely divide the space. Such walls are termed partitions. The distinction between the two is essential especially if you wish to re-arrange the interior layout of the house.

Solid walls

A load-bearing internal wall that gives major support will usually be built like an external solid wall: 230 mm (9 in) thick. Where it is of minor constructional importance, it may be only half that thickness – the width, rather than the length, of the brick. In modern homes, some types of building block are used instead of brick to make solid walls. Not all solid walls, however, are load-bearing – partitions may be solid.

Hollow partitions

In general, partitions are hollow structures, and are built on a frame of timber, with an outer covering of either lath and plaster in older houses, or plasterboard in more modern buildings. Alternatively, some form of factory-built system may be used for partitions in modern homes.

Where there is a room on both sides of the partition, there will be lath and plaster – or plasterboard – on each side of the framework. The void in the middle of the wall is often used to carry electric cables around the home.

If the partition is dividing, say, a store room from a habitable room, only the room side of it may have been faced.

Lath and plaster walls

Hollow walls in an older house may be of lath and plaster. A lath and plaster wall (Fig. 6:1) is constructed on a framework of timber, the size of which is variable, but will probably be about 75 × 50 mm (3 × 2 in). There will be a horizontal member (a ceiling plate) at the top, and a corresponding floor plate at the bottom. Between these two there is a series of vertical members, called studs. The spacing between the studs can vary between 300 and 600 mm (1-2 ft). The framework may also be strengthened by other horizontal members known as noggings, approximately halfway up the studs. Sometimes the noggings are fixed to the studs by means of half lap joints, or they can be skew-nailed. Another method is for them to be staggered, so that nails can be driven through the studs and into the ends of the noggings.

Across the studs are nailed narrow, thin timbers – the laths. These act as a key for the plaster, which is skimmed onto them.

Plasterboard walls

Hollow walls in modern homes are usually made up of plasterboard. There are two ways in which a plasterboard partition can be built. It can consist of sheets of the board, fixed on one or both sides of a timber framework (Fig. 6:2). This framework is similar to that of a lath and plaster wall, except that the vertical studs are usually spaced wider apart. Alternatively, it can be constructed of factory-built sections, made up from plasterboard sheets around an inner core, which slot together (Fig. 6:3).

How partition walls are made up: 6.1 Lath and plaster 6.2 Plasterboard on studs and noggings 6.3 Factory-built sections

6.1

Ceiling plate

Plaster

Laths

Nogging

Studs

Lath and plaster wall   Floor plate

6.2

Plasterboard

6.3

Factory-built

Telling the difference

To tell whether a wall is solid, or of plasterboard or lath and plaster, try tapping its surface with your knuckles. A plasterboard wall will have a hollow sound, unlike a solid wall. The surface of a lath and plaster wall will not be as true and flat as those of the other two types of wall, and there will be a certain amount of give if you press the surface.

If you are unsure of the type of wall, make a test boring in an inconspicuous spot. As the drill bit pentrates beyond the plaster of a solid wall, it will throw out red dust, if it is of bricks, or grey or black dust if it is made from building blocks. On a lath and plaster wall, you will get a slight amount of sawdust from the laths, before the bit bursts through into the void beyond. On plasterboard, there will be no lath, just the void. In both the latter cases, you might strike a stud, indicating that the wall is hollow. If you want to know which type (plasterboard or lath and plaster) move along the wall slightly, and drill in another place.

KNOCKING DOWN WALLS

The way that the builder – or some subsequent owner – has arranged the interior of your home might not suit you. You may prefer to have fewer, but larger rooms. Probably the wall most people wish to remove is that between two main ground floor rooms, to combine a dining room and a lounge, for example. Both load-bearing and partition walls can be removed, but the procedure is totally different for each type. So it is most important to recognize the type of wall with which you are dealing.

In any event, before carrying out a conversion of this kind, you may need permission from a local authority. So your first action should be to consult an expert about possible local regulations.

Load-bearing or partition?

To say with certainty whether an internal wall is load-bearing or a partition is not always easy. There are, however, certain guidelines. Determine the type of materials from which the wall is built. For instance, a lath and plaster or plasterboard wall is likely to be a partition. Similarly, a brick or building-block wall may be a partition but is more likely to be load-bearing. Next look at the position of the wall. If it is in the middle of the house and parallel to the floorboards of the room above (which would mean it is at right angles to the joists), then it is almost certain to be load-bearing. On the other hand, a wall at right angles to the boards, and therefore parallel to the joists, and positioned to one side of the building, could probably be just a partition. In the last resort, only an expert can tell with certainty, so always take advice on this point.

Removing any wall is a major job that will disrupt your domestic life considerably. Take precautions – for instance, put sheets over the room doors, to keep the dust as far as possible to one room. In very dusty conditions, keep the window open, wear a mask, and go outside for fresh air as often as necessary.

Decide beforehand where you are going to put all the rubble. You might bury it if you have a large garden, or you may decide to hire a skip. In either event, have a wheelbarrow to move it away.

Removing the joinery

Most walls will have at least a skirting board attached. If there is a door in the wall, there will be its architrave and door stops. The joinery is the first thing to be removed. Full instructions for doing this are given in Chapter 5.

Even if you are removing only part of a wall – as will definitely be the case with a load-bearing wall – prise away the skirting from the whole length of wall, because it is likely to be in one piece. Even if it is not, the lengths that make up the run are unlikely to coincide with the stretches of wall you want to remove.

Avoid damaging the skirting so that you can put it back in place. This is of particular importance in an old house, where it will be impossible to buy new skirting to make a precise match. Store the old skirting you do not put back, so that it can be used for any repairs that are needed in future.

Removing lath and plaster walls

Your first job is to remove the lath and plaster covering. Push a sharp instrument – an old chisel or stout screwdriver will do – into the plaster, and locate the studs. Using a lever, such as a large claw hammer or the same chisel or screwdriver, wrench the laths from the studs, bringing the plaster with them. Carry on in this way until all the laths and plaster are removed, and you are left with just the framework. Dispose of the rubble.

To complete the job, take out the framework. How you do this will depend on the way it has been fixed to the floor and ceiling joists. If, as is most likely, nails have been used, simply prise it free.

Examine the plates, studs and noggings for signs of rot or woodworm. If you detect any, then burn them immediately. If they are sound, keep them for future use elsewhere.

Removing plasterboard walls

Locate the studs as described for a lath and plaster wall. Wrench the boards away from the studs. You should be able to pull most of them away intact, which will mean there is less dust and less rubble to dispose of. Remove the framework.

Removing solid walls

To remove a minor solid wall, which you have been assured by an expert is non-load-bearing, hack off a bit of plaster at the top to reveal a brick, or some form of building block. With a bolster chisel and club hammer, chop away at the mortar joints round the brick or block until you can free it and remove it. Tackle the bricks on each side of it until the top row is clear. Now go on to remove the rest of the wall below it.

Making good

Whatever the type of wall, its removal will cause a certain amount of damage to neighbouring walls, ceilings and floors. In the case of hollow partitions, there may not be too many marks – certainly none to the ceiling and walls that cannot be made good with decorator's filler, or a bag or two of plaster. The damage might be more severe, however, where a solid wall has been hacked away, and you might have to carry out a repair with plasterboard.

Partition walls are usually built on top of the floor – they are erected after the floor has been laid. Scuffs and knocks to boards on a suspended timber floor will usually be covered up by the new floorcovering. If you want to have a sealed timber floor, with the boards on view, you might have to take up and replace a board or two.

A solid direct-to-earth concrete floor might have been covered with tiles, laid after the partition was built. You will probably find it difficult to buy new tiles to match the old. Lay down tiles of any colour or pattern, but of the same thickness, so that the floor throughout is of one level.

If there was parquet flooring in the two rooms on each side of the wall, you might be able to place strips of hard-wood in the gap where the wall previously stood, to make an attractive disguise.

Taking down load-bearing walls

Since a load-bearing wall is helping to hold the house up, you cannot remove it without putting something else in its place. That something else is invariably a rolled steel joist (known to builders as an rsj). Right at the start, enlist the help of an expert – an architect or surveyor – who will work out the size of the rsj you require and submit plans to your local authority as necessary.

Removing a wall in the average small house involves leaving a short stretch of wall (a nib) at each side of the proposed opening. The nib, probably about 450 mm (18 in) long, provides support for the rsj which is fixed just below the ceiling. This is the reason for the arch effect in a room that was converted from two small ones. In some instances further strengthening may be needed.

Support must be provided for the structure, during the removal of the wall until the rsj has been installed (Fig. 6:4). It is best to use adjustable steel props, which can be hired. For an average-sized opening, you will need three or four props on each side of the wall, but your expert will advise you on this. Place a 150 × 25 mm (6 × 1 in) board on the floor and stand the props on this. Similarly, you need a board of the same size at ceiling level, and the props should be braced between the two.

With a piece of chalk, mark on the wall the area you plan to remove, and hack away the plaster with a bolster chisel and club hammer. Now look at the wall and adjust the chalk line slightly, if necessary, so that you need to cut a few bricks as possible. Some will certainly need cutting, be-

6.4 *Supporting the structure while a load-bearing wall is being removed. How plasterboard is fixed to an RSJ (inset).*

Concrete pads

RSJ

Adjustable props

Board

Wooden wedges

RSJ

Framing

Plasterboard

cause of the bonding of the brickwork, but by moving the line slightly, you can reduce this number to the minimum.

When you have determined the exact position of the opening, use the bolster chisel to cut a line in the brickwork around its limits on both sides of the wall. This will help to give a clean edge to the bricks when the wall is demolished, and will reduce the amount of making good that will be required later. Cut carefully through the ceiling plaster where it meets the wall.

Begin to demolish the wall by removing the bricks at the centre of the top course of the proposed opening. To do this, chisel out the mortar all round the centre brick. Then hack out the one next to it, and so on. Once you have freed a couple of bricks, the work will become progressively easier, and you can go on to take out the whole opening.

Since the wall is load-bearing, it will not rest on top of the floor, but rise up from the foundations. If the floor is of suspended floorboard, the joists will pass right through the wall below floor level. Chop out sufficient of the wall below floor level to allow extra floorboards to be fitted in the space once occupied by the wall. You will probably find it easier to do this if you take up a floorboard or two on each side. Take care not to damage the joists as you work. See Chapter 9 for details of how to take up boards and fit new ones.

On a direct-to-earth floor, remove enough of the wall to allow new tiles or parquet to be fitted so that there will be an uninterrupted run of floor through the new enlarged room.

Cut out a recess from the top of the nibs at each end to provide support for the rsj. Your expert should have worked out the exact size of these. Most probably, you will be required to allow the rsj to project into each nib by 225 mm (9 in).

It is not sufficient for the rsj to rest on brickwork. Make concrete pads on top of the masonry to provide firmer support. Your adviser will determine the exact dimensions. It is likely that the pads will be at least 150 mm (6 in) thick, so cut out sufficient of the wall to allow for this. The rsj has to be in position before the pads are formed.

Hauling up the rsj is a strenuous task, and is a job that will take at least three fit men. Raise it up into its correct position under the ceiling, and place two or three props underneath to hold it in place. Now form the concrete pads. Mix the concrete, and trowel it into place. Make sure it is well formed and compacted under the rsj, otherwise it will not offer enough support. Leave all the props – those supporting the rsj, and those each side of the opening – in place for about a week to allow the concrete to set properly.

When you remove the props, there comes the task of making good. The rsj should be covered with plasterboard.

Cut wooden wedges to make a tight fit, and hammer them in between the flanges with no more than 600 mm (2 ft) between their centres. To these wedges nail a timber framing of 50 × 25 mm (2 × 1 in) battens. Nail plasterboard to these battens (Fig. 6:4).

A builder would cover the raw edges of the brickwork round the opening, and make good any damage caused elsewhere, with plaster. You will probably find it easier to use plasterboard, doing the final filling with either plaster, bought in small bags, or decorator's filler.

BUILDING A PARTITION

A simple non-load-bearing partition can be built to divide a large room into two smaller ones. The best method is to use plasterboard on a timber framework.

Plasterboard is available in two thicknesses: 9.5 mm (about ⅜ in) and 12.7 mm (about ½ in). The thinner board is less expensive, but needs more timber supports, so is not necessarily cheaper in the long run. Furthermore, it does not offer such an effective degree of sound insulation. Plasterboard sheets are 1200 mm (47½ in) wide and either 1800 mm (71 in) or 2400 mm (94½ in) long. You will need the larger size to get sufficient height for a room partition. The board can also be bought with either squared or tapered edges. Use boards with tapered edges, then it is easier to disguise the joins. The material has an ivory coloured face. It should always be worked, and fixed, with this face outwards.

Plasterboard can be cut to size with an ordinary fine-toothed woodworking saw. Or you can remove short lengths by scoring the face with a sharp knife, and snapping off the waste over a straight edge. To cut a hole in the middle of the board – usually to accommodate an electrical fitting such as a switch or socket outlet – draw the shape in pencil, drill a starting hole, using an ordinary twist bit, at each corner, and saw out with a pad saw. Lightly sand all cut edges.

The framework

The framework for the partition should be in 75 × 50 mm (3 × 2 in) softwood. Use unplaned material, because it is cheaper and thicker than prepared softwood.

Begin by fixing a length of the timber along the floor. This member is known as the sole plate, and should be continuous and unbroken, except to form a door opening. To ensure it is positioned accurately, draw a line along one outer edge of the plate before you fix it. The fixing should be with nails, but if there is a ceiling below which might be damaged by the vibration caused by nailing, fix the plate with screws instead. If the partition is to be parallel to the floor joists, place the nails or screws at 200 mm (8 in) centres; if it is to run across the joists, fix the nails or screws into each joist.

Now fix a corresponding frame member to the ceiling. This is known as the head plate and you should ensure that it is exactly above the sole plate. Do this by using a plumb line and bob or a perfectly true batten and a spirit level with a vertical. If the head plate runs across the ceiling joists, fix it with nails or screws into the joists. If it is parallel to the joists, you cannot just fix it to the plasterboard or lath and plaster of the ceiling. There are two choices. The first is that you can fix short pieces of timber (noggings) to span between two joists and receive the fixing of the plate. This job is not too difficult if the loft is tall, with no floor above, but it is very disruptive if floorboards have to be raised first. The other choice is easier, but not always workable: it involves altering the position of the partition slightly so that it is immediately below a joist. Fixing should be at the same intervals as for the sole plate.

Now fit a series of vertical members (studs) between the two plates. The studs should be of the same section timber as the plates, and they are fixed by means of skew-nailing. Drive a nail into the side of a stud, but at an angle so that it goes into the plate below or above. If you think that the vibration of nailing might cause damage, use screws instead.

Place a stud at each end of the wall and at each side of door and other openings. Then, working from one end, fit them in between so that the centres are 400 mm (15¾ in) apart, for 9.5 mm (⅜ in) thick plasterboard, or 600 mm (23½ in) apart, for 12.7 mm (½ in) thick board. The last stud will almost certainly be nearer to the end than the recommended spacing. Follow these measurements closely, because they are necessary not only to give proper support to the wall, but also to match up the width of board.

A series of horizontal members (also called noggings) is needed halfway up the studs. These too can be fixed by skew-nailing. If you are likely to fix items to the wall later – built-in furniture, for instance – then try to plot its exact position at this stage, and fit noggings at the right place to receive its fixing screws. Cut the plasterboard to a length 25 mm (1 in) less than the height of the room, and place the cut edge at the bottom of the wall. Hold the board against the framework and jam it tightly up against the ceiling. A good way of ensuring this is to make a footlifter. Place one end of this under the board, press on the other end, and it will force the board up to the ceiling.

Fix the board to the frame with galvanized plasterboard nails at 150 mm (6 in) centres along every member of the frame and about 13 mm (½ in) from the edges. Butt the boards tightly against each other along the edges. The gap at the bottom will be covered with skirting board later on and any at the top can be hidden by a cove.

If the wall divides two rooms, fix plasterboard to both sides. If there will be something such as a store room on one side, however, you need fix board to the room side only. Board of 12.7 mm (½ in) thickness on boths sides of a partition wall gives good sound insulation. If you want better sound insulation, fit two layers of 12.7 mm board on each side, making sure that the vertical joins are staggered, but

6.5 Building a partition wall: (a) How to deal with an internal and (b) an external corner. (c) Nail the plasterboard (held in position by a footlifter) to the framework of studs and noggings. Covering the joins between sheets of plasterboard using (d) filler, (e) tape, and (f) more filler.

that each edge is nailed to a frame member. In addition, fill the gap with insulating material.

Your wall may form an angle. Two types are possible. The way to deal with both of them is shown in Fig 6:5.

There is a sound method of disguising any gaps between the boards, using a special filler, tape and tools. These can be bought where you buy the plasterboard. The technique consists of applying the filler, pressing the tape into it, and covering with more filler. Full instructions are given with the pack.

If there is to be a doorway in the partition, base it on the width of a standard door, bought from a joinery supplier – it simply is not worth the time spent making your own. The inside of the door opening – both sides and the top – will need to be lined by a plate. This should be 25 mm (1 in) thick, and of a width to suit the plasterboard and studs – you may have to get one slightly oversize and plane it down. Then fit door stops. They should be about 38 × 32 mm (1½ × 1¼ in). Next, fit the architrave. All these items are simply nailed into place. Finally fit the door.

If the wall forms the outer shell of, say, a loft conversion, you will need to add insulation. Fix insulation blanket on the loft side of the wall, or fix a plasterboard that incorporates insulating material. You will also need a vapour check to prevent condensation from soaking the insulation. Such a check could consist of polythene, or a brush-on liquid.

Chapter 7
INTERIOR SURFACES

The interior surfaces of the walls of some historic buildings are left bare, and in recent years, when there has been a vogue for a return to natural materials, it is not uncommon for bare brick or stone to be used as a form of decoration. Most walls, however, are covered on the inside, usually with plaster. This material is strong, durable and presents a smooth surface that can take a wide range of decorative materials. From the do-it-yourselfer's point of view, however, plaster has one overwhelming disadvantage – applying it is probably the most skilled of the building trades, and far beyond the abilities of the average person. If you do want to give bare walls a plaster surface, however, you could apply plasterboard. This is known as dry-lining and is well within the scope of the do-it-yourselfer.

Other possible interior surfaces included timber cladding and ceramic tiles. Until timber became expensive in recent years, it was often used as a decorative covering instead of wallpaper. At one time, however, it used to be an alternative to plaster for covering bare walls and can still be seen in some old buildings. Ceramic tiles can be fixed to plaster or, provided the surface is smooth, directly on to brickwork.

THE NATURAL LOOK
If you have seen bare brickwork as a form of decoration in modern interiors, do not imagine that you can hack off the plaster in one of your rooms to reveal a similar surface. You never know how good a wall under the plaster will be. You might even find breeze blocks or some other building block there. Even if test borings with a drill in an inconspicious spot confirm that the wall is built of bricks, the wall is not likely to be attractive. The type of wall you have admired has to be specially built; it is known in the trade as fair face brickwork.

If you want natural brickwork in your home, leave the plaster intact, and apply small brick-like tiles, called 'slips', to it.

DECORATING PLASTER

Plaster is chosen as a coating for interior walls because it takes decorative treatments so well. At one time new plaster had to be allowed to dry out for several months before it could be decorated. Modern plaster settles down much more quickly, and six weeks to two months after being applied it is ready to receive any decorative finish.

In a brand new house this period would have elapsed by the time you occupy it, so you could decorate the walls as soon as you move in. If you are having a wall in an occupied house plastered – as would be the case, for instance, when you have a home extension built – it would be better to allow the plaster to dry for about a couple of months before decorating. If you are in a hurry to decorate it before then, use a thin emulsion paint, through which moisture can escape.

Plaster will take both gloss and emulsion paints, but it does not require the same protection as wood, so there is little point in applying anything other than emulsions, which are cheaper, easier to apply, and in general more convenient to handle.

Plaster also takes wallpaper readily. Especially when new, the plaster should be treated with size before you hang the paper so that the surface will have more slip. The manufacturers of some of the heavier papers suggest that walls should be cross-lined (see below) before the paper is applied.

Old plaster can sometimes become powdery, and will need to be sealed. Apply a stabilizing solution to the plaster surface and allow it to dry thoroughly before you decorate the wall.

Plasterboard can be decorated as soon as it is installed. No special preparation is required before painting it – treat the surface just as ordinary plaster. If you decide to hang wallpaper, however, apply a plasterboard primer first. This not only helps you when you are hanging the paper; it also makes it easier to strip off the paper when you come to redecorate.

REPAIRS TO PLASTER

It is unlikely that you will be able to plaster a wall satisfactorily starting from scratch, but you might well carry out repairs to a plastered surface.

Cracking caused by shrinkage of the plaster as it dries out, or even by settlement of the building, is the most common fault in a plastered wall. Stop up the cracks with decorator's filler, applied with a filling knife. This, incidentally, is often confused with a scraper, but the two are in fact totally different. The knife has a flexible blade, whereas the scraper is rigid.

Begin by running one corner of the knife blade down the length of the crack, to dislodge any loose material, and also to make the crack wedge shaped – narrower at the surface of the wall. Brush loose material from the crevice, and saturate it with water – using a brush to make sure that the water penetrates right into the crevice.

Now apply the filler. Mix it in an old cup or saucer and do not make it too runny – it should be a stiff paste. (Always add water to the filler, never the filler to water; use a wet sponge, so you can then control the flow of water easily). Take some filler on to the knife, and spread it across the width of the crack, flexing the blade as you do so, pushing the filler well into the crack. Draw the knife lengthwise along the crack, again flexing the blade, to wipe the filler flush with the surface and smooth it down. Cracks that are deep and wide should be filled in two stages. When the filler is dry, give it a light sanding, and the crack should then be undetectable when painted over. Fill small holes similarly.

If you propose to paint the wall a dark colour, you might have difficulty in obliterating the whiteness of the filler, which could persist in showing through even after two or three coats. To prevent this, add a few drops of the paint to the filler to tint it to about the final colour you have chosen for the wall.

In older houses, where the plaster is more brittle, the surface can become crazed with tiny cracks. Filling each crack individually would be impractical. The best course is to decorate the wall with a material that will cover the cracks: a heavy embossed paper, or even a woodchip paper, which you can paint, can be used. If you want a smooth, painted surface, however, line the wall first. The lining paper to apply as a base for paint has a shiny, impervious surface that does not soak up paint. If you try to paint lining paper intended for wallpapers, the surface will look like blotting paper.

Cross-lining

When lining is done as preparation for wallpaper, the lining paper should be hung horizontally – this is called cross-lining. Lining paper that you intend to paint can be hung vertically, in the normal manner. Some walls are in such bad condition that they need two layers of lining paper – the first in horizontal strips, the top one in vertical strips.

The defects in the plaster may be more serious than just a few cracks. There may, for instance, be large holes, or stretches of crumbling plaster. Hack away crumbling plaster, starting in the middle of the patch, and working outwards until you reach a firm sound edge. If the hole is small, fill it with decorator's filler, but for a large area it will be cheaper to use plaster, which is sold in small bags.

Apply the filler or plaster with a float trowel or a filling knife. Fill deep holes in two stages. First fill about half the depth of the hole. As this first layer or undercoat begins to harden, scratch it with the edge of the trowel to provide a key for the next coat. Leave for 24 hours, then apply the top coat.

Whether you fill in one or two stages, the filler should be applied so its surface is slightly raised. Then remove the excess with a batten, as described for repairs to rendering outside the house (see Chapter 3), leaving the repair level with the surrounding surface. Smooth off with the trowel or filling knife, keeping it moistened by dipping it in water.

You may not be too successful at smoothing off. This does not matter if, as is likely on a wall with crumbling patches, the rest of the surface is rough and you intend to cover it with lining paper, or if you plan to hang a heavy paper.

If the wall is generally in good condition, however, and you wish to paint it, there is a way to bring your repair up to the standard of the rest. Let it dry thoroughly then apply a sizing paste to the repaired area. Now apply wallpaper adhesive, making sure it is brushed only on the area of wall you have treated. Cut a piece of heavy-duty lining paper, so it is bigger all round than the repair. Apply it over the repair, smooth it down into place with a wallpaper brush, and let the adhesive dry. Then take hold of one corner of the paper and gently tear it round the edge of the patch. The paper will tear along the border where it is stuck, leaving an irregular and feathered edge that will not be noticed once you have painted over it.

The new plaster on internal walls can become covered with patches of a white powdery substance. This growth is called efflorescence, and it can also be seen on the external brickwork of new buildings. Efflorescence is caused by salts in the masonry drying out, and should eventually go away of its own accord. If its appearance bothers you, brush it off. On no account use water, for that will merely retard the drying-out process, and make the condition last longer. Do not decorate until the efflorescent has disappeared. If it does not disappear, this is an indication that you have a damp problem in the wall.

DRY-LINING A WALL

The easiest way for a do-it-yourselfer to plaster a wall is to cover it with plasterboard (Fig. 7:1). This is nailed to a framework of 50 × 25 mm (2 × 1 in) battens, screwed into

a Pencil mark
Spirit level

b Wall
Straight batten
Original pencil mark

c Packing
Second pencil line

d Pencil mark

e

7.1 Dry-lining a wall: (a) Mark the floor and ceiling with the aid of a batten and spirit level. (b) Use a pencil and batten to draw the line on the floor. (c) Screw a batten to the wall in alignment with the floor line. (d) Check that floor and ceiling battens are in alignment. (e) The framework is fixed to the wall and ready to receive the plasterboard.

wall plugs. Much care is needed to fix the battens to the wall. The brickwork will never be flat, so if you screw the battens down hard they will follow the contours of the wall, and when you fix the plasterboard its surface will be full of 'waves'.

First find the part of the wall that bulges out farthest – known to builders as the high spot. You can do this either by moving a long, true batten together with a spirit level along the wall, or by using a plumb line and bob. When you have found the high spot, hold the batten on it, and use a spirit level to ensure that it is vertical. Make a pencil mark where the batten touches the floor on the side nearest to the wall, and a corresponding mark on the ceiling. Next, place a long true batten horizontally on edge along the floor. Position it so that it is parallel to the wall and with its inner face on the pencil mark. Now draw a pencil line on the floor along the side of the batten farthest from the wall and remove the batten.

Screw a single batten horizontally to the wall 25 mm (1 in) up from the floor, making sure that the batten is aligned accurately with the line on the floor. To ensure that you do not screw it too hard to the wall, and thus bend it out of alignment, place packing pieces of card or hardboard behind it at the point where you insert a fixing screw.

Now fix a corresponding horizontal batten 25 mm (1 in) from the ceiling, packed out so that it aligns with the pencil mark on the floor. You can ensure that it does so by using a vertical batten and a spirit level. Now fix vertical supports at both edges of every board. Fix additional vertical supports at 400 mm (16 in) centres if you are using 9.5 mm (⅜ in) thick plasterboard, or 600 mm (24 in) centres for 12.7 mm (½ in) thick board. The battens must be vertical and aligned with the two horizontal battens already fixed. Pack them out as necessary. Now is the time to fit battens to receive the screws of any built-in furniture you may wish to add later. If at a later date you wish to fix items where you have not made such provision, it is a simple matter to drill through the plasterboard and into the masonry, where you can insert a wall plug. Nail the plasterboard to these battens in the same way as to the framework for a partition (see pages 125-6).

TIMBER CLADDING

Timber cladding can be fixed directly to the bare brickwork of a wall as a substitute for plaster, or it can go on top of existing plaster as a form of decoration. The cladding can be matchboarding – lengths of shaped natural timber – or in sheets of hardboard or thin plywood with a surface pattern that simulates matchboarding.

Matchboarding is often confused with tongued and grooved boards (Fig. 7:2). Tongued and grooved boards have squared sides so that when two boards are joined they fit snugly together. Matchboarding has additional moulding, so that a V-shaped groove is formed where two boards meet. Tongued and grooved boards are, in general, fitted as flooring, matchboarding being unsuitable because of its grooves.

Matchboarding, however, is more suitable for cladding because the heat of the room will in time make the boards shrink, and cause gaps to appear between them. Such gaps look unsightly in tongued and grooved boards, but because of the V-shape they are not noticeable in matchboarding.

The planks of matchboading are fixed to horizontal battens screwed to the wall. You need one batten at floor level, another near the ceiling, and a third half-way between. If you are fitting the timber to a wall that has a skirting board, use this instead of the bottom batten (Fig. 7:3). The two higher battens should then be of the same thickness as the skirting. A width of 50 mm (2 in) is suitable. If there is no skirting board, use 50 × 25 mm (2 × 1 in) battens.

The battens must be level with each other and with the skirting so that the cladding will present a flat surface. Pack out the battens as necessary when you fix them to the wall.

Matchboard

Tongued and grooved

7.2 Matchboarding (above) and tongued and grooved

7.3 Matchboarding nailed to wall battens

Packing

Existing skirting

The planks are fixed to the battens by 'secret nailing', so that no fixing nails are visible. Pins are driven into the front of the tongue, but emerge on the other side through the main body of the plank to pass into the batten (Fig. 7:4). When the next board is fitted, its groove locates on the tongue, which holds it into place. On the other edge it is fixed by pins driven through its tongue, and so on.

7.4 Secret nailing

Begin by fitting the first plank with its groove towards the end of the wall. Make sure, by using a plumb line or a spirit level, that this first plank is vertical, for its alignment will determine that of the rest. If the surface of the other wall at the corner (the return wall) is badly out of true, tack the first plank slightly away from it, making sure it is vertical. Place a small block of wood so that it touches the return wall and overlaps the plank. Place a pencil along the block and move both to trace out the profile of the return wall on to the plank (Fig. 7:5). Trim the plank along the pencil line.

To trim to the correct width the plank at the other end of the wall, place it on top of the last whole plank, and lightly tack it in place. Now take a short offcut of plank plus a pencil. Jam the offcut hard against the return wall at the top, and hold the pencil tightly against the offcut. Now move offcut and pencil slowly downwards to the bottom, tracing a line on the plank to be trimmed. Saw or file the plank to this line and it should be a tight fit in the gap.

When you use secret nailing, the planks at each end are not held in place on their outer edges. Usually, this does not matter. Tap the face of the planks lightly to check that they are firmly fixed. If not, drive three pins – one for each batten – through their face. These pins will not be hidden, but can be punched home and covered with stopping.

7.5 Making planks to fit the contours of a return wall: (a) The first plank and (b) the plank at the end of the run.

7.6 Moulding, quarter round or triangular (top inset), neatens the top of timber cladding, and skirting (bottom inset) is fitted at the base.

The floor, and especially the ceiling, may be out of true, as well as the return walls. Measure the height required for each plank individually. Even so, there will be slight gaps top and bottom. Disguise the bottom one by fitting skirting, which you can buy at wood yards. The skirting is nailed to the bottom of the planks. You can also use skirting turned upside down, at the top, or you might prefer a smaller moulding (Fig. 7:6).

If you are cladding adjacent walls and the angle where they meet is an internal one, a vertical length of quarter-round or triangular section moulding will neaten the join. Fig. 7:7 shows two methods of treating an external angle.

Fixing sheet cladding

Sheet cladding, since it is based on hardboard or plywood, comes with a maximum length of 2440 mm (8 ft). It is not suitable for rooms with a ceiling height greater than that dimension.

There are two ways in which it can be fixed. The first is to

a

b

Batten

Wall

7.7 Two ways of neatening an external corner in timber cladding:
(a) Chamfering a plank and (b) pinning quarter round moulding.

fit a framework of battens to which the sheets can be nailed. You need a batten on each edge, an intermediate vertical one, and two intermediate horizontal ones. To make sure these are all in the same plane, pack them out as necessary.

The second method is to stick the sheets directly to the wall, provided you are working on a flat plaster surface. Remove any skirting, spread the adhesive on the wall and on the back of the sheets in a pattern similar to that suggested for the battening. You can use a glue gun with which to apply the adhesive to speed up the work. Fig. 7:8 shows both methods.

It is not easy to cut a large sheet to fit the irregularites of a floor and ceiling, so aim to disguise these with skirting at ground level and moulding at the top.

To fix this type of cladding in an alcove that is narrower than the width of a sheet, first cut the sheet to the correct height. Using a plumb line and bob, or a spirit level and true batten, draw on the alcove wall a vertical line about 75 mm (3 in) from one end of the alcove (Fig. 7:9). Place the sheet flat on the floor nearby, and on it draw a pencil line a little more than 150 mm (6 in) from one edge. At about 150 mm (6 in) intervals, measure the gap between the line on the wall and the end of the alcove. Transfer these measurements to the sheet, then join up the marks, and you have a line to which to saw or file. This edge of the sheet should now be a perfect fit against one end wall.

Now draw a second vertical line on the wall 150 mm (6 in) from the other end of the alcove. Measure the gap between the two lines. Use this measurement to draw a second line on the sheet, the same distance from the first line. Then measure the narrow gap between the second vertical line

7.8 *Timber cladding can also be carried out with sheet material, glued and pinned to a timber framework. Inset shows glue being spread on back of sheets, and a mastic gun which can also apply the adhesive.*

7.9 *Cutting sheet cladding to fit an alcove: (a) Draw a vertical line (Line A) on the alcove wall. (b) Measure the distance between Line A and that end of the alcove wall at 150 mm intervals. (c) Draw a second line (Line B) 150 mm from the other end of the alcove. Measure the distance (x) between the two lines on the wall. (d) Transfer these measurements to the sheet. (e) Saw along the two outer lines and the sheet should be a perfect fit in the alcove.*

on the wall and the end of the alcove. Transfer these measurements to the sheet, join them up, and saw to the line. The whole sheet should now be a perfect fit in the alcove, with only minor adjustments necessary here and there with a file.

When timber cladding was fixed in old cottages as an alternative to plaster, it used in general to be painted – normally white. One of the objects of installing timber cladding in modern interiors, however, is to introduce the beauty of natural timber into the home, so it is usually treated with a polyurethene varnish.

CERAMIC TILES

Ceramic tiling gives a permanent, hygienic, easily cleaned surface that is particularly suitable in kitchens, bathrooms and lavatories. Tiles can be fixed to a wide range of materials, including plaster, brick, synthetic boards, and even old ceramic tiles. In fact, they can be fixed to any flat surface that is clean and free from flaking material, except wood. If tiles are fixed to wood, the movement caused by gain or loss of moisture will cause cracks to appear in the tiles.

Fixing the tiles into place is easy, using modern adhesives. A space needs to be left between the tiles to allow them to expand and contract with temperature changes. Until recently, most tiles have had lugs on the edges to ensure that the spacing is equal. A new development, however, is the Universal tile. This has a slightly chamfered edge, tapering towards the face of the tile to provide the correct spacing for expansion and grout. This tile also dispenses with the need for specially-made border tiles, because it is glazed on two adjacent edges, so can be used where these will be exposed. The adhesive is spread on the wall, and you merely place the tiles in their correct position on it. Do not slide them into position, however, as this forces adhesives up between the cracks.

To cut a tile (Fig. 7:10), place it on a flat surface, with a straight edge on its face. Draw a tiler's spike along the straight edge, to cut through the glaze. Press firmly to make sure the glaze is cut, but not so hard as to break the tile. Also score the glaze on the edges. Now place the tile with the cut line accurately on the edge of a bench, with just the waste overhanging. Press on the waste with a short sharp jerk, and the tile will break cleanly along the line.

Alternatively, use a tile cutter. One type looks like a pair of pliers with enlarged jaws. Grip the tile in the jaws and press. The tile will split along the line. If a tile has to be cut to an L-shape, or any other irregular pattern, score it, then snip off the waste bit by bit with a pair of pincers.

The tricky part in tiling comes in making sure the tiles will be arranged neatly on the wall – the 'setting-out'. On a plain, straight wall, you merely arrange the tiles so that the cut ones at each end of the wall are not too small, and are of equal size. Where there are obstructions – doorways, windows, bathroom or kitchen fittings – make sure that your setting-out does not leave small unsightly cut tiles round their edges.

7.10 *How to cut a tile: (a) Score its face with a tiler's spike. (b) Place it on the bench and press. Alternatively place it in the jaws of a tile cutter (inset). (c) To make an L-shaped tile, snap out the waste with pincers.*

Tiling a simple wall

First, prepare the wall. Plaster surfaces should be washed down and rinsed, and allowed to dry. High spots should be sanded off, and any large holes or cracks filled. Remove grease and dirt from other surfaces and fill any large holes or depressions.

Find the lowest point of the floor – or skirting board, if this is to be retained. Make a pencil mark on the wall one tile's height up from this point (Fig. 7:11). Cut a long, true batten to the length of the wall. Tack the batten in place on the wall, its top edge level with the pencil mark. Use a spirit level to ensure that the batten is truly horizontal. Tile adhesive is not a contact adhesive – it takes a short time to act. The batten gives a true line to which you can work, and it also prevents tiles from sliding down the wall before the adhesive has started to grip.

Measure the batten, and mark its centre. You can set out your tiles to ensure that the centre tile is located centrally on this point, or that there are two centre tiles, one each side of it. Adopt the arrangement that will give the largest cut tile at the edges. To find out the best arrangement, make a measuring staff from a long true batten, just over half the length of the one on the wall. Lay it flat on the floor or bench, and on it place a run of dry tiles. Mark off with pencil the width of a tile (including the spacer lugs if any) along the entire length. Place the measuring staff along the batten that is tacked to the wall, and determine which arrangement to adopt. Begin tiling at one edge of the batten – right-handed people will usually find it more convenient to begin on the left, but it is up to you.

Measure the width of the cut tile that will be needed at this edge. Mark this distance from the edge of the wall. Draw a vertical line at the mark, using a true batten and a spirit level.

Usually a combed spreader is supplied with the adhesive. Hold the spreader at an angle of 45° to apply the adhesive, in a series of combed ridges. Cover as much of the wall as you think you can conveniently cope with – a square metre (10 ft) is about right for most people. Place the tiles on the wall one by one. Position the first with extreme accuracy, and butt the others carefully against each other. Make sure the spacer lugs on the side just meet. If any adhesive oozes out, wipe it off before it dries.

Cover the wall with all the whole tiles needed. When the adhesive has set, remove the wall batten and fill in the border with cut tiles. Measure the space for each one individually – inaccuracies in the plaster and floor will make each space slightly different. The cut tiles should not butt up against the end walls, but should be the width of the spacer lugs away from it. The cut edge should go to the wall. As each tile is cut, spread adhesive on the back and place it on the wall, tapping it accurately into position. Wipe away any surplus adhesive.

Leave the tiles for at least 12 hours, then apply the grout. This is necessary to fill the space between the tiles. The grout usually comes as a powder to which you add water. You can buy ready-mixed grout, and there is a mixture that can be used as combined adhesive and grout. Apply the grout with a sponge, which you draw across the face of the tiles, pushing the grout well into the spaces. Wipe off the excess grout with a damp sponge. Draw a round pointed length of wood along each joint to give a really neat finish, then polish up the tiles with a dry cloth.

7.11 *Tiling a wall: (a) Mark one tile's height up from the floor. (b) Tack a batten at this height, using a level to ensure that it is horizontal. (c) Make a measuring staff. (d) Use the staff to determine the best starting point. (e) Draw the vertical line near the end of the wall. (f) Apply the adhesive with a combed spreader. (g) Place the tiles in position. (h) apply the grout. (i) Neaten the grout.*

7.12 Tile arrangements: (a) Tile round a washbasin (b) Support the tiles over a window opening. (c) How to take tiles round an external corner.

Complex tile arrangements

Walls with obstructions are tackled in much the same way as simple walls.

Plan the setting-out thoroughly. Make several trial runs with the measuring staff. Your aim should be not only to get the largest possible cut tiles at the ends of the rows, but also to avoid small cut tiles round the fixtures. In many instances you will have to compromise. Once you are satisfied you have the best setting-out possible, you can start to tile. When you come to a fitting such as a washbasin, continue to tile to the nearest full tile. Such a fixture cannot be relied on to be level, so nail a short horizontal lath (Fig. 7:12) above it, checking with a spirit level that it is true. Lay tiles on top of this batten. The cut tiles can be filled in later along with the border tiles.

If you are tiling only half-way up a wall and not using Universal tiles, border tiles – which have an edge without space lugs, and are slightly rounded – should be used on the top row. They are also required when you are tiling into a doorway or window reveal. Use ordinary tiles up to the edge of the reveal, and border tiles in the reveal with the rounded edge covering the edge of the standard tile. If you wish to tile on the underside of a door or window opening, fix the tiles and hold them in place with a batten wedged underneath with long lengths of timber.

Seal the gap round a basin or bath with ceramic bath trim. This is fixed with a sealant that acts both as flexible adhesive and grout. Alternatively, apply silicone bath sealant, which is available in different colours.

Chapter 8
CEILINGS

Domestic ceilings are normally covered with plaster. If the floor above is of concrete, as in modern high-rise buildings, the plaster is applied to the underside of the concrete. Where the floor above is laid on joists the ceilings are fixed to the joists. Traditionally such ceilings are of lath and plaster, but in modern homes plasterboard is often used instead.

Occasionally other materials, such as tongued and grooved boards or matchboarding, are used to form a ceiling. In many older cottages, the timber is fixed directly to the joists, and takes the place of plaster. If you came across a tongued and grooved ceiling in a modern house, however, it will usually have been installed as a decorative measure, and will be a false ceiling, with the original plaster one more than likely still above it.

Another type of ceiling that you will occasionally come across is the hollow-joisted ceiling. In this, the joists are fully on view. If there is a room above, you are likely to see the underside of its floor. On top storeys, plasterboard may have been fixed over the joists. On lower floors, the space between the joists under the floor might have been lined with plasterboard, to give a good, clean effect; although fitting it would be a very tedious job. The advantage of such a ceiling is that, in order to comply with building regulations, the room height may be measured to the underside of the top covering, not the bottom edge of the joist – an important point in some loft or basement conversions.

REPAIRS
You might be surprised to learn that ceilings have to withstand stresses. If there is a room above, then as feet pass across the floor they cause the joists below to move, even if only slightly, putting a strain on the fixings of the ceiling. Even on top storeys, there can be natural movement of the timber that might cause problems. Moreover, older ceilings would be fitted in the days when no one bothered about insulation, and the extremes of heat and cold in the loft could cause the joists to move. Rainwater getting through defec-

tive roofs and snow blown through the eaves are other hazards.

Lath and plaster ceilings are usually the ones that give the most trouble, if only because they are older, but you can also have problems with modern, plasterboard ceilings.

Cracks in the ceiling

Because of the problems of movement, ceilings are much more likely to have cracks than are walls. You can often, too, get rough surfaces caused by extensive cracking, or by areas where the smooth surface skin of the plaster has fallen away, leaving porous patches.

Small defects can be filled with ordinary filler, as part of the process of redecorating. Where the blemishes are widespread, however, it is better to use heavy-duty decorative material, such as thick ceiling paper applied over lining paper, or a textured finish when you decorate.

A ceiling needs more thorough washing and rinsing prior to redecoration than does a wall, because the movement of air in a room carries dirt and tar upwards.

Powdery surfaces

The surface of old lath and plaster ceilings is often perpetually dusty; brush your hand across it, and it will leave a powdery deposit on your palm. Seal the surface before carrying out any decorative treatment. Use a stabilizing solution, sold in paint shops or builders' merchants.

Ceilings that bulge

A common defect with lath and plaster ceilings is that they bulge away from the joists – they 'belly out'. The remedy for this depends on the cause. If the laths have worked loose, nail them back to the joists, using galvanised clout nails. The nail heads will be disguised later in subsequent redecoration. If the bulge has come about because the plaster has separated from the laths, nailing back will not work.

One method that is often effective is to work from above – either in a loft, or by raising floorboards in the upstairs room. Brace the bulge back into place by placing a wide length of timber under it, held by a stout timber prop wedged against the floor. Trowel new plaster from above over the laths so that it bonds with the old.

Such treatment might not give a smooth surface on which to paint, but you will get a satisfactory result if you cover it with a thick paper. In fact, thick paper, or textured finishes, are often the best solution to the problem of defective ceilings.

If the ceiling is not easily accessible from above you will have to scrape bulging plaster off, then fill the hole with decorating filler or plaster, according to the extent of the damage (Fig. 8:1).

Loose plasterboard

Structural stress can cause the nails holding plasterboard to pop, leaving an ugly edge where the board parts from its neighbour, and spots where the nail heads break through. Brace the board hard against the joist – a helper can do this for you – and re-fix the board by driving in extra galvanized plasterboard nails about 38 mm (1½ in) from each loose one. Drive home the loose nails. Fill in the cracks and disguise the nail heads with ordinary filler before you redecorate.

Patching plasterboard

Plasterboard ceilings are not unduly difficult to repair.

Begin by locating the joists at each side of the damage. You might see them from above in a loft. If you cannot, then tap the ceiling and listen to the sound. From below, push up a saw through the damage (Fig. 8:2), and cut sideways in each direction until you meet the joists. Make up a frame from 50 mm (2 in) square timber, half-lapped at the corners and strengthened with screws. The width of the frame should be such that it will just fit between the joists; its length should allow it to cover the entire damaged area. A frame longer than 600 mm (2 ft) should be strengthened with a cross member in the middle.

Offer up the frame to the ceiling, position it carefully between the joists, and pencil a line round its outer edges over the damaged area. Now saw out the area you have marked, beginning perhaps with a pad saw and finishing up with a handsaw.

You need a piece of plasterboard to fill this cut-out. To cut a piece to the right size, place the frame on a sheet of plasterboard (you might be able to buy an offcut, if you need only a small patch), draw a line round it, and cut 3 mm (⅛ in) inside this line.

Nail 50 × 25 mm (2 × 1 in) battens to the sides of the frame so that the battens will not touch the joists. Position the frame inside the hole you have cut in the ceiling, and fix it into place with 75 mm (3 in) screws driven through pre-drilled holes and into the sides of the joists. The frame should be positioned on the joists so that the new patch will be level with the old ceiling.

Place the patch in position on the frame, and fix it with galvanized plasterboard nails. Fix down any free ends of the plasterboard of the existing ceiling, by nailing to the joists or the battens fixed to the frame. Disguise the join between new and old plasterboard as detailed in Chapter 6.

8.1 *Repairing a bulge in a lath and plaster ceiling: (a) Scrape off bulging plaster. (b) Fill the hole with decorating filler or plaster.*

Half-lapped joints

Pencil line

e   Joist   No. 10 screws driven into joist

Galvanized plasterboard nails   Old ceiling

Frame   New plasterboard patch   Batten

8.2 *Patching a plasterboard ceiling: (a) Locate the joists with a saw. (b) Make up a frame that will eventually fit between the joists and cover the damaged area. (c) Mark and saw out area covered by frame. (d) Use frame as pattern for marking out plasterboard patch. (e) The patch is nailed to the frame, free ends of the main ceiling to the joists or battens fixed to the side of the frame.*

Pulling down a ceiling

An old ceiling, particularly a lath and plaster one, can get into such a bad state that complete replacement becomes necessary. The first stage is to take down the old ceiling. This is not a job that calls for any particular skills, but it is not one to be undertaken lightly. Especially in an older house, you will be showered by a large amount of dust as the ceiling, along with the debris of 100 years or more lying on top of it, pours down. Do not underestimate the amount of dust there will be, especially on top floors: the cloud can be so dense that visibility can go down to a couple of feet.

Begin by opening the window. Warn the neighbours what you propose to do. Dust will billow out to such an extent that they might think it is smoke and that you have a fire. Wear goggles and a mask – improvise this from a handkerchief, if need be.

Work with an old stout chisel, screwdriver, small crowbar or any similar blunt instrument or even a large claw hammer. Push the tool up through the plaster and try to locate the joists. When you have found the joists, wrench the laths free, letting them and the plaster fall to the ground. Finding the joists will be easier as the work proceeds.

When the entire ceiling is pulled down and the dust has

settled, inspect the joists and pull out any nails or remnants of lath.

This is a good opportunity, too, to inspect the joists for damage or decay (see Chapter 9). Look particularly for signs of woodworm attack, both in the joists and in the underside of the floor above.

Decide whether you are going to put up a new ceiling, or leave the joists on view. Much depends on the condition of the joists and on the underside of any floor above. Only if these are attractive will you want to have them on view.

If you decide to leave the joists uncovered, you can get a pleasing effect by staining the joists a dark colour, and painting the underside of the floor above white.

A NEW CEILING

Modern ceilings are nearly always made of plasterboard. If you decide to put up a new ceiling, then this is the obvious choice. A timber ceiling is an alternative, but for most purposes it is prohibitively expensive.

Erecting a plasterboard ceiling

As already explained, plasterboard comes in two thicknesses. For joists spaced with the centres up to 450 mm (18 in) apart use 9.5 mm (⅜ in) board; if they are wider apart – up to 600 mm (24 in) – use 12.7 mm (½ in) board. Plasterboard incorporating an insulating material is available, and this is particularly suitable for top-storey ceilings. Choose a length of board that suits the spacing of the joists.

The boards should be fixed with the longest edge across the joists, and the ends should lie along the middle of a joist. They must not be left flapping free. Noggings (intermediate strips) should be fixed between the joists along the sides of the board, so that each is supported on all edges (Fig. 8:3).

Plasterboard is a heavy material, especially the larger thicker sheets, so you will need a helper. You must have proper access so that you can reach the ceiling. Do not attempt to balance on a pair of household steps: rest each end of a scaffold board on a strong support.

With the aid of a helper, lift a sheet of board and carry it on edge to a corner of the room, which is where the first one should be fixed. Turn it flat, and hoist it up. The helper should stand at one end, supporting the board with the head and outstretched hands. You stand at the other end, also using your head for support, and drive in the first few fixing nails. When sufficient nails have been driven in for the board to stay in place you can both drive home the fixing nails. Nails should be driven in at 150 mm (6 in) centres, and no closer than 13 mm (½ in) from the edge.

8.3 *Erecting a plasterboard ceiling: (a) Fix noggings between the joints. (b) Lift up the plasterboard. (c) The board is nailed to joists and noggings. (d) Start off second row with a cut piece in order to stagger the joins.*

Leave a gap of 3 mm (⅛ in) between this board and the next one you erect. Eventually, when you come to the end of a row, cut a board to fit. Use the waste from this to start off the next row, so the cross joins of the boards will be staggered. If an exact number of whole boards make up a row, start off the second row with half a board, in order to stagger the joints.

Full instructions for working with plasterboard and disguising the joins are given in the section on internal walls.

A false ceiling

Pulling down an old defective ceiling is extremely messy and disruptive so, where the ceiling height permits, it might be better to erect a false ceiling just below the existing one. The way to do this is to fix a network of battens to the ceiling, with screws driven through them and the plaster into the joists (Fig. 8:4). If you decide on a plasterboard ceiling, the network should go both along and across the joists, to give the necessary fixing points, as detailed in the previous section.

Finding the ceiling joists can be difficult, but in cases such as this – where there will be a good cover-up – you can make a series of test borings. Once you have determined

Skirting

Existing upstairs floor boards

Batten screwed to wall for end support

Battens screwed through existing ceilings into joists

Plasterboard nailed to battens

Battens across joists skew nailed to those running along joists

Joist

Existing lath and plaster ceiling

Straight edge

Spirit level

Sagging ceiling

the position of two joists you should easily locate the others, because usually the spacing between them is regular.

To get a good, level ceiling, all the battens should be at the same height. Check that they are by placing a long, true batten, with a spirit level held against it, across them. To adjust the level, withdraw the battens' fixing screws or drive them in further as necessary. Where the ceiling joists have twisted badly out of true, and the ceiling bows heavily in the middle, fix the battens at the perimeter of the room to the top of the wall, rather than the ceiling (Fig. 8:4 inset).

The battens should have a cross-section of about 50 mm (2 in) square, so long screws will be required – a minimum of 100 mm (4 in) to get through batten, plaster and lath, and give a good, firm fixing.

A false ceiling serves a useful function in a top-storey room, where there is no accessible attic space above. You can place insulation materials above the plasterboard, to make the house warmer, and so reduce heating bills.

Timber ceilings

Many do-it-yourselfers putting up a false ceiling prefer to use lengths of matchboarding instead of sheets of plaster-board, because these are much easier to handle. Be

8.4 Battens screwed through existing lath and plaster and into joists provide fixing points for a false ceiling. (Inset) Check with a spirit level and true batten that the fixing battens are all level. Those at a room's perimeter may have to be fixed to the top of the wall, instead of to the ceiling, to ensure that they are true.

8.5 *False ceiling of matchboarding 'secret nailed' to battens screwed to joists*

Joists

Batten screwed across joists

warned, however, that many authorities feel that this repre-sents too much of a fire risk.

Matchboarding used on a ceiling (Fig. 8:5) should be fixed to battens at each end and at spacings of about one metre (40 in). It will probably be easier to fix the battens across the joists, rather than along them, with a screw driven into each joist. The planks should be fixed to the battens with secret nailing (see page 135).

Illuminated ceilings

Until recently, illuminated ceilings were to be found mainly in shops and supermarkets, but they have become increasingly popular in the home. They consist of a series of plastic panels, suspended below a set of fluorescent tubes. The light from these ceilings is not suitable for living rooms and bedrooms, but is ideal for kitchens and bathrooms. Moreover, the warm surface of the plastic can help to re-duce, if not eliminate, condensation – a problem to which such rooms are prone. An illuminated ceiling is also a good means of hiding one in a bad condition. It is particularly suitable for high-ceiling rooms, but could be a problem with rooms that already have a low ceiling.

Plan the height of the ceiling carefully. It should not be so high that there is no room for the tubes, or so low that the light becomes diffused. The manufacturers give advice on suitable heights. Many people think it a good idea to paint the original ceiling in brilliant white gloss before fixing the panels. With some brands, the panels can be used to change the colour of the light from the tubes. Using a com-bination of plain and coloured panels it is also possible to build up interesting patterns.

A TRAP DOOR TO THE LOFT

Many homes, especially those built in the last century, have no means of access to the loft, which is often necessary nowadays to lay insulation, fit a cold supply tank, or carry out electrical work.

A landing is usually the best place for a trap door, because you can enter the loft without inconveniencing anyone in a bedroom, and without showering the bedroom with dust when the door is opened.

Draw in pencil on the ceiling the shape of the opening you wish to cut. Ideally, this should be close to a joist on two sides, so be prepared to adjust its position if necessary. Push a chisel through the middle of the piece of plaster you wish to remove, and make a slot. Push a saw through the slot and cut out the shape with a saw. Get a helper to stand by as you do so, to support the cut-out. Lower it gently to the ground to minimize dust.

If you are dealing with plasterboard, it will be easy to take down the cut-out in one piece, and with the minimum of dirt; lath and plaster will be more messy, so saw through each lath carefully.

If the space between two joists is not big enough for a hatch, support the ceiling, then saw out a section of the joist in the middle of the opening. For the support use a stout post wedged between two lengths of timber (at least 50 mm (2 in) thick) – one on the floor and the other on the ceiling. These pieces of timber should be long enough to span at least two joists on both floor and ceiling. Saw through the joist squarely.

At each end of the opening fit a 'trimmer' (Fig. 8:6). This is

8.6 (a) Framework for door to left (b) How to fix trimmers and tailers to sides of joist (c) Detail of how opening is lined with planed timber, and underside framed with moulding a length of timber (of the same size as the joists) that spans the gap between the two uncut joists. Butt the trimmer up against the end of the cut joists. If you want an opening narrower than the space between two joists, fit a 'tailer' – a similar piece of timber spanning the gap between the two trimmers.

Professionals would fix the trimmers and tailers with 100 mm (4 in) round wire nails. This will be secure enough only if the ends of the cut joists are square. If in doubt, screw battens to the sides of the cut ends of the joists, and notch the trimmers over them.

When the timber framework forming the opening is fixed securely, remove the timber supports. Line the inside of the opening with planed timber about 19 mm (¾ in) thick. Frame the underside with moulded timber, then make good any damaged plaster. Cut the door from a sheet of block-board.

If the door will be used infrequently, you can line the loft opening with timber to form a ledge. The door can merely rest on this ledge, and be pushed up when you want to enter the loft. You might prefer to hinge the door instead. To enable you to fit a loft ladder you should fix the hinges so that the door opens downwards. Then you need a catch to hold the door closed when it is pushed back into place.

Chapter 9
FLOORS

There are two entirely distinct types of floor – those that actually rest on the ground below, and those that are fixed some way above it. These are known as 'direct-to-earth' and 'suspended' floors. Floors on the first storey and above must, by their very nature, be suspended; those on the ground floor can be either. In general, however, only direct-to-earth floors are found in basements.

SUSPENDED FLOORS

In small homes suspended floors are nearly always of timber, and that usually means floorboards. However, because of the high price of timber, some modern homes have floors of chipboard. Suspended floors can also be of concrete, but these are usually confined to high-rise buildings. There is little to go wrong with this material, and if cracks do develop they indicate faults way beyond the scope of the do-it-yourselfer. If tamping marks are visible on the surface of this sort of floor, a floor-levelling compound should be applied before fixing any floorcovering; no other repair should be attempted.

The joists

Suspended wooden floors are supported by, and fixed to, a network of joists. The normal fixing of each board is by floorboard nails, two driven into each joist.

The spacing between joists and their size will have been determined by the architect according to their span (the length across which they are unsupported) and the load they would be expected to carry. It is important to bear in mind that domestic suspended floors may have been designed to support only normal furniture and living stress. They can be damaged if subjected to excessive strain – unusually heavy furniture, for instance (water beds have recently been found to be a problem in some situations), or dancing. Natural stone fireplaces that spread beyond the chimney breast to incorporate shelves and so on can also pose a threat: they should never be installed on a sus-

Iron wall plate

Notched wall plate   dpc   Sleeper wall

Joist hanger

9.1 *Three ways in which the ends of floor joists can be supported: (a) In sockets, (b) on a sleeper wall and (c) in joist hangers.*

pended timber floor without extra support being added. The joist spacings will be at centres of from 300 mm (1 ft) upwards – you can see at a glance the spacing in your case (if the boards are not covered) by looking at the heads of the fixing nails. The size will usually be 100×50 mm (4×2 in) or perhaps 150 mm (6 in) depth and 38 mm ($1\frac{1}{2}$ in) width.

Fig. 9:1 shows three ways in which a ground floor joist can be supported at the ends:

1 It can be let into a socket left for this purpose in the brickwork. In such instances, there will often be an iron wall plate running under the joists, to spread the load along the entire wall.

2 It may rest on a low wall, built just inside the main walls of the house, and known as a sleeper wall. On top of the sleeper wall will be a damp-proof course (dpc) strip, then a length of timber known as a wall plate. The joist will usually be notched into and over the wall plate (although some just rest on top of it) and be held in place by skew-nailing.

3 It might rest in a device known as a joist hanger, a sort of galvanized metal stirrup built into the brickwork.

Any intermediate support that is necessary will be provided by extra sleeper walls in the middle of the span. Such sleeper walls have gaps to allow extra circulation of air, ventilation being an important factor in keeping damp at bay.

The ends of upper floor joists can also be fixed in sockets or joist hangers; intermediate support will be provided by an internal wall in the house.

Repairing joists

Fortunately, joists do not develop as many faults as floorboards, but defects can occur, especially if unseasoned wood was used in the first place. A joist can twist out of true. A symptom of this would be that a floorboard would be seen to be twisted, but could not be nailed down flat. Or a joist can be attacked by woodworm or dry rot. The floor will seem weak or unstable if this is the case. If you suspect a weak floor you should always lift a board or two to discover what is wrong.

It must be stressed that repairs to joists are a major undertaking, and not to be embarked upon lightly. They involve a great upheaval, especially on upper floors, for your work will almost certainly damage the ceiling below. Since each joist carries every board in the room, a large part of the floor – if not the whole lot – will have to be taken up, which will mean the room will be unusable, as will any room below if you interfere with its ceiling.

A joist might be damaged along part of its length – a tendency for the floor to sag, or feel unstable at one point is an indication of this. In such a case, saw out the damaged section as detailed below, buy a new length of timber of the same size, and bolt it to the cut ends of the old joist.

If a joist is twisted or bowed it is often possible to straighten it by fitting struts between it and the joist on each side. Should all the joists be twisted, struts of fairly strong timber, 25 mm (1 in) thick, and almost as wide as the joists are deep, will have to be fitted between each of them. They are cut to a length equalling exactly the spacing between the joists, and are fixed by skew-nailing. If this remedy does not work, the joists will have to be replaced.

Replacing joists

Begin by taking up all the boards fixed to the joist. If the joist is in an upper storey, you will need to free the ceiling below by pressing gently on top of the ceiling to push the fixing nails down. One way of finding these nails is to push a very thin blade under the joist and move it along until the nails are located. If the ceiling is made of lath and plaster you will probably have to cut a large area, if not take down the whole lot.

If the joist is supported at its end on joist hangers, or fixed to the top of a wall, it can be lifted clear. The new joist, which obviously should be of the same size as the old, can then be dropped into place. Should the joist be resting on wall plates, withdraw any fixing nails, then once again remove it and fit the new joist. If the joist is built into a slot, get someone to hold it while you saw through it near its ends. Lift the main body of the joist away, then pull out the short stub still in the slot. You cannot push a new joist back into these slots, so they will have to be bricked up and joist hangers mortared into the brickwork.

An electric cable may have been passed through a joist you are replacing. Disconnect it – having turned the supply off at the mains first – from the nearest connection and draw it clear. Bore a 19 mm (¾ in) diameter hole in the new joist 50 mm (2 in) from its top to accommodate the cable.

Timber floor surfaces

Floorboards, nowadays, are often tongued and grooved ('t and g') so that as shrinkage of the timber occurs over the years there will not be a gap for dirt and draughts to pass through. But this was not always so: in the last century, and occasionally in this, boards without tongues and grooves – 'square-edged' boards – were fitted.

Warped floorboards

Warping can cause boards to curl up at the edges, making it difficult to lay floorcoverings. If this is not too pronounced, overlaying it with hardboard will be a sufficient cure. Alternatively, you can sand the boards flat again with a floor sander, using a course abrasive belt. Normally when sanding boards you should work along – not across – their length, because crosswise sanding causes score marks that are difficult to remove. Work at an angle of 45° to the side of the boards. If you mean to seal the boards and leave them uncovered, treat them along their length in the normal way first with a medium, then with a fine abrasive.

Lifting and replacing floorboards

The commonest reason for having to lift a floorboard is to work on plumbing or electrics below. First check whether your boards are 't and g' or square-edged. Push a knife blade down between two boards, but not so far that you might strike a cable. If there is no resistance, the board is square-edged; if the blade will not pass through, there is a tongue. If there is a tongue you will have to remove it on both sides of the board. The traditional tool for doing this is the floorboard saw, but a powered circular saw is just as good (Fig. 9:2).

You must set the saw blade so that it protrudes just below the tongue you are going to cut, for not only does this ensure that the saw teeth strike the work at the best angle for sawing, but also that there is less risk of cutting into the joists or striking cables and pipes. The tongue occupies the middle third of the side of a board, so its lower edge would be about 8 mm (⅓ in) below the surface of a 25 mm (1 in) thick board, and 6 mm (¼ in) below that of a 19 mm (¾ in) board. When you have removed the tongues, you must saw across the width at each end of the section of board you wish to raise. These cuts should be done with a pad saw, for which you might have to drill a starting hole; the cut should be made immediately to the side of a joist – you will be able to locate

Drilled starter hole

Existing floorboard

Batten

Joist   d

these easily with a knife once the board tongues have been removed.

The board now has to be wrenched up. You can shove a strong screwdriver, old chisel, or small crowbar under the fixing points and heave, but you risk marking the boards this way. On an old floor that you intend to cover up completely this may not matter, but if you want the board to be on view, a better way is to wrench up a set of nails near a cut end, then push a hammer handle flat under the board and press down sharply on the free end. This will send a shock wave down the length of the board that will loosen nails further along You will then be able to push the hammer farther along and repeat the process. The farther you push the hammer, the more effective this method will be, for you will be able to exert greater leverage. Pull the nails out as they loosen with either a claw hammer or pincers.

With one board up and out of the way, it is easier to remove subsequent boards. If you need to take up boards that are side by side, it will probably be enough to remove the tongues on each outer edge, leaving the ones between intact.

When you come to refix the board, you cannot nail it to the joists at the end since you have to cut just to the side of them. You must screw a small length of timber – 38 mm (1½ in) square is suitable – to the side of the joist. The length of the timber should be greater than the width of the board. Fix it with its top edge hard against the underside of the boards on each side, and it will be in the correct position to make the replaced board level.

If you have raised the board to install an electrical or plumbing connection, fix it back with screws, so that it will

9.2 *Lifting up a floorboard: (a) Cut off tongues with a circular saw. (b) Saw across width of board. (c) Prise board from cut end. (d) When board is replaced, its end is nailed to a batten screwed to side of joist.*

be easy to raise should you need access again. Otherwise use floorboard nails, unless it is an upstairs floor over a dubious ceiling, in which case hammering might loosen the ceiling's key.

A floorboard that is badly damaged can be replaced. Take it up and discard it. If just one board is involved, the replacement should be square-edged – a 't and g' board cannot be fitted. You may not be able to buy a board of exactly the right width, so get one larger and plane it to a close fit. Your new board should be of the same thickness as the old, but if it proves impossible to buy one of the correct thickness, you can choose one slightly thinner and place a little packing – hardboard, perhaps – on each joist. Or buy a thicker one and plane it to size – this is not too much trouble if you have a power planer.

Squeaking boards

A board squeaks because, as you walk over the floor, it moves and rubs against its neighbour. To stop such movement you must refix it. At its simplest, such refixing could consist of punching home nails properly. However, the movement of the board may have so enlarged the hole round the nails that this will not be effective. The obvious remedy then might seem to be to drive in extra nails elsewhere in the board. But you have to be careful to avoid cables and pipes.

Electricity cables are not such a problem because, if they have been properly installed, the holes in the joist through which they pass will be at least 50 mm (2 in) below the floor. Pipes are a different matter, however, because they are likely to be sitting in notches cut in the joist immediately below the boards. To find out where pipes are likely to be, look at whatever items supplied by gas or water are in the room and try to work out where the pipe runs. If all else fails, take the loose nails out of the loose board and replace them with screws driven in exactly the same holes.

Gaps between boards

Gaps that develop due to shrinkage or bad fitting between the boards can be a problem. Even if there is a tongue the gap makes it difficult to lay a floorcovering smoothly. There are several ways in which these gaps can be plugged. For instance, you can take thin strips of wood, taper them slightly with a sander on the lower edge, and tap them down into the gap. They should be left slightly proud, then smoothed down flush with a plane or, better still, a floor sander. Another method is to make papier mâché with old newspapers to fill the gap, but this, although cheap, is tedious. In both cases, if the floor is left bare it will be obvious what you have done.

The best method is probably to overlay the floor with hardboard. This presents a superb surface on which to lay floorcoverings and, if sealed, or even painted, can make an attractive flooring in its own right.

Hardboarding a floor

Hardboard comes in a range of sheet sizes, the biggest normally being 2440 × 1220 mm (8 × 4 ft). The bigger the sheets the more quickly you can work, but large sheets can be unwieldy and you might prefer to settle for a sheet 1220 mm (4 ft) or even 900 mm (3 ft) square.

Hardboard should always be conditioned before use, and this process is essential when it is to be laid over floorboards. Brush a litre (1⅘ pints) of water into the reverse side of each 2440 × 1220 mm (8 × 4 ft) sheet (use correspondingly less water on smaller sheets), then stack them flat, back to back, in the room where they will be laid. Leave them for approximately 48 hours – not much less or much longer. The sheets then dry out once they are fixed, and tighten up like a

Sequence of laying

9.3 *Order in which sheets of hardboard are fixed to a floor. Fixing is best done with ring shank nails (inset).*

drum skin to form a perfect surface on which to lay a floor-covering.

Hardboard is fixed with ring-shank nails (Fig. 9:3). Lay it smooth-side down if you intend to cover it, so that the mesh will hide the nail head and present a good surface to receive the covering. You need a nail at 225 mm (9 in) centres in the middle, and 150 mm (6 in) centres round the edges.

Begin laying the sheets in the corner of the room farthest away from the door. This corner will probably not be a perfect right angle because most rooms are out of true, but it does not matter if the sheet does not fit perfectly against the wall. Butt the next sheet up against the first, and fix that. Eventually you will come to the end of the row, where you will have to cut a sheet to the size of the gap – again it does not have to be a perfect fit. Take the waste from this sheet and use it to start the next row. Not only is this an economical use of the material, but also it staggers the joins – breaks the bond – between the sheets thus making for a better job. The final row of sheets at the end of the room will probably need to be cut to width.

Re-laying a floor

Where large gaps have developed between floorboards, often the only remedy will be to take the floorboards up and re-lay them. Begin at the side of the room away from the door. Take up about seven or eight boards, but leave the one under the skirting undisturbed. The tongues should remain intact where possible. Clean off the edges and undersides of all the boards you left, and get rid of any dust or dirt on top of the joists. Take out any nails or tacks still left in the boards.

Now take one of the raised boards and push it into position up against the board still remaining under the skirting. Follow with about five more boards. You now need sets of two wedges cut from softwood and preferably slightly thicker than the floorboards. The wedges should be about 150 mm (6 in) long, and tapered from, say, 50 mm (2 in) at their widest to a narrow point. A set of wedges is required for every metre (39 in) of board length.

Place the wedges in pairs on their sides up against the last row out from the skirting, then nail a spare board to the joists hard against the wedges. Use two hammers to knock the wedges so they slide against each other, working on each set alternately. This will drive the boards as close as possible against each other. When you are satisfied they are tight, nail them in place, beginning with the one nearest the wedges. Use floorboard nails, two per board per joist.

Now you can remove the wedges and take up further boards to allow you to re-lay the next half dozen. Eventually you will come to the far side of the room. Once again leave the board half under the skirting alone. When you have re-laid all the rest, there will be a gap between this board and the rest of the floor. Fill it with a new board that will have to be cut to size.

Repairing and installing chipboard floors

In many modern buildings chipboard is used on top of the joist instead of floorboards, because it can be up to 30 per cent cheaper. It must, however, be a special type of chipboard suitable for the job. Chipboard is a good base for all types of floorcovering and can be an attractive surface in its own right when sealed.

Flooring-quality chipboard can be bought in three different edge profiles – square-edged, tongued-and-grooved on two sides or four, or loose-tongued. It is available in two thicknesses – 18 mm ($1\frac{1}{16}$ in) and 22 mm ($\frac{7}{8}$ in) – and in various sheet sizes, 2440 × 1220 mm (8 × 4 ft) and 2440 × 600 mm (8 × 2 ft) being the most common. It is fixed to the joists with nails.

Chipboard has one other big advantage over floorboards, apart from cost: it is a more stable material than natural timber, and therefore less likely to twist, shrink or warp. It is not, of course, as strong, but is perfectly adequate for the job.

If any of the panels that make up a chipboard floor become damaged, replace them. Should the panel be a large one, you might be able to minimize costs by replacing just half of it.

First ascertain by probing as before, whether a 't and g' board has been used. If it has, the tongues on all sides will have to be removed, in the same way as for floorboards. Prise up the board, using a large, old screwdriver or chisel. Begin along one edge. Once you work this free, the rest will come up easily.

When the board is raised, measure its thickness, and buy a replacement of the same dimension. In the meantime, leave the damaged board loosely in place so that no one will fall down the hole. No matter what type of edge profile was used previously, the replacement will have to be square edged. Chipboard can also be used to replace a damaged plank floor. As already mentioned, flooring-grade chipboards come in two thicknesses – 18 mm ($1\frac{1}{16}$ in) and 22 mm ($\frac{7}{8}$ in). For the former the joists must be no more than 450 mm (18 in) apart, while for the latter they can be up to 610 mm (24 in). Local building regulations may specify minima.

Square-edged boards should be supported on every edge (Fig. 9:4). Their long edges go parallel to – and should

9.4 *Fixing a chipboard floor: (inset) Three types of board – square edged, loose-tongued, and tongued and grooved. (a) Square edged boards fixed parallel to joists with ends supported on noggings (b) Tongued and grooved boards run across the joists.*

fall in the middle of – the joists. This means that, if you cannot buy a standard sheet size to match your joist spacing, you will have to cut the sheets to width. The ends of the sheets are fixed to short lengths of timber, skew-nailed to the side of the joists. These lengths of timber are known as noggings, and they should be 38 mm (1½ in) wide. The boards should be nailed in place, the nails being about 9 mm (⅓ in) from the edge of the board, and 200-300 mm (8-12 in) apart round the perimeter, 400-500 mm (16-20 in) on intermediate joists.

Tongued-and-grooved boards go with their long edges across the joists. They must, however, be supported at the ends, so cut them to a length that ensures their short edges fall in the middle of joists, one 25 mm (1 in) from each edge, the others spaced between.

Study the foregoing information, look at the joist spacing in your home, get from your supplier a list of the sizes of board he can offer you, then work out which it would be best for you to buy.

The temptation will be to get the biggest boards possible because that would speed up the work. However, do remember that chipboard is such a heavy material that some of the larger sheets are unwieldly, so unless you can be sure of help, you might get along better with a smaller size.

When your chipboard arrives, it must be properly stored until you are ready to use it – bad storage can cause permanent distortion of the boards. Stack them flat, indoors. It is a good idea, too, to loose-lay them in the room where they will be fixed for at least 24 hours in order to condition them to the moisture content of the room.

The edges of all types of board should be tightly butted up against each other, and you will get a stronger result if you smear a pvc woodworking adhesive on the meeting surface. But where the boards meet the walls of the room you should leave an expansion gap. This gap should be 2 mm ($\frac{1}{12}$ in) for every metre (40 in) of floor, with 10 mm ($\frac{2}{5}$ in) as the minimum.

Just as when you are laying hardboard, you should break the bond so that the cross joins are staggered, and you achieve this in just the same way: when you saw a board to length to complete the end of the row, use the waste to start off the next row.

Should there be electrical or plumbing connections under a chipboard floor it is a good idea to form a trap above them. Make sure it is supported by joists or noggings on all edges, and fix it with screws rather than with nails so that it can be raised easily.

You can bond all types of flooring, both sheet and tile, directly to chipboard. If you will be using an adhesive with a high water content, seal the floor first with a polyurethane lacquer.

DIRECT-TO-EARTH FLOORS

A direct-to-earth floor, sometimes known as a solid floor, is one that is laid directly on the ground beneath. At one time most ground floors were of this type: typical were floors consisting of flagstones or quarry tiles embedded in mortar directly on the earth. They suffered from one overwhelming defect: they were subject to rising damp.

Timber direct-to-earth floors were a little more sophisticated. They consisted of timber floor plates lying on the earth, to which would be fixed a series of joists, with floorboards on top. The resulting cavity made for a warmer, drier floor than was possible with flagstones or quarry tiles, but it was still subject to damp. In some cases, large-section timber, looking something like railway sleepers, would be bedded directly to the earth. This type was very prone to damp.

Because of these considerations, direct-to-earth floors fell out of favour for many years, and were revived only after 1945. Two factors made for the revival. First, at that time timber was so scarce as to make the joist-and-boarded floor prohibitively expensive. Second, improved methods of

9.5 *Construction of a modern direct-to-earth floor*

damp-proofing meant that the rising damp could be kept at bay. And so homes with tiles – usually thermoplastic – throughout the ground floor made their appearance (or reappearance).

The modern direct-to-earth floor (Fig. 9:5) will be laid on well compacted earth. It will consist of a layer of hardcore, topped by concrete; then will come a damp-proof membrane, which will tie in with the damp-proof course of the walls; and finally there will be a finishing screed, with a floorcovering on top of that. Such a floor will be perfectly dry.

However, just because a floor has a concrete screed, you cannot assume that it has been correctly built. Before 1945 and, indeed, on occasions since, concrete floors were laid without proper damp precautions being taken.

Damp

If you have a direct-to-earth floor that was built before the last war, damp may be patently obvious, with marks covering the floor, and evidence of rotting in the floorcovering. In other cases, damp may be there without your being aware of it, and its presence would not matter unless you wanted to lay a floorcovering. There are various rough-and-ready tests you can carry out.

For instance, heat a brick in the oven for about an hour, then place it on the floor (so long as it is not a decorative one that can be damaged by heat). If the floor becomes stained, damp is present. Or you can take a sheet of metal, heat it on a blowlamp or gas ring, and lay it on the floor – again provided that it is one that will not be damaged by heat. Moisture beads will gather on the underside of the plate and a patch will appear on the concrete if the floor suffers from damp. Another test is to place a piece of glass on the floor and seal its edges with putty. Damp will cause moisture to form underneath it.

The snag with these tests, however, is that if they are negative you still cannot be absolutely sure that the floor is dry. Some floors are wet only during very damp weather, and in some cases the level of the local water table can vary. In the last resort, the only way to be absolutely sure is to call in an expert to make tests with special instruments – a hygrometer or protimeter.

If you have a floor – of concrete, perhaps – that is in good condition (level and smooth, for instance) except that it suffers from rising damp, then a cure can be effected fairly easily. Liquid preparations that can be brushed on to the floor are available at builders' merchants and home improvement centres. These can then be over-laid with the normal floorcoverings such as carpet, linoleum, or vinyl, and some can be left exposed as a floor surface in their own right. Follow the manufacturer's instructions when using them.

Laying a new floor
An old direct-to-earth floor, of flagstones, quarry tiles or timber, if damp or defective in some other way, has to be taken up and a concrete one built in its place. You must first of all remove the existing flooring (if you wish to retain the period flavour of an old house, this can be removed carefully, then re-laid on top of the new floor).

To lift flagstones, ram a crowbar or stout garden spade in between the joins, and lever up. The first quarry tiles should be chipped up with a cold chisel and club hammer, although later on you may get on faster with a garden spade. Quarry tiles that are cemented in place will be more difficult to lift without breakages. Timber can be prised up with a claw hammer, bolster chisel, or old screwdriver. There is no need to be gentle with this wood, as when dealing with floorboards: timber from a direct-to-earth floor will probably be so wet – and more than likely affected by rot or woodworm – that it will be fit only for burning.

Now you must excavate to get sufficient depth for your new floor. You will probably find it convenient to make this on the same plane as the original one, otherwise you will run into trouble with door openings and perhaps a change of level from other rooms.

The base of the excavation should be well compacted, and of the same depth throughout. You can ensure the latter by hammering in a series of timber pegs 25 mm (1 in) or 38 mm (1½ in) square. Span a batten from one peg to the next, and use a spirit level to ensure the tops of the two are level. Dig down to the same depth round each peg. The base on which the concrete slab rests will vary according to the site condition, and in particular to the relationship of the floor to the level of the soil outside the house and the nature of the soil. It could be that hardcore dressed with sand, or graded granular material, would be suitable. In some cases wet lean concrete – i.e. a very weak mix consisting of from 1:16 to 1:20 of cement to aggregate – would be best. Get expert advice from someone with detailed knowledge of local conditions.

The concrete should be at least 100 mm (4 in) thick, and consist of a mix of 2½ parts of sharp sand to 4 of coarse aggregate, by volume. It should be well compacted to obtain maximum density and strength, and be finished to a smooth surface. It is normal to top it off with a sand and cement screed, on which you can lay virtually any type of flooring.

A vapour-resistant membrane should be fitted between the concrete and the screed, and this should tie in with the damp-proof course of the walls. The damp-proof membrane (dpm) is necessary because although watertight, concrete is not vapour-tight, and vapour could pass through the slab to attack the floorcovering, or the adhesive with which it is fixed.

The dpm can be in either liquid or sheet form. However, the most effective liquid dpms must be hot-applied, and are really only for professional use. Of the sheet materials, polythene is probably the most convenient for the do-it-yourselfer.

A sheet 0.12 mm thick (500 gauge) is sufficient to keep out the damp, but might tend to get damaged in subsequent operations, so it is often as well to use material of twice that thickness. Joins in the material should overlap by at least 150 mm (6 in) and be taped down with vapour-resisting tape. The screed should be of Portland cement and clean sharp sand in a mix of 1:3 by weight, where the flooring finish will be of thin or flexible material (e.g. thin tiles or carpet); and 1:4 by weight if thick or rigid flooring, such as concrete or quarry tiles, are planned. Because it cannot be bonded directly to the concrete below, the minimum thickness of the screed should be 50 mm (2 in).

There is no need to split the floor into bays when dealing with domestic-sized rooms – you can cover the whole floor at one go. However, place down battens temporarily to give a depth to which to tamp down the screed. You must make sure that the material is well compacted, and that there are no hollows in the concrete. To help in this you can make a tamper from scraps of timber and a broom handle. Smooth off finally with a float.

When finished the floor should be cured for four days by being covered with a 0.12 mm sheet of polythene 500 gauge, well lapped and held down all round the edges. Since the floor is inside a building, there will normally be no need to provide protection against frost.

Chapter 10
PLUMBING

The plumbing system of your home has two distinct functions: it supplies water to the points where it is needed and it carries away waste water when you have finished with it.

Any work you do on the plumbing must comply with the regulations of your local water authority. You are not required to get permission beforehand, but the authority can inspect the work and demand changes if they are not satisfied. The rules vary from area to area, and are changed from time to time.

You do not need to consult anybody to carry out minor maintenance work, such as re-washering a tap, but if you plan major additions or alterations, check on the requirements first with your local water authority; this is equally true of changes to drains.

THE SUPPLY
The main supply pipes are under the street, and an underground branch line runs from them to bring water to your property. From the point at which the pipes leave public property (Fig. 10:1), they become the responsiblility of the householder. So a stop tap is fitted, usually at the limit of a private property – perhaps somewhere near the garden gate – in order that the supply can be turned off by the supplier whenever necessary. The pipe then continues into the building and usually surfaces near the kitchen sink, where there will be another stop tap. Just beyond this stop tap there will be a branch line to the cold tap at the kitchen sink so that water drawn there for cooking and drinking will be pure from the main. The supply pipe continues upwards, and from this point on is known as the rising main. It feeds a cold supply tank, which is usually, though not necessarily, in the loft – it is the one that freezes up in winter if it is not lagged properly. Like all storage tanks, this one has an overflow pipe to carry water away harmlessly, should the tank ever overfill.

The entry of water into this tank is controlled by a ball valve. This comprises a lever connected at one end to the

Cold supply tank

Hot water expansion pipe

Overflow pipe

Hot cylinder

Cold water supply

Mains supply

Rising main

Boiler

Stop cock

Stop tap

Drinking water supply

Boiler to cylinder (flow)

Cylinder to boiler (return)

inlet valve and a ball on the other end. The ball floats on the water. When water is drawn from the tank, the water level drops, taking the ball with it and opening the valve. As the tank fills the ball rises and shuts off the valve when the correct water level is reached. If the valve fails to close, excess water will be carried away via the overflow.

The cold supply normally feeds all the cold outlets in the house, except for the kitchen sink. These outlets include the cold taps at all baths, washbasins, and lavatories (collectively known as fittings), as well as washing machines. To save on pipework the builder of the house might have connected all or some of the cold outlets – most probably cold taps of basins and baths, perhaps even a lavatory cistern – directly to the rising main. This practice is frowned on by some water authorities, however.

Water reaches the cold tank because of the pressure in

10.1 *Typical supply system in modern domestic plumbing*

the main. It flows from the cold tank because of gravity. The cold tank must, therefore, be high up in the house, which is why it is usually located in the loft. Water stored in this tank can be contaminated by dust and insects, for example, and become unfit for drinking, so the kitchen cold tap must have a direct pure supply from the main.

The height at which the tank is installed determines the strength of the flow of water at the various outlets: the greater the height, the faster water will gush out. Plumbers refer to the differences in height between the bottom of the cold tank (you do not measure from the top, in case the tank is half empty) and the water outlet as the head of water.

At various points throughout the system there may be other stop taps so that parts of the system can be turned off for maintenance without depriving the whole house of water. Such stop taps might be fitted to the supply to a lavatory, for instance, or to the hot water system.

Hot water

Domestic hot water (plumbers use the word 'domestic' to distinguish it from the water in a radiator system) is usually heated by a boiler. This may be free-standing in a kitchen or boiler house, mounted on a wall, or incorporated as a back boiler behind, say, a living room fire. Hot water for heating and domestic use is provided by the same boiler. When it has been heated it is stored in the hot cylinder, which may be housed in an airing cupboard.

Various fuels can be used to power the boiler, including gas, solid fuel and oil. Electric boilers are also being introduced. Whatever fuel is used, it is a wise economy to maintain the temperature of the heated water, and to achieve this the hot cylinder should be well insulated. Special jackets are sold for this purpose. At one time a jacket 25 mm (1 in) thick was considered adequate, but with escalating fuel costs a thickness of 75 mm (3 in) or more is now the rule. If your cylinder has only a thin jacket, do not discard it, but place a new one on top of it. You cannot have too much insulation on a hot cylinder, and lower fuel bills will soon cover the cost of an insulation jacket.

In normal circumstances, the water heating system will be of the gravity type, which works because hot water is lighter than cold. Water heated in a container will lie in layers of different temperatures, with the hottest at the top. So water heated by the boiler will rise to the hot cylinder through one pipe (the flow primary), and water that is cooler than this will fall to the boiler by another pipe (the return primary), to be heated in turn.

For such a gravity system to work effectively, the hot cylinder must be sited at a higher level than the boiler, and, indeed, in the average home it is customary for the boiler to be downstairs, with the hot cylinder in an airing cupboard conveniently by the bedrooms on the first floor. Even in bungalows and flats it is usually possible to raise the hot cylinder to a high enough level for the gravity system to operate.

For greatest efficiency, however, pumped primaries can be installed. Water from the cold tank (to replace the hot drawn off at the taps) is fed into the system at the bottom of the hot cylinder, where it will quickly drop down to the boiler through the return primary, and be heated. The draw-off point for water from the hot cylinder needs to be near its top, because that is where the water will be at its hottest.

Modern boilers are self-regulating (thermostatically controlled) so they maintain the water at a required temperature without overheating. In case a regulating thermostat fails, however, overheated water would rise up a pipe (known as the vent pipe) from the top of the hot cylinder to the cold tank, and would discharge there harmlessly. Should the cold tank become overfull as a result, excess water would run away through the overflow. Even so, if you ever hear water boiling in the hot cylinder (something that used to be more common when thermostats were not so general), shut down the heating immediately and draw off hot water by opening a hot tap somewhere in the house. Then have the system serviced by a heating engineer.

An immersion heater may be fitted to the cylinder, occasionally as a sole form of heating, but more usually as a standby if the boiler system fails.

The hot cylinder may be either 'direct' or 'indirect'. In a direct system the water heated in the boiler goes direct to the cylinder where it is stored until it is drawn off at the domestic taps. In an indirect system, water in a heating circuit is circulated through the boiler and a coil of piping within the cylinder. This coil serves as a heating element for the main body of water. Thus the water in the boiler and that for the taps are kept quite separate. Normally indirect cylinders are found where there is a radiator system of central heating, so that domestic and radiator water are never mixed, but you do come across them where the boiler is used just for domestic hot water.

Instant hot-water systems

The system described above is very common in modern homes because it makes use of the boiler that is necessary to heat water for radiators. If, however, there is an alternative form of space-heating, the hot water supply may be of the instant type. With such a heater, which can work off gas or electricity, no hot water is stored and there is, therefore no hot cylinder. Instead, the gas jets or electric elements come into play only when you turn on the tap and water passes across them.

Instantaneous heaters may be multi-point, with one heater serving all (or most) of the house. Or they can be single point, placed over a sink, washbasin or bath, for instance.

Such heaters are usually installed in conversion and modernization schemes because they simplify, and therefore usually reduce, installation costs, and because they are space-saving – one heater takes the place of a boiler and hot water cylinder. They can also save money in operating costs, because you heat up only as much water as you need; and they have the further advantage that they can supply unlimited hot water, whereas a hot tank once emptied of hot water takes time to reheat. In a home with this type of system it is often the case that all cold outlets are fed directly from the rising main, so that a cold storage tank will not need to be installed either.

Your own system

You should aim to get to know the plumbing system of your home, so that you will be ready to deal with emergencies. Try to trace the run of the pipes from the point at which the rising main starts. And, with the boiler or other water heater shut off, turn off one at a time any stop taps you come across. Then turn on the taps and flush the lavatories to determine which outlets are controlled by each stop tap.

Lagging

If the water in your supply pipe freezes you lose your supply temporarily. As the water freezes it expands, and may burst the pipe. Therefore any pipes in your supply system that are exposed to the weather should be lagged.

Lagging for pipes is available in two principal forms. One comes as a roll, and is wrapped like a bandage with large overlaps round the pipes. The other consists of cylindrical lengths of foam plastic, split lengthways so that they can be fitted round a pipe, then taped or clipped in place.

The cold tank, too, needs to be protected by lagging, especially if it is in the loft. Lagging kits consisting of four sides and a top are available. Also, never insulate the area of the loft below a cold tank because warmth rising from the house below helps to keep the tank from freezing.

Copper pipes

The first metallic plumbing systems were made of lead (the word plumbing comes from the Latin word *plumbum* for lead). Later on iron was used for a time. Today copper is used extensively; and plastic is gaining favour.

Most people altering or extending their plumbing system will be working with copper. If your supply pipes are in lead or iron, your whole plumbing system is out of date, and needs to be renewed – this is a job for a professional.

Pipes of three dimensions are found in modern plumbing systems. At one time they were in imperial sizes, which you will still come across when working on older installations. The modern (metric) sizes are 28 mm (used for the primaries), 22 mm (for the main runs), and 15 mm (for branch lines). The former imperial sizes were 1 in, ¾ in, and ½ in. If you convert pipe dimensions, it is important to note that the metric dimension refers to the external diameter, whereas the imperial refers to the internal.

Working copper pipe (Fig. 10:2) may involve cutting, joining, connecting up (a type of joining) or bending.

In any job using pipe, it will probably need to be cut to length. Copper is so soft that this can be done easily with a hacksaw – even a junior one. You will find, however, that there is a tendency to flatten the pipe with this method. You might also fail to make the cut square. Either distortion will make it impossible to achieve a fully watertight connection. The solution is to use a pipe cutter, which cuts squarely and does not flatten. Small portable ones are available. When you are cutting into a pipe that is already installed, however, there may not be enough room to wield a pipe cutter, and you will have to use a hacksaw. If so, take care not to flatten the pipe; and once the pipe has been cut, use a file to get rid of any burr on the end and also to square it up properly, if this is necessary.

In many plumbing jobs, pipes have to be joined – for instance to connect up two short lengths or to take off a branch line at a T-junction. Ready-made joints are needed for this and there are two kinds – compression and capillary. With both types of joint the 28 and 15 mm pipes can be connected up directly to the old 1 in and ½ in. However, to join 22 mm to ¾ in you must use an adapter.

A compression joint consists of a threaded body, known as a union, a small chamfered copper ring, called an olive, and a nut, the cap nut.

To fit a compression joint, slip first the cap nut, then the olive, with its shortest chamfer pointing towards the nut, on to the end of the pipe. Push the pipe as far as it will go into the union, and slide first the olive then the nut towards the body. When the nut is tightened it will crush the olive, forming a watertight joint. It is important to get just the right degree of tightness, however: too much, and the olive will be crushed too much; to little, and it will not be crushed sufficiently. In both cases, the joint will leak. To ensure the correct tightness, tighten the nut as far as you can by hand,

10.2 *Working copper pipe: (a) The three types of joint – threaded, compression and capillary. (b) Cut the pipe with a small portable cutter. (c) Pipe running under the floor is supported in joist notches. (d) A bending spring stops the pipe from flattening while being bent. (e) Bending a pipe on the knee as an alternative to using an 'elbow joint' (inset). (f) Two types of support clip.*

then give one complete turn with a spanner. When the water is turned on, inspect the joint for signs of weeping. If you find any, give quarter turns with the spanner until they stop.

One of the advantages of a compression joint is that you can make it while the pipes are wet, which enables repairs or additions to be made to an existing system. With capillary joints, you have to wait for all the parts to dry thoroughly.

A capillary joint is much smaller and neater, and less expensive than a compression joint, although it is a little more difficult to handle. It is sealed by solder, a small ring of which is inserted inside the joint during manufacture.

All the parts of a capillary joint must be spotlessly clean, so begin by burnishing both the end of the pipe and the inside of the joint with fine steel wool. Take care neither to damage the solder nor to grease any burnished surface with your fingerprints.

Apply soldering flux to the end of the pipe, push the end fully home, and apply a blowlamp flame on the joint. The heat will cause the solder to flow out and seal the joint, making it watertight. Once again, you have to make sure that you get things just right, for if you leave the flame on the joint for too long the solder will flow too far out, and if you do not heat the joint sufficiently, the solder will not flow far enough. The trick is to watch carefully until a ring of bright solder appears round the pipe, then withdraw the flame instantly. Allow the solder to cool off and harden before disturbing the joint. It is also necessary to make all parts of a capillary joint at one go, because heat will travel along the body of the joint causing all the solder rings to melt.

If a pipe needs to be connected up – to a radiator valve or some taps, for instance, a threaded joint is used. The joint is formed by screwing a 'male' part, which is threaded on its outer surface, into a 'female' part, which is threaded on its inner surface. The two parts cannot just be screwed together to make a waterproof joint, however. The joint must be reinforced with either plumber's hemp or PTFE tape, together with a jointing compound such as Boss White.

Plumber's hemp, which is sold by the hank, does not make such a neat joint as the tape, but it is more effective with deeper threads, such as you get on a boiler. To use it, first smear a little Boss White on the male fitting, then pull a few strands of the hemp off the hank. Wind the strands round the fitting in the same direction it will turn when being tightened, to ensure that it will be pulled into the fitting (rather than being unwound) when the joint is being tightened. Smear a little more Boss White on top of the hemp, insert the male fitting into the female, and tighten as hard as you can with a spanner.

Most of the hemp should be snugly inside the fitting. If much of it has pulled outside, there are three possible causes – you did not wind it on tight enough; you wound on too much; or you did not wind it in the right direction. In any case, you must unscrew the joint and make it again. Drawing a hacksaw blade lightly across the threads of the male fitting to form burrs that will grip the hemp may help keep it in place.

PTFE tape is easier to use, and is neater than hemp. Wind it on in the same direction as hemp, taking it two or three times round the fitting, and allowing it to overlap. Smear Boss White on the female thread, insert the male, and tighten.

Some thread should still be visible after the tightening, whether you have used tape or hemp. If it is not, you will probably find that the joint is too loose and will leak, so it will have to be remade.

Pipes can be bent into complicated shapes to pass round obstacles, or into simple curves to go round corners. If you are dealing with 22 mm and 15 mm pipe, bending is easy, but you must prevent it from flattening at the centre of the curve. You do this with a bending spring, which you can hire. Tie a length of string to one end of the spring, smear a little oil on its coil and push it into the pipe until its middle point is roughly at the centre of the required bend. Then take hold of one end of the pipe in each hand, place it on your knee at the centre of the proposed bend and give a short sharp tug. The pipe will then bend to the required curve.

Bend the pipe slightly more than required, then take it back to the required angle. If the process hurts your knee, tie a protective rag on it. Twist the spring clockwise, and you will be able to pull it out easily. You cannot make a bend near the end of a length of pipe in this way, so form a curve before cutting the pipe to length.

Pipe of 28 mm diameter is too strong to be bent by hand. Plumbers use a bending machine, but it is hardly worth hiring the pipe bender and a spring for one or two bends, so make use of elbow couplings instead. You can, in fact, always use elbow couplings instead of hiring a spring to bend narrow-gauge pipes, too, and although they are expensive it might pay you to use them for a small job, where only one or two bends are required.

Pipes should be supported by clips. Recommended spacings on vertical runs are 2.4 m (8 ft) for 28 mm and 22 mm pipes, 1.8 m (6 ft) for 15 mm pipes and 1.2 m (4 ft) for all three on horizontal runs. Use stand-off clips, which hold the pipes clear of the walls, rather than the kind that fits like a saddle over the pipe and holds it close to the surface. This is especially important for hot water pipes, which need to have air circulating round them to prevent them overheating the wall.

Pipes under floors and at right angles to floor joists can sit in notches cut in the top of the joists. Such notches should be directly under the middle of floorboards, so that when the board is nailed back there is no risk of puncturing the pipe.

Plastic pipes

Plastic pipes have been used for many years in waste systems, and for some time have been available as cold supply pipes. Because they were not suitable for hot water, there was little point in installing them just for cold. Now, however, pipes in cpvc (chlorinated polyvinyl chloride), which can be used for hot supply and for central heating, are available.

Plastic pipe has many advantages. It does not corrode, and scale does not form easily on the inside. It is a good insulator, so hot water does not cool so quickly and condensation does not form so readily on the outside. It is light and easy to handle, and does not dent easily.

A wide range of joints and stop taps is supplied for use with plastic pipe, and there are connectors to allow you to join it to copper. It is worked and joined, using the solvent welding method, in the same way as plastic waste pipe (see below).

There are some snags, however: plastic pipe cannot be used within 380 mm (15 in) of a boiler – you must use copper for this length, then connect it to the plastic; it is necessary to leave space for expansion under heat – about 6 mm (¼ in) per 3 m (10 ft) length; and an expansion loop, formed with two elbow couplings and a 300 mm (1 ft) length of pipe must be fitted to any run exceeding 10 m (25 ft). Nevertheless, plastic supply pipe will, in years to come, offer many advantages to DIY plumbers.

THE WASTE

Waste pipes, like supply pipes, were once made of lead, then of copper and are now almost exclusively of plastic. Each waste pipe must incorporate a trap, which is a loop of pipe filled with water, which stops drain smells coming back up into the home. Lavatories, too, have a trap, which may be a separate fitting or incorporated into the pan.

Two different systems are used to dispose of waste water to the drains. These are the two-pipe and the single-pipe (sometimes called the single-stack) systems (Fig. 10:3).

Two-pipe drainage

Two-pipe systems get their name because waste from fittings and appliances is kept separate from lavatory waste. Waste pipes from ground floor fittings and appliances discharge into open gullies that are connected to the drains. Baths, basins, bidets and other fittings on upper storeys empty into a hopper fitted to the top of a downpipe. This then conveys the water to an open gully at ground level – it may, in fact, be the one into which some or all of the ground floor waste discharges.

The lavatory in a two-pipe system is connected to a soil pipe leading to the sewer. It is easy to see at a glance whether a pipe on the outside wall of your home is a soil pipe or downpipe, besides looking for the connections from the lavatory. A soil pipe extends upwards above eaves level and well away from windows, to act as a vent for the escape of sewage smells. It should also be topped by a small wire

a

b

Basin and
bath waste pipes

Hopper

WC waste
pipe

Basin and
bath waste pipes

To sewer

Sink
waste pipe

To drain

To drain

Sink waste
pipe

10.3 *The types of waste system: (a)
Two-pipe and (b) one-pipe.*

cage to prevent rubbish getting in and causing a blockage.
If this cage is missing from the soil pipe, you should fit a
replacement.

To tell whether your home has a two-pipe drainage system, look ouside for a soil pipe, in addition to the downpipe,
and for open gullies and hoppers.

Single-pipe drainage

In a single-pipe system one stack carries all the waste to the
drains. It is fitted in high-rise buildings, and some modern
two-storey homes. The stack will usually be inside the building. Older stacks were made of cast iron; modern ones are
plastic.

Fittings and appliances in a single-stack system often
need deep-seal traps, which prevent water being sucked
out of them by back-siphonage as waste rushes down the
stack. For the same reason, fittings may require larger diameter wastes (this is likely to be a matter of local regulation).

To test whether or not your home has single-pipe drainage, follow the course of the waste pipes to see if they end
up at a stack, which you will usually find inside the building,
and cross-check by the absence of gullies or open drains
outside.

Installing plastic waste pipes

Modern waste systems are of plastic. Four types of plastic are used: upvc (unplasticized polyvinyl chloride); mpvc (modified polyvinyl chloride); abs (acrylonitrile butadiene styrene); and pp (polypropylene). Two sizes of pipe are used in domestic work – 43 mm (1½ in) diameter for baths and 36 mm (1¼ in) for fittings such as basins and sinks. As with supply pipes, the metric dimension is an external one and the imperial an internal one.

Plastic pipe is cut with a saw – a fine-toothed general purpose one is better than a hacksaw for ensuring a square cut (Fig. 10:4). As a guide to cutting, wrap a piece of paper with a straight edge round the pipe, making sure the ends line up. Once the pipe has been cut, clean off the burr both inside and out with fine glasspaper.

Lengths of pipe are connected up with small jointing pieces: a range of straight couplings and elbow fittings is available. Two methods are used – push-fit and solvent welding.

Push-fit joints have a small sealing ring inside. Usually this is inserted during manufacture but you may have to fit it yourself. In any case, you must make sure it is seated properly. To make a joint by this method, draw a line round the pipe about 10 mm (⅜ in) from its end, using a paper guide as described above. With a file, form a chamfer from the end back to this line. Clean the pipe and the inside of the socket and smear either a silicone jelly, supplied by the manufacturer, or petroleum jelly, on the end of the pipe. Push the pipe home as far as it will go, and make a pencil mark on it where it meets the edge of the fitting. Then pull it back by 10 mm (⅜ in) – using the pencil mark as a guide – to form an expansion allowance. The joint will now be fully watertight.

Solvent-welded joints are more difficult to make, but they are neater (note that pp cannot be solvent-welded, however). Use glasspaper to roughen the inside of the socket, and a file to roughen the part that will fit inside. To determine how much of the pipe should be roughened, push it fully home into the socket and draw a line all round the pipe. Apply the solvent with a small, clean paint brush both to the end of the pipe and to the inside of the socket. Make sure that the whole surface is covered – you will probably find this easier if your brush strokes go along the length of, rather than round, the pipe. Push the pipe home and hold the joint securely for about 15 seconds to allow the solvent to set, wiping off any that oozes out. Don't let hot water pass through a solvent-welded joint until 24 hours after welding.

One of the problems with solvent-welded joints is that, unlike the push-fit kind, they do not allow the pipe to expand

10.4 *Plastic waste pipe: (a) Cut it to size. (Note paper wrapped round pipe to act as a cutting guide.) Lengths of pipe are connected with jointing pieces. These can be (b) solvent welded, as with this T-fitting, (c) expansion coupling, or (d) push fit. To connect to a single pipe waster system, (e) mark where the waste will join the main stack. (f) Cut stack with hole saw. (g) Fit boss to which plastic waste pipe can be connected.*

as hot water passes through. So on long runs, fit expansion couplings at 1.8 m (6 ft) intervals. These are similar to ordinary joints but at one end they are push-fit, and at the other solvent-welded. It is unlikely that you will need to fit a coupling, however, because you do not get such long runs in the home.

Plastic waste pipe should be supported by clips at 750 mm (30 in) intervals. The pipe can be bent, but, even more than with supply pipes, it is not worth while; you would do better to use elbow couplings.

The pipe has to empty into the drains. With either a two- or one-pipe system, you may have nearby an existing waste pipe to which you can connect by means of a T-joint. If not, then in the case of a two-pipe system arrange for it to discharge into a convenient open gully or hopper. To reach one, chop a hole through a wall, using a club hammer and bolster chisel. Work from both sides of a cavity wall, making sure that debris does not fall into the cavity. With a solid wall, you can make the entire hole from inside.

On single-pipe systems, the pipe is joined to the stack by means of a boss. Various types are available; most are solvent-welded to the stack. Then the waste pipe is connected to the boss by either a push-fit or solvent-welded joint. A hole has to be cut in the stack for the boss, and this is best done with a hole saw fitted to a drill.

There are various rules about joining up to the stack, and this is one of the points on which you should consult your water authority. For instance, the boss must not be fitted within 200 mm (8 in) of a lavatory waste connection. And remember to slope the waste pipe, as you would slope a gutter, to allow the water to flow.

JOBS TO TACKLE
Before cutting into any part of the system, shut off the supply and open an appropriate tap to empty the pipe completely. Even so, a certain amount of water will come out, so be ready with bucket and mopping-up rags.

Fitting a stop tap
Few homes have enough stop taps, so whole sections of the system are deprived of water when even a minor job has to be done. In extreme cases the supply has to be shut off at the rising main and the whole system drained, just because a tap needs a new washer. A good system would have stop taps in the supply pipes from the cold storage tank, in the hot supply, and in the feed to lavatories. If your system lacks them, fitting one or two is a good introduction to simple plumbing.

Measure depth of shoulder

Flow

Measure length of body

10.5 *Fitting a stop tap*

Begin by measuring how much of the pipe you must cut out to take the tap. In doing so, remember that the pipe must fit right up to the shoulder inside. So measure the length of the body, then the depths inside the shoulders (Fig. 10:5). The difference between these measurements is the correct dimension. The tap is fixed by means of a compression joint at each end; the arrow on its casing should point in the direction of the flow. Place it in position – you will be able to spring the pipes far enough apart to do this – and tighten the joints.

New taps for old
Fixing mixer taps at a kitchen sink or, indeed, just ordinary modern single taps in place of the old ones on any fitting, is a good way to update your kitchen or bathroom. If you plan to

10.6 *Fitting new taps: (a) Use a crow's foot spanner to remove old taps. (b) Bed the new tap in with putty. (c) Tighten the back nut.*

fix a mixer, check before you buy one that it will locate in the existing holes of the sink.

The biggest difficulty lies in removing the old taps. Disconnect the supply from the taps. Unscrew the nut if a compression joint has been used, or saw through the pipe in the case of a capillary joint. There will probably not be enough room to use an ordinary spanner on the nut underneath, so you must use a crow's foot spanner, in which the jaws that grip the nut are at right angles to to the main body (Fig. 10:6). Even using a crow's foot spanner you may find that everything is so corroded that the nut will not turn. If so, apply penetrating oil, or one of the products designed to free corroded joints. Alternatively, grip the nut with the spanner, while a helper taps the spout of the tap with a rubber hammer – carefully so as not to damage anything. When the nut is loosened, remove the tap and scrape off the old putty that was underneath it.

Usually full instructions are given with the new tap – follow them closely. Place the tap in position, bedding it in putty, and with the washers in place (there may just be one for underneath the fitting, or one above and another below) tighten the back nut. A second locking nut may be supplied. A tap connector is fitted to the tail of the tap by means of a threaded joint, and this in turn is connected to the supply, usually with a compression joint.

Plumbing in a washing machine

It is much more convenient to have a clothes washing machine, or a dishwasher, plumbed in, rather than to have to connect its supply hoses to the taps every time you want to use it. The installation is easy, and kits containing all you need can be bought.

The instructions with the machine will tell you whether it takes both a hot and a cold supply, or just a cold. Find a convenient spot in the supply pipes and fit a T-joint there

(Fig. 10:7) – the technique is similar to that for fitting a stop tap. To the branch of the T fit a short length of pipe with a stop tap in the middle, so that you will be able to shut off the supply to the machine and remove it for maintenance and repairs without having to close down the whole system. At the end of this pipe, fit the coupling to which the hose of the machine is connected.

Another method is to use a self-cutting tap. This is fitted to the supply pipe; it has a piercing tip that cuts into the pipe and makes a connection. No water can escape during this process, so you do not even have to turn off the supply while you fit the tap. The device also acts as a stop tap. Self-cutting taps are sold at do-it-yourself shops, and full instructions are supplied.

Next fit a waste system to the machine (Fig. 10:8). This consists of a vertical length of pipe, open at the top, that runs to an existing waste pipe, out to a gully, or to a boss on a one-pipe stack. The instructions received with the machine specify what diameter of pipe to use, and the required height of the vertical section.

The machine has a flexible waste hose pipe with a permanent bend formed during manufacture. This hooks into the open end of the plastic waste pipe.

Fitting a shower

An electrically heated shower, which heats the water as it is being delivered, is the easiest (and usually the cheapest) to install. The heater unit should be positioned so it can discharge into a bath, and perhaps a basin as well, so it can be used for hair washing too. Fix it to the wall according to the manufacturer's instructions. Then connect it, by means of a T-joint, to the rising main.

Run pipe from this T-joint to the heater, and connect up according to the manufacturer's instructions. Carry out any final assembly – for example of the shower rose and flexible hose. The heater must then be wired up by a competent electrician.

Although the rising main should ensure that there is sufficient water pressure, the flow out of the rose of an electric shower is restricted by the heater. If you want a shower at a comfortable temperature, water can come out only as quickly as the heater can warm it.

If you have a cheaper means of heating the domestic hot water – especially if you have a radiator central heating system – your running costs would be lower with a shower unit fed from your existing hot and cold supply system.

For a shower unit to work effectively off the hot cylinder and cold tank you must have a strong enough head of water – probably at least 900 mm (3 ft). The greater the difference

10.7 *Fitting a T-joint*

10.8 *Plumbing in a washing machine*

Cold water tank

Separate cold feed to shower

To hot water taps

Domestic
cold supply

Separate hot feed to shower

Hot water tank

Rising main

10.9 *How a shower is fitted*

in height between the shower rose and the bottom of the cold tank, the better the flow of water (Fig. 10:9). If you do not have such a head of water, consider re-siting the tank at a higher level (see next section) – or choose an electric shower, which will give a stronger flow than a shower unit with a poor head of water.

A shower unit can take the place of the existing bath taps, in which case the installation is similar to that of a kitchen mixer tap. Or you could install a separate unit, with its own supply.

There is, however, a caution to observe. A person might be taking a shower when somewhere else in the house someone turns on another tap – causing what the plumber calls an auxiliary draw-off that reduces, or indeed might cut off entirely, the flow of water to the shower. If the auxiliary draw-off is in the hot supply, then the bather gets a cold douche – uncomfortable, but not too serious. If the auxiliary draw-off is from a cold supply, however, scalding hot water might surge out of the rose (one of the advantages of an electric shower is that there can be no auxiliary draw-off).

The way to prevent auxiliary draw-off in a shower unit is to choose one that is thermostatically controlled. These are expensive, but they ensure that the temperature of the flow remains constant. If you fit a shower without such thermostatic control, give the unit its own direct cold supply from the cold storage tank. This will eliminate the most dangerous (scalding) type of auxiliary draw-off, by ensuring the cold supply is never interrupted. The direct cold supply must be fixed low down in the side of the tank by means of a tank connector (see next section).

A new cold tank

Cold supply tanks were at one time made of galvanized iron, a material that eventually corroded. Modern tanks are of either glass fibre or plastic. The plastic type is flexible, so can be squashed to go through a narrow loft opening, but may well need support under the entire base. Glass fibre tanks are rigid.

Your local water authority will have rules about the size of the cold tank, which it will express as something like 40/50. The latter figure (50 gallons/227 litres) is the amount the tank will hold when full to the brim; the former (40 gallons/181 litres) its capacity in practice.

When a tank is being replaced the house will be deprived of water for some time, so do as much of the preparatory work as you can beforehand. Begin by shutting off the rising main, and opening cold taps to empty the tank. The draw-off points are in the side, rather than the base, of the tank, so some water will be left behind. Beware later of spilling any of this. The tank needs to be disconnected from its various pipes. Do not bother trying to free corroded nuts to do this. The pipe runs will probably need modifying anyway, so just saw through them near the tank, making sure your cuts are square. Do not worry either, if the tank is too big to come out through the loft opening. Just leave it up there.

No holes are bored in the side of the tank when it is delivered – the manufacturer could not possibly know where you want them. You have to make them yourself, with a hole saw in either a hand drill or an electric drill. So decide on a site for the tank (remembering that if you want a shower it might be wise to site the tank on a stout platform as high as possible to increase the pressure of water at the rose). Plot the pipe runs, and determine the position of the holes in the tank (Fig. 10:10). The pipes are linked to the tank by pipe connectors. These have a threaded sleeve with a back plate. Push the sleeve through the hole from inside the tank, with a washer on each side, then tighten the fixing nut. The supply pipes are fixed to this connector with a compression joint.

You will need a cold supply from the rising main, a cold feed to the cold outlets, perhaps a special cold feed to a shower, and an overflow. Also the vent pipe from the hot cylinder must bend over the top of the tank. Modify existing

10.10 *Fitting a new cold tank: (a) Mark the position of the pipes on the side of the tank. The pipes are linked to the tank by pipe connectors on (b) the inside and (c) the outside. (d) Fit a stopcock. (e) A ball valve must be fitted. (f) The installation is complete.*

runs and add new ones as needed and connect them to the tank. A ball valve will be needed to control the entry of water from the rising main.

Your local water authority may have regulations about the position of the various pipes. A rule of thumb, however, is that the ball valve inlet should be 55 mm (2¼ in) from the top of the tank; the overflow should be 25 mm (1 in) below that (so that water from the tank cannot be sucked back into the main); and the various feeds to the supply should be 50 mm (2 in) from the bottom of the tank.

Finally, having connected up all the pipework, restore the supply and check for leaks.

EMERGENCIES

In even the best of plumbing systems, things can go wrong from time to time. One possible result is flooding, so deal with faults before any more serious damage is done.

Frozen pipes

This is one emergency that should never happen, because efficient lagging that will prevent it is readily available. The worst result of frozen plumbing is not so much that you are temporarily deprived of water at the particular taps affected, troublesome as that can be, but that when water turns to ice it expands and in so doing can fracture a pipe, or force a compression joint apart. When the ice melts, there will be a flood.

If you do have a frozen pipe, begin by opening the affected taps slightly and turning off the relevant stop tap. Working back from the tap, gradually apply heat (preferably with a hair dryer, but possibly with an electric fan heater) until water starts to flow. If you have no such heat source try wrapping the pipe with rags soaked in water as hot as you can handle. When water runs freely again, you can close the tap, and restore the supply.

As you work, look for signs of damage caused by the ice. If you find any, put a bucket underneath to catch the flow that will come as the ice melts. Then carry out the remedies suggested in the next section.

Bursts

When a supply pipe is burst, by frost or for any other reason, put a bucket underneath the pipe or get a helper to put his/her thumb over the hole. Then shut off the stop tap controlling the supply to that pipe, and open the tap at the end of the supply to empty the pipe as quickly as possible. When the flow has stopped, begin the repair. Fit a straight coupling compression joint at the break, in just the same way as a stop tap is fitted. If the damage (typically a split) is too long to be covered by one coupling, fit a short length of copper pipe with a coupling at each end.

If a leak occurs at a compression joint, try tightening the coupling nut a quarter of a turn at a time, until moisture stops oozing out. Do not test for this with your finger, because skin is always moist. Instead, wipe round the joint with a tissue or lavatory paper, and look to see if this gets wet. If you cannot stop the leak by tightening the joint, it may be that the olive has been damaged. If so, you will have to remove the joint and fit a new one.

If a leak develops at a capillary joint, remove the joint by cutting through the pipe on each side, and repair it as you would a damaged pipe.

Air locks

You will know there is an air lock in a supply pipe if the water comes in spurts instead of flowing out smoothly. There is a quick ploy that often clears it: run a length of hose pipe from the kitchen cold tap to the affected one, and secure both ends. This is simple when it is the adjacent hot pipe that is affected, but it can often be done with other taps too. Now turn on both taps and leave for a few minutes. The water from the kitchen cold tap, because it has the pressure of the mains behind it, will travel up the affected pipe and clear out the air bubble.

Some authorities frown on this procedure, saying there is a danger of impure water being sucked back from the air-locked tap into the main. Others argue that the pressure of the main is so strong that this cannot happen. Check with your own authority.

An alternative method is to use a pump operated through the appropriate outlet of the cold storage tank.

Blocked traps

The trap in a waste pipe can trap other things besides the pool of water it is designed to hold. Debris can collect there, especially from sinks, and block the waste. Two types of trap are in general use. First, there is the kind formed simply by a bend in the pipe, and known because of its shape as either the P or the U trap. The other kind is the bottle trap.

On modern plastic systems the trap can be removed by hand. P traps are held in place by a couple of nuts, bottle traps by just one. Unscrew the nut, remove the trap, empty out solids and wash it out (at another sink or basin).

It is more difficult to remove older, metal traps, so try to clear the blockage by using a plunger first. This consists of a rubber or plastic cup, with a short wooden or plastic handle. Run some water into the sink, block up the overflow with a rag bung, place the plunger's cup over the waste outlet, and pump the handle up and down. This will force water down the waste outlet, and ought to clear the blockage. If it does not, try poking wire down the waste pipe, then use the plunger again. If this still produces no result, tackle the problem from the base of the trap. There you will find a large nut. It may be knurled so that you can grip it by hand, or you may have to use a large spanner. In some cases there are small lugs against which you place a short length of wood and hammer it. Place a bucket under the trap, open it, and water should pour out, bringing debris with it. You might have to force debris along by poking around with a length of wire from below or above.

When a lavatory trap becomes blocked you have to clear it with a lavatory plunger. This looks something like a sink plunger, but there is a metal plate behind the cup to stop the cup from becoming inverted. Such plungers can often be hired. Place the cup in the lavatory pan and work it up and down to force water round the bend and drive the blockage away. Once it has gone, flush the lavatory to fill the trap again.

Washer

Overflows

When you hear an overflow running from the cold tank or a lavatory cistern it may simply be that the ball is riding too high in the water, and as a result the water level has passed the overflow pipe before the inlet valve shuts off the supply. For this there is a simple remedy. Support the lever with one hand at the valve then bend the lever arm down so that the ball rides lower, shutting off the water at a lower level (Fig. 10:11).

If the ball is punctured it will take in water and be too heavy to float, so it will not rise enough to close the inlet valve. Do not bother trying to mend the puncture – you would never get the water out. Remove the ball, which is threaded on to the end of the lever arm, and fit a new one in its place.

While carrying out this – and, indeed, any other – repair you will have to shut off the water supply. If the cistern does not have its own stop tap, to avoid shutting down the whole system, place a stick across the top and tie string to it to hold the ball lever up high.

If the ball is neither submerged nor riding too high, raise the lever as high as it will go and notice whether water drips in through the inlet. If it does, the valve needs re-washering.

10.11 Cures for a cistern overflow: (a) Bend the lever arm so the ball will be lower in the water. (b) The arm is tied to a stick to stop the entry of water as an alternative to shutting off the supply. (c) Withdraw the split pin holding the lever arm. (d) Remove the cap on the end of the valve case. (e) Unscrew the two parts of the piston. (f) Insert a new washer in the smaller end of the piston.

The whole mechanism may have become so damaged that a new one will have to be fitted. Unscrew the nuts and remove the valve. Slip one of the washers provided with the new kit over the threaded tail of the new valve, push the tail through the hole in the side of the tank. Fit the other washer on the outside, and tighten up the retaining nut. Connect the tail to the supply pipe.

Chapter 11
THE ELECTRICAL SYSTEM

The benefits that electrical systems provide are taken so much for granted that it is easy to forget that they are made and installed by fallible beings. It is also easy to overlook the fact that the components of the system tend to decay and therefore need replacement.

The dangers of a faulty or decayed wiring system are electric shocks and fires. The consequences of these are so serious that you should never allow your system to fall into disrepair. Do not wait to receive a shock before you heed the warning signs of a faulty system. And if a fire starts in the wiring, it can burn inside walls throughout a house before it breaks out, engulfing the entire structure. Always, therefore, treat electrics with respect.

THE SYSTEM'S CONDITION

A properly installed modern system should give no cause for concern. In some older homes, however, replacement is long overdue. In particular, cables insulated with rubber, which by now may well have perished, are hazardous. Also the insulating material of which old switches and sockets are made can become brittle and may crack, giving you a shock or even causing a fire. Moreover, the wiring systems of 20 or 30 years ago were rarely designed to cope with today's heavy loads.

Modern systems are insulated in plastic, which is extremely durable. If you are doubtful about the state of your system, judge its age by the appearance of the light switches and the socket outlets. If they are square or rectangular in shape, and the sockets are all the same size, then the system is modern. If the fittings are circular, with the sockets in two or three different sizes, then it is likely that the installation is due for complete replacement. This is not a job the average householder should tackle; it requires a professional electrician.

It is, however, possible for a do-it-yourselfer to work on a modern system – to improve, extend or repair it. Some of those jobs are detailed in this chapter. If you do not understand the instructions fully, and if you are in any doubt about what you are doing, call in an electrician.

Always switch off at the mains before you carry out any work on the system.

HOW THE SYSTEM WORKS

Electricity is brought into your home from the main supply by a service cable, which ends at a service terminal box. This box contains a fuse that protects the whole installation and allows engineers to switch off the supply when they need to carry out maintenance work. Close by the box is the meter. From the mains to the meter the installation is the property and responsibility of the supplier and you should not tamper with it. Beyond the meter the installation is the responsibility of the consumer.

11.1 *Typical domestic wiring*

Meter

Consumer unit

Service cable

Key
——— power
– – – lighting
·········· heavy duty

At the heart of the consumer's installation is a consumer unit or fuse box. This is a metal or plastic box housing the mains switch that governs the supply to the whole house, and the fuseways that protect each individual circuit within the house. The various power and lighting circuits lead off the consumer unit. It is normal, for example, to have an upstairs lighting circuit and a separate one for downstairs. Similarly, there would normally be separate power circuits – see Fig. 11:1.

Each of the circuits goes from a fuseway, which consists of a fuseholder housing a fuse. A fuse is a weak link inserted in the circuit so that it will burn through should anything go wrong, thus cutting off the supply of electricity before damage can be caused. Each circuit must have its own fuseway, unless it is fitted with a Miniature Circuit Breaker (MCB), also known as a 'trip-switch'. It is useful to have a unit with spare fuseways or MCBs because you will need these should you ever wish to install extra circuits.

There are two types of fuse. The most common is the rewireable fuse, in which a length of fuse wire is looped through a holder and connected to a terminal at each end. Less common are cartridge fuses which are similar to, but not interchangeable with, those in the plugs of portable appliances. It is much easier to change a cartridge fuse, but you cannot immediately see which one has blown, as you can with the rewireable kind.

Modern fuseholders have a small coloured dot so that you can tell their rating at a glance. The colour coding is; white – 5 amp (for lighting); blue – 15 amp (for power); red – 30 amp (for cookers and immersion heaters). Your consumer unit may have a fuseway for two or more of some of them.

The consumer unit is connected to the meter by two cables called meter leads – one live and the other neutral. The live one has pvc insulation coloured red, whereas the insulation of the neutral lead is black. There is also an outer sheathing. This in some cases is the same colour as the inner insulation, but in others it is grey. There is also a third cable, insulated in green or green and yellow pvc, but with no outer sheathing; this is the earth lead. In modern installations, it is good practice to provide an earth by means of a Residual Current Breaker (RCB); previously this was called an Earth Leakage Circuit Breaker (ELCB).

It is a good idea to mark on the back of the consumer unit cover which fuseway governs which circuit – in fact, there is often a small card on which to do this – so that you can immediately identify the various circuits.

The cable used in house wiring is described as being flat pvc – sheathed and insulated two core and earth. It's worthwhile knowing what that specification means. The fact that the cable is flat is stressed, because leads and non-domestic cables are circular in cross-section. The term 'pvc-sheathed' refers to the outer covering, which is white when the cable will be on view, but grey, which is slightly cheaper, when it will be out of sight. Some cables – those used out of doors, for instance – have a different kind of sheathing. The 'two-core' refers to the conductors – the wires that actually carry the electricity – which are, as the specification says, insulated with pvc. The live conductor has a red covering and the neutral a black (the international brown – live – and blue – neutral – coding is used only for flexes, not cables). Finally there is the earth, a bare strand of wire. When the outer sheathing is stripped off to make a connection, a sleeve of pvc sheathing must be slipped over the end of the earth wire. This earth sheathing used to be green, but is now green and yellow, just like that used to distinguish the earth wire on an appliance flex.

SWITCHING OFF

Before carrying out any job on the electrics of your home, you must shut off the supply at the main. There is no need to deprive the whole house of electricity. Turn off the mains switch at the consumer unit, remove the fuse controlling the circuit on which you will be working, then restore the supply.

But do check that it is the right fuse you have removed. If you are dealing with a lighting circuit, then even before going to the consumer unit, switch the relevant lights on to make sure the bulbs are working. Then turn off at the main, remove the circuit fuse and check that the lights are off. If they are, you can go ahead safely. If it is a power circuit you wish to check or change, switch off the supply, then plug in an appliance you know to be in good order and verify that it does not work. It is easy to forget as you become absorbed in your work, but you cannot be too careful about shutting off the supply.

THE CIRCUITS

There are three types of circuit – lighting, power (supplying socket outlets) and special heavier duty circuits for items such as cookers and water heaters. Cable of different size is used according to the kind of circuit. Ring circuits start out from the return to the consumer unit; radial circuits come to a stop when they reach the farthest points on their routes.

Power Circuits

The normal circuit used to supply the socket outlets into which portable appliances are plugged is the ring circuit. It consists of a loop of cable 2.5 sq. mm in cross-section, running from a 30 amp fuseway. The ring circuit can supply appliances up to a rating of 3 kilowatts – table lamps, televisions, washing machines, room heaters. Anything above that rating – for example, cookers and water heaters – must have its own circuit.

One advantage of a ring circuit is that only one size and type of plug is used no matter what the appliances (under previous systems, different sizes of plug were used for appliances of different ratings). There is, however, a cartridge fuse inside the plug, and this should be changed according to the amount of power the appliance takes.

For appliances up to a rating of 720 watts the fuse is 3 amp, coloured red; for those between 720 and 3000 watts (3 kilo-

11.2 *A domestic ring circuit*

Single socket spur

Double socket spur

watts) the fuse should be 13 amp, coloured brown. When you buy a new plug it usually comes with a 13 amp fuse. The shopkeeper should change it for a 3 amp if you ask for one. It is a good idea to keep a stock of fuses of both sizes, because they may blow because of a fault, and if you transfer the plug from say, a table lamp to a room heater, you will need to uprate the fuse in the plug from 3 to 13 amps.

To prevent dangerous overloading, a ring circuit must not supply an area of your home greater than 100 sq. m (1000 sq. ft). In fact it is usual for small homes to have one ring for the ground floor and another for upstairs, even when it is not strictly necessary, so that the whole house will not be deprived of power if one circuit fails.

In addition to the main loop, a ring circuit can have branch lines, known as spurs, used for supplying outlets some distance from the main ring (Fig. 11:2). Each spur may supply only one socket, though this can be a double.

11.3 *Radial circuits supply socket outlets*

To supplement the sockets of the ring main, a radial circuit can also be used to supply socket outlets – this can be useful in small areas, such as a kitchen, where there are many appliances.

The number of outlets that can be connected to a radial power circuit (Fig. 11:3) is unlimited, but the area supplied by such a circuit must not be greater than 50 sq. m (500 sq. ft). The circuit must be in 4 sq. mm cable and run from a 30 amp fuseway, controlled either by a cartridge fuse, or by a miniature circuit breaker, not by a rewireable fuse. When the area is only 20 sq. m (200 sq. ft) the cable can be 2.5 sq. mm and the fuseway 20 amp. Moreover this circuit can be controlled by a rewireable fuse, instead of a cartridge or an MCB.

Besides socket outlets, a ring can have Fused Connection Units (FCUs), to which appliances are permanently wired and which have a fuse housed inside the unit. Such units are useful for appliances that you do not wish to keep unplugging – for example, waste disposal units, fridges, freezers and dishwashers. FCUs have a switch, and often a neon indicator as well to show when a current is flowing.

Lighting Circuits

There are two distinct types of lighting system, both of which use radial circuits. The more modern type is the loop-in system (Fig. 11:4). Cable goes from the consumer unit to each of the roses of the lighting system in turn, and is connected to them (or looped-in), hence the name. Separate cable connects the rose to the lampholder, and a third cable connected inside the rose leads to the switch – the 'switch drop'. So there will be at least three sets of wires inside each rose – the incoming and outgoing circuits and the switch

11.4 *Loop-in wiring*

11.5 *Junction-box wiring*

drop. There may also be a branch line leading to another lighting point, but the number of terminals available restricts such branches to only one per rose.

Lighting systems used to be wired according to the joint-box (or junction-box) system (Fig. 11:5). Cable passed from the consumer unit to a series of joint boxes. From each of these there was a lead to its light point and another to the switch.

The reason that the loop-in system is preferred is that all connections are made inside the rose, which is easily accessible, so it is much easier to check the system or add to it. Nevertheless, a joint-box system has advantages in some applications. For instance, if you cannot hide the cable to a lighting point it is better to expose just one cable (that from a joint box) rather than three – the cable to the rose, the return cable and that to the switch. Where a lighting point is a long way from the next light or the switch, it will involve less work and fewer materials if you connect it to the circuit via a joint box. There are hybrid systems that are mainly loop-in but incorporate elements of joint-box wiring.

Both types of system are wired in 1 sq. mm cable governed by a 5 amp fuseway. Previously, lighting circuits did not incorporate an earth wire, but because of safety considerations – especially in view of the increasing use made of metal light fittings – modern installations invariably do.

Since fewer connections are made inside a rose in a joint-box wiring, fewer terminals are needed, and so you might imagine that such a rose would cost less. For single or small purchases, however, it does not, and since there is much less demand for joint-box roses, most retail outlets do not stock them. Accordingly, roses intended for loop-in systems are found in joint-box wiring. But you can tell at a glance on which system a rose is wired. Unscrew its cover, and observe how many wires enter it. If there is only one set (live, neutral and earth, if the cable carries an earth wire) then, in general, the system is the joint-box one. If there are two or three cables, it will almost certainly be a loop-in wiring system.

Most of the points supplied by lighting circuits are known as plain pendants – they consist of flex hanging from a ceiling rose and supporting a shade held on a lampholder. There are, however, special pendant fittings, many of which carry more than one bulb and incorporate their own rose cover, such as close-mounted ceiling fittings (usually found in kitchens and bathrooms) batten fittings and wall lights. Switches are normally on the wall, but there are also cord-operated ceiling switches. These are fitted in bathrooms to minimize the risk of shock (a person who is wet is at greater risk from shock than one who is dry).

Installing cable

Cables can be hidden, according to need, in a variety of ways.

Under the floorboards is the normal place for running cable to socket outlets above skirting boards, or to lighting points in the ceiling below. To install cable here, lift up the floorboards (see page 156-7). If the cable is parallel with the joists it can lie loosely on the top of the ceiling below, if there is one. On ground-storey suspended floors, with just a void below, clip the cable to the side of the joists (Fig. 11:6). When the cable has to cross the joists pass it through holes bored through them at least 50 mm (2 in) from their tops. If this clearance is not possible, perhaps because the joists are not big enough, the cable must be protected by metal inserts sold for this purpose.

Above the ceiling is the normal place to run cable supplying roses in rooms. In a house with a loft, the installation is easy. Run the cable either parallel to the joists (tucked well down below the insulation at the side of the joist) or across. If it runs across, there is no need to bore holes through the joists unless you are going to floor the loft: fix the cable with clips on each side so that it lies neatly and close. If there is cable on top of the joists in any areas where you are likely to walk (for example, around the cold water storage tank) protect it with plastic channelling.

Even if there is no loft you can run cable parallel to the joists above a ceiling. Make a hole at the start of the run, feed the cable along, then bring it out through a hole at the end (see page 201 for the technique). Patch the holes with filler when you have finished. Running cable across the joists of such a ceiling presents problems, because you have to by-pass each joist. The method is to cut holes in the ceiling each side (Fig. 11:7), and then cut a channel in the bottom of each joist. Bring the cable out of one hole, pass it along the

Cable clip

Metal insert in hole

11.6 Cable passing through and clipped to a joist

Channel in bottom of joist

11.7 Passing cable above a ceiling

channel into the other, and then make good. Crossing joists is thus laborious and to be avoided except for short runs.

Inside hollow walls is the natural way to run cable from one floor to the next, when you can, or to feed socket outlets or wall lights. If the cable is to pass through the top member of a stud wall in the top storey, bore the hole from the loft; if it is to pass through the top member of a lower-storey wall you merely have to lift floorboards. Sometimes there are intermediate horizontal frame members, which can obstruct the cable's passage. Electricians have long wood augers with which to bore holes as much as 1 m (3 ft) from the top. It is not worth a do-it-yourselfer's while acquiring one, so use the method already outlined for passing across ceiling joists – pass the cable through a hole cut in the wall above the frame member, along a channel chopped out of its side and into a hole in the plaster below it. Since there will normally be one intermediate horizontal timber in a wall frame, this is not such a bothersome task as it is in a ceiling where there are many joists.

Inside cavity walls is a convenient place to hide cable – provided there is no insulation. If a vertical drop in a cavity wall exceeds 4.6 m (15 ft), however, regulations demand that it should have an intermediate fixing. Make this by boring a hole in the wall's inner leaf, under the first-storey floor, then loop the cable out and secure it to a joist.

Behind an architrave is a small gap between the timber lining the doorway opening and the wall itself. Cable can be pushed into this gap and covered by the architrave. This is an ideal place for hiding cable going to a switch, which can be next to the architrave, or for passing cable from one storey to another if there is no adjacent hollow wall.

Behind a skirting board the plaster of the wall does not usually extend to meet the floor, so there is a gap behind the skirting board where cable can be hidden. This is a convenient spot for hiding cable supplying socket outlets low down on the wall – indeed it is the only place if the floor is a direct-to-earth one, under which cable cannot be passed.

Buried in the plaster. Cable passing along a wall that is not hollow, or along a cavity wall filled with insulation, can be buried in the plaster. To do this, cut out a chase or channel. If there is paper on the wall, first trim away a strip about 25 mm (1 in) wider than the cables. Make two firm lines on the plaster surface, the width of the cable apart, using a craft knife and a straight edge.

Run the blade of an old wood chisel or screwdriver along the grooves cut by the knife, then use it to chop out the plaster back to the masonry behind. In many cases, a chase the depth of the plaster will be sufficient to take the cable; if not, deepen it by cutting into the masonry with a bolster chisel and club hammer. Place metal channelling, bought from electrical suppliers, over the cable and nail or screw it to the wall. This is to prevent the cable being pierced or cut accidentally. Make good with filler. If you want to run cable in two adjoining rooms there is no need to cut a chase on both sides of the dividing wall. Just make the chase on one side double width, put both cables into it, and feed the cable for the next-door room through a hole in the wall.

Making cable move

Cable weighs little, so when you want to drop it down a confined space – inside a cavity or hollow wall, for instance – you cannot always rely on gravity. To solve the problem devise a mouse, a weight tied to a length of string (see the section on renewing sash cords in Chapter 4).

Drop the mouse down the cavity then tie the cable to the weight end of the string, if you want to haul the cable up-wards, or to the free end if you aim to draw it down. A mouse can also be used to determine how far down any obstruc-tions – such as horizontal frame members of a cavity – may be, so that you know where to cut into the surface of the wall to make a bypass.

It can also be difficult to move cable horizontally – for instance, when you drop it under a suspended timber floor at one end of a room and want it to emerge at the other; or if you are trying to run it above a ceiling where there is no loft. This is accomplished by using a length of stout wire bent at one end into a hook shape. Form the cable into a loop and push it under the floor, or above the ceiling. Insert the wire from the other end, then push it along so its hook catches the loop of the cable. Then pull it back. Electricians refer to this as 'fishing' for cable.

Stripping the ends

The ends of the sheathing and insulation of cable must be stripped off to allow you to make connections to a terminal. To remove the outer sheathing, cut with a small knife drawn lengthways between the wires forming the inner core. It does not matter if you nick into the insulation at the start, for the ends of the core insulation will have to be stripped off anyway; as the cutting proceeds, however, you will be able to hold the cores far enough apart to avoid nicking the in-sulation. Peel the sheath back, and cut across its width.

The core insulation is best removed with a wire stripper, which you use to cut through the insulation and then bare the core – there is a depth regulator to stop the cutter's jaws from biting into the core itself.

SOCKETS AND SWITCHES

Socket outlets (sometimes incorrectly called power points) and the switches that control ceiling lights consist of two parts – a faceplate and, behind it, a box.

In the best installations, the box is buried flush with the wall's surface. Sometimes, though, the box is fixed to the surface of the wall, because this is easier. Surface-mounted boxes for use in homes are usually in white plastic. Flush-mounted ones are always in metal, usually aluminium alloy or black-coated steel.

Boxes come in three main sizes. For square-plate accessories (single switches and socket outlets) there is the 1-gang box. Such boxes usually have four lugs to take the accessory's fixing screws. There are only two screws, so it does not matter which way up you fix the box. Next there is the 2-gang box, used for double socket outlets. These have four fixing lugs positioned to take the four screws of a double socket outlet. The third type is the dual box, which you should not confuse with the 2-gang type. This has extra lugs so that you can fix two square-plate accessories to it.

Boxes also come in varying depths. The shallowest is a square-plate accessory box which is only 17 mm (about 5⁄8 in) deep. On most walls, that would be no more than the thickness of the plaster, and it is, in fact, often referred to as a plaster-depth box. It is designed to take room light switches only – there is not enough space for a socket outlet.

The normal depth for a box is 25 mm (1 in). There are, however, deeper boxes – at 35 and 46 mm (about 1½ and 2 in) – and the extra space can prove useful when you need to fit many cables inside a box, for instance when you are running a spur from a socket ring circuit. Special boxes are also available for such items as cookers, control panels and shaver sockets.

On the sides and back of plastic boxes there are thin sections, known as push-outs or knock-outs. You do as the phrase suggests – push them out to form a hole through which cable can pass. A metal box has perforated knock-out blanks. Once a blank has been pushed out for cable a small grommet, in plastic or rubber, must be inserted so that the cable's insulation will not be chafed.

The terminals to which the cable is connected are on the back of the faceplate. It is therefore important to draw enough cable through the box to allow the faceplate to be connected without undue labour, but not so much that it cannot fold comfortably into the space left in the box. In the case of switches, the earth wire is fixed to a terminal in the box.

When fixing a box to the wall, take care to make it horizontal, or at least parallel to some prominent feature, such as a skirting board, architrave or the grout pattern on a tiled wall.

11.8 *Fitting a box in a hollow wall: (a) Tie the string to a small batten. (b) Pull the batten into place. (c) Screw the box to the batten.*

Fixing surface-mounted boxes

On a brick or stone wall, the screws should be driven into wall plugs. Such a fixing might be suspect in breeze block, however, because the outlets need to withstand some force when plugs are withdrawn. It is better to cement or glue to the wall a thin piece of wood slightly smaller all round than the box, then make the fixing with woodscrews driven into this timber.

On a hollow wall, aim wherever possible to position the box so that you can drive its fixing screws into the timber framework behind the plaster. If you must have the box between pieces of the framework, fit a deadman – a thin batten inserted behind the plaster (Fig. 11:8). Drill a small hole at one end of the batten and thread a length of string through it. Hold the string in place with a knot tied at the back. Make an incision in the plaster, slip the batten through, and use the string to pull it to the correct spot. Drive screws through the surface of the lath and plaster or plasterboard to fix the deadman in place. Fixing screws for the box can then be driven through the plaster and into this timber. The box can be positioned to hide the incision. Otherwise make good with filler.

Flush-mounted boxes

On solid walls, make this job as easy as you can for yourself by choosing as shallow a box as you can get away with. Should a deep box be necessary, make sure the wall is thick enough to take it. Place the box on the surface of the wall and draw round its outline in pencil. Run a sharp knife along these lines, using a straight edge. If there is wallpaper, peel off the waste. Using a cold or bolster chisel and a hammer, carefully chop out the plaster to the masonry below. Check whether the hole is deep enough for your box. If it is not, cut into the masonry. Aim to make the bottom of the hole flat. Should this prove too difficult, chop out a hole that is too deep, cover its base with cement, then press the box into place to level off the cement. Remove the box, wipe off excess cement that has seeped through the holes, and let the cement set before drilling holes for the wall plugs.

Hollow walls constructed from plasterboard should pose no problem. In fact, on these walls it pays you to choose a site between frame members, for the fixing is then easier. You can buy special lugs that clamp on the side of a metal box, and are then fixed to the plasterboard. Should you want to site the box directly above a frame member, then you merely cut a hole in the board equal in area to that of the box. Where that does not give you sufficient depth, cut out a notch, making sure it is absolutely flat, in the frame member, and fix to the timber.

Lath and plaster walls present a problem. It is not too bad when you are fitting a shallow box to a stud or nogging, or when you have deep plaster. But if you have to cut into the laths, then the end of one or more will be left flapping free. The only way to remedy this is to push a thin piece of wood behind one or more laths and smear glue on the meeting surfaces to provide support.

Do not attempt to fix between frame members on a lath and plaster wall. There is no way of making the fixing firm enough to withstand use.

Extra socket outlets

There are rarely sufficient electrical socket outlets in a modern home. If your system is in good order, you can install extra ones.

Singles into doubles

One of the easiest ways to increase the number of sockets is to convert any existing singles into doubles. Any single socket on a ring circuit can be doubled, but if you are working on a spur with two sockets, you cannot convert either of them to a double. You can, however, double a single socket if it is the only one on a spur.

To establish whether a socket is on the ring, or if it is the only one on a spur, switch off at the main and remove the faceplate. If there are two sets of wires, the socket is either on the ring or it is the first one of two on a spur. To determine which, you need a continuity tester. This you can easily improvise from a battery and bulb holder (Fig. 11:9). Connect one lead of the tester to one of the red wires in the socket, and the other lead to the other red wire. The bulb

11.9 *A simple continuity tester*

Bulb and holder

Battery

will light if the cable is part of a ring, but not if it is a spur.

If the socket has only one set of wires it is on a spur, but it could be the last of two. A test helps you to be sure. Call the first socket A. Look for another socket nearby that, because of its position, could be on the same spur. Call this socket B. Remove the faceplate of B and twist together the black and the red cores of the cable going towards socket A. Remove the faceplate of A and connect the bulb tester to its red and black wires. If the bulb lights, both sockets are on the same cable and you must not double either. Do be sure to re-connect all the cables properly before restoring the power.

Assuming that you can proceed, there are various possibilities. If the single socket is flush mounted, an easy conversion is to make the new double a surface one. Modern surface boxes do not protrude as far as the older kind, so the result need not be obtrusive. You can buy a 2-gang plastic box that can be screwed to the fixing points of the existing flush single box. Then draw the cable(s) through a knock-out in the back of the new box, connect them to the terminals of the new double faceplate, and screw this to the new box.

If you wish to retain the outlet as flush, remove the existing single box, enlarge the hole and fit a new 2-gang box. Then fix the double socket to the box.

When you are dealing with a surface-mounted box, the procedure will usually vary according to whether the cable is surface-run. If it is, there is nothing to gain by making the new outlet flush mounted. Merely fit a 2-gang box in place of the existing single, and fix the new double socket to it. If the wiring to the surface box is concealed, use the same method, but it might be worth while making the socket flush fitting. This involves chopping out a hole for the new 2-gang box.

Instead of one double socket, you can fit two singles side by side, but you must then use a dual box, not a 2-gang one. Buying one new single faceplate instead of a double would not be much less expensive. But if you are thinking of turning two singles into doubles you need buy only one double to put alongside the two singles in a dual installation.

Installing a spur

All the sockets in your rooms may be doubles already. And even converting all the existing singles may not give you sufficient socket outlets. Moreover, you may want a socket in an entirely new position. A new socket is installed by means of a spur. You can have only one socket on this spur, but it can be a double so you might as well make it that. Use 2.5 sq. mm cable for the spur.

Begin by switching off at the consumer unit and then fixing the socket either flush- or surface-mounted. Connect the cable to its terminals, and run it to the point at which you propose to connect it to the supply. There are three possible places at which you can make the supply connection.

The first is at an existing socket outlet to which no spur is already connected. Choose one that is conveniently situated. It need not be in the same room as your new socket. For instance, if you are fitting the new socket on the dividing wall between two rooms, consider connecting it to a socket on the other side of the wall. Fit the new socket directly opposite the existing one. If the wall is not thick enough, fit the new socket slightly to one side of the old. In either case you will get an easy installation.

Another possibility (though as a last resort only) is to connect to a socket on another floor. A short length of cable, for instance, dropping down from a bedroom to a living room, perhaps through a hollow partition wall, would also be an easy installation. You will have to remember, though, when carrying out work in the future that you remove the fuses controlling both the upstairs and the downstairs rings. This is a good example of why it is essential always to check that a socket or lighting point is dead before touching it.

To make the connection, first remove the supplying socket's faceplate. If the socket is flush-mounted, remove the mounting box from the hole to allow you to remove a knock-out blank, through which the spur cable will enter. Also, it is easier to fish for a new cable with the box out of the way. You may, however, be able to push out the blank of a plaster surface-mounted box without removing it from the wall.

Once the new cable is brought through into the box, connect its wires to the same terminals as those of the ring, making sure that the terminal screw grips all three. Replace the faceplate.

The second place at which you can make a supply connection is at a joint box inserted in the ring circuit. This is

11.10 *Connections inside a three terminal joint box.*

Red tape indicating live neutral wire

Switch

Earth

Live

Mains

Mains

Key
Neutral
Live
Earth

Switch return wire to light

Light

Neutral

worth considering only if the ring runs conveniently close by and under the floor. The ring is usually out of sight, so you have to make an inspired guess at its route, taking into account the position of existing sockets in the room. You can then remove the faceplate of a socket, and perhaps the box, too, to get an idea of where the cable runs before finally lifting a floorboard or two to confirm your guess.

Connect to the ring by means of a three-terminal joint box (Fig. 11:10). Fix this into place by screwing it to a length of 75 × 25 mm (3 × 1 in) timber spanning two joists, about 75 mm (3 in) from their top edge. Support this timber with screws on to two short battens nailed to the sides of the joist. There will be nine wires to be connected – six from the ring, and three from the spur. Make sure all three reds go to the same terminal, all three blacks to another, and all the earths to a third.

The third place to make a supply connection is at a ring circuit fuseway in the consumer unit. This is a method it might pay you to adopt if the new socket is near to the consumer unit.

Extra lights

If you wish to fit extra lights, make a simple check to ensure that the loading will not be too great. On a domestic lighting circuit the loading must not exceed 1200 watts.

To determine the loading you must first find out which lights are on the circuit. So switch on all the lights in your home, then switch off the mains at the consumer unit, and remove a lighting fuse. Restore the power and check which lights do not light up: these are all on the same circuit. Repeat with the second lighting fuse, then the third, until you have plotted all the lighting circuits in your home.

Now inspect the bulbs on the circuit you wish to work on and add up the total wattage. Bulbs of 100 watts and over should be taken at their face value; those of less than 100

11.11 *Connections inside a loop-in rose (left) and a junction box rose*

Mains — To switch

Red tape on black switch return to indicate it is live

N   LOOP   SW

From joint box

N   LOOP   SW

Flex to light

Key
Neutral
Live
Earth

watts should be counted as 100. Provided the extra light will not take the load beyond 1200 watts on that circuit you can go ahead. Use 1 sq. mm cable.

Fig. 11:11 shows typical connections inside a loop-in and a joint-box system rose. There is one point you should note about the switch drop: both of its cores are, in fact, live. One core (the neutral) goes straight to the light, and the other (the live) passes to it via the switch. Ordinary cable is used for the switch drop, so inside a loop-in rose or a joint box you will see a black core connected to a live terminal. To avoid any dangerous confusion, a piece of red sticky tape should be fastened to this black wire, but the electrician who worked on your home might not have bothered.

Your first job when installing a new light is to select the position for the rose, then fix it into place. To fix a rose, unscrew its cover and drive 38 mm (1½ in) woodscrews through two of the fixing holes in its base. The fixing must be completely secure, for the rose will have to bear the weight of the light fitting, which can be heavy. In a building with a concrete ceiling, a secure fixing presents no problem. The fixing screws can be driven into wall plugs fixed in the concrete, so the rose can be positioned almost anywhere you like. On a plasterboard or lath and plaster ceiling, you will make things simpler if you fix directly to a joist, by driving the fixing screws through the plaster and into the timber. There will be sufficient room to feed the cables through, although you may have to chisel a slight notch in the joist. Otherwise, provided there is access above, you can fit a short length of 100 × 25 mm (4 × 1 in) timber on top of the ceiling, immediately above the site of the rose, and attach it at each end to a joist. The fixing screws go into this timber.

A loop-in system. If you wish to have the new and existing lights controlled by the same switch, so that both come on and go off together, then connect up your new rose as for the joint-box in Fig. 11:10. Run the mains cable from this rose to the existing one. There connect its red wire to the SW terminal, the black to the N and the earth to the E.

You may wish to have the new light independently switched. In that case you can still loop-in to a rose in the same room, if there is one. Otherwise, look for the most convenient rose in another room nearby, on the same circuit. At the existing rose, the red wire of the new cable goes to the LOOP terminal instead of the SW one. The black goes to the N terminal, and the earth to the E.

You also need to install a switch, and the wiring at the new rose is as in Fig. 11:10.

A joint-box system. The job is still simple if the new light is not to be independently switched. Install the new rose, then run cable from it to the rose of the light with which it will work in tandem. The red, black and earth wires go into terminals already occupied by wires of that colour.

Installing a new independently switched light on a joint-box circuit is complicated – this is why the system has been superseded – and involves much disturbance to the house as you try to trace hidden lighting cables, so it is better to call in an electrician.

WHEN THINGS GO WRONG
Not much should go wrong with a modern electrical system. The most common fault is that the room light will not work when you turn on the wall switch. Usually, the fault is a defective bulb. Turn off the wall switch while you change it.

Occasionally, however, the bulb will not have been at fault. In that case check whether other lights in the same and adjacent rooms – those likely to be on the same circuit – are working. If all are out, the trouble is probably a blown fuse.

If none of the lights in the house works, look outside to make sure that the whole neighbourhood does not have a power failure.

Check at the consumer unit. If you have previously noted which fuse controls which circuit, you will know the fuseway you should inspect. Otherwise, deal with each one in turn. If, like most homes, yours has the rewireable type of fuse, you can see immediately if anything is wrong, for the wire will be broken, and there may even be charring. But you cannot tell merely by looking at a cartridge fuse if it is defective. You can, however, carry out a simple test using a metal torch. Remove the bottom end cap of the torch, place one end of the fuse on the metal casing and the other on the end of the battery. Switch on. The bulb will glow only if the fuse is sound. You can use this test on the cartridge fuse of an appliance plug. If you have an MCB system, you will be able to see immediately which switch has tripped.

It is easy to rewire a fuse, or to change it if you have the cartridge type. If the fault that caused the fuse to blow in the first place persists, however, the fuse will blow again immediately you restore the power. The most probable cause of such a fault is a short circuit brought about because one of the wires in the cable has become detached from a terminal and is touching the other wire. To check this, make sure all the lights in the circuit are switched off. Replace the fuse and restore the power at the main. Now go round the house switching on each light in turn to discover which causes the fuse to blow. Switch off at the main again and examine the connections inside the bulb holder, rose and switch. You may find a loose connection. If not, you had better call in a professional electrician.

Very rarely it may be that neither a bulb nor a blown fuse is at fault. If all the lights in the circuit are off, and there is no power cut, then there is a break somewhere in the circuit.

Dealing with this is probably a job for an electrician, although if you have surface-run wiring you might just as well inspect it to see if anything is obviously wrong. If just one light is not functioning, it might be that a terminal connection has come loose without causing a short. Check. If you can see nothing wrong, call in an electrician.

If you get no power when you plug into a socket outlet, the trouble is most likely to lie with the appliance rather than the circuit. The reason for this is that the fuse in the appliance plug will blow before the fuse controlling the circuit burns through.

If you plug in, say, a vacuum cleaner, and when you switch on the motor does not start, unplug it and plug in a table lamp. If this works, then (except for the extremely rare occurrence that a connection inside the socket has come loose, and is making contact only intermittently) you can be certain that the fault lies with the vacuum cleaner. If the lamp does not work, try it on an adjacent socket to test the circuit. If the lamp does not light, check the circuit fuse. If it does light, switch off at the main, remove the faceplate of the first socket and check its terminals. If there is nothing wrong with the connections, you need an electrician.

If the fault seems to lie in the appliance, replace the fuse in its plug with a fuse you have tested in another plug. If the appliance still does not work it needs repairing.

Glossary

A

Abutment wall: Wall at the end of, and projecting at least as high as, a pitched roof. It is square at the top, and is capped off with either stone coping or rendering.

Access tower: Metal framework for reaching high parts of the house.

Acoustic tiles: Sound absorbent material for fixing to walls or ceilings to reduce noise or improve the sound quality of a room.

Aggregate: Natural sand or gravel, or crushed stone that is added to cement to make concrete.

Air brick: Perforated brick, of earthenware or cast iron, built into a wall to provide ventilation.

Allen key: L-shaped steel tool, hexagonal in cross section and in various sizes, used to turn round-head bolts with hexagonal slot.

Anchor bolt: Device for making extra strong fixing in a wall – it has a steel, rubber or plastic sleeve that expands as the bolt head is tightened.

Angle bead: Right-angled metal strip reinforcing external corners in plasterwork.

Annular nail: Nail with ridged serrations along its shank which gives extra strong fixing. They are often used for fixing hardboard to a suspended timber floor.

Anodizing: Protective film – glossy, matt or coloured – given to metal, especially aluminium, by electro-chemical methods.

Architrave: Decorative moulded timber surrounding a door or window opening.

Arris: Sharp edge where two angled surfaces meet – for example, the corner of a brick or stone.

Arris rail: Triangular-section rail running horizontally between fence posts to provide a fixing for the fence boards.

Asbestos cement: Mixture of cement and asbestos fibres used in the manufacture of building materials – for example, corrugated roofing sheets and rainwater goods.

B

Back boiler: Boiler fitted behind an open fire – gas or solid-fuelled – used to supply heating or hot water.

Ball valve: Valve operated by a float at the end of a lever, used to control entry of water into a cold water tank.

Baluster: Vertical length of wood, often decoratively moulded, supporting the handrail of a staircase.

Balustrade: Row of balusters along the sides of a staircase.

Bargeboard: Length of timber fixed to the top of a gable wall where it joins up with the end of a pitched roof.

Barrel bolt: Surface-mounted bolt that slides open or closed in a cylindrical sleeve – the barrel.

Batten: Originally a long thin piece of squared timber used in flooring, and to support laths, tiles and slates. Now widely used to describe any small-section timber.

Beading: Originally, moulding carved like a row of beads, but now any small-section moulding of timber or other material.

Belly out: Bulging or bowing in a wall or ceiling.

Bending spring: Flexible former inserted in plumbing pipes, to stop them being flattened when bent.

Bleeding: Blemish on decorative surface caused by, for example, resins from knots, or colours of previous paints or wallpapers seeping through to the surface.

Blockboard: Manufactured board with a core of parallel strips of softwood faced on each side with one or more layers of veneer. Most commonly 19 mm (¾ in) thick.

Bond: Overlapping of bricks in a wall so that the vertical joints between courses are staggered.

Boss: Device for connecting waste pipes to a drainage stack.

Boss White: Compound for use with plumber's hemp and PTFE tape to make plumbing joints watertight.

Box gutter: Gutter built up on site, as opposed to being factory-made. It is found where, for instance, a pitched roof meets a parapet wall.

Bottle trap: See **Trap**.

Brace: 1. Carpenter's tool which, when fitted with a bit, is used to bore holes.
2. Length of metal or timber used to strengthen the construction of building.

Building block: Rectangular blocks, other than bricks, used in building. They can be solid, hollow or cellular and are sometimes used for the inside leaf of cavity walls, or for internal walls. Some are load bearing; others are lightweight. They have better insulating qualities, and are cheaper than bricks.

Butt joint: Joint formed when two squared pieces of timber meet without overlapping.

C

Came: Metal strip holding the glass in a leaded light window.

Capillary groove: Channel cut into, for example, a window frame, to stop water being forced up the frame by natural suction.

Capillary joint: Sleeve with internal rings of solder, for joining plumbing pipes.

Capping: Protective or decorative finish on the top of a wall or fence.

Cap sheet: Top layer of felt fixed to a roof.

Carriage: Length of timber that supports a staircase from the underside.

Chase: Groove cut in a wall or floor to take concealed cables or pipework.

Caulking: The act of filling the gap between door and window frames or a bath or kitchen worktop and surrounding walls. The material used for such filling.

Cavity fixing device: A sort of wall plug for hollow walls.

Ceiling plate: Horizontal member at the top of a timber framework for a hollow wall of lath and plaster, or plasterboard.

Cement: Material used as a binder with sand to form mortar, or with aggregate to make concrete.

Cess pit: Underground chamber (in brick, concrete or plastic) into which domestic sewage is discharged, to be emptied at intervals.

Chair rail: Moulding at the top of a dado, fitted to stop chair backs from scratching the wall.

Chamfer: Sloping surface of a bevelled edge or corner.

Chipboard: Manufactured board made from particles (and therefore sometimes known as particle board) of wood, or occasionally flax, bonded with resin and compressed to a high density.

Cill: See **Sill:**

Cladding: Material applied to a wall or vertical framework as either a decorative or protective covering (or sometimes both).

Cleat: 1. Piece of timber fixed under a staircase to provide extra support.
2. Metal or plastic anchorage to which cords, for example blinds or clothes lines, are tied.

Clout nail: Nail with extra large head. Used for fixing roofing felt and sash cord.

Coach bolt: Dome-headed bolt in which a short part of the shank nearest the head is of square-section.

Compression joint: Plumbing joint formed by tightening a nut to compress a ring-shaped seal.

Coping: Finishing detail on the top of a wall to make it look neater and protect it from the weather.

Corbelling: Courses of brickwork projecting from a wall in an inverted triangular pattern – the lower courses stick out less than the higher ones – usually to support masonry above.

Cornice: Ornamental moulding, usually in plaster, where a wall joins up with the ceiling.

Corrugated fastener: Short length of corrugated steel sharpened along one edge so that it can be driven into timber to strengthen a butt joint.

Coupled sash: Type of double glazing in which a pane of glass in a wood, metal, or plastic frame is fixed to an existing sash in the window.

Coving: Prefabricated cornice, in plaster or polystyrene.

Cramp (clamp): Tool for holding joined pieces of wood together while the glue sets.

Cross lining: Practice of applying lining paper horizontally so that its joins will not coincide with those of the top decorative wallcovering hung in the normal vertical manner.

Crow's foot spanner: Spanner in which the jaws are at right angles to the body.

D

Dado: Lower half of a room wall, often given a different decorative treatment from that above, and topped off with a decorative moulding, known as a chair rail.

Damp-proof course (dpc): Bed of impervious material running horizontally in a wall to stop moisture in the ground from rising up the structure.

Damp-proof membrane: Layer of waterproofing material in a direct-to-earth floor to stop damp from rising.

Dentil slip: Place of material used to fill the cavity under a deep-profile ridge tile (such as a pantile) on a roof. Dentil slips can be bought specially, or bits of broken tile can be used instead.

Direct-to-earth floor: Floor resting directly on the ground.

Door furniture: Accessories, such as handles, finger plates, locks, street numbers and letter boxes that can be fitted to a door.

Dog leg stair: A staircase with two non-parallel flights separated by a half-landing.

Door stop: Part of a door frame against which the door closes.

Down draught: Draught set up when a cold panel (usually a window) sets up a movement of air, as opposed to one caused by air passing through gaps around doors and windows.

Downpipe: Pipe that carries rainwater from the gutter down to the drains.

Drip bead: Shaped piece of timber that forms part of the top rail of a window frame, to throw off rainwater.

Drip channel: Groove in the underside of a window cill, cut out or formed with moulding, to prevent rainwater running back on to the house wall.

Drop: Length of wallpaper needed to cover the wall from ceiling (or picture rail) down to the skirting or chair rail.

Dry lining: Cladding an internal wall with plasterboard, as opposed to using plaster.

E

Eaves: Point where a roof meets the top of the house walls.

Efflorescence: White deposit on the surface of walls caused by soluble salts, which crystalize as brickwork or plaster dries out; it can be brushed off but will eventually disappear of its own accord.

Elbow coupling: Right-angled joint used in plumbing.

Escutcheon: Surround that neatens a keyhole.

Expanded metal: Mesh formed by perforating a sheet of metal then expanding it.

Expansion joint: A flexible joint that allows a structure to expand or contract as the temperature changes, without causing damage.

Expansion loop: Length of pipe inserted in a run to allow for expansion.

Expansion tank: Empty tank that accommodates water expelled from a radiator central heating system as the temperature rises, then feeds it back when the water contracts as its temperature falls.

F

Fair face brickwork: Interior brickwork laid particularly neatly to a decorative surface.

Fascia: Horizontal timber, to which the gutters are fixed at eaves level.

Fibre building board: Sheet material made by compressing wood or vegetable fibres. Hardboard and insulating board are different forms of fibre board.

Firring piece: Tapered length of timber fixed to the rafters to slope a flat roof and ensure that rainwater runs off.

Flashing: Strip of material fitted to give a waterproof joint where a roof joins up with a wall or chimney stack.

Flaunching: Mortar into which chimney pots are set on top of a chimney stack.

Flooring brad: Nail for fixing floorboards to joists.

Floor plate: Bottom horizontal member of the timber framework for a hollow wall.

Flow and return pipe: Pipe used to carry hot water from the boiler of a central heating system, round the radiators and back to the boiler.

Footlifter: Tool used to position wall boards when they are being fixed to a timber framework.

Frass: Tiny brown pellets, like sawdust, that are left behind by the grubs of wood-boring insects such as woodworm.

Frenchman: Improvised tool used for trimming mortar when repointing a wall.

Frieze: 1. Part of a wall between picture rail and ceiling.
2. Thin strip of wallpaper applied as a border – for example, horizontally below the ceiling or just above the skirting board.

Frog: Inset part on one face of a brick.

G

Gable wall: Wall at the end of a house with a two-way pitched roof; the top is triangular in shape, to conform with the shape of the roof.

Glazing bar: Small-section intermediate frame member that divides a window into small pieces.

Glazing spring: Small headless nail that holds a window pane in its frame before putty is applied.

Glue block: Small (usually triangular) piece of timber held in place by glue under a timber construction (for example, a staircase, chair or sideboard) to strengthen the joint.

Grout: Adhesive-like material used to fill the gaps between tiles after they have been fixed into place.

Gully: Opening in the ground through which rainwater is conveyed to the drains; usually a glazed earthenware fitting with a trap.

H

Hanger: Timber member of a roof truss.

Hardcore: Rubble such as broken bricks, stone and concrete, placed on the ground as a base for concrete.

Hawk: Tool used for carrying plaster or mortar. It consists usually of a small, square sheet of wood about 12 mm (½ in) thick attached to a short handle.

Header: Brick laid across a wall, usually to form a bond or coping.

Head plate: Top horizontal member of the framework for a stud partition wall.

Herringbone: Flooring pattern in which parquet, bricks, tiles or other materials are laid in a zig-zag arrangement.

High spot: Part of a surface (a wall or floor, for instance) that bulges slightly from the surrounding area.

Hinge bolt: Also known as stud or dog bolt. Fitted to the hinge edge of a door to locate in the frame to stop this edge from being forced by burglars.

Hip: Line where two slopes of a hipped roof meet.

Hip iron: Curved strip of iron at the foot of a hip, which prevents the hip tiles from sliding down before the mortar holding them has set.

Hip rafter: Main corner rafter of a hipped roof.
Hipped roof: Type of pitched roof that has a second slope at its end instead of a gable wall.
Hollow-joint ceiling: Ceiling without any cladding; the joists and the floor of the room above are fully on view.
Hollow wall: Partition wall with cladding (plasterboard, or lath and plaster) on a timber frame.
Hopper head: Open top of a downpipe into which waste pipes from baths, sinks and basins above ground level discharge.
Horn: Part of a window frame or door frame that projects beyond the main structure.
Hygrometer: Instrument used to test for damp.

I

Illuminated ceiling: False ceiling, usually in opaque plastic, above which are fluorescent lights.
Inspection chamber: Brick-built chamber in a drainage system (sometimes called a manhole).
Insulating glass: Another name for a double glazing sealed unit.

J

Jack rafter: Intermediate rafter on a hipped roof.
Jamb: Vertical member at the side of a door or casement window frame.
Joist: Horizontal structural timber supporting floors and ceilings.
Joist hanger: Galvanized metal stirrup built into brickwork of a house to support a joist at one end.

K

Keeper plate: See **Striking plate**
Knotting: Liquid, based on shellac, applied to knots and other resinous areas of timber to stop resin from oozing out later to spoil the paintwork.
Knuckle: Point where two leaves of a hinge join.
Kraft paper: Strong, smooth brown paper.

L

Ladder stay: Device to hold the top of a ladder away from a wall so it does not rest on a gutter or window.
Laminboard: High quality blockboard in which the core battens are thin and the structure strong.
Latch: Locking device in which the bolt is spring loaded and opened by the operation of a handle or key, unlike a lock, which can be opened and closed only by a key.
Lath and plaster wall: Internal partition wall built on a timber framework to which small horizontal pieces of timber (the laths) are nailed to provide a key for the plaster which is skimmed on to them.
Lead boat: Wooden tool, so-called because one end is shaped like the bow of a boat; used by glaziers to close the beading that holds the glass in leaded lights.
Lintel: Horizontal structural member, in stone, concrete or even wood, holding up the masonry above a door or window opening.
Lipping: Thin strip of timber or plastic used for disguising a raw edge.

Lock block: Block of wood fitted inside a flush door to take locks, handles and other furniture.

Lock nut: Second nut threaded on to the end of a bolt to stop the first one from working loose. A nut that incorporates a retaining washer.

Lock rail: Middle horizontal member of a panelled door.

Loose fill: Insulation material in the form of pellets or flakes.

M

Mastic: Non-hardening material used for sealing gaps, such as in rainwater fittings, round baths and between door and window frames and walls.

Matchboarding: Timber similar to tongued and grooved boards but with additional moulding so that a V groove is formed where two boards meet.

Melamine: Resin applied to synthetic boards (especially chipboard) to give a protective, easily-cleaned surface.

Microbore: System of radiator heating based on very small pipework – even smaller than those used in **Small bore.**

Mirror plate: Small, shaped piece of brass or chromium-plated metal used for hanging pictures, small cupboards and mirrors on a wall.

Mixer valve: A control valve that mixes hot and cold water so that it emerges from the tap at the desired temperature.

Mortise bolt: Bolt that is housed in a recess cut into the door.

Mortise lock: Lock housed in a recess cut into the door.

Mouse: Small weight, attached to the end of a length of string, that is dropped into gaps and cavities so that electric cable or sash cords, for example, can be drawn after it.

Mullion: Intermediate vertical member of a large window frame.

N

Newel cap: Piece of wood, often decorative, fixed to the top of a newel post.

Newel post: Stout post that forms the end of a staircase balustrade at the bottom of the stairs and on landings.

Nib: 1. Short stretch of wall left at each end to support the rsj that is inserted when a load-bearing wall has been removed.
2. Projection of a roofing tile that hooks on to the roofing batten.

Night latch: Rim latch operated by a key from outside the door and a small handle inside. A small catch stops the handle or key from turning the latch and can hold the latch open.

Nogging: Subsidiary supporting member in a timber framework – such as horizontal cross-pieces between the main uprights (or studs) in the framework of a wall, or a minor cross-member between the joists of a ceiling.

Nosing: A rounded front edge – especially of a stair tread.

O

Offset: Section of a downpipe that leads from the gutter to the main pipe under the eaves. Also called a **Swan's neck.**

Opening light: A window that can be opened.

Open tread: Staircase in which the risers (the vertical sections between the treads) are omitted.

Outer bead: One of three beads that form the channels in which vertical sliding windows run. See also **Staff bead** and **Parting bead.**

P

Pantile: A decoratively shaped roofing tile.

Parapet gutter: Gutter formed *in situ* between a roof and the back of a parapet wall.

Parapet wall: External wall that extends higher than the eaves of a pitched roof.

Pargetting: Decorative plasterwork on the outside of buildings.

Particle board: See **Chipboard.**

Parting bead: Central bead that forms the channels in which sliding sash windows run. See also **Outer bead** and **Staff bead.**

Parting slip: Vertical piece of timber that divides the weight compartment of a vertical sliding window in two, keeping the two weights apart.

Penetrating damp: Caused by rainwater finding its way through the structure of a building.

Piano hinge: Long hinge, with several holes in each leaf, of the sort used on piano lids.

Pilot hole: Starting hole drilled for screw, slightly less in diameter than the screw itself, making it easier to drive home the screw without splitting the wood.

Planed all round (PAR): Term used to describe softwood that (as is the norm) is sold planed on every edge, and is therefore slightly smaller than its nominal size – reduced about 3 mm ($\frac{1}{8}$ in) in each dimension.

Plasterboard: Plaster-based material sandwiched between paper to form a hard rigid board, which is applied to walls and ceilings, instead of plaster.

Plasticizer: Compound added to mortar to make it more workable.

Plumber's hemp: Fibre used in making joints watertight.

Plunger: Wooden or plastic handled tool with a small rubber cup at one end, used for clearing blockages in waste pipes.

Pocket piece: Timber covering the weight compartment of a vertical sliding sash window.

Pointing: Facing of mortar applied to the joints between courses of brickwork.

Primaries: Plumbing pipes that carry water between a boiler and a hot water cylinder.

Protimeter: Instrument used to test for damp.

PTFE tape: Plastic used in plumbing to make joints watertight.

P-trap: See **Trap.**

Purlin: Intermediate cross-member of roof timbers.

Q

Quoin: Large stone inserted in the corner of buildings built mainly of brick.

R

Raft: A slab of concrete.

Rasp: Coarse file used to shape, reduce or smooth material.

Rebate: Small recess cut out along the edge of a length of timber. Used, for example, in window frames to provide housing for glass and in door frames.

Rendering: Facing of sand and cement applied to a wall.

Retaining wall: Wall built to hold back earth piled up behind it.

Reveal: The opening for a window on the room side of the frame.

Ridge: Point at which the two slopes of a pitched roof meet.

Ridge board: Timber support under the apex of a pitched roof.

Ridge tile: V-section tile fixed to cover and weatherproof the ridge of a pitched roof.

Rim latch or lock: Security device fitted on the surface of the door – not housed in a mortise.

Ring shank nail: Nail with raised ring along the shank; used for fixing hardboard to a timber floor because it is less likely to be shaken loose than a conventional nail.

Riser: Vertical section between the treads (steps) of a staircase.

Rising butt: Hinge that raises a door as it opens so that it is lifted clear of, say, a floorcovering.

Rising damp: Damp that rises up into the structure from the moist earth below.

Rolled steel joist (RSJ): Strong supporting member for buildings, usually inserted in the top of an interior load-bearing wall that is removed to convert two rooms into one.

S

Sash: Fixed, opening or sliding frame of any material holding a pane of glass and forming part of a window. Commonly describes a vertical sliding window.

Saw horse: Four legged trestle that supports large-section timber while it is being sawn.

Scratch coat: First coat of rendering on a wall; it is scratched just before it sets, to provide a key for the next coat.

Screed: Layer of sand and cement used to top off a concrete floor.

Secondary sash: Double glazing in which sashes are installed just inside, and separate from the existing ones.

Secret gutter: Gutter formed behind a parapet wall.

Secret nailing: Method of fixing tongued and grooved planks or match-boarding, by driving nails at an angle through the tongue and out via the main body of the plank, so that they are covered by the groove of the next plank to be installed.

Self-levelling compound: Viscous liquid applied to a floor to make it level before a floorcovering is laid.

Septic tank: Container in which sewage is purified by bacteria, before being filtered into the soil.

Shake: Split in timber.

Sharp sand: Coarse sand used in making concrete.

Shoe: Section at the bottom of a downpipe that directs the water into a gully.

Shuttering: Wooden formwork that makes a mould for concrete.

Sill: Bottom horizontal member of a window or door frame.

Skew nailing: Method of fixing timber framework by driving a nail at an angle through the side of one member and into another that meets it at right angles.

Skin coat: Smooth top coat of plaster or sand and cement rendering.

Sleeper wall: Low wall used to give intermediate support to the joists of a ground-storey suspended floor.

Slip: Thin piece of brick-like tile stuck to the surface of an interior wall to give the impression of natural brickwork.

Slurry: Mortar mixed to a cream-like consistency.

Small bore: Central heating based on small-diameter pipes.

Soffit board: Horizontal length of timber fixed under the rafters and behind the fascia board, at the eaves of a building.

Soft sand: A fine sand containing stone particles, used in mortar and certain renderings.

Soil pipe: Pipe leading from a lavatory to the drains.

Solvent welding: Use of adhesive to join plastic pipes.

Spalling: Surface flaking of bricks.

Stack: Main drainage pipe.

Staff bead: The inner of the three beadings that form the channels for a vertical sliding window. See also **Parting bead** and **Outer bead**.

Stile: Vertical side member of a door or ladder.

Stop bead: Part of the lining round a door opening.

Stopping: Material used to fill holes in woodwork.

Strawboard: Form of building board, often used on flat roofs.

Stretcher: Brick laid lengthways to bond a double-skin wall.

Striking plate (keeper plate): Housing for a bolt or latch in a door frame.

String: Timber member at the side of a staircase into which the steps and the vertical sections between them (risers) are fixed.

Stucco: Smooth external rendering with a painted finish.

Stud: Vertical member of the timber framework for a hollow wall.

Stud partition: Non-load-bearing hollow wall that consists of cladding (usually lath and plaster or plasterboard) on a timber framework.

Swan's neck: Term for an offset – a section of downpipe shaped to run under the eaves and connect the gutter with the main vertical run.

T

Tack rag: Fabric impregnated with slow drying varnish, used for dusting off surfaces prior to repainting.

Tail piece: Shaped piece of timber at the end of a **bargeboard.**

Terrazzo: Floor-finish consisting of marble chippings in cement.

Thixotropic paint: Jellied (non-drip) paint.

Threaded joint: Plumbing joint in which a threaded insert fits into a threaded hole.

Threshold: Strip (of wood, metal or plastic) across the foot of an external door opening to make it weatherproof.

Tile hanging: Roofing tiles used vertically on an external wall.

Tiling batten: Strip of timber fixed at right angles to the roof rafter to support tiles or slates.

Tilting filler: Triangular piece of wood used at the eaves to lift the slates or tiles of the roof slightly so that they bed properly on the nails.

Tongued and grooved ('t and g'): Lengths of timber moulded along both edges – one with a groove, the other with a matching tongue. Used mainly for floors, where the tongue of one board locates into the groove of the next to provide a draught- and dust-free seal.

Toothing: Brickwork in which alternate courses are left projecting (like teeth) so that the wall can be extended later.

Top-hung: Opening casement window hinged at the top.

Torching: Mortar used to fix slates and tiles to a roof and to seal the gap between rows.

Transom: 1. Horizontal part of a window frame that separates a fixed from an opening window.
2. Horizontal member between a door and a fanlight.

Trap: Bend in a waste pipe to contain a small pool of water that stops drain smells from coming up into the home.

Trimmer: Timber member used to support the ends of rafters that have been cut (for example, to make a window opening in the roof).

Trussed rafter: Roofing support in which the rafter joist, strut and other members are delivered to the site as one unit.

U

U-valve: Measure of the performance of insulation material. The lower the U-valve, the better the insulation.

V

Valley: Angle formed when two slopes of a pitched roof meet at the bottom.

Ventilating pipe: Open-ended pipe leading from a soil pipe.

Vent pipe: Pipe leading from the top of a hot water cylinder to allow excess overheated pressure to escape.

Vent stack: A ventilating pipe.

Varge: Roof projection beyond the gable.

Vermiculite: Loose-fill insulating material based on mica.

W

Wall plate: Horizontal length of timber fixed to a wall to provide anchorage for floor joists or rafters of a lean-to building.

Wainscot: Wood panelling on an interior wall.

Wall tie: Strip of metal, wire or plastic bedded into mortar courses in the middle of a cavity wall to hold the two leaves together.

Waste pipe: Pipe that carries water from sinks, basins and baths.

Water bar: Strip of metal under a door to stop rainwater finding its way through.

Waterhammer: Noise caused by vibration in water pipes.

Weatherboard: 1. Shaped piece fitted to the bottom of a door to throw rainwater clear; usually made of timber, but sometimes of metal or plastic.
2. Horizontal timber cladding on the outside of a building.

Weep holes: Holes left in a structure to allow moisture to flow out.

Weight compartment: Housing for the balancing weights of a vertical sliding sash window.

Welted apron: Overlap of roofing felt projecting from a flat roof to throw rainwater into the gutter.

Wet and dry: Abrasive paper that can be used dry, but is normally used wet so that it produces no dust.

Winder: Angled step used where a staircase changes direction.

Wire balloon: Metal cage that prevents debris from falling down a ventilation pipe.

Index